T0329942

THE WELFARE STATE REVISITED

INITIATIVE FOR POLICY DIALOGUE AT COLUMBIA
CHALLENGES IN DEVELOPMENT AND GLOBALIZATION

INITIATIVE FOR POLICY DIALOGUE
AT COLUMBIA: CHALLENGES IN
DEVELOPMENT AND GLOBALIZATION

JOSÉ ANTONIO OCAMPO AND JOSEPH E. STIGLITZ,
SERIES EDITORS

Escaping the Resource Curse, Macartan Humphreys, Jeffrey D. Sachs, and Joseph E. Stiglitz, eds.

The Right to Know, Ann Florini, ed.

Privatization: Successes and Failures, Gérard Roland, ed.

Growth and Policy in Developing Countries: A Structuralist Approach, José Antonio Ocampo, Codrina Rada, and Lance Taylor

Taxation in Developing Countries, Roger Gordon, ed.

Reforming the International Financial System for Development, Jomo Kwame Sundaram, ed.

Development Cooperation in Times of Crisis, José Antonio Ocampo and José Antonio Alonso

New Perspectives on International Migration and Development, Jeronimo Cortina and Enrique Ochoa-Reza, eds.

Industrial Policy and Economic Transformation in Africa, Akbar Noman and Joseph E. Stiglitz, eds.

Macroeconomics and Development: Roberto Frenkel and the Economics of Latin America, Mario Damill, Martín Rapetti, and Guillermo Rozenwurcel, eds.

Too Little, Too Late: The Quest to Resolve Sovereign Debt Crises, Martin Guzman, José Antonio Ocampo, and Joseph E. Stiglitz, eds.

Efficiency, Finance, and Varieties of Industrial Policy: Guiding Resources, Learning, and Technology for Sustained Growth, Akbar Noman and Joseph E. Stiglitz, eds.

THE WELFARE STATE
REVISITED

EDITED BY

José Antonio Ocampo
and Joseph E. Stiglitz

COLUMBIA UNIVERSITY PRESS

NEW YORK

Columbia University Press
Publishers Since 1893
New York   Chichester, West Sussex
cup.columbia.edu

Library of Congress Cataloging-in-Publication Data
Names: Ocampo, José Antonio, editor. | Stiglitz, Joseph E., editor.
Title: The welfare state revisited / edited by José Antonio Ocampo and
Joseph E. Stiglitz.
Description: New York : Columbia University Press, [2018] |
Series: Initiative for policy dialogue at Columbia : challenges in development
and globalization | Includes index.
Identifiers: LCCN 2017028027 (print) | LCCN 2017029625 (ebook) | ISBN
9780231546164 (electronic) | ISBN 9780231185448 (cloth) Subjects: LCSH:
Social policy—21st century. | Equality. | Welfare state. | Welfare state
—History.
Classification: LCC HN18.3 (ebook) | LCC HN18.3 .W45 2018 (print) |
DDC 361.6/5—dc23
LC record available at https://lccn.loc.gov/2017028027

Cover image: ©sbk_20d pictures/Getty Images
Cover design: Jordan Wannemacher

INITIATIVE FOR POLICY DIALOGUE AT COLUMBIA: CHALLENGES IN DEVELOPMENT AND GLOBALIZATION

JOSÉ ANTONIO OCAMPO AND JOSEPH E. STIGLITZ, SERIES EDITORS

The Initiative for Policy Dialogue (IPD) at Columbia University brings together academics, policy makers, and practitioners from developed and developing countries to address the most pressing issues in economic policy today. IPD is an important part of Columbia's broad program on development and globalization. The *Initiative for Policy Dialogue at Columbia: Challenges in Development and Globalization* book series presents the latest academic thinking on a wide range of development topics and lays out alternative policy options and trade-offs. Written in a language accessible to policy makers and students alike, this series is unique in that it both shapes the academic research agenda and furthers the economic policy debate, facilitating a more democratic discussion of development politics.

This book, *The Welfare State Revisited*, argues that, more than ever, there is a need for a strong welfare state. In particular, it is essential to face the strong inequality trends that have been in place in large parts of the world since the last decades of the twentieth century. The welfare state should be strengthened in developed countries where its advancement has been incomplete (as in the United States) or where it has been weakened in response to ideological political shifts (in several countries since the Thatcher-Reagan era) and to austerity policies put in place over the past decade (in some European countries). And it should spread in the emerging and developing countries that have not yet subscribed to its principles.

The book also argues that a twenty-first-century welfare state will have to be different from those of the nineteenth and twentieth centuries. It must be redesigned in a way that is consistent with a coherent vision of its role in the economic and social system today. And it must respond to the demands generated in many parts of the world by demographic changes, the changing role of the family, new features of labor markets, technological change, and the fiscal constraints created by tax competition in the globalized world. To do this, it must borrow from research in recent decades that has provided new insights into the roles that the welfare state has to perform and how to design a better, more efficient, and equitable system, research that is summarized by the authors in this volume.

The volume is organized in two parts. The first analyzes the conceptual issues associated with the challenges outlined above. The second focuses on the experience of specific regions or countries. These experiences are those of the European Union, Scandinavia, the United States (also analyzed in several chapters in the first part), Latin America (the region of the developing world that has had the most significant advances in social protection in the early twenty-first century), and one of the most interesting initiatives put in place in the developing world in recent times, India's National Rural Employment Guarantee Act.

CONTENTS

PART II

ACRONYMS

ACA	Affordable Care Act of 2010
AI	Artificial intelligence
AWI	Agricultural wages in India
BLS	Bureau of Labor Statistics
CEQ	Commitment to Equity Project
CCT	Conditional cash transfers
DC	Defined contribution
ECLAC	UN Economic Commission for Latin America and the Caribbean
ELR	Employer of last resort
EPS	Entidades promotoras de salud/health-promoting entities
EU	European Union
FLSA	Fair Labor Standards Act
FONASA	Fondo Nacional de Salud/National Health Fund
GDP	Gross domestic product
GMI	Guaranteed minimum income
GRA	Guaranteed retirement account
ILC	International Labor Conference
ILO	International Labor Organization
IMF	International Monetary Fund
IPS	Instituciones prestadoras de salud/health-provisioning institutions
IRA	Individual retirement account
ISAPRES	Instituciones de salud previsional/private health insurance companies

MGNREGA	Mahatma Gandhi National Rural Employment Guarantee Act
NCEUS	National Commission on Enterprises in the Unorganized Sector
NLRA	National Labor Relations Act
NREGA	National Rural Employment Guarantee Act
NSS	National sample survey
OECD	Organisation for Economic Co-operation and Development
OHCHR	Office of the UN High Commissioner for Human Rights
OOP	Out-of-pocket (health expenditures)
SDGs	UN Sustainable Development Goals
SPS	Social protection systems
UBI	Universal basic income
UN	United Nations
SC	Scheduled Caste
SNAP	Supplemental Nutrition Assistance Program
ST	Scheduled Tribe
WEF	World Economic Forum
WHO	World Health Organization

José Antonio Ocampo and Joseph E. Stiglitz

For a third of a century, the welfare state has been under attack, even more so since the crisis of 2008. The idea that the state has a responsibility for social protection dates back at least to the nineteenth century. Bismarck is usually given credit for creating the first social security program.[1] There were both economic and political objectives: Bismarck believed that social insurance would increase productivity and that it would stave off more radical reforms.

Since then, critics of the welfare state have argued the opposite. They claimed that it attenuates incentives and encourages a dependency mentality. Somehow, as Europe and the world grow richer, the welfare state increasingly appears to be a luxury out of reach, given today's economic and budgetary constraints. European Central Bank head Mario Draghi, in some of his press interviews, seemed to go so far as to blame the welfare state for Europe's woes, declaring: "The European social model has already gone."[2]

The central thesis of the papers in this volume is that Draghi and those who argue similarly are wrong. Now, more than ever, there is a need for a welfare state. A stronger welfare state is part of the answer to Europe's problems, not the cause of them. Those countries in Europe with the strongest welfare states weathered the crisis better and have higher living standards. The development of welfare states is also essential for equitable development in middle- and low-income countries. Furthermore, it is critical to reverse the adverse domestic inequality trends that have been in place throughout the world since the last decades of the twentieth century.

But a twenty-first-century welfare state will have to be different from that of the nineteenth century, when it began under Bismarck, or the twentieth century, when it was extended, reaching new heights, for instance, in the United Kingdom with Clement Attlee implementing the Beveridge Report.

Thus, this book deals with two interrelated issues that are central challenges of the twenty-first century. The first is the welfare state. How can it be redesigned for the twenty-first century in a way that is consistent with a coherent vision of its role in the economic and social system. How can the spread of the welfare state be facilitated throughout the whole world, especially in the developing countries that have not yet subscribed to its principles. How can it be strengthened in developed countries where its advancement is incomplete (as in the United States) or where it has been weakened in response to ideological political shifts (in several countries since the Thatcher-Reagan era) and austerity policies put in place over the past decade (in some European countries). The redesign of the welfare state must respond to the demands generated in many parts of the world by demographic changes, the new features of labor markets, technological change, and the fiscal constraints created by tax competition in the globalized world. Moreover, research in recent decades has provided new insights into the roles that the welfare state has to perform and how to design a better, more efficient, and equitable system.

The second challenge is rising inequality, a fairly widespread trend of the world economy since the 1980s—with some exceptions, notably the improvements that took place in most Latin American countries in the early twenty-first century, which still left this region as one of the most unequal in the world. This challenge is, of course, related to the first, as the welfare state was historically the major institutional framework to manage the inequalities generated by the functioning of markets, inequalities that have been magnified by globalization.

These two challenges were central to the world's agenda put forth in the Sustainable Development Goals (SDGs) approved by the UN General Assembly in 2015. The commitment to reduce inequality is clearly stated in SDG-10: "Reduce inequality within and among countries." The objectives of the welfare state are captured in SDG-1: "End poverty in all its forms everywhere," and this goal includes a particular commitment to social protection: "Implement nationally appropriate social protection systems and measures for all." Social protection is also included in the objectives set out in SDG-3, to "ensure healthy lives and promote well-being for all at all ages"; in SDG-4, to "ensure inclusive and equitable quality education and promote lifelong learning opportunities for all;" in SDG-5, on the commitment to "end all forms of discrimination against all women and girls everywhere"; and through the particular emphasis placed on children, the elderly, and persons with disabilities in several goals.

The volume is organized in two parts. The first part analyzes the conceptual issues associated with the two challenges outlined above, while the second focuses on the experience of specific regions or countries. The two parts intersect throughout. For instance, there are specific analyses of the U.S. welfare system in chapters 1 and 2, and some chapters in the second part of the volume deal with the broader issues of the design of the welfare state.

—⚬⚬⚬—

The conceptual framework of the project is laid out in chapter 1 by Joseph Stiglitz, as well as in the contributions by Sandra Polaski and Isabel Ortiz (from the International Labor Organization), in chapters 2 and 3, by Jody Heymann and Aleta Sprague in chapter 4, and more specifically by many other contributors to this volume. As Stiglitz argues, the welfare state's major defense is ethical: a desire for social justice, based on a sense of solidarity and social conscience that must be at the center of adequate social arrangements. Underlying the welfare state is the question of what kind of society do we want to belong to and create. Of particular concern are those that cannot care for themselves, children and others who, without the help of the state, might face severe deprivations.

Beyond this ethical argument, the authors of this volume argue that a well-designed welfare state also improves *economic* performance. Stiglitz underscores the pervasiveness of market failures—including their incapacity to provide insurance against major risks that people face, such as severe sickness, unemployment, and old age—and the inability of markets to mitigate, and rather, their tendency to increase, inherited inequalities. Imperfections in capital markets means that without the assistance of the government, talented individuals with poor parents would never be able to live up to their potential. One of the major market failures is, of course, the absence of any mechanism to guarantee cross-generational risk sharing, which would have entailed contracts with unborn generations. A greater awareness of the breadth of these market failures has led to a broadening out of the meaning of the welfare state. It embraces not just that the state takes responsibility for social protection but also that it engages in a range of investments in arenas where, in the absence of the government, there would be underinvestment. So too, because of pervasive market failures, the welfare state may offer a more efficient way of providing a variety of needs that individuals confront at various stages of life, from education to children, to retirement income for the aged, to mortgages for homeowners. This theme—that a twenty-first-century welfare state is broader than just social protection—is a central one of this volume.

Correcting these market failures may not only enhance social justice, but also improve economic performance. In particular, the social insurance provided by the welfare states results in more innovative societies and economies where individuals are more willing to accept change and its associated risks. These features are key to faster productivity and economic growth. The absence of adequate systems of social protection may well have contributed to the growth of protectionist sentiments that have spread in many parts of the world in recent years. These positive results go against the view of critics of the welfare state, who argue that welfare attenuates market incentives and creates a culture of dependency that blocks change.

Stiglitz points out that the welfare state has proven itself robust, able to adapt to differences in circumstances. Thus, while this volume focuses on welfare states in Latin America and Europe, Stiglitz notes that there are successful cases in Africa (Namibia, Mauritius, and the Seychelles). The papers in this volume explore the variety of forms that the welfare state has taken around the world.

Stiglitz also argues that changes in the world necessitate changes in the structure of the welfare state. In particular, work-based welfarism of the mid-twentieth-century variety—where much of the burden of social protection was imposed on individual employers—will not work today. And changes in social structures imply that social institutions, like the family, may not be able to play the role that they did in the past.

Workers' increasing vulnerability is, of course, partly a result of their weaker bargaining power, so addressing the concerns of the welfare state entails addressing the broader issue of why that is so and what can be done about it—what changes in, say, labor market rules would enhance workers' bargaining power?[3]

Changes in the world and our understanding of how the economy functions[4] have also broadened the instruments and refined the design of the welfare state. Cash transfers and microcredit schemes[5] represent two important innovations within developing countries. Even more importantly, as the relevant chapters in the book show, several Latin American countries have been putting in place universal health, pension, and child and maternity benefits, and India created the very novel National Rural Employment Guarantee.

Stiglitz emphasizes new understandings, too, of the areas in which the state may have a comparative advantage based, say, on lower transactions costs (taking advantage of economies of scale and scope, including those arising from its role in collecting taxes) and weaker incentives to engage in abusive practices.[6] The design of the welfare state also has to take into account changing views on the role of individual responsibility and choice, which look more askance at mandates and more favorably at programs that expand the range of choices that individuals face. But any move away from universal, mandatory programs confronts problems of adverse selection ("cream skimming"), which can at least partially be addressed through appropriate tax and regulatory policies.[7]

These ideas form the basis of some of his suggestions for a twenty-first-century welfare system for the United States, which includes a public option for supplementary coverage of Medicare (the U.S. program of health care for the aged) and basic coverage of those below retirement age, a public option for supplementary retirement insurance, going beyond the mandatory levels required of all individuals, income-contingent loans, not only for education but also for unemployment and other areas currently provided through grants and insurance,[8] and a public option for mortgages, including income-contingent mortgages.

Beyond the significant impacts of social welfare systems on individual workers, households, and firms, these systems also generate short-term macroeconomic benefits, as argued by Polaski in chapter 2. Most obvious is the fact that systems of social protection act as automatic stabilizers. By contrast, as Ortiz argues in chapter 3, the weakening of social welfare systems as a result of short-term austerity programs has contributed to the poor social and economic performance of those countries over the past decade.

These arguments are closely linked to the debates on inequality, where there is a growing body of theory and evidence showing that societies that are more equal have better economic performance. Several chapters in this volume confirm this relationship. Polaski notes that productivity and economic growth were much stronger during the earlier postwar period when labor and social protections were arguably at their peak. Torben Andersen argues in chapter 7 that human capital, and its more equitable distribution, enhances economic growth. Similarly, José Antonio Ocampo and Natalie Gómez-Arteaga (chapter 10) find that the spread of social protection had stronger effects on poverty reduction in Latin America in 2003–2013 than did economic growth.

In chapter 4, Heymann and Sprague propose four essential pillars of a welfare system: healthy development, economic opportunities, foundation for resilience, and nondiscrimination. The first includes policies for infants and paid leave for their mothers, as well as policies that support children's education. The second pillar states that access to a decent job is an essential pathway out of poverty and requires adequate wages and a work-life balance for workers. The third pillar entails basic support during illness, unemployment, and old age—a system of social protection. The last pillar overlaps with the former two, and should guarantee the equal social treatment of people of all genders, races, and abilities or disabilities.

Polaski proposes in chapter 2 five major elements that are necessary for successful social protection reform for the United States. These elements can be applied in broad terms to other countries: (1) to preserve, defend, and improve the already established rights and social protection systems; (2) to close existing loopholes in labor laws; (3) to improve enforcement of labor laws; (4) to adapt and expand contributory social insurance systems; and (5) to fill the gaps in the social protection floor in comparison to other economies.

In turn, based on the current world debates on social protection, Ortiz argues in chapter 3 that reducing inequality in the twenty-first century will require strengthening welfare systems by (1) expanding social protection until universal coverage is achieved at adequate benefit levels; (2) reducing informality, incorporating youth and informal workers into the labor market, and regulating precarious forms of work (e.g., digital employment); (3) enhancing labor standards and social rights, strengthening collective bargaining and social dialogue; (4) re-reforming pensions to ensure pension adequacy and old-age income security; (5) investing in the care economy, creating millions of jobs in long-term care and childcare, which will additionally increase female labor force participation; and (6) supporting other redistributive policies outside social protection.

Some conceptual debates cut across the whole volume. One particularly important debate relates to the role of universalism versus targeting in the design of social policies—or, in the specific realm of protection between the design of social security and social protection systems versus more limited social safety nets. The views expressed in this volume are definitely inclined to the universal character that the welfare state must meet its broader societal goals, but also generate its full expected economic benefits.

A second conceptual debate relates to what Stiglitz calls "income fetishism": the belief that well-being is enhanced by cashing out benefits and allowing individuals to make choices of their own. Income fetishism is tied to the substitution of market instruments—in pensions, but also health or education—for public sector arrangements. As Ortiz argues, the introduction of individual accounts, pension privatization, and other reforms in a number of countries weakened the redistributive components of social security systems. In chapter 12, Uthoff forcefully argues how the pension privatization in Chile—a model that received significant attention in other countries, including in the United States, and was championed by the World Bank for several years—failed to guarantee both universal access and adequate pensions.

Several other issues with the welfare system are underscored in different chapters. These problems include particular policies for children and the challenges of aging societies—a major obstacle faced by several developed countries, but also by China and other developing countries. There is also a discussion of novel debates and policies, including the proposal to design a universal basic income (UBI), raised in chapter 3 by Ortiz, and more extensively in chapter 14 by Richard McGahey. In chapter 15, Amit Basole and Arjun Jayadev analyze India's National Rural Employment Guarantee.

The issue of financing and its redistributive effects are discussed in detail in chapter 5 by Nora Lustig. An essential point she makes is that, although social policies generally improve income distribution and reduce poverty, there are actually cases in which they leave the poor worse off in terms of actual consumption of private goods and services, and thus increase income poverty. Such cases occur when there are taxes on basic foods that are consumed by the poor, or when there are taxes on agriculture in poor countries.

In turn, the importance of intrahousehold distribution is analyzed in detail in chapter 6 by Ravi Kanbur. He underscores that intrahousehold distribution has a major effect on some traditional social policies, including, in particular, a minimum wage. Kanbur therefore argues that intrahousehold effects must be incorporated in the design of transfer programs to guarantee that they maximize social welfare.

———

The selection of regional and national experiences covered in the second part of the volume is not meant to be comprehensive, but the range of issues discussed reflects the challenges that welfare states face around the world. The experiences included are the European Union, Scandinavia, Latin America (the region of the developing world on which we focus, largely because of its significant advances in social protection in the early twenty-first century), the United States (also dealt with in chapters 1 and 2), and India's National Rural Employment Guarantee.

Chapter 8, by Ernst Stetter, deals with the EU welfare states. As the author indicates, these welfare states have undergone major transformations in the past to respond to surges in unemployment, to adapt the systems to aging populations, to account for shifting gender roles within households, and more recently, to accommodate the austerity measures put in place after the 2008–2009 financial crisis. Changes in the welfare systems have also been accompanied by labor market reforms and a reduction in the power and role of labor unions and collective bargaining. While Stetter underscores the need to reaffirm the role of the European welfare state (the EU social model), in particular in the light of new emerging social risks due to the crisis (higher unemployment and dualism between insiders and outsiders of the labor market), international competition, as well as the expansion of new forms of unprotected (including digital) labor, he also notes that these developments are challenging the scope of the welfare state and providing less room to maneuver for nation-states.

Chapter 9, by Kalle Moene, analyzes the experiences of the Northern European countries (Scandinavia in particular) and how they are relevant to the developing world. The welfare state, he argues, raises the individual labor productivity of poor workers, empowers weak groups, and generates a continuous and politically sustained redistribution. The chapter starts with a broad-based discussion on how the welfare state raises the productivity of low-skilled workers and reduces poverty. The welfare state also enables weak groups to take more control over their lives, to be more resistant against shocks and deprivation, and to be better protected against abuse of power by employers and landowners. The chapter emphasizes the political popularity of welfare programs in these countries, which is key to their sustainability. Northern Europe's experience provides important guidance for other countries, though obviously benefit levels must be set in accordance with the local living conditions in each country. As Stiglitz also emphasizes, experiences within Scandinavia support the theory that the model is supportive of innovation.[9]

The next three chapters deal with experiences in Latin America. The first, by Ocampo and Gómez-Arteaga (chapter 10), shows the significant improvements in the social indicators that took place in the region over the 2003–2013 decade, including reductions in income inequality in most countries. Aside from favorable external conditions (high commodity prices and ample access to external financing), improvements can be attributed to the construction of new forms of social protection as part of the development of stronger and innovative welfare states. Broadening coverage to guarantee universal access has been the best guarantee for strong redistributive impacts of social spending. The authors point out that, despite much progress, many challenges remain: the limited social protection coverage of informal workers (particularly in pensions), and the low redistributive impact of fiscal policy. These challenges are becoming more important in the new era of slower economic growth that the region is facing.

In chapter 11, Ana Sojo argues that efforts of diverse nature and magnitude will be required in Latin America for continued expansion of social protection coverage, improvement of its quality, and an increase in the equitable features of its financing schemes. The strategy of universalization cannot be exclusively focused on increasing resources, but must rather target institutional changes to break the fragmentation and segmentation built into the very structures of the region's social protection systems. Coverage expansion requires continued improvements in formalizing employment and a mix of contributory and noncontributory pillars.

The experiences in Latin America are similar to those elsewhere: the presumed advantages that market systems allegedly offer to consumers have not materialized. This is forcefully argued by Uthoff in chapter 12, which presents a critical evaluation of Chile's 1981 reform, the earliest and best-known case of a reform that replaced the old social insurance with a system of compulsory individual pension accounts and health plans managed by the market. The system has shown poor results in terms of guaranteeing universal access, affordable risk coverage, and sufficient benefits for the poor and vulnerable. Overall, he argues, the system is inconsistent with the solidarity principles that should be at the center of well-designed social protection systems. He proposes a series of reforms to repair it. In health insurance, this would require regulation to access a single and open health plan, and risk-pooling to compensate across insurers by risk exposure. In the pension system, this implies providing a universal flat benefit for all; defined contributions financed in a tripartite way, with cross-subsidies topped to a level that guarantees an income similar to the minimum wage; and a self-funded benefit out of individual savings accounts.

Chapter 13, by Teresa Ghilarducci, complements the analysis of the deficiencies of the U.S. welfare system by Stiglitz and Polaski in the first two chapters of the volume. She underscores that, for the first time in two generations, the risk of elderly people being poor or nearly poor will increase because the American pension system has failed. She attributes the failure to the ideological emphasis on individual asset building. Extending large tax breaks and encouraging more voluntary participation in individual accounts may have boosted participation, but the costs of the system were very high, and its distributional aspects were ineffective, and in fact enhanced inequality. In her view, a pension system should do three basic things to smooth life-course consumption: accumulate sufficient assets over the life course, invest those assets well, and distribute them as a lifelong stream of income. These objectives are most successfully attained through a guaranteed retirement account plan, in which sufficient accumulation is achieved through mandatory participation, with other rules that ensure both that contributions are not dissipated in transaction costs and that the investment risks are managed so that the risks facing the retiree are limited.

The last chapters of the volume analyze two interesting innovations. Chapter 14, by McGahey, analyzes the proposal to introduce a UBI as a complement to existing welfare state policies, or in some cases, as a replacement for the welfare state as currently constructed, with its myriad of programs directed at particular needs. His chapter highlights the economics of different versions of this idea, discusses the social welfare policy issues associated with a UBI (with special reference to the United States), and outlines an agenda for future research on how it would function in relation to existing welfare state policies. In McGahey's view, much of the current interest in UBI stems from a belief that robots and technology will rapidly eliminate jobs, but the evidence in this regard is still uncertain. The author argues, therefore, that the UBI debate might be better linked to the analysis of changing economic and power relations between business and labor and the growth of the "precariat"—the large number of individuals who view their station in life as highly precarious. He believes that focusing on the continuing decline of job quality, labor standards, and dependable income returns us to the core arguments about the design and efficacy of the welfare state.

The final chapter, by Basole and Jayadev, analyzes an innovation that has actually been implemented: India's employer of last resort program, the

(Mahatma Gandhi) National Rural Employment Guarantee Act (NREGA). NREGA guarantees 100 days of wage employment in a year to every rural household whose adult members volunteer to do unskilled manual work. Work is undertaken to produce durable assets that will contribute to environmental conservation, irrigation, and infrastructure. In terms of its coverage, it is perhaps one of the largest social programs in the world. Equally interesting, while relief through employment under public works programs has been part of poverty alleviation in many pre-industrial contexts, the idea of a programmatic employment program such as this one is a great novelty. The authors argue that India's peculiar structural transition has created significant employment challenges. In this regard, the NREGA has been a step toward providing the country's workers some security and dignity. Such an intervention also has the advantage over an unconditional income transfer in that it can simultaneously create meaningful work, develop skills, and provide economic goods.

⸺꙰⸺

Finally, we want to thank all of the organizations that supported Columbia University's Initiative for Policy Dialogue on this project: the International Labor Organization, the Roosevelt Institute, the University of Oslo, the Foundation of European Progressive Studies, and the Ford Foundation. This project was part of a broader agenda on inequality of the Ford Foundation and represented the international complement to the Roosevelt Institute's work on inequality. Their work has centered on how the rules of the market economy have been rewritten over the past third of a century, beginning in the Reagan-Thatcher era, in ways that have led to poorer economic performance and more inequality. One aspect of this "rewriting the rules" has been stripping away the protections of the welfare state, at the same time that changes in the economy, and in the rules themselves, exposed individuals to more risks, and seemingly inhibited the ability of the state to perform the social functions that it has in the past. The central theme of the Roosevelt Project is that rewriting the rules once again can increase societal well-being, promote equality, and strengthen economic performance. One important aspect is rethinking the welfare state. We hope that this project and volume serve as significant contributions to some of the most important debates of our time.

NOTES

1. According to the U.S. Social Security Administration, "The idea was first put forward, at Bismarck's behest, in 1881 by Germany's Emperor, William the First, in a ground-breaking letter to the German Parliament. William wrote: '. . . *those who are disabled from work by age and invalidity have a well-grounded claim to care from the state.*'" www.ssa.gov/history/ottob.html.

2. *Wall Street Journal*, February 24, 2017.

3. This is one of the central themes of several Roosevelt Institute reports, including J. E. Stiglitz, *Rewriting the Rules of the American Economy*, with Nell Abernathy, Adam Hersh, Susan Holmberg, and Mike Konczal (A Roosevelt Institute Book; New York: Norton, 2015), available at www.rewritetherules.org.

4. Including the development of behavioral economics, which recognizes that individuals do not necessarily act in the rational way hypothesized in standard economics and that an individual's beliefs and preferences are endogenous.

5. The role of microcredit schemes and their design has been a subject of immense debate, especially after the infamous collapse of the largest such scheme in India. See A. Haldar and J. E. Stiglitz, "Group Lending, Joint Liability, and Social Capital: Insights from the Indian Microfinance Crisis," *Politics & Society* 44, no. 4 (2016):459–497.

6. Recent work by Akerlof and Shiller have emphasized the pervasiveness of this kind of exploitation. See G. A. Akerlof and R. J. Shiller, *Phishing for Phools: The Economics of Manipulation and Deception* (Princeton, N.J.: Princeton University Press, 2015).

7. Standard economic theory has addressed the problems of moral hazard and adverse selection separately. There is very limited literature addressing the interaction of the two, which often plays an important role in policy, and especially in the design of the welfare state. See J. E. Stiglitz and Jungyoll Yun, "Optimality and Equilibrium in a Competitive Insurance Market Under Adverse Selection and Moral Hazard" (NBER Working Paper 19317, National Bureau of Economic Research, Cambridge, Mass., August 2013). See also Richard Arnott and J. E. Stiglitz, "Moral Hazard and Optimal Commodity Taxation," *Journal of Public Economics*, 29(1986):1–24; and "The Welfare Economics of Moral Hazard," in *Risk, Information and Insurance: Essays in the Memory of Karl H. Borch*, ed. H. Louberge (Norwell, Mass.: Kluwer Academic, 1990), 91–122.

8. Bruce Chapman has championed income-contingent loans. Higher education is now financed through such loans in Australia. See B. Chapman, T. Higgins, and J. E. Stiglitz, eds., *Income Contingent Loans: Theory, Practice and Prospects* (Houndmills, U.K. Palgrave Macmillan, 2014); J. E. Stiglitz, "Income Contingent Loans for the Unemployed: A Prelude to a General Theory of the Efficient *Provision* of Social Insurance," in Stiglitz, Chapman, and Higgins, *Income Contingent Loans*, 180–204; and J. E. Stiglitz and J. Yun, "Income Contingent Loan as an Unemployment Benefit" (Columbia University Working Paper, Columbia University, New York, 2017). Stiglitz and Yun argue that there are distinct advantages of integration of different social protection schemes. See J. E. Stiglitz and J. Yun, "The Integration of Unemployment Insurance with Retirement Insurance," *Journal of Public Economics* 89(2005):2037–67. All of these are reforms that, at any level of risk mitigation, reduce the adverse incentive effects.

9. See also K. O. Moene, "Scandinavian Equality: A Prime Example of Protection Without Protectionism," in *The Quest for Security: Protection Without Protectionism and the Challenge of Global Governance*, ed. M. Kaldor and J. E. Stiglitz (New York: Columbia University Press, 2013), 48–74; and the special issue of the *Journal of Public Economics* (2015) on Scandinavia edited by K. Moene and S. Blomquist, including J. E. Stiglitz, "Leaders and Followers: Perspectives on the Nordic Model and the Economics of Innovation," *Journal of Public Economics* 127 (July 2015):3–16; and E. Barth, K. O. Moene, and F. Willumsen, "The Scandinavian Model—An Interpretation," *Journal of Public Economics* 127 (July 2015):60–72.

PART I

CHAPTER 1

The Welfare State in the Twenty-First Century

Joseph E. Stiglitz

Designing the twenty-first-century welfare state is part of a broader debate redefining the role of the market, the state, and "civil society"—non-state forms of collective action.

One of the tenets of the Reagan-Thatcher revolution was questioning the welfare state. Some worried that the financial burdens of the welfare state would drag down growth. Some worried about the effect of the welfare state on the sense of individual responsibility, others that the welfare state provides an opportunity for the lazy and profligate to take advantage of hardworking citizens. A sense of social solidarity had united citizens around the world during World War II. Some thirty years after that global conflict, that solidarity was eroding, and economic arguments quickened its disintegration. Even two decades after the doctrines of the Reagan-Thatcher revolution of the 1980s had taken root—and long after its shortcomings had become obvious—others argued that the welfare state had contributed to the euro crisis.[1]

This chapter argues that these arguments criticizing the welfare state are for the most part fallacious and that changes in the global economy have even increased the importance of the system. It then describes some of the key elements of a twenty-first-century welfare state.

1. BASIC PRECEPTS OF THE WELFARE STATE

To understand the principles and philosophy of the welfare state, it is useful to contrast it with the "neoliberal" or market-oriented state.[2]

The central economic doctrine of neoliberalism is that markets are efficient. (There are limited exceptions to this belief; for example, many who believe that markets are normally efficient still believe that the government should intervene in certain cases, for example, to ensure macroeconomic stability or to prevent pollution.) Moreover, market advocates believe that every (Pareto-) efficient outcome can be supported by a free-market economy, with the appropriate (lump-sum) redistributions.[3] This implies that one can separate issues of efficiency and distribution, and that the task of economics is to maximize output (as reflected, say, in GDP), leaving the distribution to the political process. When the conditions required for these results to hold are not satisfied, the job of the economist is to advise governments on how to ensure that they are. For example, markets must be made competitive through effective enforcement of antitrust laws.

Of course, politicians who have argued against the welfare state typically do not frame their critique in the formal language of economics. Rather, they talk about how the provision of social insurance attenuates incentives, for example, through the taxes that are used to finance it. Many politicians go further, saying that the welfare state creates a culture of dependency, implicitly arguing that it changes the nature of the individual. This argument moves beyond standard welfare economics, which takes preferences as fixed and given. This is an important argument, to which I return shortly.

By contrast, the advocates of the welfare state believe that markets are not, in general, efficient; that market failures are pervasive and not easily correctable; and that as a result, government needs to take a more active role. Of course, government should do what it can to ensure that markets work well, more in accord with how they are described in standard textbooks—for example, making sure that there is strong competition and that firms do not exploit ordinary individuals through questionable practices.

Later in this chapter, I will briefly recount the theoretical research done over the past forty years that helped us understand that pervasive market failures indicate that markets are often not efficient and that there is an important role for government, including those roles typically associated with the welfare state. The political debate was framed differently: the demand for the welfare state was driven by hard-to-ignore imperfections in markets that sometimes had a devastating effect on people's lives and well-being. It was obvious that markets were not providing insurance against many of the important risks that individuals faced, such as unemployment and inadequately financed retirement. The annuities that were available were expensive, and none had provisions against important risks, like the risk of inflation. The absence of these insurance markets had profound effects both on efficiency and individual well-being. Indeed, it can be shown that the provision of well-designed unemployment benefit programs can not only increase well-being but even increase GDP (Stiglitz and Yun 2017).

So too, many individuals had substandard housing, suffered from hunger, and had inadequate access to medicine. Access to these necessities was declared a basic human right under the UN's 1948 Universal Declaration of Human Rights. Whether one framed these deprivations in terms of basic economic human rights or in other ways, there was a call for *specific equalitarianism*, focusing not just on income but on specific goods (Tobin 1970). Economists might debate why individuals faced these specific deprivations—whether it was a result of market failures or individuals' poor decisions or the failure of the political process to make the necessary redistributions—but the fact of the matter is that the deprivations were deep and pervasive.

Of especial concern were those deprivations confronting children, which were in no way a result of their own choices or behavior. Here again it was clear that such deprivations represented a social injustice but also led to lower GDP—these individuals would not be able to live up to their potential.

Thus, the creation of the welfare state was motivated by observed failures in the economy and society, outcomes that seemed socially unacceptable. Developments in economic theory only helped explain why these failures should have been expected.

Twenty-first-century advocates of the welfare state begin with the premise that something is not working when large sections of society face such deprivations and that government can and should do something about these failures. Moreover, ordinary individuals are having difficulty coping with unanticipated financial stresses. In the United States, what was once viewed as a basic middle-class life is no longer attainable for large swaths of society. Matters are so bad that life expectancy across important parts of the population is actually in decline (see Case and Deaton 2015; 2017). The welfare state cannot remedy all of the ills facing our society, but the advocates of the welfare state believe it can make a difference. The traditional welfare state focuses on a particular set of "market failures" associated with the markets' ability to help individuals confront important risks that they face,[4] such as providing for social protection, through, for instance, retirement insurance (annuities) and health insurance.[5] Markets have also failed to provide insurance against unemployment and disability, and again the welfare state stepped in.

In some ways, there is a parallel between the welfare state and the developmental state. In the latter, it was recognized that markets on their own often did not succeed in the structural transformations that were required if countries were to achieve their developmental ambitions. As in the case of the welfare state, the rationale for state intervention was partly pervasive market failures of both the static and dynamic varieties. The developmental state corrected these market failures and had a catalytic role in promoting structural transformation. It helped change mind-sets—to understand that change was possible and to understand the scientific and technological bases of change.

Advocates of the twenty-first-century welfare state argue that it should go beyond the traditional welfare state model in six critical ways:

1. *Risk and innovation.* They argue that imperfections of risk markets may dampen the ability and willingness of individuals to undertake risky investments, including in innovation. Thus, the welfare state leads not only to better outcomes within a conventional static framework but also to a more dynamic and innovative economy (Stiglitz 2015a).

2. *The country as a community: social solidarity.* Neoliberalism begins from very individualistic premises. The central theorem underlying reliance on the market is Adam Smith's invisible hand theorem, that individuals in the pursuit of their own self-interest are led, as if by an invisible hand, to the well-being of society. Greenwald and Stiglitz (1986) showed that the reason that the invisible hand often seemed invisible was because it wasn't there: with imperfect information and imperfect risk markets, markets are not Pareto efficient. But the welfare state is based not just on this critique; it begins from quite different premises. Think of a country as a community, as a large family. Family members take care of one another. That is one of the most important things they do. There is solidarity among the members of the family. Many advocates of the welfare state thought of society in much the same way: national solidarity implies that those who can do so take care of those who are less fortunate. At the very least, they provide some form of social protection.

Families (or corporations) operate on quite different principles than markets do. Even if there is some reciprocity, there is not the well-defined quid pro quo. We think of ethical norms as governing relationships, not just self-interest and markets. Interestingly, though, the market works best when those participating in it are ruled by strong norms, such as those that discourage cheating or that encourage fulfilling contracts. It becomes expensive to enforce contracts through the law, and markets break down in the presence of extensive cheating. The law is designed in part to reinforce norms, severely punishing those who stray too far from them.

3. *Endogenous preferences.* The construction of society—including the rules of the economic game—affects the nature of the individual—his or her beliefs, preferences, and behavior. Indeed, we noted that some critics of the welfare state emphasize that it may undermine its beneficiaries' sense of individual responsibility. Supporters make precisely the opposite argument: the welfare state encourages social solidarity, making the individual think more about the community of which he or she is a part and, in doing so, improving social behavior in a myriad of other ways.[6] Neoliberalism has encouraged selfishness and has led to pervasive moral depravities, evidenced so clearly by the bankers in the run-up to the Great Recession: a willingness to do almost anything that enhances profits, so long as one could get away with it. For the bankers who caused the financial crisis, this greed meant in some cases crossing the line of legality—massive fraud, multiple instances of insider trading and market manipulation, and racial and ethnic discrimination. More often, though, it meant skirting the law, with practices such as abusive credit card practices and predatory lending. The head of Goldman Sachs trumpeted the new set of norms: bankers used to pride themselves as being trustworthy; now, it was every man for himself—a new standard of caveat emptor.

4. *Social justice.* The welfare state is essential to achieving social justice, broadly understood. Rawls (1971) provides a convincing case for thinking about social justice as choosing rules for society behind a veil of ignorance, before one knows one's ability, or one's station in life. I would add: and before one knows the risks that one will confront. Clearly, if individuals are averse to risk, and if markets fail to provide adequate insurance, one would want society to provide social protection.[7]

5. *Life-cycle support.*[8] Earlier, we noted that there was a compelling argument for government support for children, and especially provision of health care and education. There is another set of arguments for government provision of annuities (retirement) insurance and health insurance. As individuals go through their lives, they face a variety of other basic needs—for instance, housing. Neoliberalism simply assumed that markets provided the most efficient way of providing for these life-cycle needs, at

least at a basic level. In some countries or circumstances that might be true. But it was also obviously not so in certain other circumstances. The largely private health sector in the United States is far less efficient than that of European countries with greater state involvement, and delivers poorer outcomes with greater expenditures. Australia's system of public income–contingent student loan programs is far more equitable and efficient than America's privately based student loan system. The American public social security annuity program is far more efficient than any private annuity— with a smaller fraction of resources going into overhead.

6. *Cross-generational risk sharing.* No matter how one views the trade-offs or complementarities between the welfare state and the market, there are some forms of risk sharing in which the market cannot engage but the state can. Cross-generational risk sharing is one. Individuals within a generation can pool their risks, but it is not possible for an individual to make a contract with someone in a generation yet to be born. Society as a whole can, however, make such social contracts, and it does so all of the time. Some of the costs of fighting World War I and World War II were borne by later generations. Of course, the societal expenditures occurred during the war. And aggregate consumption during that period was reduced. But later generations' effective transfer of goods to the working-age people of the 1940s—via social security and other society-wide expenditures— meant that the World War II–era generation's consumption was probably reduced by less than it would have been otherwise. Well-designed social security systems are in part structured to facilitate this intergenerational risk sharing.

GOVERNMENT AND MARKET FAILURE

There are some who acknowledge the pervasive market failures that we have described and the ability of government, *in principle*, to correct them. But they argue that government failures are so deep and pervasive that, in practice, government interventions are unlikely to correct the market failures.

There is, of course, ample evidence of both government and market failure, without highlighting one and underestimating the other. How far the government should go in correcting market failures and with what instruments may depend on the capacities and capabilities of the state. The best-performing societies (using almost any measure) have created a well-functioning state—these societies have shown that the welfare state *can* work. In other societies, there may not yet be comparable state institutions. But it should be noted that in those societies that have achieved the best-functioning welfare states, such as those of Scandinavia, markets also work better. This is probably no accident: a well-functioning welfare state may contribute to the functioning of the market.

A VARIETY OF PRACTICES

In the twenty-first-century welfare state, there is no ideological attachment as to the best way of addressing the failures with which the state is concerned. Whether the welfare state operates through government provision of services, government regulations, or interventions in markets is not important, so long as it is effective. In some circumstances, the evolution of the market—sometimes as a result of the catalytic effects of government—reduces the magnitude of the market failure and changes the nature of public-welfare-state intervention. Thus, some might say that annuity markets are better today than they were at the time retirement social insurance programs were created (in the 1930s for the United States). Though this is true, they still do not provide insurance against critical risks like inflation, and the private market still makes much of its profits from exploiting consumer ignorance or behavioral irrationalities–for example, systematically overestimating the probability of the occurrence of certain risks. There are still unacceptably high transactions costs.

When we look around the globe, we see a range of practices. Some countries have retained the welfare state, modifying it here, strengthening it there, as they identify problems and opportunities for improvement. The Scandinavian countries are all thought to have a welfare state, but remarkably, there are also a few developing countries, like Namibia, Mauritius, and the Seychelles, that can be said to have a form of the welfare state, adapted to their (much) lower standards of living. These countries think of the welfare state as advancing a broad range of societal objectives—including economic growth. They have done well (well above the average for Africa), and many in these countries attribute at least part of that success to their having a welfare state. At the other extreme, some countries, including the United States, have at most limited social protection. The safety net is just something to prevent citizens from starving, but is not designed to enable them to live a life with dignity or to give them the capabilities to be more self-supporting.

There are many institutions, laws, and programs that make up the welfare state, and many of these overlap with what occurs in governments that do not think of themselves as having a welfare state. For instance, in all governments, there is some investment in infrastructure, though in the welfare state—more sensitive to the social benefits, with a more comprehensive societal analysis of what those benefits are—they may be larger relative to GDP. I want to focus on those aspects of the role of government that are particularly associated with a twenty-first-century welfare state.

I begin with a discussion of the developments in ideas, especially in economic theory, that have influenced—or should have influenced—thinking about the welfare state. This is followed by a discussion of some of the changes in the world that also have had an effect on the evolution of the modern welfare state. Section 4 then analyzes the principles of a twenty-first-century welfare state. The chapter then turns to two particular issues, the welfare state and deprivations (section 5) and a twenty-first-century American welfare state (section 6).

2. CHANGES IN IDEAS AND THE EVOLUTION OF THE WELFARE STATE

There have been large changes in the world—and in our understanding of the world—that have affected views of the welfare state.

The welfare state came into its own in the aftermath of World War II and the social solidarity to which it gave rise. This was a period of rapid economic growth in both Europe and America, and it was a period of shared prosperity. Every group grew, but those at the bottom saw their incomes grow faster than those at the top.

A third of a century later, this sense of solidarity seemed to wane, and neoliberalism seemed to triumph. It is worth noting that neoliberalism did not come into fashion as a result of the failure of the welfare state. There were many problems that did smooth the way for neoliberalism's growing popularity. The United States, for instance, was beset by inflation, as it tried to fight a war in Vietnam without having anyone pay the price. This macro-mismanagement was then aggravated by the oil price shocks, which variously led to price increases, recessions, inflation, and stagflation. But these problems were not *caused* by the welfare state, and abandoning the welfare state was not the solution. Still, they provided an opportunity for the ever-present critics of the welfare state to push for another model, which promised faster growth—so much faster that all would benefit. The pie would increase so much that even though those in the middle and bottom would be receiving a smaller proportion, the size of their piece would increase. But the supply-side reforms did not pan out: the economies grew more slowly, rather than faster; inequality was even greater than "promised," with the result that, in the United States, the incomes of the bottom 90 percent basically stagnated (Stiglitz et al. 2015). The welfare state, weakened but not gone, softened the consequences, especially in Europe, but did not reverse them: inequality grew in most countries around the world.

DEVELOPMENTS IN ECONOMICS

The irony was that this seeming faith in markets grew just as economists were beginning to understand the limits of markets and why market failures were so pervasive. Adam Smith's presumption—that markets would lead the economy, as if by an invisible hand, to societal well-being—was reversed. The first welfare theorem, that every competitive market economy was efficient, was turned on its head. Economists had always understood that markets are often not competitive; they understood, too, that when there are externalities, markets would not be efficient. Greenwald and Stiglitz (1986, 1988) showed that even competitive economies were almost always inefficient, so long as there were imperfections (asymmetries) of information and incomplete risk markets—that is, always.[9] These market failures were different from the kinds of market failures that economists had focused on following Arrow and Debreu's work, such as imperfections of competition and externalities, which presumably could be easily identified and corrected. Externalities, for instance, could be addressed through Pigouvian corrective taxes; anticompetitive behavior, through antitrust policies. The pervasive market failures identified by Arnott, Rothschild, Greenwald, Geanakoplos, Polemarchakis, and Stiglitz could not so easily be addressed.[10] This line of research has thus established that markets are efficient only under highly restrictive conditions, *which were essentially never satisfied*; hence the new presumption that markets are not efficient.

Arrow and Debreu provided sufficient conditions under which these results were true. For markets to be efficient in the management of risk, there has to be a full set of securities, called Arrow-Debreu securities. It is clear that such a full set does not in fact exist. Indeed, most individuals have a hard time buying insurance against some of the major risks that they confront. Subsequent research (focusing on the economics of information) has explained why markets for insurance are incomplete.

There followed a quest to answer two questions: (1) Would the results be approximately true if these assumptions were, in some sense, approximately satisfied? (2) And were there weaker conditions under which the theorems were still valid? Market advocates hoped that so long as the imperfections of information were not too great, the standard model would provide a good description of the economy and the economy would be, if not fully efficient, at least approximately so. They also hoped that there were weaker conditions than those assumed by Arrow and Debreu under which the economy would be fully efficient.

Unfortunately for market advocates, both of these hopes were disappointed. Rothschild and Stiglitz (1976) and Diamond (1971) showed that even a little bit of imperfection of information could have very large consequences. Some had hoped, for instance, that one could obtain efficiency in the absence of a complete set of insurance markets (Diamond 1967), but that proved to be wrong (Stiglitz 1982).

The central concerns of traditional welfare economics—social protection—were thus at the heart of this growing recognition of the limits of the markets.

Imperfections of information also implied that one could not separate issues of distribution from issues of efficiency: the second welfare theorem was also true only under restrictive and unrealistic conditions. Distribution affected the magnitude of agency costs in a society.[11] Moreover, imperfections of information meant that lump-sum taxes targeted at correcting distributional inequities could not exist. Greater inequalities in market incomes put a greater burden on redistribution through the tax and transfer system, and such redistributions were not costless.[12]

Not only has there been greater understanding of the inefficiency of markets, but there has also been greater understanding of the origins and adverse effects of inequality. Nineteenth-century justifications of inequality ("just deserts," marginal productivity) are increasingly unpersuasive. Increasing inequality arises only partially as a result of changes in factor prices—for example, as a result of skill-biased technological change. There may be increased intergenerational transmission of advantages—not just wealth—because of changes in our education system and increases in economic segregation. Furthermore, our tax system may also have facilitated increased intergenerational transmission of advantages (see Stiglitz 2015b).

In addition, developments in game theory and markets with information imperfections provided understandings of why imperfections of competition were so pervasive, as well as understandings of the links among this market power, inequality, and the precariousness felt by so many ordinary citizens. Market power was often exercised by the rich (often through corporations) to exploit the disadvantaged, or even ordinary individuals. Because markets do not exist in a vacuum, they have to be structured: how they are structured affects efficiency and distributions. The rules of the game are set through political processes. But economic power too often gets translated into political power. The political power of the rich enabled them to write the rules of the game to enhance their market power and incomes—and to exploit workers and consumers. A vicious circle emerged (Stiglitz 2012).

One of the most profound implications of this new understanding of inequality was that it became clear that there was not necessarily a trade-off between economic performance (broadly understood as growth, efficiency, and stability) and equality. Older doctrines held that if one wanted more equality, one had to pay a price. I, along with an increasing number of other economists and institutions, including leading mainstream institutions like the IMF and the OECD, have argued that we pay a high price for inequality and that, especially once we take into account what gave rise to this inequality, we could get better economic performance if we reduced inequality from the extremes to which it is rising in the United States and many other Western countries.[13]

The research just described explained how it was that even with most of the standard assumptions of conventional economics—including fully rational individuals—market outcomes were inefficient and inequitable. But in recent decades not only have assumptions such as perfect information, perfect risk markets, and perfect competition that underlie the neoliberal model been questioned, the rational actor model itself has also been discredited thanks to the development of behavioral economics. Firms have ruthlessly exploited these irrationalities.[14] Among those who are most vulnerable to such exploitation are the poorest.

Government has made less use of these insights than it might, whether to combat this exploitation or to develop programs that better meet the needs of society. Government and economic theorists have paid too little attention to understanding *endogeneity of preferences* and the implications that this has for policy—though the private sector spends considerable efforts in shaping preferences.[15] Additionally, government and economists have paid too little attention to the importance of the allocation of resources that occur within the household and firms, both of which occur without the mediation of prices and markets.

All of these increases in our understanding of the economy, the limitations of markets, the limitations of individual rationality, and the importance of equality should lead to a renewed focus on the welfare state—a reexamination of what it should do and how it should do it. Twenty-first-century welfare states should and will be different from those of the mid-twentieth century.

3. CHANGES IN THE WORLD

While changes in ideas provide a renewed interest in the welfare state and the role it can play in improving societal well-being, changes in the world have increased the imperative for reconstructing the welfare state.

For instance, there have been marked changes in the labor market—there are no longer lifetime jobs, implying less incentive for firms to invest in their workers and less loyalty between workers and firms. Workplace-based welfarism of the mid-twentieth-century variety won't work today.[16] Matters have been made even worse because of the "sharing economy" and "innovations" in worker-employer relations—converting workers into "independent contractors." Firms that have embraced these new models are motivated in part by the desire to avoid taxes and circumvent employer regulations.

At the same time, the enormous growth in inequality makes it clear that the market on its own, at least as it has been structured under neoliberalism, won't achieve anything approaching something that is socially acceptable, let alone any higher ambition, such as the just society. At the bottom, those in the United States confront the same real wages as they did sixty years ago. In the middle, the income of a full-time male worker—and it is increasingly difficult for those without a college education to get a full-time job—is comparable to what it was more than four decades ago.

There is an especially strong consensus that something needs to be done about childhood poverty—with approximately one in five people in the United States growing up in families in poverty. While the United States committed itself to the elimination of discrimination, the large wage gaps in gender, race, and ethnicity are evidence that discrimination still abounds. (The financial crisis of 2008 provided further evidence of racial and ethnic discrimination in lending.) Not only do the changes in the economy make it clear that the corporation cannot play the role in social protection that it once did, changes in the structure of our society limit the role of social institutions. Changes in demography mean that we have gone from the extended family to the nuclear family and, increasingly, to the non-family, as marriage becomes increasingly unpopular, especially among low-income individuals. As urbanization has progressed, social bonds have weakened, and with that the kind of social protection provided by communal solidarity (Putnam 2000, 2015).

Finally, there have been a number of changes that have weakened the bargaining power of workers—including poorly managed globalization—and increased the market power of firms. Some of these have led to weakened unionization, and weakened unionization has led in turn to workers' weakened bargaining power. Rents have taken on greater importance: the competitive model provides an increasingly poor description of many (or even most) sectors of the economy (Council of Economic Advisers 2016).

This means that without the protection of the state, there will be more individuals at the bottom, and the deprivations they suffer will only be addressed by state action, providing further impetus for a twenty-first-century welfare state.

4. PRINCIPLES AND PRACTICES OF A TWENTY-FIRST-CENTURY WELFARE STATE

The twenty-first-century welfare state is about achieving a just society and improving the well-being of ordinary citizens, recognizing that markets on their own won't necessarily do this and that corporate interests and national interests (interests of ordinary citizens) are often markedly different.

The modern welfare state focuses on inequalities in initial distribution of assets, asymmetries of market power (including those arising from asymmetries of information and associated with discrimination, past and present), and market failures, with special attention to those least able to fend for themselves, especially children, and to ensure that the basic prerequisites of a middle-class life (appropriate to the country's GDP) are accessible for most citizens.

Similarly, the modern welfare state does more than just provide a safety net, a subsistence floor. The focus of the traditional welfare state is on social protection—making up for the failure of private risk markets.

But the modern welfare state is more than that: it is also a system of consumer, investor, and worker protection, including a system trying to increase competitiveness and transparency of markets, in the belief that more competitive and transparent markets enhance the welfare of society.

A central tenet of a twenty-first-century welfare state is ensuring equality of opportunity, and that, of course, entails a particular focus on children and their health and education, fighting against the intergenerational transmission of advantages and disadvantages and against discrimination in all its forms. And there is increasing recognition that one can't have equality of opportunity in a society with large disparities in income and wealth.

MULTIPLE INSTRUMENTS

Earlier we observed that the twenty-first-century welfare state is focused on creating opportunities and improving outcomes but is not wedded to any particular mechanism for achieving these. It sometimes employs market mechanisms but rejects income fetishism—the idea that well-being is necessarily enhanced by cashing out benefits—and allows individuals to make choices of their own. This rejection is not a matter of paternalism, though it is partially motivated by a concern about children who are not allowed to make choices for themselves and may not be in good positions to make good decisions. Behavioral economics has shown that individuals may make short-run choices that are not in their long-run interests, and persistent irrationalities can and are exploited by profit-maximizing firms. But even absent these, market mechanisms may not be appropriate: pervasive market failures may make access to certain basic necessities difficult at best for those of modest income. Private sector firms can take advantage of those who are less informed and have shown the willingness and capacity to engage in broad and deep exploitation. This means, at a minimum, that relying on the private sector necessitates tight monitoring and regulation; but both monitoring and regulation can be difficult—and once a private sector has been established, a political economy process is set in play to weaken regulation and its enforcement.

Moreover, there can be social consequences from the way the private sector works, which in turn have important societal consequences. In education, for instance, it can result in segregation by income or ability.[17] Again, one can imagine regulation to prevent this, but the design and implementation of such regulation is difficult. Further, education has shown itself to be one of the areas where exploitation is particularly easy: those from poor backgrounds may be in a weak position to judge what is being "sold," and in the United States, private for-profit colleges have proved particularly adept at taking advantage of this. The industry has also proved to be particularly adept at fighting off attempts to regulate it—even attempts to force disclosure of information (such as graduation rates, employment rates and average salaries for degree holders) that would facilitate good choices on the part of potential enrollees.

One can think, moreover, of there being social externalities, with the education of one child being affected by who else is in the classroom. But it is more than that: the provision of public education, with children from all backgrounds sharing similar experiences, helps shape society, providing an example of the endogeneity of preferences and attitudes discussed earlier in this chapter.[18]

While market power and asymmetries of bargaining power can arise in any market, the consequences can be particularly important in the provision of basic necessities. There can be, and typically is, more concern about the redistributive consequences. (By contrast, the social consequences of market power in diamonds are likely to be more limited.) Here, if the market is relied upon, a welfare-state government has to be particularly sensitive to the importance of the rules of the game; changing the rules of the game can change relative bargaining positions.

For instance, in a twenty-first-century welfare state, most jobs will be provided by the private sector, but there must be rules that facilitate workers engaging in collective bargaining. And the government will need to impose constraints on the market processes, setting minimum wages, maximum hours, minimum overtime pay, minimum family leave benefits, and so on.

All of the instruments relevant to reducing inequality might be considered part of "welfare policies," going well beyond the usual tax and transfer policies. Antitrust and consumer protection policies may be especially important in preventing exploitation. Changes in corporate governance and bankruptcy laws over the last thirty years in the United States have played an important role in the increase in extremes of inequality at the top and have even contributed to the increase in poverty. Creditor-friendly bankruptcy laws encouraged, for instance, predatory lending, with lenders knowing that it would be more difficult for individuals to discharge their debts.

GOVERNMENT AS PRODUCER AND REGULATOR (AND ENTREPRENEUR)

The neoliberal agenda attempted to discredit government in many of its roles, except perhaps in providing a safety net for corporations, as was evident in the aftermath of the 2008 crisis. The oft-noted irony is that an agenda focused on minimizing the role of the state had resulted in the largest intervention of the state ever. But while corporations were provided with social protection, much more limited social protection was provided to those losing their homes and jobs. In the United States, of the hundreds of billions of dollars that went to "saving the economy," a very small fraction went to helping homeowners. Many conservatives opposed providing bankruptcy relief or extending unemployment insurance, even as many reached even the extended time limits for support.

However, government-run programs can play an important role in the twenty-first-century welfare state. The next section will illustrate the role they can play through income-contingent loan programs; and our previous discussion has noted problems associated with the private provision of education.

Government has marked advantages in information, transactions cost, risk pooling, and the avoidance of exploitation. There at least needs to be strong government oversight in areas like insurance, education, and health, recognizing not only market failures but also the opportunities for exploitation.

As we noted earlier, in some areas government has proved to be an effective catalyst and entrepreneur, and not just in innovation.[19] Public social insurance for retirement has perhaps provided the spur leading to the development of the private annuity markets, though again, as we noted earlier, private annuities remain expensive, partly because of the large profits, sales costs, and other transactions costs.[20]

At the same time, a better understanding of economics has enabled an improvement in the design of the programs provided by the welfare state. Behavioral economics, for instance, has provided insights into how "nudges" can increase retirement security (see Sunstein and Thaler 2008). Combining income-contingent loan programs with standard unemployment insurance can lead to more efficient provision of insurance (Stiglitz and Yun 2014; 2017), as can the integration of various social insurance programs (Stiglitz and Yun 2005). Advances in the economics of information have also made it clear that the intertwining of adverse selection and moral hazard made reliance on private markets for health insurance at best problematic,[21] and that care even had to be taken in allowing private supplementation of public provision.[22]

5. DEPRIVATIONS

The growth of the welfare state was associated with the recognition that there were large groups in society suffering from significant deprivations—even in wealthy countries. For simplicity, we can divide them into three groups: youth, the elderly, and the poor of working age.

THE ELDERLY

The distinction between neoliberalism and the welfare state is perhaps clearest in the context of the treatment of the elderly. If the elderly have insufficient income to live a decent life, the neoliberal response is: they should have saved for their retirement. Those that did not save enough are getting the just deserts of their profligacy, of their failure to save and manage risk appropriately. The nanny state undermines incentives for individuals to take care of themselves, according to the neoliberal view, and almost inevitably results in those who are responsible subsidizing those who are not. Since it was realized that individuals might not save enough, and that our humane society was too soft not to bail out an elderly person who hadn't saved adequately, there needed to be a *minimal* compulsory savings program with minimal or no discretion over the management of funds.[23] And because some individuals had so low an income during their lifetimes that there was no way their savings could finance a retirement with a minimum of human decency, there was a need for supplementing what these workers would receive on an actuarial fair basis.

Yet this twentieth-century perspective ignored multiple failures in the market for annuities and retirement products: (1) Before social security, the market did not provide adequate annuities; and indeed, the market for annuities has been very slow to develop. (2) Even as it developed, premiums were high, partly because of high administrative costs compared with the government, which could take advantage of certain economies of scale and scope, including lower transactions costs in collecting and dispersing funds. (3) Even today, those who manage retirement accounts are often not required to obey fiduciary standards, resulting in large transfers of wealth from retirees to those managing the funds. (4) Today, markets do not provide adequate insurance against some of the important risks, which are sometimes hard to anticipate. Private annuities do not provide insurance against inflation. Those buying safe government bonds can't buy insurance against the risk that the government will push interest rates down to zero for an extended period of time.

Modern theory has explained why, with adverse selection, important insurance markets (like the market for annuities) may not exist. Government can force pooling and risk sharing in ways that the private sector cannot.

Ironically, much of the interest in privatization of social security arose from the desire of the financial sector to increase its profits: they wanted to increase transactions costs, and they knew that there were huge opportunities for them to "phish for phools"[24]—to find individuals who were relatively financially unsophisticated and could be exploited.[25]

Thus, today, many elderly in the United States who prudently put their savings into government bonds are bereft of income. They acted responsibly: who could have anticipated a decade of zero interest rates? Neoliberalism simply accepts that they were unlucky. The welfare state says that societal well-being can be improved by providing social protection—social insurance—against the vagaries of markets.

CHILDREN

We have argued that the neoliberal philosophy of putting the onus for deprivation among the elderly on the individual is questionable; but even most of those who believe that there should, in general, be reliance on markets agree that the same approach cannot be adopted for children. One cannot claim that they should have done a better job at picking their parents.

Admittedly, there are real concerns with state paternalism. What happens, for instance, if parental views about education differ from those of the government? But such issues arise with or without the welfare state. The welfare state is concerned about access to resources—including educational resources—not who directs how those resources are used.

Even with children, there are moral hazard/incentive issues: parents may not work as hard knowing that the state will provide some support. The magnitude of these effects is almost surely not large; but in any case, advocates of the welfare state put primacy on the well-being of the child and the long-run consequences of the child facing deprivations. Though this is an ethical stance, from a long-run efficiency view, the economic benefits of ensuring that each child lives up to his or her potential almost surely outweigh any adverse incentive effect, if one exists.

There is one more philosophical issue: many parents may believe that they have a fundamental right to advantage their children over others. This conflicts with a principle of equality of opportunity. In some societies, such inequities would be viewed as intolerable. In others, circumscribing them would be viewed as intolerable. The welfare state begins with the premise that *at a minimum* every child should have the opportunity to live up to his or her potential. This entails access to good preschool education and to affordable higher education, either through low tuition (subsidized by the state) or income-contingent loans (as in Australia).[26] And most of those subscribing to welfare-state principles, while not proscribing individuals from attempting to give some advantage to their children—how could one even imagine doing that—want to tilt the scale at least slightly toward equality. Thus, there is free public education, and parents wishing to send their children to private school forgo this benefit. But the charter school movement is in part an attempt at circumvention of this attempt at creating a more egalitarian educational system, unless strict regulations are imposed on the socioeconomic and racial mix of students. Local education in the United States suffers from a similar problem: with increasing economic segregation, rich parents move to rich suburbs to get their children a "private-school quality" education. If one is committed to maintaining a modicum of equality of opportunity, one has to ensure more economic integration and less dispersion in spending.

THE WORKING-AGE POPULATION

Neoliberalism and the welfare state have the greatest conflict when it comes to the working-age population. The young cannot be held accountable for their state. The elderly can be, but it's too late to lecture them that they should have saved more. But what about those who are able to work but do not. Should one let them suffer?

Here, the advocates of the welfare state again emphasize the presence of market failures. With high levels of unemployment, it may be hard to get jobs. India has made the most important contribution to the welfare state agenda: the rural guaranteed-employment scheme, which guarantees a job for everyone willing to work in a public works project, at a wage at or slightly below the minimum wage.

Even a full-time worker may be in poverty, if market wages are too low. Neoliberals and welfare state advocates often agree that if someone works full time, he or she should not be in poverty; there needs to be an earned income tax credit to ensure that all full-time workers deserve to live above the poverty level. (Some advocates of a welfare state believe that there are other tools the government should use—namely, a minimum wage.)

Welfare state advocates are typically concerned not just with income but with access to certain basic goods, like food, medical care, and shelter. Presumably, if everyone had an income large enough to guarantee adequate access to these basic goods, then there would not be such a concern about these goods. But no country has achieved that ideal, and in its absence, welfare state advocates argue that some attention must be paid to ensuring that individuals have access to adequate amounts of these basic necessities. But there is another reason for their focus on these markets: the belief that they often do not work well, in ways that lead to large numbers of the poor and middle class facing deprivation. Direct intervention is needed. Today, as our understanding of market failures has improved, there is a better grasp of why the markets for these goods often fail, and this knowledge can be used either to design ways of correcting the market failure and/or to create better systems of public provision. Neoliberal economists, by contrast, tend to ignore or minimize these market failures; and even when they recognize them, they suggest that government actions are not likely to improve matters. In some cases, they believe that the market failures have been exacerbated by the government.

The growing concern about labor-saving technological progress—the notion that robots may replace humans, and that jobs for all but the highly skilled will be scarce—has led to growing support for a universal basic income (UBI), a grant given to everyone. This proposal also has the support of many who believe that targeted welfare programs (aimed at the "needy") are sufficiently cumbersome and inefficient that they often do not reach those in need, and when they do, they do so in ways that undermine human dignity. While recognizing the merits of these arguments, I still believe that work is an essential part of human dignity and a meaningful life, and that our economic system must be designed to provide work that pays a livable income to any who are able and willing to engage in it. Besides, we are far from the point, even in our richest countries, where there is a public willingness to tax at a level that would ensure that the UBI benefit would be sufficient to sustain a decent life.

6. ELEMENTS OF A TWENTY-FIRST-CENTURY SYSTEM FOR THE UNITED STATES

Any welfare state program has to be tailored to the country and its history, institutions, and problems. In advanced countries like the United States, the scope for tax evasion is limited, and most transactions now occur digitally. Indeed, it would be easy to move to a completely digital system (see Stiglitz 2016a, 2016c, 2017). By contrast, in Latin America, where there is a strong welfare state tradition, many people still fall within the informal sector—those small-scale economic activities that the government often does not fully monitor or tax and that typically provide few of the fringe benefits and job security associated with the formal sector. Much of the social protection is directed at those in the formal sector—who are typically better off than those in the informal sector—and the worry is that, if there is a fiscal deficit in these programs to be made up for by support from general revenues, the beneficiaries of such state support are those who are better off on average. The response is to make more of the schemes universal and less contingent on income (because income is not accurately observable for large portions of the population). But moves in that direction result in the programs providing less social insurance—evening out income across good and bad "events." Income-contingent public loan programs (described in greater detail later) may be one way of squaring the circle.

In many quarters, there has been resistance to the notion of the welfare state, with even Democratic presidents justifying the strength of our corporate welfare system (but not the weakness of our system of social protection for the rest of society) by saying that we're different from Scandinavia.[27] That puts a special onus on those proposing public programs. Yet, while there is widespread skepticism of public programs, there is very strong support for both Social Security and Medicare. Indeed, in a famous incident at a 2009 town hall meeting with a congressman from South Carolina, an audience member shouted for the representative to "keep your government hands off my Medicare": evidently, because the program was so successful, it was presumed it must be a private program.

In the following sections, I briefly describe elements of a twenty-first-century welfare state for the United States.

PROGRAMS AIMED AT THE ELDERLY

Medicare and Social Security should continue to be at the center of programs for the elderly. These programs have elements of both intergenerational and intragenerational distribution. It is not clear that the design of these programs takes into account differences in life expectancy and retirement ages across income classes to the extent it should. These differences may be becoming even more important.[28] Changing the structure of retirement income with retirement age can rectify existing inequities, at least on average.

But there are at least three important extensions that should be considered:

1. PUBLIC OPTION FOR SUPPLEMENTARY COVERAGE FOR MEDICARE, STRONGER FIDUCIARY REGULATIONS FOR PRIVATE SUPPLEMENTARY COVERAGE, AND TAXES ON CERTAIN TYPES OF SUPPLEMENTAL COVERAGE

The provision of supplemental insurance interacts with the public provision of base coverage. Again there is an irony: neoliberals consistently worry about the moral hazard effect, the effect of coverage on the likelihood of the insured-against event occurring. They worry that people will not take as good care of themselves if they have health insurance or that they will overuse medical care. Yet when it comes to advocating for private supplemental coverage, these concerns are suddenly forgotten. If such coverage were provided by a competitive, nonexploitative market, there would be excessive coverage, because the private sector firms would ignore the additional costs their coverage imposes on the public sector. But the sector is often far from perfectly competitive, and there is ample opportunity to exploit the elderly, especially given the complexities of the coverage, that is, describing what is and is not covered.

That is why it may be desirable to have a public option, one that enables consumers to feel they are not being exploited. The public option would likely be less expensive (more value per dollar premium), simply because it can take advantage of economies of scale and scope—the government is already providing Medicare coverage to everyone. Moreover, because so much of private insurance companies' costs are associated with marketing, cream skimming (efforts to ensure that one is insuring only good risks), and collecting insurance premium and other charges, overall "transaction costs"—dollars that go to running the insurance system rather than to providing health care benefits—would be lower with the public option than under the current regime.

The pervasive incentive of private providers to engage in cream skimming, the attempt to recruit as customers only the most healthy—imposing a kind of externality on others—provides a rationale for forbidding private coverage, regulating it to ensure that it does not engage in cream skimming, or taxing it in a way that reduces the incentives for cream skimming.

2. RETIREMENT INSURANCE

The United States has created a multitiered system—an efficient, universal basic coverage provided by government; corporate pensions for those lucky enough to work for a corporation providing these tax-preferenced benefits; and a supplemental retirement program that, up to a point, also receives tax preferences. In these programs, individuals are left to invest in the market, with the individual drawing down his or her savings post-retirement or purchasing annuities. Corporate programs have switched from defined benefits to defined contributions, and thus both corporate and individual supplementary programs leave huge risks on the shoulders of ordinary citizens; and as we have noted, market annuities leave much to be desired. Criticism of the basic universal coverage is not based on its lack of efficiency but on the fact that, in some central forecasting models of the evolution of the economy over the next seventy-five years, its expenditures will exceed its revenues. Critics argue, moreover, that political economy considerations make it difficult to bring the public program back into balance.

The fact of the matter is that the deficit is relatively small, sufficiently small that reasonable alternative estimates of, say, migration would bring it back into balance. Alternatively, small adjustments either to taxes to finance it or to the design of the program itself would bring it back into balance. Part of the reluctance to make large changes now in the anticipation that fiscal gaps would appear later is that the models on which the projections of fiscal deficits depend are highly sensitive to the assumptions.

Prior to the 2008 financial crisis, there was a big push, especially by those in the private financial sector, to at least partially privatize social security. The argument was that the private sector was more efficient; the reality was just the opposite. It was simply an attempt by the private sector to grab more rents for itself; the incomes of those selling the annuities increase as transaction costs increase—all at the expense of retirees. Results from the partial privatization of social security in the United Kingdom suggested that retirement benefits might be reduced by as much as 40 percent (Orszag and Stiglitz 2001).

A further critique of private programs is that, here again, there is an incentive to "phish for phools" (Akerlof and Shiller 2015)—profits can be increased more readily by developing better ways of exploiting the unwary than by lowering transactions costs or "beating the market" in one's investments, both extremely difficult. Indeed, the resistance the financial sector put up against fiduciary standards to prevent conflicts of interest was remarkable. They seemed to argue that they could not function if they were not allowed to continue with practices rife with conflicts of interest.

Again, a public option provides effective competition to the private sector and security against exploitation: the government would simply allow individuals to make contributions to social security, treating such contributions as if they were received as a result of employment. That is, what a retiree receives is based on contributions made into his or her account over the many years before retirement, both by the worker and by the employer on the worker's behalf. Those with greater contributions receive more back in their social security benefits. Now, there is a cap, because contributions are limited; in 2017, individuals and their employers only made contributions on incomes up to $127,200. The "public option" would allow individuals to choose to make contributions beyond that—and to put aside, in their social security account, more of their income than the 6.2 percent they currently contribute.

3. NURSING HOME CARE

The facts that individuals are living longer, families are getting smaller, and the cost of housing is high in the urban areas where an increasingly large proportion of families live mean that increasingly large numbers of the elderly are left to themselves in their old age. They have to turn to nursing homes, which they cannot afford. Through Medicare, the government is picking up a large fraction of these costs. Over the years, there have been discussions of adding nursing home care to the Social Security program. Private insurance again has proven very costly. Such insurance could be provided by a modest increase in the Medicare or Social Security contributions.

PROGRAMS FOR CHILDREN

There is an increasing recognition of the inequities faced by children from poor families and that investing in these children can pay large social dividends. There is a need for stronger prenatal and preschool programs. Earlier programs aimed at ensuring nutrition and health for all children have proven their worth.

Reducing inequities at birth requires not just equal access to education but compensatory education systems.

Children live in families, and income support for low-income parents redounds to the benefit of children. That, of course, is part of the philosophy of the earned income tax credit. That program has to be extended and strengthened.

Children from poor families get off to an unfair start even when compensations are attempted, but when it comes to tertiary education, they are again placed at a disadvantage. America used to be the leader in the fraction of the population that goes on to college; it no longer is, because it is more difficult for a young American of modest means to go to college or get access to a quality education to live up to his or her potential than is the case in other developed countries. President Obama recognized this, but he only offered to have universal access to community colleges. While these institutions have played an important role in extending access, the quality is typically not the same as in the country's best schools. Some critics say that we cannot afford even this much. But somehow, at the end of World War II, as we emerged with an enormous debt—130 percent of GDP—the country said that it could afford to provide education to all who had fought in the war, essentially every young man and many women, for as many years at as good a school as the person was qualified to attend. The country is much richer now; anyone who says the country can't afford this is making a statement about *choices* and *preferences*—that he or she thinks there are better ways of spending that money, such as leaving it in the pockets of the very wealthy or the banks or the corporations and letting them determine how it is spent. By contrast, anyone committed to a twenty-first-century welfare state would argue that one must ensure affordable access to college for *all*.

Around the world, there are two approaches: low tuition (financed by government subsidies) or income-contingent loans. The latter have proven particularly effective in Australia. With the government providing the loans, the transaction costs will be low. Repayment can be done through the tax system, and the cost of capital for the government is far lower than for the private sector.

This is another area where more regulation is required—both on those providing finance and those providing higher education.

PROGRAMS TO GUARANTEE FULL ACCESS TO THE LABOR MARKET

There is also increasing recognition that the poor, and many middle-class Americans, do not have equal access to labor markets. Discrimination is pervasive. America has done less to make it easy for women to participate in the labor market and get ahead—which is why female labor force participation rates in the United States trail those of the best performing countries. Public transportation systems are weak, and when they exist, they often do not provide connections between the locations where low- and middle-income Americans live and where the jobs are situated.

Furthermore, an excessive focus on inflation and an unwillingness to engage in sufficiently large and effective fiscal policies has meant that the economy is often at less than full employment. Unemployment puts downward pressure on wages, especially when combined with provisions that have weakened workers' bargaining position.

The remedies for these problems are clear: stronger antidiscrimination laws more effectively enforced; active labor market policies to help those who lose a job get the skills needed for the new jobs being created; childcare and family leave policies; public transportation policies focused on connecting people and jobs; and a renewed commitment to full-employment policies.

BASIC ELEMENTS OF A MIDDLE-CLASS LIFE

The basic elements of a middle-class life seem increasingly out of reach for many Americans. Among those requisites are health care, housing, education for one's children, and a modicum of security, including retirement security and social protection in case one loses a job. I have already discussed several aspects of these. Here, I identify programs that might address other deficiencies in current arrangements.

1. HEALTH

The Affordable Care Act (ACA) made great strides in increasing access to health care, but twenty-six states refused to extend Medicaid so that more of the previously uninsured were covered. This extension was a central part of the "design" of ACA, so there are still large gaps in coverage, though the numbers without insurance are, at the same time, markedly lower than before ACA. (This fact was brought home forcefully in 2017, as Republicans attempted to "repeal and replace" ACA. They simply could not come up with a new program that didn't leave some twenty million Americans who now have health insurance coverage without coverage. While many Americans still did not fully recognize access to medical care as a basic human right, the vast majority believed that millions *more* should not be left uninsured.) Beyond ensuring that *everyone* has health insurance, there are three further reforms needed. First is to recognize that health and access to health care are basic rights, as other countries have done.

Second is to improve competition in health care provision. There has been disappointment in the level of competition in many of the so-called exchanges that the ACA mandated, which are supposed to be marketplaces where consumers can compare plans. In some cases, there may be scope for stronger antitrust enforcement. In many cases, though, it may not be easy to prove collusion, and thus competition laws will not suffice.

What is required for competition is a public option, which can simply be provided by extending access to Medicare to everyone. (This had been originally proposed as part of the ACA, but got scuttled as the law was debated.) The presence of the public option will lead to more competitive pricing by private firms.

Third and finally, there must be policies aimed at behavioral changes and ensuring the availability of good nutrition. An increasing proportion of health problems are associated with social diseases, like obesity. The market has left large parts of the country as "food deserts," places, for instance, where it is hard to access fresh fruits and vegetables. In New York, former mayor Michael Bloomberg showed how public policy could remedy such shortcomings.

Many of these social diseases are in part the result of corporate avarice—corporations that enrich themselves by selling unhealthy foods, including to children, or, as in the case of cigarettes, making their products more addictive. What is required are strong regulations curbing these purveyors of disease and death.

2. HOUSING

Many Americans face inadequate housing and obtain housing finance only at excessively high costs. The private sector model of providing housing finance proved its inadequacies in the 2008 crisis, in which the housing bubble played such a large role. But as the practices of the private sector came under scrutiny, it became clear that they were more focused on exploitation—exploiting both consumers and investors—than on risk management. Remarkably, nine years after the crisis, the private sector model is still broken; the government provides more than 90 percent of all housing finance.

While there is an open question about how best to provide housing for low-income individuals, there is a simple solution for providing housing finance, which I call the public option for housing finance. There are two pieces of information that are critical in determining an individual's eligibility for a mortgage—the value of the house and the individual's income—and both of these pieces of information exist in public records. Transferring this information from the public sector to the private sector is costly. This would become unnecessary under the public option. Moreover, the cost of collection would be greatly reduced; there are economies of scope in using the tax-collection system. Repayment could even be made on an income-contingent basis. Thus, a better product could be provided at a lower cost. The loan could be provided at just a little more than the rate at which the government borrows.

3. SOCIAL PROTECTION SYSTEMS

Individuals are averse to risk; they care about the risks they face, and security has a value. The market overcharges—or simply doesn't provide the security that individuals want and, as has been suggested, government could provide. Much of what we have already discussed is part of society's social protection system. Here, I want to make two observations.

Most individuals are unemployed for periods that represent a small fraction of their working lives. Unemployment, especially for the young or average wage earners, has a high cost, because they cannot engage in intertemporal smoothing. Providing unemployment loans (possibly income-contingent) would enable individuals to smooth their incomes without the adverse incentive effects sometimes associated with unemployment insurance. It would allow them to continue to search for jobs appropriate to their skills and preferences, thus increasing GDP (Stiglitz and Yun 2005).

But there are some individuals who face repeated and/or extended bouts of unemployment; thus "interstate insurance"—insurance against this risk—is important. But the risk of future unemployment decreases the unattractiveness of a conventional loan (even if one could get one) to tide one over a short bout of unemployment, since it lowers consumption in some states where the marginal utility of income is very high. There is an easy solution: income-contingent unemployment loans. The optimal unemployment benefit program thus consists of a combination of income-contingent unemployment loans and unemployment insurance. The optimal design looks markedly different from that of the U.S. unemployment system (Stiglitz and Yun 2014, 2017).

More broadly, the design of optimal systems of social protection entails maximizing risk mitigation while minimizing market distortions (adverse incentive effects), and this can be done by pooling risks, that is, having a single individual lifetime account addressing a variety of risks, along the lines of Singapore or Malaysia's provident fund. It provides for a high level of individual responsibility—because of the risk pooling, individuals can themselves take care of most of the risks they face—while allowing social insurance against large cumulative calamities.

7. CONCLUDING REMARKS

Many critics of the welfare state believed it would bring down the economy, as the weight of social obligations and the security provided by social insurance both eroded incentives. It turned out that none of the major crises have been related to the welfare state but were instead brought on by the excesses of the financial sector (the sector that employs many of the welfare state's critics). Even after the crisis, some in the financial sector (including the European Central Bank) found it difficult not to seize the opportunity to warn against the dangers of the welfare state, even though countries with the strongest welfare states were among those with the strongest recoveries.

The question is sometimes posed: Is a welfare state viable today? Globalization has in many ways increased the need for a modern welfare state, but at the same time reduced the fiscal capacity to provide it, because of tax competition.[29]

There are two responses. The first is that we must reform globalization, limit the scope for tax competition, and design effective systems of taxation of multinational corporations. In Europe, this is an especially important issue, because of the ease with which goods, money, and people can move. On the Continent, there is a need for a progressive Europe-wide income tax, the revenues from which could in part be used to provide some basic social protection.

The second is to note that a well-designed welfare state would actually *increase* overall economic performance. As we noted, there is now a large body of theory and a wealth of evidence that societies that are more equal perform better, having both higher growth and more stability. We noted earlier, for instance, that equity can lead to more innovative societies, because individuals are more willing to take risks. [30] Karl Ove Moene and his co-authors (Moene 2013; Barth, Moene, and Willumsen 2015) have also noted the benefits in creating a politics that supports openness: with a modicum of social protection, individuals are more willing to accept change and openness. The evident growth in protectionist sentiments among Americans and Europeans who have been left behind bears testimony to this insight.

Thus, the welfare state is not *only* a matter of social justice. Still, I believe the most compelling case for the welfare state goes beyond these narrow economic arguments. It even goes beyond standard arguments for social justice. We must ask ourselves: What kind of society do we wish to live in, and what kind of individuals do we wish to be? For those who support the welfare state, its central role is in creating compassionate individuals with a social conscience and a sense of solidarity with their fellow citizens.

NOTES

1. Interview of Mario Draghi in the *Wall Street Journal* (Blackstone, Karnitschnig, and Thomson 2012).

2. As in any set of doctrines, there are large differences in views among the adherents of these market-based philosophies. I ignore those subtleties here and refer to doctrines that argue against the welfare state and for the reliance on markets as "neoliberalism."

3. These are referred to as the first and second fundamental theorems of welfare economics. For further elaboration on these issues, see Stiglitz (1994).

4. The welfare state can thus be contrasted with the *developmental state*, which focused on the role of government in promoting development (especially in East Asia—see, for example, Chang 1999), and the *entrepreneurial state* (Mazzucato 2015), which focused on the role of government in promoting innovation.

5. In the United States, for example, Medicare provides health insurance for the elderly. In the United Kingdom, the National Health Service provides such insurance more broadly.

6. Hoff and Stiglitz (2016) emphasize the endogeneity of preferences and the role that society plays in structuring beliefs. See, in particular, their citations to evidence concerning the effects of banking on greed and dishonesty.

7. The discussion of endogenous preferences above poses difficulties for this framework of social justice.

8. Section II elaborates on these issues, with a particular focus on the implications for social justice.

9. In particular, they showed that the economy was not *constrained* Pareto efficient, that is, there exist interventions within the given market structure that would make some individuals better off without making anyone else worse off. See also Arnott, Greenwald, and Stiglitz (1994); and Geanakoplos and Polemarchakis (1986).

10. Rothschild and Stiglitz (1976) showed that even a slight amount of information imperfections (asymmetries) had very large effects on equilibrium outcomes—or even the existence of equilibrium. In short, the standard theory was not robust.

11. See Shapiro and Stiglitz (1984); and Stiglitz (1993b, 1994).

12. See Stiglitz (1998, 2016b).

13. This was the central point of Stiglitz (2012). There have been a rash of empirical studies from the IMF (Ostry, Berg, and Tsangarides 2014; Dabla-Norris et al. 2015), the OECD (Cingano 2014), and elsewhere corroborating this perspective.

14. Evidenced so strongly in the Great Recession. See chapter 10 in Stiglitz (2010). See also Akerlof and Shiller (2015).

15. See Hoff and Stiglitz (2016); World Bank (2015); Sunstein (2016); and the references cited therein.

16. Just as earlier, the decline in the extended family and urbanization, with the weakening of the sense of community and the decreased role of religion, placed increasing burdens on the state for social protection.

17. For instance, if the rich prefer having their children go to school with the rich, profit-maximizing schools for the rich will be economically segregated.

18. Given the centrality of education to our society, it is not surprising that there is a large literature on these subjects—the effects of choice on the quality of education and on educational segregation; the consequences of particular market and market-like mechanisms, such as vouchers and charter schools; the political economy of private education; and market failures in education, particularly once one sees education not just as part of the formation of human capital but as at the center of how society screens individuals, differentiating among those with different abilities. Stiglitz (1973) discussed social externalities and the efficient provision of education; Stiglitz (1974) discussed the interactions between private and public educational systems, with a majoritarian political economy model; Stiglitz (1977) analyzed more broadly the inefficiencies associated with the provision of public goods by local authorities; Stiglitz (1975) discussed the inefficiencies of the market provision of education, when there is screening; and Stiglitz (1988) analyzed how market inefficiencies even extended to the market provision of textbooks.

19. See Mazzucato's book, *The Entrepreneurial State* (2015), describing the central role that government has played in the big innovations in recent decades.

20. And, like all insurance markets, they face problems of adverse selection.

21. See Stiglitz and Yun (2013)

22. There are important externalities that can be addressed, at least in part, by appropriate taxation. See Arnott and Stiglitz (1986, 1990).

23. See Stiglitz (1993a).

24. In the words of Akerlof and Shiller (2015).

25. The financial sector has engaged in extensive and well-documented fraud, but what we are talking about here is more subtle—selling products to individuals with higher fees that cannot be justified by performance.

26. See Chapman, Higgins, and Stiglitz (2014).

27. This was Obama's defense for his bank bailout, when it was pointed out that there were far better ways of dealing with banks in trouble—ways that are more consistent with the "rules" of capitalism. See Stiglitz (2010).

28. See Case and Deaton (2015, 2017).

29. This is a theme I analyzed in Stiglitz (2013). See also the other papers in that volume, in particular Moene (2013).

30. See Stiglitz (2015a).

REFERENCES

Akerlof, G. A., and R. J. Shiller. 2015. *Phishing for Phools: The Economics of Manipulation and Deception*. Princeton, N.J.: Princeton University Press.

Arnott, Richard, and J. E. Stiglitz. 1986. "Moral Hazard and Optimal Commodity Taxation." *Journal of Public Economics* 29:1–24.

———. 1990. "The Welfare Economics of Moral Hazard." In *Risk, Information and Insurance: Essays in the Memory of Karl H. Borch*, ed. H. Louberge, pp. 91–122. Norwell, Mass.: Kluwer Academic.

Arnott, R., B. Greenwald, and J. E. Stiglitz. 1994. "Information and Economic Efficiency." *Information Economics and Policy* 6(1):77–82.

Blackstone, B., M. Karnitschnig, and R. Thomson. 2012. "Europe's Banker Talks Tough—Draghi Says Continent's Social Model Is 'Gone,' Won't Backtrack on Austerity." *Wall Street Journal*. Retrieved from www.wsj.com/articles/SB100014240529 70203960804577241221244896782.

Barth, Erling, Karl O. Moene, and Fredrik Willumsen. 2015. "The Scandinavian Model—An Interpretation." *Journal of Public Economics* 117(July):60–72.

Case, A., and A. Deaton. 2015. "Rising Morbidity and Mortality in Midlife Among White Non-Hispanic Americans in the 21st Century." *Proceedings of the National Academy of Sciences*, 112(49):15078–83.

———. 2017. "Mortality and Morbidity in the 21st Century." Brookings Papers on Economic Activity, Spring 2017. Washington, D.C.: Brookings Institution.

Chang, Ha-Joon. 1999. "The Economic Theory of the Developmental State." In *The Developmental State*, ed. Meredith Woo-Cumings, pp. 192–99. Ithaca, N.Y.: Cornell University Press.

Chapman, B., T. Higgins, and J. E. Stiglitz, eds. 2014. *Income Contingent Loans: Theory, Practice and Prospects*. Houndmills, U.K.: Palgrave Macmillan.

Cingano, F. 2014. "Trends in Income Inequality and Its Impact on Economic Growth." OECD Social, Employment and Migration Working Papers 163. Paris, France: OECD Publishing.

Council of Economic Advisers. 2016. *Economic Report of the President (2016)*. Executive Office of the President. Washington, D.C.: U.S. Government Printing Office. Retrieved from www.gpo.gov/fdsys/pkg/ERP-2016/pdf/ERP-2016.pdf.

Dabla-Norris, M. E., M. K. Kochhar, M. N. Suphaphiphat, M. F. Ricka, and E. Tsounta. 2015. "Causes and Consequences of Income Inequality: A Global Perspective." IMF Staff Discussion Notes, 15/13. https://www.imf.org/external/pubs /ft/sdn/2015/sdn1513.pdf.

Diamond, P. A. 1967. "The Role of a Stock Market in a General Equilibrium Model with Technological Uncertainty." *American Economic Review* 57(4):759–776.

——. 1971. "A Model of Price Adjustment." *Journal of Economic Theory* 3(2):156–168.

Geanakoplos, J., and H. Polemarchakis. 1986. "Existence, Regularity, and Constrained Suboptimality of Competitive Allocations when the Asset Market Is Incomplete." In *Uncertainty, Information and Communication: Essays in Honor of KJ Arrow*, vol. 3, ed. W. P. Heller, R. M. Starr, and D. A. Starrett, pp. 65–96, Cambridge: Cambridge University Press.

Greenwald, Bruce, and J. E. Stiglitz. 1986. "Externalities in Economies with Imperfect Information and Incomplete Markets." *Quarterly Journal of Economics* 101(2): 229–264.

——. 1988. "Pareto Inefficiency of Market Economies: Search and Efficiency Wage Models." *American Economic Review* 78(2):351–355.

Hoff, K., and J. E. Stiglitz. 2010. "Equilibrium Fictions: A Cognitive Approach to Societal Rigidity." *American Economic Review* 100(2):141–146. Shortened version of Policy Research Working Paper 5219 (same title), World Bank Development Research Group (February 2010). Accessible at http://elibrary.worldbank.org/docserver /download/5219.pdf?expires=1304012730&id=id&accname=guest&checksum=5 428C2B3013CF8ECBB54953BAC3F328C.

——. 2016. "Striving for Balance in Economics: Towards a Theory of the Social Determination of Behavior." *Journal of Economic Behavior and Organization* 126(June):25–57.

Mazzucato, M. 2015. *The Entrepreneurial State: Debunking Public vs. Private Sector Myths*. London: Anthem.

Moene, K. O. 2013. "Scandinavian Equality: A Prime Example of Protection Without Protectionism." In *The Quest for Security: Protection Without Protectionism and the Challenge of Global Governance*, ed. M. Kaldor and J. E. Stiglitz, 48–74. New York: Columbia University Press.

Orszag, P., and J. E. Stiglitz. 2001. "Rethinking Pension Reform: Ten Myths About Social Security Systems." In *New Ideas About Old Age Security*, ed. R. Holman and J. E. Stiglitz, 17–56. Washington, D.C.: World Bank.

Ostry, M. J. D., M. A. Berg, and M. C. G. Tsangarides. 2014. "Redistribution, Inequality, and Growth." IMF Staff Discussion Notes, 14/2. https://www.imf.org /external/pubs/ft/sdn/2014/sdn1402.pdf.

Putnam, R. D. 2000. *Bowling Alone: The Collapse and Revival of American Community*. New York: Simon & Schuster.

——. 2015. *Our Kids: The American Dream in Crisis*. New York: Simon & Schuster.

Rawls, John. 1971. *A Theory of Justice*. Cambridge, Mass.: Belknap Press of Harvard University Press.

Rothschild, M., and J. E. Stiglitz. 1976. "Equilibrium in Competitive Insurance Markets: An Essay on the Economics of Imperfect Information." *Quarterly Journal of Economics* 90(4):629–649.

Shapiro, C., and J. E. Stiglitz. 1984. "Equilibrium Unemployment as a Worker Discipline Device." *American Economic Review* 74(3):433–444.

Stiglitz, J. E. 1973. "Education and Inequality." *Annals of the American Academy of Political and Social Sciences* 409:135–145.

——. 1974. "Demand for Education in Public and Private School Systems." *Journal of Public Economics* 2:349–386.

——. 1975. "The Theory of Screening, Education and the Distribution of Income." *American Economic Review* 65(3):283–300. Reprinted in *Selected Works of Joseph E. Stiglitz*. Vol. 1. *Information and Economic Analysis*, 99–121. Oxford: Oxford University Press, 2009.

——. 1977. "Theory of Local Public Goods." In *The Economics of Public Services*, ed. M. S. Feldstein and R. P. Inman, 274–333. London: MacMillan.

——. 1982. "The Inefficiency of the Stock Market Equilibrium." *Review of Economic Studies* 49(2):241–261.

——. 1988. "On the Market for Principles of Economics Textbooks: Innovation and Product Differentiation." *Journal of Economic Education* 19(2):171–177.

——. 1993a. "Perspectives on the Role of Government Risk-Bearing Within the Financial Sector." In *Government Risk-Bearing*, ed. M. Sniderman, 109–130. Norwell, Mass.: Kluwer Academic.

——. 1993b. "Remarks on Inequality, Agency Costs, and Economic Efficiency." Prepared for a workshop in Economic Theories of Inequality, Stanford Institute for Theoretical Economics, Stanford University, Stanford, Calif., March 11–13, 1993.

——. 1994. *Whither Socialism?* Cambridge, Mass.: MIT Press.

——. 1998. "Pareto Efficient Taxation and Expenditure Policies, with Applications to the Taxation of Capital, Public Investment, and Externalities." Paper presented at a conference in honor of Agnar Sandmo, Bergen, Norway, January 1998.

——. 2010. *Freefall: America, Free Markets, and the Sinking of the World Economy*. New York: Norton.

——. 2012. *The Price of Inequality: How Today's Divided Society Endangers Our Future*. New York: Norton.

——. 2013. "Social Protection Without Protectionism." In *The Quest for Security: Protection without Protectionism and the Challenge of Global Governance*, ed. M. Kaldor and J. E. Stiglitz, 24–47, New York: Columbia University Press.

——. 2015a. "Leaders and Followers: Perspectives on the Nordic Model and the Economics of Innovation." *Journal of Public Economics* 127(July):3–16.

——. 2015b. "The Origins of Inequality, and Policies to Contain It." *National Tax Journal* 68(2):425–448.

——. 2016a. *The Euro*. New York: Norton.

——. 2016b. "In Praise of Frank Ramsey's Contribution to the Theory of Taxation." *Economic Journal* 125(583):235–268.

——. 2016c. "The Theory of Credit and Macro-economic Stability." NBER Working Paper 22837. National Bureau of Economic Research, Cambridge, Mass.

——. 2017. "Macro-economic Management in an Electronic Credit/Financial System." NBER Working Paper 23032. National Bureau of Economic Research, Cambridge, Mass.

Stiglitz, J. E., and J. Yun. 2005 "The Integration of Unemployment Insurance with Retirement Insurance." *Journal of Public Economics* 89:2037–2067.

——. 2013. "Optimality and Equilibrium in a Competitive Insurance Market Under Adverse Selection and Moral Hazard." NBER Working Paper 19317. National Bureau of Economic Research, Cambridge, Mass.

——. 2014. "Income Contingent Loans for the Unemployed: A Prelude to a General Theory of the Efficient Provision of Social Insurance." In *Income Contingent Loans: Theory, Practice and Prospects*, ed. J. E. Stiglitz, B. Chapman, and T. Higgins, 180–204. New York: Palgrave Macmillan.

——. 2017. "Income Contingent Loan as an Unemployment Benefit." Columbia University Working Paper. Columbia University, New York.

Stiglitz, J. E, Nell Abernathy, Adam Hersh, Susan Holmberg, and Mike Konczal. 2015. *Rewriting the Rules of the American Economy*. A Roosevelt Institute Book. New York: Norton.

Sunstein, Cass. 2016. "People Prefer System 2 Nudges (Kind Of)." July 19, 2016. *Duke Law Journal* 66:121.

Sunstein, Cass, and Richard H. Thaler. 2008. *Nudge: Improving Decisions About Health, Wealth, and Happiness*. New Haven, Conn.: Yale University Press.

Tobin, J. 1970. "On Limiting the Domain of Inequality." *Journal of Law & Economics* 13(2):263–277.

World Bank. 2015. *World Development Report 2015: Mind, Society, and Behavior*. Washington, D.C.: World Bank.

CHAPTER 2

Adapting Labor and Social Protection Systems to Twenty-First-Century Capitalism

Sandra Polaski

Over the past several decades the economic prospects facing U.S. households and workers have changed in substantial ways. For most, it has been a change for the worse: less job security, less or no wage growth, erosion of employment-based pensions and health care, fears about future employment prospects, fears about the solvency of Social Security and Medicare. The causes have been widely analyzed and the growth of data and computing power have gradually enabled a better understanding of what has been driving the changes. However, there is still no universal consensus among economists on the relative weight of different factors and the most appropriate policy responses. Among politicians, views are highly polarized along ideological and party lines.

With this decades-long evolution as a backdrop, the advent of new forms of work and services arranged through the Internet have added a new element and—for some—a new urgency to the question of how society and policy makers should respond. Still further into the future, questions loom about the impact of technology, in particular artificial intelligence and robotization, on overall employment levels.

Thus, long-standing debates in the United States—over inequality, the declining share of national wealth going to labor rather than to capital, the future of Social Security, the need for labor law reform—have now been stirred and expanded by debates over the future of work and the on-demand economy. To some extent, the addition of these new elements has served to confuse rather than illuminate the longer-term trends and the underlying causes.

This chapter is intended to bring analytical clarity and focus to the issues that currently confront workers, households, and policy makers in the spheres of employment and social protection. It addresses the issues from a U.S. perspective, but includes references to other advanced economies and the global economy to illuminate broader forces at work, while distinguishing what is specific to the United States.

The organization of the chapter is as follows. First, the policy challenges are defined, and available evidence is used to estimate the size of the component elements. The second section lays out the specific policy objectives that would have to be met to address these challenges effectively. The third section proposes a framework of principles to guide choices among policy alternatives. It provides illustrations of how these principles could be applied in practice within the specific U.S. context. The fourth section discusses the prospects for political and legislative action to create a viable modern social and labor protection system in the short- and medium-term. The fifth section explores the relative merits of alternative proposals to address these challenges. A final section concludes.

1. WHAT IS THE NATURE AND SIZE OF THE POLICY CHALLENGE?

It has been widely noted that the U.S. social and labor protection systems built over the twentieth century have eroded in terms of coverage and adequacy and that the erosion has contributed to stagnation of incomes for middle- and lower-income groups and to widening inequality.[1] This in turn has had negative impacts on aggregate demand by reducing household consumption, the main motor of the U.S. economy, or on macroeconomic stability through unsustainable borrowing to maintain that consumption.[2] It also reduces investment, as firms do not see the demand or future markets that would justify expanded productive capacity. The changes have also had the effect of transferring economic risk from firms and investors to households and workers.[3]

CAUSES AND IMPACTS

These broad changes are the result of many forces, not only the erosion of U.S. labor and social protection systems. They include the expansion of the globally available labor force after the Cold War ended, China's entry into the global economy, and the liberalization of trade (Polaski 2004). This large expansion of the global labor supply tilted bargaining power away from workers and toward owners of capital. Changes in technology also changed the demand for various types of labor skills, improving prospects for some and worsening them for others.[4] Changes in the overall incentives facing firms also shifted, with an increasing emphasis on maximizing short-term shareholder returns, stock prices, and executive compensation at the expense of workers' wages and benefits.[5]

While these forces also affected other advanced industrialized economies, and indeed the entire global economy, their impact on wages and social protection differed significantly across countries. The differing impacts can be traced in large part to the differences in legal regimes governing labor markets, the structure of national social protection systems, and the norms governing distribution of economic risk. They also reflect the social and political views in different countries on what is fair and politically acceptable, sometimes called the social contract. In the United States, for most of the last four decades, the federal government adopted a deregulatory stance and policies that favored owners of capital rather than labor. For example, financial deregulation benefited the owners of capital, as did lower taxation on capital earnings than on earnings from labor. Meanwhile, relatively weak labor laws were further eroded through weak enforcement. Increasingly unequal economic power translated into increasingly unequal political power. The expansion of the U.S. social safety net came to a virtual halt after the 1960s, with rollbacks in existing programs starting in the 1980s. The one major exception—the expansion of health-care coverage by the Obama Administration—was contested from the beginning and is at continued risk of being reversed.

THE PURPOSE OF A SOCIAL AND ECONOMIC FLOOR

Taken together, employment and labor rights laws, social insurance systems, and other publicly provided or mandated support to households constitute a nationally defined set of minimum guarantees that is constructed over time. They constitute a social floor or social contract that households can count on regarding labor income and rights, access to health care, and income in old age and in case of unemployment or injury.

The social floor serves multiple policy and economic purposes. It can prevent or reduce poverty and smooth income across economic cycles or individual setbacks. It can insure individuals and households against risks that could otherwise have long-term deleterious effects on their incomes, well-being, and productivity. It enables workers to invest in education and training and make decisions on employment and mobility based on a set of expectations about the likely returns to their effort. It constrains firms to respect certain rights and standards and prevents externalization of their costs to society or beggar-thy-neighbor approaches toward competitor firms. It can help ensure that wages and living standards rise for the broad population in line with productivity growth. These microeconomic effects then contribute to macroeconomic outcomes by way of channels that include income distribution, consumption, and further productivity increases.[6]

These policy objectives are compelling in social and political terms, and they are supported by robust economic research showing that they are also important factors in achieving and maintaining positive long-term economic performance (Stiglitz 2012). They are an important stabilizing and equalizing foundation for modern advanced economies. If existing U.S. labor and employment laws, social insurance arrangements, and welfare benefits no longer provide the population with this politically and economically desirable social floor, they eventually must be reformed, both to restore social and political cohesion and to avoid economic stagnation or decline.

THE STATE OF THE U.S. SOCIAL FLOOR

To evaluate the need for reforms to the U.S. social floor, it is first essential to understand the extent of erosion and any existing exclusions and gaps in the protection provided to workers and households. What do we know about the current state of the social floor?

We begin with coverage of employment laws, because they establish the basic rules under which the large majority of U.S. households gain most or all of their income and social benefits. These laws define whether or not a working person is considered an employee and thus entitled to key labor rights and minimum protections for wages, working time, and working conditions. Employee status also provides access to most social insurance systems, including Social Security, unemployment insurance, and workers' compensation in case of workplace illness or injury.

Under various labor laws at the federal and state level, whether a working person is covered by the law depends on whether he or she is an employee.[7] Working persons who are not employees are categorized in different ways, with the status of "independent contractor" being a predominant one.[8] An employee is protected by the Fair Labor Standards

Act (FLSA), which sets minimum wages, regulates hours, mandates overtime payments, and sets other basic workplace standards; the National Labor Relations Act (NLRA), which establishes the right to form unions and engage in collective bargaining; and laws prohibiting employment discrimination based on race, gender, age, and other personal characteristics. An employee also enjoys coverage of Social Security, Medicare, unemployment insurance, and workers' compensation based on payroll contributions to these social insurance systems by the employer and employee. A working person who is not an employee does not enjoy the rights listed above (although he or she may have some antidiscrimination protection under other laws) and is solely responsible for contributions to social insurance schemes, if he or she is entitled to participate at all. This distinction makes clear that in terms of labor protections, social benefits, and exposure to economic and other risks, there is a sharp difference between working as an employee and not being accorded that status. It suggests that this is an important area of policy to be addressed. We will return to this issue in the section on policy principles and responses.

The difference in rights, entitlements, and costs between employees and those who lack this status has led some U.S. employers to misclassify employees as independent contractors in order to avoid obligations. Misclassification is enabled in part by differences in the definition of employee status under different labor and social insurance laws and the subsequent, often complex tests created by courts when applying those definitions. It has expanded as a result of the evolution of complicated contracting, third-party hiring practices, and other arrangements that can be used to blur the employment relationship and the employee status of those providing their labor.

This complexity is reflected in statistical measures designed to assess employment status and its evolution over time. Public survey instruments such as those carried out by the Bureau of Labor Statistics (BLS) use a wide array of categories regarding working status, including employee and independent contractor, but also the categories of self-employed, contract employee, temporary agency worker, and on-call worker. There are many relevant sources of data, including the surveys undertaken by the BLS, the U.S. Census Bureau, private surveys, and administrative data such as tax records and contributions to social insurance programs. Table 2.1 presents a sample of findings on the changes in the share of working people in each of these categories over time as recorded by different surveys and studies.

Table 2.1 Employees, Independent Contractors, and Others as Percentage of the Employed U.S. Labor Force (1990–2017)

Status (source)	1990	1995	2005	2010	2015	2017
Employee, standard full-time (CWS,CPS[a])		67.9	69.4			
Employee, standard part-time (CWS,CPS)		13.6	13.2			13.5[b]
Part-time for economic reasons						3.8[c]
Part-time, all[d]	19.0				19.2 (2013)	17.3[e]
Independent contractor (CWS)		6.7	7.4			
Independent contractor (GSS[f])			13.5 (2006)	12.9		
Self-employed[g]	11.4	11.8	11.1	10.9	10.1	
Self-employed unincorporated[g]	8.5	8.4	7.4	7.0	6.4	6.2[h]
Direct-hire temps[i]		2.8	2.1			
Temporary agency workers		1.0[j]	0.9[k]		1.6[l]	
On-call and day laborers		1.6[j]	1.8[k]		2.6[m]	
Contract company workers[a]		0.5	0.6			
Alternative work arrangements[l] of which contract workers					15.8–17.2 / 3.1–3.3	
Core contingent (GAO[m])			5.6 / 7.1 (2006)	7.9		
Online platform on-call workers					0.4[n] / 0.5[o] / 0.7[p]	

[a] U.S. GAO (2006): calculations based on U.S. BLS Contingent and Alternative Employment Arrangements, from the 1995 and 2005 Contingent Worker Supplements (CWS) to the Current Population Survey (CPS).

[b] CPS January (2017): "Part-time for non-economic reasons."

[c] CPS January (2017): "Slack work or business conditions or could only find part-time work."

[d] Bernhardt (2014): calculations based on CPS.

[e] CPS January (2017).

[f] The 2006 and 2010 General Social Surveys (GSS), a project of the independent research organization National Opinion Research Center (NORC) at the University of Chicago.

[g] Hipple (2010); Hipple and Hammond (2016).

[h] CPS January (2017).

[i] U.S. Bureau of Labor Statistics (1995, 2005).

[j] U.S. Bureau of Labor Statistics (1995).

[k] U.S. Bureau of Labor Statistics (2005).

[l] Katz and Krueger (2016).

[m] GAO (2015): calculations based on CWS (2005); GSS (2006); GSS (2010).

[n] Farrell and Greig (2016a).

[o] Katz and Krueger (2016).

[p] Jackson, Looney, and Ramnath (2017): based on 2014 income tax filings.

Finding a clear pattern in the results of these surveys and studies is complicated by the different definitions and aggregations and also by a lack of consistently available time-series data and other measurement problems. There have been various efforts to combine these different categories into broader groupings that capture common elements, including "nonstandard forms of work," "contingent employment," or "core contingent employment."[9] The purpose of these efforts is to make sense of the complex information that is available in order to detect changes and trends and assess possible impacts on the affected workers. Understanding the significance of the different categories of work is also complicated by the lack of close alignment of the existing categories with clear indications of vulnerability or other disadvantages.[10]

Despite the difficulties, it is possible to gain at least a sense of the order of magnitude of different categories of work relationships and employment status from the currently available data and studies. What emerges is a rough portrait of a labor market in which the large majority of the U.S. working population still works in a standard employment relationship but up to 17 percent of workers have either no direct employer, an intermediary employer, or a temporary or on-call relationship to employment. While the component elements of this aggregate have shifted over time, with some growing and some declining, the overall proportion of the workforce in these nonstandard arrangements appears to have been growing slowly over recent decades. This suggests that a substantial and gradually increasing subsegment of the U.S. workforce may be excluded from the protections of labor law and social insurance systems.

It is interesting to note that various attempts to measure the extent of new online work arrangements (the on-demand gig economy) find that only about 0.4–0.7 percent of U.S. workers engage in this type of work.[11] This arrangement has emerged only recently and may grow in the future; however, it currently involves a very small part of the overall workforce and even of that segment of the workforce involved in nonstandard, contingent, or vulnerable employment. A recent study of growth patterns of participation in online work found that after a short period of rapid growth, the number of new entrants typically levels off and more than half of participants exit within twelve months (Farrell and Grieg 2016b).

With regard to part-time work, about 17.5–19.2 percent of the U.S. workforce works less than full-time, including both voluntary and involuntary part-time work. This proportion has been very stable over the long-term, with short-term fluctuations around recessions. While the large majority work part-time by choice, this is a significant share of the workforce, and so it is also necessary to examine part-time workers' access to labor protections and social insurance. This is addressed in the section on policy principles.

Have these patterns or changes in work relationships had differential impacts on different groups of workers, for example, by age or gender? One study in late 2015 found that the percentage of workers engaged as independent contractors, freelancers, temporary help agency workers, on-call workers, or contract workers was highest among older workers (aged 55–74), at 23.9 percent, lowest among young workers (aged 16–24), at 6.4 percent, and that workers in the 25–54 age group were in the middle, at 14.3 percent (Katz and Krueger 2016). The study also found that the incidence of these alternative work relationships was growing fastest among older workers. This runs counter to a common perception that contingent work disproportionately affects young workers and that growth in nonstandard work is most rapid among the young. It serves to illustrate the crucial importance of obtaining good information before drawing conclusions about changes in the labor market, their impacts, and appropriate policy responses. The same study found that in 2015 women were more likely than men to be employed in these alternative work relationships, reversing an earlier pattern when such workers were more likely to be men.

Nonstandard employment is an area of active current investigation in the United States, and the greater availability of data and computing power will likely produce much better information on the distribution and changes in these categories of work over the next few years.[12]

How do the changes in the U.S. labor market compare with those in other advanced economies? It is difficult to make a precise comparison, because the status of employee and other categories of work are based on different legal definitions and data-gathering practices in other countries. Nonetheless, it is possible to compare broad patterns based on national data that are then adjusted for comparability by international organizations. For example, the rate of *self-employment* as a share of the total working population ranges from about 6 percent to about 25 percent in the high-income countries that belong to the Organisation for Economic Co-operation and Development (OECD), with Greece an outlier at 36.9 percent, compared with an adjusted estimate for the United States of 6.6 percent.[13] The percentage of workers in *temporary employment* as a share of all employees varies from 5.6 percent in Australia to 23.1 percent in Spain, compared with a U.S. rate of about 5 percent.[14] The share of workers in *part-time employment* ranges from about 10 percent to 26 percent in advanced economies, with the Netherlands as an outlier at 38.7 percent and the United States in the middle at about 17.5 percent.[15] These substantial differences in patterns of employment suggest that government policies and laws as well as social attitudes, preferences, and economic options can lead to a broad range of outcomes.

2. POLICY OBJECTIVES

As noted earlier, there is robust empirical evidence that labor and social protections that guarantee rights, distribute risk, and support domestic demand are necessary for the long-term success of a modern economy. Further, as evidenced by current political processes in the United States and elsewhere, public perceptions that economic policies favor the rich and are disadvantageous to working households can have destabilizing political and social effects, which can further undermine economic stability and growth.

When seeking to achieve broad objectives such as fairness, adequate social protection, and equitable apportionment of risk, those who design actual policies must make detailed choices on a range of questions and policy options. These include, for example, how to assign rights and obligations to different economic actors; how to correct for market failures; how to establish social insurance systems that are adequate, efficient, and affordable; and how to decide between contributory and noncontributory sources of funding for social protection.

Given this complexity, it is clearly necessary to establish priorities based on the specific context and the nature and size of the challenges. In the United States, the current context includes rising inequality; stagnant or declining incomes for middle- and lower-income groups; changes in the structure of the economy; a gradual increase in nonstandard forms of employment; and the need to adapt social protection to be sustainable in light of changing demographics. Against this background, the following objectives provide a framework for thinking about the policy reforms needed to achieve balanced and fair social and economic outcomes. Reforms should be sufficient to:

- provide income security at adequate levels across the life cycle and mitigate economic risks to individuals and households;

- correct any exclusion of particular groups and ensure the adequacy of protections for more vulnerable groups and individuals; and
- improve overall income distribution, given high and increasing inequality.

These broad objectives can be pursued through various combinations of labor, social, and tax policies.

Labor protection policies that address these objectives include minimum wages, maximum or minimum hours, and acceptable minimum working conditions, including safety and health, and terms of employment. They also include nondiscrimination laws and the rights of workers to organize and bargain. The extent of coverage of labor laws in different sectors, types of establishments, and work relationships is an important aspect that can determine the reach and effectiveness of labor policy.

Social protection policies that address these objectives include guaranteed income programs such as pensions, unemployment benefits, welfare benefits, and compensation in case of workplace injury or illness and access to affordable health care. They should be structured to address any exclusion of particular groups and should improve the distributional impact of these social programs. Their credibility and long-term economic viability are also important considerations.

Tax policies are essential for addressing questions of distribution and for raising adequate funding for social protection systems. They can also provide incentives or disincentives to workers and firms that can affect behaviors and outcomes and assist governments in achieving desired objectives.

3. PRINCIPLES THAT SHOULD GUIDE POLICY REFORM

The existing U.S. social and labor protection system was built over the course of the twentieth century, with some additions in this century. Major elements were enacted in the 1930s as part of the New Deal (basic labor rights under the FLSA and NLRA, Social Security, etc.) and during a period of concentrated policy innovation in the turbulent 1960s (civil rights, Medicare, etc.). In both periods public awareness, political movements, and activism had built a demand for change over many years. Nonetheless, sharp economic or social crises were still required to provide the final push that led to legislative action. Similar examples can be found in agitation for and enactment of the Occupational Safety and Health Act of 1970, the Family and Medical Leave Act of 1993, and the Affordable

Care Act of 2010. This history provides an important starting point for any reform going forward.

FIRST PRINCIPLE: PRESERVE, DEFEND, AND IMPROVE HARD-WON RIGHTS AND SOCIAL PROTECTION SYSTEMS

It is extremely difficult for governments to rebalance markets and change economic and social behavior by providing major legal rights to the less powerful actors in markets. In the labor market, the employee has substantially less power than the employer. Because they are so difficult to establish, legislatively created rights for employees (as under the FLSA, NLRA, and civil rights legislation) should be maintained and safeguarded. Any reform that could erode access to and protection of rights acquired through employment status as an employee should be avoided. This fundamental political economic reality is reinforced by other advantages of employment-based rights and benefits, discussed later.

Similarly, major social insurance systems such as pensions and health care are extremely difficult to create due to their complexity, expense, and shifting of risk. Once established they will need to be adapted and reinforced; but changes that fundamentally weaken their nature as broad-based social insurance should be avoided. Thus, changes that would shift the risk for basic retirement income security from society as a whole (as currently achieved through payroll-based financial contributions to Social Security by both employees and employers) to the individual would be historically regressive and economically undesirable. Similarly, changes that would eliminate the administrative efficiencies of a single fund and the benefits of a large risk pool (as is the case with both Social Security and Medicare) and instead create multiple entities with separate financing arrangements and fragmented risk pools would sacrifice fundamental advantages and undermine historically effortful achievements. This would be the case with privatization or creation of alternative, more fragmented arrangements for Social Security or Medicare. In addition, ex post studies confirm the ex ante intuition that management by a not-for-profit entity such as the government is far less expensive than management by private for-profit entities.[16]

This starting principle on the need to preserve established rights and social protection systems cannot be overstated. The historical foundation should be adapted or expanded to address gaps or erosion in coverage or other weaknesses in existing labor and social protections but should not be weakened or replaced.

SECOND PRINCIPLE: START THE PROCESS OF ADDRESSING GAPS OR EROSION IN COVERAGE BY ELIMINATING EXISTING EXCLUSIONS AND CLOSING EXISTING LOOPHOLES IN EMPLOYMENT LAWS

A first step should be to eliminate inappropriate existing exclusions from coverage by employment laws. By way of illustration, some labor laws exclude coverage of agricultural or domestic workers. There is no economic logic to these sectoral or occupational exclusions, and they disproportionately affect vulnerable groups of workers, such as the low-skilled, women, and migrant workers. Part-time workers are often excluded from coverage or protection if they work below certain thresholds of working hours, but again there is no economic logic to denying equal rights and prorated benefits to these workers. Extending coverage of labor laws to part-time workers and establishing their right to prorated benefits can also eliminate perverse incentives to keep workers below designated hour thresholds. Similarly, coverage of labor laws should extend to all firms, regardless of size. Exclusions for small firms introduce perverse incentives to stay small and create uneven playing fields between different firms. Eliminating these existing exclusions would bring very substantial numbers of workers under the protection of existing laws.

Beyond ending these explicit legal exclusions, there is a clear need to close loopholes or constrain practices that have been exploited to exclude workers from coverage or evade rights and benefits. The most fundamental step is to reaffirm and reestablish the definition of employer as all those who "suffer or permit" an individual to work for their benefit; and to accord the status of employee to all who perform such work. This is the clear and expansive definition of employer and employee in the FLSA; however, it has been blurred by subsequent practice and court applications.[17] A 2015 interpretation by the Department of Labor's Wage and Hour Division Administrator addresses the de facto erosion of the FLSA's protections as a result of employer claims that certain workers fall outside the scope of the act's coverage.[18] The interpretation reasserts that the terms "employ," and in turn "employer" and "employee," were intended to be broadly construed, consistent with the meaning of "suffer or permit" to work. The interpretation provides guidance to employers and workers regarding the act's broad application and the limited circumstances in which a working person can be excluded from its protections. If this interpretation is respected by the new Administration and the courts, it could substantially narrow exclusions and begin to reverse the erosion of coverage.

A number of states have also begun to address the gaps in coverage of state labor laws through new legislation that clarifies the duties of employers and/or the status of employees.[19] For example, Massachusetts, Indiana, and New Hampshire have created a presumption of employee status with regard to employer compliance with minimum wages and wage payments. Some states have legislatively established joint employer responsibility (for example, between contractors and their subcontractors in heavily subcontracted industries) for compliance with some labor laws (New York and California) or between temporary labor agencies and their clients (Illinois). As often happens in the United States, the states can serve as laboratories by providing experience with different policy innovations. They can also serve as natural experiments that provide evidence of the relative impacts of different approaches across the states.

Reestablishing the definition of employer and employee as clearly as originally intended is one essential step required to address gaps and erosion of coverage, and the effect could be substantial. One area of impact would be to rein in the misclassification of employees as independent contractors.[20] A credible estimate of misclassification based on multiple sources suggests that as much as 1–2 percent of the U.S. labor force is misclassified.[21] At current employment levels, this would mean that 1.5 to 3 million workers would benefit from consistent application of the clear and intended definition of employer and employee in the FLSA. It could also help to clarify the status of workers engaged in new forms of online work platforms. Such platforms often classify those providing labor for digitally arranged services as independent contractors. Challenges to this status are currently wending through U.S. courts. An unambiguous application of the "suffer or permit" definition would suggest that firms that provide such platforms and charge a fixed fee or percentage of the payment for transport or other services provided are clearly "permitting" the work to be done for the firm's financial benefit and as such are employing those who provide the labor. The practical implications for coverage of gig economy workers are discussed later.

THIRD PRINCIPLE: STRENGTHEN, ADAPT, AND INNOVATE ENFORCEMENT STRATEGIES TO ACHIEVE COMPLIANCE WITH LABOR LAWS AND PARTICIPATION IN SOCIAL INSURANCE SYSTEMS

One factor contributing to the erosion of protections provided by labor laws and coverage under payroll-based social insurance has been the mismatch between the challenge of enforcing these rights and entitlements compared with available enforcement resources. Federal and state enforcement budgets have been reduced, while the number of workplaces has increased through overall growth of the economy and has grown in complexity due to the use of contracting and other business strategies that disperse or disguise employment relationships.

In response, some U.S. labor enforcement agencies have optimized their use of the limited budgets available to them by strategically targeting resource use. For example, they have focused on particular localities, sectors, and business models that have high occurrences of noncompliance and on vulnerable workforces that are often exploited. They have worked to identify industry structures and business strategies that suggest points of influence and leverage in order to seek voluntary compliance or pursue enforcement action. These approaches have been developed and improved over time, with the increasing availability of data and computing power contributing to progress. But clearly, much remains to be done, and enforcement and compliance strategies are only effective with sufficient budgets for staff and technological capabilities to implement them. It goes without saying that consistent political will is also essential to achieve acceptable levels of compliance.

There is also great scope for progress through better linking of regulatory systems and sources of leverage and data that are available to different parts of the government, ranging from enforcement agencies (such as the Department of Labor's Wage and Hour Division and Occupational Safety and Health Administration) to the Internal Revenue Service, Social Security Administration, Commerce Department, and state regulatory agencies. Effective linking of government data and enforcement systems would also create additional and powerful incentives for voluntary compliance, since some of these agencies have more effective remedies than others.

A reinforcement and expansion of employee status to more workers is also a part of the solution to the funding of enforcement and financing of social insurance systems. Payroll withholding of income taxes and contributions to Social Security and Medicare is a highly effective and efficient method of ensuring required payments.

FOURTH PRINCIPLE: ADAPT AND EXPAND EXISTING CONTRIBUTORY SOCIAL INSURANCE SYSTEMS TO INCREASE COVERAGE, PARTICIPATION, AND SUSTAINABILITY

The major social insurance systems built in the 1930s and 1960s—Social Security and Medicare—have largely achieved the objectives of such systems: the elimination of poverty among elders, universal coverage, large risk pools, broad-based contributory financing, and portability across different employers and employment relationships. They also benefit from the relative ease of collecting contributions through employer payroll deductions and transmissions. As such, they should be preserved and strengthened. However, as is evident, increasing life expectancies increase their costs, and therefore, their financing must be strengthened.

The obvious place to start is to raise the limit on annual earnings subject to Social Security contributions, which is currently set at $118,500. (A similar cap on the earnings limit for contributions to Medicare's hospital insurance was completely eliminated in 1994.) When the current approach to limiting Social Security contributions was instituted in 1977, the expressed congressional intent was to make 90 percent of wages subject to Social Security contributions. The earnings limit set at the time achieved that, and Congress mandated inflation-based adjustments to the cap that were intended to maintain coverage of about 90 percent of all wages. Over the intervening years, however, the disproportionate and above-inflation growth of income for high earners has shifted the pattern of earnings, with the result that the system currently requires contributions on only 83 percent of all wages (AARP 2015). This both weakens the financial sufficiency of the system and further expands the rising inequality from which it stems, as the top 17 percent of earnings are exempted. Raising the earnings limit to once again cover 90 percent of wages (and achieve the result intended by Congress) would translate to a contributions cap of about $274,200 at 2016 earnings levels (AARP 2015). Alternatively, the cap could be eliminated entirely, as Congress did for Medicare in 1994, which would largely erase the deficit in funding of the system caused by the retirement of the large baby boom generation. An argument against eliminating the cap is that Social Security funding has historically been based on the combination of two principles: social adequacy and individual equity. To achieve social adequacy, the system redistributes contributions to provide pensions to all that are sufficient to avoid poverty among the elderly. Individual equity means that the size of an individual's pension bears a relationship to the level of his or her contributions over the course of working years. However, Social Security pensions are capped for high earners, and thus the cap on contributions can be seen as an element of the individual equity aspect of the system. On the other hand, it would affect only a small percentage of the working population—namely the highest earners who have benefited from rising inequality.

If the funding deficit is addressed, Social Security will continue to be largely fit for its purpose, given its full portability, individual equity, and social redistribution. In addition to raising the contribution cap, an important policy principle to be pursued is to make more workers eligible to participate as employees, with contributions shared by their employers. This can be achieved in part by clarifying the definition of employee status, as discussed earlier. Misclassification of employees as independent contractors shifts the full burden of contributions—which amounts to 12.4 percent of earnings for Social Security and 2.9 percent for Medicare—to the employee, along with the administrative responsibility for payment. For low-paid workers, this can be a significant burden. Those engaged in new online forms of work would benefit if their status as employees were recognized, as the responsibility for contributions would be shared by the firm organizing the provision of service and the worker providing the service. This could be achieved by deducting the contributions from the online payments made by the firm to the worker. This is technologically feasible, as evidenced by the fact that payments by customers and the division of those revenues between the platform firm and the workers providing the service are done through online financial transfers. Adding a function that deducts the platform firm and online worker contributions to Social Security and Medicare (as well as income tax withholding) and transmitting them to the government is no more burdensome than payroll practices required of other firms.[22] The Social Security and Medicare systems could easily be adapted to receive and credit these online payments, analogous to current electronic payroll transfers to those systems.

Similar considerations apply to eligibility for and contributions to the federal and state unemployment insurance systems and to workers' compensation systems covering occupational injury and disease. Reestablishing the definitions of employer and employee as originally intended is hence an essential step to address gaps and erosion of coverage of social protection systems as well as protection of labor laws themselves. Extending this status to workers whose labor is dispatched online would update the system to include this currently small but potentially growing group and would also help shore up the finances of these systems.

With respect to health and medical coverage, employment-based insurance provides this coverage to about 44 percent of the working age population (Gallup-Healthways Well-Being Index 2017). Employment-based health insurance is the largest single source of such coverage in the U.S. for those below the Medicare eligibility age of 65, but it also gives rise to large gaps in the U.S. social protection system. It is not portable, meaning that a worker changing jobs loses coverage at some point and must rely on finding new employment with health coverage or purchasing insurance as an individual in the market. Medicaid, the public health care system funded out of general tax revenues, provides coverage only for low-income workers and households, for the disabled, and, for the low-income elderly, coverage of long-term, which is not covered by Medicare. The gaps in coverage have been partly addressed by the Affordable Care Act of 2010 (ACA), which expanded access to health insurance, including for those with existing conditions. It created a mandate for employers with more than 50 employees to provide health insurance; provided subsidies for those with moderate to low-incomes who exceed the Medicaid eligibility thresholds; and expanded Medicaid coverage in states that chose to participate. This new social protection program has been politically controversial, and the current administration and Congress have tried (although thus far failed) to repeal it. However, the ACA has expanded health care coverage over the course of its short existence to roughly 20 million previously uninsured individuals and reduced the share of uninsured from 15.7 percent to 9.2 percent of the population as of the first quarter of 2015.[23]

While the combination of employer-based insurance, Medicare, Medicaid, and access to health insurance through the ACA provides major elements of health care to the majority of the population, it is worth noting that, by contrast, most advanced economies organize health-care coverage through a single, large social insurance system that covers almost everyone and is based on payroll or other tax contributions. This approach provides the greatest advantages in terms of universality, efficiency, cost containment, and risk sharing.

Summing up, some major elements of the U.S. social protection system are basically sound but in need of adaptations to address both long-existing gaps and erosion of coverage over time; to make their financing adequate and sustainable; and to extend them to cover new ways of working, including online work. Because of the complexity and size of these large social insurance systems, it would be extremely unwise to eliminate them and substitute other systems rather than adapting existing programs to the maximum extent possible to deal with contemporary labor market and demographic circumstances. Any new approaches should be treated as experiments that are piloted, tested, and evaluated for efficacy, equity, efficiency, and any unintended consequences or externalities. In any case, to the extent that some existing programs (notably Social Security and Medicare) already satisfy basic principles of social insurance—including scale efficiencies, large risk pools, and near universality—it is difficult to envision alternatives that would perform better.

FIFTH PRINCIPLE: FILL THE REMAINING GAPS IN THE U.S. LABOR AND SOCIAL FLOOR

Creating an adequate twenty-first-century labor and social protection system in the United States obviously requires additional work to fill the existing gaps in coverage and reverse the erosion of the twentieth-century system discussed earlier. However, the United States has always lacked important elements of social protection that are typically provided—indeed mandated—in many other advanced economies. Adequate paid time off for vacation, sickness, and maternity and family leave stand out as major gaps in U.S. social benefits compared with those in peer economies. They should be established through legislative action that mandates broad and inclusive coverage from the beginning. These benefits are typically prefunded through employer and/or employee contributions and to the extent that they are organized by government can offer the advantages of large pools, risk-sharing, and relatively low administrative costs. A number of U.S. states are currently initiating such benefits and these provide welcome laboratories and models for action elsewhere. The experience of other advanced economies that provide these benefits is also a useful source of guidance.

In terms of protection of labor rights, U.S. laws that enable workers to organize and defend their own interests through collective bargaining have long been in need of reform. The original National Labor Relations

Act of 1935 was a reasonably robust, workable approach that achieved impressive progress toward its goal of encouraging collective bargaining. However, it was dramatically weakened through amendments in the late 1940s and 1950s and has suffered further erosion through administrative and court decisions in subsequent decades.[24] Reforms are needed to eliminate coverage gaps, reverse the major weakening amendments and the further erosion of this law in practice, and eliminate waivers that allow states to compete with each other by weakening rights. Additional progress should be made in terms of streamlining procedures and rules that are unnecessarily difficult and time-consuming. Restoring the effective rights of workers and unions to improve wages, working terms, and conditions is an important step in addressing the erosion of living standards for middle- and lower-income workers and countering rising inequality in the United States.

With respect to the noncontributory, tax-funded aspects of social and income protection (often referred to as "welfare" in the United States), these programs have been cut back over recent decades and fragmented in terms of eligibility. Such programs constitute the safety net of last resort, including when contributory, employment-based income protection fails. Many individuals and families fall through the current safety net, with 43 million living in poverty in 2015, almost half in deep poverty (U.S. Census Bureau 2016).[25] This aspect of social protection is in need of profound rethinking. If employment laws and other social protection systems were strengthened as discussed earlier, that would relieve some pressure on these safety-net programs. Eliminating lifetime limits on receipt of income support is clearly essential, as shown by the spikes in poverty that occurred during recessions after the enactment of these limits in the 1990s. However, much more must be done, including to ensure that work is available as a way out of poverty. One promising area for experimentation is for the government to serve as the employer of last resort, through public service employment or support for programs run by nonprofit organizations. Such work was an important aspect of poverty mitigation during the Depression of the 1930s. More recent experiments have shown success and should be expanded.[26]

These five principles provide a systematic, element-by-element approach to updating and strengthening U.S. labor and social protection for twenty-first-century economic and labor market conditions. They represent a careful, precautionary approach, in that they do not destroy or weaken the rights and benefits enjoyed by current generations as a result of the efforts and struggles of earlier generations. They also recognize that U.S. labor and social protections have, in the past, provided relatively strong protection to much of the population and that the legal framework on which they rest has been and can once again be a sound foundation—if major existing gaps are filled. If steps in line with these principles are taken, tens of millions of currently excluded workers would be brought under their protections. The current system would also be better adapted to cope with the impact of future technologies on work and employment relationships.

4. POLITICAL PROSPECTS FOR REFORM

As already noted, the major innovations in labor and social protection of the twentieth century were the result of growing awareness of problems, public debate and protest over the need for solutions, expert analysis of options, and—in most cases—social or economic crises. It was only then that electorates selected lawmakers who promised and then mustered the courage to act. Today, it is reasonable to assume that public discontent with economic insecurity and rising inequality will continue to mount and will be reinforced by the sense that labor and social protections are slipping away from many workers and households in a winner-take-all economy. The 2016 election in the United States reflected a wide range of sentiments and views across the public, but a large and arguably decisive component was the economic angst felt in large swaths of the country. It demonstrated that the economic grievances of middle- and lower-income groups are becoming an increasingly explicit political force. History provides abundant examples that this force can power progressive reforms to labor and social policy. Unfortunately, there are also abundant examples of candidates and parties that use it for scapegoating and diversionary policies that increase social conflict and leave problems to fester. Real progress depends upon public education and mobilization and political parties that offer sound strategies to address the underlying sources of discontent and the political will and leadership to undertake them.

In addition to political and electoral pressures to strengthen economic and social security for the broad population, there are compelling macro-economic reasons to do so, which could provide additional pressure for reform. Labor and social protections have clear and significant impacts on individual workers, households, and firms. However, these effects also translate into major and long-term macroeconomic effects, as discussed earlier. Perhaps most obvious is the relationship of wages and other sources of household income (such as pensions) and labor income security to aggregate demand. In the United States, consumer demand makes up 68.6 percent of gross domestic product (GDP), more than twice the contribution of private investment and government expenditure combined (U.S. Department of Commerce, Bureau of Economic Analysis 2017). Thus, policies on wages, labor protections, and social insurance that affect the level and stability of household income have major impacts on demand and help to determine whether the economy is growing, stagnating, or contracting.[27] While business cycles, particularly the financial crisis of 2007–2008 and its aftermath, have had cyclical impacts on consumer demand, the overall trend of income stagnation, rising inequality, and erosion of income and social protection coverage has persisted and worsened over the last forty years, indicating that structural factors are a major cause.[28] Policies that restore the purchasing power of households through adequate minimum wages, strengthened collective bargaining, the inclusion of more workers under legally mandated employee protections, and access to social insurance would have a significant positive impact on consumer demand and therefore on sustainable growth of the U.S. economy.

Recent research shows that rising inequality slows economic growth in the medium- and long-term as well, as mentioned earlier.[29] Strengthened labor and social protections would thus improve short-, medium-, and long-term economic prospects, in addition to their equity and redistributive advantages. When the next cyclical crisis hits and exacerbates the long-term adverse trends, attention to these macroeconomic effects is likely to intensify.

In addition to these macroeconomic considerations, there is also robust evidence that labor and social protection can have positive impacts on productivity and innovation at the microeconomic level. U.S. productivity growth has been uneven, but generally much lower over the last forty years than during the postwar years when labor and social protections were arguably at their peak. While many factors determine productivity growth, labor and social policies are important elements. For example, minimum wage increases have been shown to increase both firm-level and macroeconomic productivity growth through channels such as worker effort, reduced turnover, additional worker training provided by firms, and the replacement of less productive firms by more productive firms.[30] The same channels also lead to higher productivity growth at higher than minimum wage levels, particularly when wage structures are perceived as fair. Other labor protections (such as regulation of working hours) and social protections (such as unemployment insurance) are associated with higher levels of productivity.[31] If productivity growth continues to be slow, the quest for ways to increase it can also contribute to a reexamination of the beneficial effects of good labor and social policies.

5. EVALUATING ALTERNATIVE PROPOSALS

Given the gaps in U.S. labor and social protection, the further exacerbation of inequality and wage stagnation since the financial crisis, and the emergence of new forms of work, it is not surprising that a robust debate over suitable policy responses is emerging. I evaluate three alternative approaches that have been proposed that differ in important ways from those suggested in this chapter and consider their efficacy, equity, costs, and unintended but foreseeable consequences.

The first is the idea of establishing a universal basic income (UBI), an idea that is being debated not only in the United States but also in some European countries and Canada. A UBI would provide a uniform social welfare payment to every individual in a country, without income thresholds or other eligibility requirements. Advocates claim that this approach would avoid the costs and inefficiency of targeted income-based welfare programs and would eliminate unintended consequences of current programs, such as discouraging recipients from working due to loss of benefits.

Given the complexity of modern welfare systems and the real potential for adverse incentives based on income thresholds, this approach has attracted support from some progressive commentators as well as conservatives. However the UBI approach poses large challenges in terms of equity, adequacy, and affordability. With regard to equity, giving tax-financed monthly payments to wealthy and upper-income individuals poses a clear issue of equity, particularly at a time when their incomes have grown enormously compared with middle- and lower-income groups. Proponents argue that payments to the wealthy could be recovered through progressive taxation. However, the U.S. income tax system has become less progressive, and tax avoidance by the wealthy is a known problem. With respect to adequacy, monthly payments in the range of $500 to $1,000 are contemplated in current proposals or pilot versions of basic income.[32] For the poor, that range would not lift an individual above the poverty line and even the upper end would leave a household with fewer than five members in poverty, while for the elderly it would represent a steep cut compared with current Social Security benefits. With respect to affordability, a system that provides substantial payments to 100 percent of the population is obviously much more expensive than current welfare and income-support programs that cover only the population below the poverty line and in some cases an additional cohort just above it. A monthly UBI of $1,000 for the entire U.S. adult population would cost approximately $3 trillion per year, compared with a *total* U.S. federal budget of $3.8 trillion in 2016.[33] Of that budget, social spending amounts to about $2.3 trillion, including Social Security, unemployment insurance, Medicare, Medicaid, ACA subsidies, and other health-care programs. If the UBI were intended to replace not only income support to the poor, but all of these other federal social welfare payments, the impact of substituting a single payment of $1,000 per person would be to sharply worsen incomes for low- and middle-income retirees, the unemployed, and many others. For example, the average monthly Social Security payment is $1,341, and monthly unemployment payments range from about $800 in low-income states to about $1,800 in high-income states. Purchasing health insurance to replace lost Medicare, Medicaid, and other coverage could consume most or all of the UBI. If instead of replacing all social welfare spending, the UBI were to leave these important but relatively costly programs in place, it would be necessary to find additional funding for most of the $3 trillion in additional cost, requiring massive, unprecedented increases in taxation.

It is also important to consider the relative merits of providing a basic income with no requirement to work compared with public employment programs in which the government serves as the employer of last resort. These programs have been used at times of high unemployment in the United States and other advanced economies and are currently being used in emerging economies such as India with impressive success. Such an approach is based on a preference for providing socially or economically useful work to individuals or households in exchange for guaranteed income. The contrast between the two approaches serves to illuminate fundamental questions such as the social and psychological importance of work and perceptions of rights and responsibilities as factors in creating and sustaining social solidarity. It is beyond the scope of this chapter to fully discuss these profound questions.

Some countries are currently considering or experimenting with pilots of basic income programs without work requirements, and it will be interesting to observe the experience and lessons learned. It is worth noting that none of the current pilots are universal; instead, they replace either traditional welfare payments and/or unemployment benefits. Therefore, they require targeting mechanisms just as current programs do; and their cost will be only a fraction of the cost of a universal basic income. However, they may provide some insight on behavioral responses to the reduction of conditionalities.

A second approach that has been suggested to address the exclusion of some workers from labor protections and employment-based access to social insurance has been to create a new category of work status falling between that of employee and independent contractor. The motivation is to partially cover the cohort of workers in working relationships that may not meet all current regulatory or judicial criteria for determining employee status but who are not fully independent of the firm that engages their labor. Such an intermediate category has some initial appeal as a way to partly address the exclusion of such workers from the benefits of employee status. However, as a new and intermediate category, this group would not be entitled to the full range of employee rights and benefits. For example, under a prominent current proposal, these "independent workers" would gain protection against discrimination based on sex, age, or disability and antitrust immunity to enable them to negotiate as a group. However, they would not be eligible for minimum wage guarantees, maximum hours and overtime pay protections, unemployment insurance, or workers' compensation (Harris and Krueger 2015). There is also a risk of unintended consequences in creating a new category. As noted previously, perhaps 1.5 to 3 million workers are currently misclassified as independent contractors. Given the extent of misclassification, it is quite foreseeable that some employers would find it even easier to misclassify employees into the new intermediate category, thus eliminating major obligations and costs by transferring existing employees to this new status.

A third alternative approach is the proposal to lower payroll-based taxes and contributions (sometimes called the "labor tax wedge") to reduce the overall cost of labor, with the expectation that this will encourage more hiring. (An extreme version calls for eliminating all payroll taxes for social insurance and breaking the link between employment and social protection altogether.) This approach is based on the standard partial equilibrium economic model of labor markets, in which employers will hire labor up to the point at which its marginal revenue product equals its marginal cost. Reducing employers' contributions to pensions and other social programs would reduce their labor costs.

The economists (and some international organizations such as the International Monetary Fund) that advocate this approach often do not address the loss of revenue to the social insurance systems that are funded by the payroll taxes, and therefore hold out a gain in terms of labor demand without addressing the loss in terms of income protections and overall demand. When advocates do address this loss, they typically call for the revenue to be made up through increased consumption (e.g., value-added) taxes or property taxes. These alternatives pose several problems. First, payroll contributions to Social Security, Medicare, and other social insurance programs are progressive, as contributions rise with income (up to the cap in the case of Social Security), whereas consumption taxes are regressive, since lower-income groups spend a higher proportion of their incomes on consumption rather than savings. In the context of high and rising inequality, a shift from more to less progressive taxation is clearly undesirable. Second, property taxes are typically paid to subfederal entities such as cities and counties, whereas payroll taxes support federal social programs. This mismatch between the entity accruing the revenues and the entity paying the benefits would be difficult or impossible to resolve. Third, payroll taxes fund social benefits such as unemployment insurance and workers' compensation as well as Social Security and Medicare, benefits that are enjoyed by or provide risk protection to those who pay the taxes (directly or indirectly through wages diverted by their employers to cover the employer contribution). Increased consumption and property taxes would be paid by workers, but also by those outside the labor market, including retirees and more than a third of the working-age population. Finally, in a macroeconomic context of weak aggregate demand, shifting taxation from production and income to consumption would seem to go in exactly the wrong direction.

6. CONCLUSION

In conclusion, political, social, and economic trends reveal the damage done by the erosion of the U.S. social contract. Reversing that damage and building an adequate framework of labor protections and social benefits for the twenty-first century is a complex and politically challenging project. However, it is one that is essential if we are to avoid further erosion of living standards for the majority of people and further fraying of social cohesion. The alternatives discussed in section 5 offer flawed approaches that are not adequate to the task and likely to have adverse side effects. Instead, the same forces that built earlier labor and social protections can again be harnessed to produce meaningful reforms such as those proposed in this chapter. It will take a combination of education, public mobilization, organization, and courageous political leadership to achieve it.

NOTES

1. This has been discussed in a range of popular and scholarly works, e.g., Polaski (2007); Weil (2014).

2. A discussion that places this in a global context can be found in International Labor Organization et al. (2015).

3. An overview of the shifting burden of risk can be found in Hacker (2006) and a discussion of risk in retirement in Hacker (2011).

4. Dabla-Norris et al. (2015) provide a recent overview of this factor at the global level and for advanced economies.

5. A review of analytical work on these topics can be found in Davis and Kim (2015).

6. Dabla-Norris et al. (2015) provide a useful survey of the channels through which this occurs and add to current knowledge by evaluating the impacts on the middle class and the poor and their role in overall growth.

7. Different employment laws may have slightly different definitions of "employee" and "employment" depending on the purpose of the law.

8. Those found not to be employees have been characterized as independent contractors, self-employed, or "in business for him or herself" according to various court decisions.

9. Bernhardt summarizes nonstandard employment as "departing from the standard employment relationship on at least one dimension: (1) the job is temporary, (2) the job is part-time, (3) the worker is employed by an intermediary, or (4) there is no employer at all" (Bernhardt 2014). The BLS definition of contingent work is "any work arrangement which does not contain an explicit or implicit contract for long-term employment" (Polivka and Nardone 1989). The U.S. Government Accountability Office notes that "no clear consensus exists among labor experts as to whether contingent workers should include independent contractors, self-employed workers, and standard part-time workers, since many of these workers may have long-term employment stability. There is more agreement that workers who lack job security and

those with work schedules that are variable, unpredictable, or both—such as agency temps, direct-hire temps, on-call workers, and day laborers—should be included. We refer to this group as the 'core contingent' workforce. We estimate that this core contingent workforce comprised about 7.9 percent of employed workers in the 2010 GSS and also made up similar proportions of employed respondents in the roughly comparable 2005 CWS and 2006 GSS—5.6 percent and 7.1 percent, respectively" (GAO 2015).

10. For example, some independent contractors (who may also be described in surveys as self-employed or "in business for themselves") are highly skilled professionals or technicians whose work is in demand and who choose to create their own businesses. Others may be self-employed (or misclassified as such) as a result of lack of opportunities for (or denial of) a standard employee-employer relationship and may face low wages, few or no benefits, and income instability. Contract workers, a relatively small but rapidly growing group, includes workers with a wide range of skill levels. They may or may not have a steady employment relationship with the contracting company that deploys them, and such contracting firms may or may not provide all required labor law protections and the full range of social insurance.

11. Katz and Krueger find that about 0.5 percent of all workers identify customers through an online intermediary (Katz and Krueger 2016). Farrell and Greig estimate the group at about 0.4 percent of the workforce based on the frequency of bank deposits from online work platforms (Farrell and Greig 2016a). A study by analysts at the Office of Tax Analysis of the U.S. Department of Treasury based on tax filings for 2014 found that about 109,700 tax filers, amounting to 0.7 percent of all workers, reported income based on participation in the gig economy (Jackson et al. 2017).

12. The BLS is once again conducting the survey on contingent and alternative employment as part of the May 2017 Current Population Survey (CPS), the first update since 2005. Abraham et al. have undertaken a project to link records for CPS respondents to administrative data derived from federal income tax filings for wage and salary workers (Abramson et al. 2016). Bernhardt provides a careful assessment of available data and identifies specific gaps to be filled by future research (Bernhardt 2014).

13. OECD Self-employment rate indicator for 2013 (OECD 2017a).

14. OECD Temporary employment indicator for 2013 (OECD 2017b); the U.S. rate is for 2005, from the Bureau of Labor Statistics "Contingent and Alternative Employment Arrangements February 2005."

15. OECD Part-time employment rate indicator for 2013 (OECD 2017c); the U.S. rate is from BLS Current Population Survey April 2016.

16. For example, a 2004 study by the Congressional Budget Office compared the administrative costs of four systems for funding retirement in the United States: Social Security, the federal government's Thrift Savings Plan, private retail mutual funds, and private defined-contribution plans. It found that the administrative costs of the Social Security system reduced assets available to beneficiaries in retirement by 2 percent, whereas mutual funds and private defined-contribution funds reduced assets available to beneficiaries by 21–30 percent, depending on the size of the plan (CBO 2004).

17. The Fair Labor Standards Act of 1938, as amended 29 U.S.C. 201, et seq. § 203. Definitions: (g) "Employ" includes to suffer or permit to work.

18. U.S. Department of Labor Wage and Hour Division Administrator's Interpretation No. 2015–1 was issued by Administrator David Weil on July 15, 2015.

19. A useful discussion of state-level initiatives can be found in Weil (2014).

20. Misclassification is by definition in contravention of legal requirements, so as with any nonlegal behavior, reliable data is difficult to obtain.

21. Bernhardt (2014, 7n8) notes: "In 1984, the IRS made its last misclassification estimate, finding that 15 percent of employers misclassified 3.4 million workers as independent contractors. Since then, a number of states have conducted their own audits, of varying quality; Planmatics extrapolated a range of 1–2 percent based on these."

22. Similar challenges related to the collection of sales taxes on online transactions have been addressed.

23. U.S. Department of Health and Human Services (2016). The figure of roughly 20 million is the total number estimated to have gained coverage through the ACA "marketplace" of insurance for purchase, expansion of Medicaid eligibility, young adults staying on their parents' plans, employer mandate, and other coverage provisions (ObamaCare Facts 2017).

24. It is worth noting that the other major law governing organizing and collective bargaining, the Railway Labor Act covering air, rail, and other transport sectors, has been eroded less.

25. Deep poverty is defined as living in a household with a total cash income below 50 percent of the poverty threshold. According to the Census Bureau, in 2015, 19.4 million people lived in deep poverty.

26. Haskins provides an overview and summary of current examples and analysis of costs and benefits of such programs (Haskins 2017).

27. For example, the high growth of the U.S. economy in the quarter century after World War II was highly dependent on wage growth, private health and pension benefits negotiated by strong unions, income stability, and public pensions, in addition to other factors.

28. It is also well documented that borrowing by lower- and middle-income households to sustain their consumption in the face of weak income growth, for example, through subprime mortgages, was a major contributor to the financial crisis.

29. See: Berg and Ostry 2011; Stiglitz 2012; Ostry, Berg, and Tsangarides 2014; Dabla-Norris et al. 2015.

30. Several studies found these microeconomic effects after minimum wage increases in the United States and United Kingdom (Owens and Kagel 2010; Dube, Lester, and Reich 2013; Georgiadis 2013; Riley and Bondibene 2015). At the macroeconomic level, minimum wage increases force firms to become more efficient and lead to more productive firms replacing the less productive, with overall productivity increases. A study of eleven OECD countries, including the United States, found that a 10 percentage point increase in the ratio of the minimum wage to the median wage was associated with an increase in the long-run level of both labor and multifactor productivity of between 1.7 and 2 percentage points (Bassanini and Venn 2007). Other studies found similar positive productivity impacts at the macroeconomic level

in China and the United Kingdom (Mayneris, Poncet, and Zhang 2014); Croucher and Rizov 2012.

31. Long hours produce fatigue that reduces productivity. Several studies find that increases in overtime or annual hours worked resulted in decreased productivity (Cette, Chang, and Konte 2011; Golden 2012). In the realm of social protection, programs such as unemployment insurance can allow workers to invest in their skills or take the time to find employment that matches their abilities, thus contributing to productivity. Access to health care along with adequate nutrition and basic education, make up the very foundations of human productivity.

32. The Netherlands has launched an experiment to provide a basic income of €900 (about $1,000) per month to welfare recipients in several cities in the Netherlands. Finland launched a two year pilot project to provide €550 (about $630) per month to a test group of up to 10,000 working-age adults. The payment would replace unemployment and some welfare payments. Switzerland held a referendum in June 2016 on a UBI proposal that does not specify a level of benefits. It was rejected by voters.

33. U.S. Department of the Treasury Bureau of the Fiscal Service 2016.

REFERENCES

AARP, Inc. 2015. "Updating Social Security for the 21st Century: 12 Proposals You Should Know About." Retrieved February 13, 2017 from: www.aarp.org/work /social-security/info-05-2012/future-of-social-security-proposals.html.

Abraham, Katherine G., John Haltiwanger, Kristin Sandusky, and James R. Spletzer. 2016. "Measuring the Gig Economy." Presentation for the Society of Labor Economists Meeting May 2016. Retrieved February 13, 2017 from: www.sole-jole. org/16375.pdf.

Bassanini, Andrea, and Danielle Venn. 2007. "Assessing the Impact of Labor Market Policies on Productivity: A Difference-in-Differences Approach." OECD Social, Employment and Migration Working Paper 54. Paris: OECD. Retrieved February 13, 2017 from: www.oecd.org/social/soc/38797288.pdf.

Berg, A., and J. D. Ostry. 2011. "Inequality and Unsustainable Growth: Two Sides of the Same Coin?" IMF Staff Discussion Note 11/08. Washington, D.C.: International Monetary Fund. Retrieved February 13, 2017 from: www.imf.org/external /pubs/ft/sdn/2011/sdn1108.pdf.

Bernhardt, Annette. 2014. "Labor Standards and the Reorganization of Work: Gaps in Data and Research." IRLE Working Paper No. 100–14. Berkeley, Calif.: Institute for Research on Labor and Employment. Retrieved February 13, 2017 from: http:// irle.berkeley.edu/workingpapers/100-14.pdf.

Cette, Gilbert, Samuel Chang, and Maty Konte. 2011. "The Decreasing Returns On Working Time: An Empirical Analysis on Panel Country Data." Working Paper No. 315. Paris: Banque de France. Retrieved February 13, 2017 from: www .banque-france.fr/uploads/tx_bdfdocumentstravail/DT315_02.pdf.

Congressional Budget Office (CBO). 2004. "Administrative Costs of Private Accounts in Social Security." Retrieved February 13, 2017 from: www.cbo.gov/sites/default /files/cbofiles/ftpdocs/52xx/doc5277/report.pdf.

Croucher, Richard, and Marian Rizov. 2012. "The Impact of the National Minimum Wage on Labour Productivity in Britain." *E-Journal of International and Comparative Labour Studies* 1(3–4). Retrieved February 13, 2017 from: http://adapt.it /EJCLS/index.php/ejcls_adapt/article/view/43/50.

Dabla-Norris, Era, Kalpana Kochhar, Frantisek Ricka, Nujin Suphaphiphat, and Evridiki Tsounta. 2015. "Causes and Consequences of Income Inequality: A Global Perspective." IMF Staff Discussion Note 15/13. Washington, D.C.: International Monetary Fund. Retrieved February 13, 2017 from: www.imf.org/external/pubs /ft/sdn/2015/sdn1513.pdf.

Davis, Gerald F., and Suntae Kim. 2015. "Financialization of the Economy." *Annual Review of Sociology* 41:203–221.

Dube, Arindrajit, T. Willian Lester, and Michael Reich. 2013. "Minimum Wage Shocks, Employment Flows and Labor Market Frictions." IRLE Working Paper No. 149–13. Berkeley, Calif.: Institute for Research on Labor and Employment. Retrieved February 13, 2017 from: http://irle.berkeley.edu/workingpapers/149-13 .pdf.

Farrell, Diana, and Fiona Greig. 2016a. "Paychecks, Paydays and the Online Platform Economy." JPMorgan Chase & Co. Institute, February 2016. Retrieved February 15, 2017 from: www.jpmorganchase.com/corporate/institute/report-paychecks-paydays-and-the-online-platform-economy.htm.

——. 2016b. "The Online Platform Economy: Has Growth Peaked?" JPMorgan Chase & Co. Institute, November 2016. Retrieved February 15, 2017 from: www. jpmorganchase.com/corporate/institute/document/jpmc-institute-online-plat-form-econ-brief.pdf.

Gallup-Healthways Well-Being Index, January 9, 2017. Gallup. Retrieved February 10, 2017 from: www.well-beingindex.com/u.s.-uninsured-rate-holds-at-low-of-10.9-in-fourth-quarter.

Georgiadis, Andreas. 2013. "Efficiency Wages and the Economic Effects of the Minimum Wage: Evidence from a Low-Wage Labor Market." *Oxford Bulletin of Economics and Statistics* 75(6):962–79.

Golden, Lonnie. 2012. *The Effects of Working Time on Productivity and Firm Performance: A Research Synthesis Paper*. Conditions of Work and Employment Series No. 33. Geneva: ILO. Retrieved February 13, 2017 from: www.ilo.org /wcmsp5/groups/public/@ed_protect/@protrav/@travail/documents/publication /wcms_187307.pdf.

Hacker, Jacob. 2006. *The Great Risk Shift: The Assault on American Jobs, Families, Health Care, and Retirement and How You Can Fight Back*. New York: Oxford University Press.

Hacker, Jacob. 2011. "Restoring Retirement Security: The Market Crisis, the 'Great Risk Shift,' and the Challenge for Our Nation." *Elder Law Journal* 19(1):1–48.

Harris, Seth D., and Alan B. Krueger. 2015. *A Proposal for Modernizing Labor Laws for Twenty-First-Century Work: The "Independent Worker."* Hamilton Project Policy Brief 2015–10. Washington, D.C.: Brookings Institution. Retrieved February 13, 2017 from: www.hamiltonproject.org/assets/files/modernizing_labor_laws_for_twenty _first_century_work_krueger_harris.pdf.

Haskins, Ron. 2017. "Helping Work Reduce Poverty." *National Affairs* 30(Winter). Retrieved February 17, 2017 from: www.nationalaffairs.com/publications/detail /helping-work-reduce-poverty.

Hipple, Steven F. 2010. "Self-employment in the United States." *Monthly Labor Review*, September. Retrieved February 13, 2017 from: www.bls.gov/opub/mlr/2010/09 /art2full.pdf.

Hipple, Steven F., and Laurel A. Hammond. 2016. "Self-employment in the United States." U.S. Bureau of Labor Statistics. Retrieved February 10, 2017 from: www. bls.gov/spotlight/2016/self-employment-in-the-united-states/pdf/self-employ-ment-in-the-united-states.pdf.

International Labor Organization (ILO), International Monetary Fund, Organization for Economic Co-operation and Development, and World Bank Group. 2015. *Income Inequality and Labor Income Share in G20 Countries: Trends, Impacts and Causes.* Report prepared for the G20 Labour and Employment Ministers Meeting and Joint Meeting of Finance Ministers, September 3–4, 2015. Retrieved February 10, 2017 from: www.ilo.org/global/about-the-ilo/how-the-ilo-works/multilateral-system/g20/reports/WCMS_398074/lang—en/index.htm.

Jackson, Emilie, Adam Looney, and Shanthi Ramnath. 2017. *The Rise of Alternative Work Arrangements: Evidence and Implications for Tax Filing and Benefit Cover-age.* Office of Tax Analysis Working Paper 114. U.S. Department of the Treasury. Retrieved February 13, 2017 from: www.treasury.gov/resource-center/tax-policy /tax-analysis/Documents/WP-114.pdf.

Katz, Lawrence F., and Alan B. Krueger. 2016. *The Rise and Nature of Alternative Work Arrangements in the United States, 1995–2015.* Retrieved February 13, 2017 from: http://krueger.princeton.edu/sites/default/files/akrueger/files/katz_krueger _cws_-_march_29_20165.pdf.

Mayneris, Florian, Sandra Poncet, and Tao Zhang. 2014. "The Cleansing Effect of Minimum Wage: Minimum Wage Rules, Firm Dynamics and Aggregate Pro-ductivity in China." CEPII Working Paper No. 2014–16. Paris: Centre d'Etudes Prospectives et d'Informations Internationales. Retrieved February 13, 2017 from: www.cepii.fr/CEPII/en/publications/wp/abstract.asp?NoDoc=7139.

National Opinion Research Center (NORC). 2006. "2006 General Social Survey (GSS)." Chicago, Illinois: University of Chicago.

——. 2010. "2010 General Social Survey (GSS)." Chicago, Illinois: University of Chicago.

ObamaCare Facts. 2017. ObamaCare.com. Retrieved February 10, 2017 from: http://obamacarefacts.com/2015/04/13/us-uninsured-rate-drops-11-9-in-first -quarter-2015.

Organisation for Economic Co-operation and Development. 2017a. Self-employment rate (indicator). OECD iLibrary Statistics. Retrieved February 9, 2017 from: www .oecd-ilibrary.org/employment.

——. 2017b. Temporary employment (indicator). OECD iLibrary Statistics. Retrieved February 9, 2017 from: www.oecd-ilibrary.org/employment.

——. 2017c. Part-time employment rate (indicator). OECD iLibrary Statistics. Retrieved February 9, 2017 from: www.oecd-ilibrary.org/employment.

Ostry, Jonathan D., Andrew Berg, and Charalambos G. Tsangarides. 2014. "Redistribution, Inequality, and Growth." IMF Staff Discussion Note 14/02. Washington, D.C.: International Monetary Fund. Retrieved February 13, 2017 from: www.imf.org/external/pubs/ft/sdn/2014/sdn1402.pdf.

Owens, Mark F., and John H. Kagel. 2010. "Minimum Wage Restrictions and Employee Effort in Incomplete Labor Markets: An Experimental Investigation." *Journal of Economic Behavior & Organization* 73(3). Retrieved February 13, 2017 from: www.econ.ohio-state.edu/kagel/JEBO24871.pdf.

Polaski, Sandra. 2004. "Job Anxiety Is Real—and It's Global." Carnegie Endowment for International Peace Policy Brief 30, April 2004. Washington, D.C.: Carnegie Endowment for International Peace. Retrieved February 13, 2017 from: http://carnegieendowment.org/2004/04/21/job-anxiety-is-real-and-it-s-global/3qe5.

———. 2007. "U.S. Living Standards in an Era of Globalization." Carnegie Endowment for International Peace Policy Brief 53, July 2007. Washington, D.C.: Carnegie Endowment for International Peace. Retrieved February 13, 2017 from: http://carnegieendowment.org/2007/07/17/u.s.-living-standards-in-era-of-globalization/i7pj.

Polivka, Anne, and Thomas Nardone. 1989. "On the Definition of 'Contingent' Work." *Monthly Labor Review*, December. Retrieved February 13, 2017 from: www.bls.gov/opub/mlr/1989/12/art2full.pdf.

Riley, Rebecca, and Chiara Rosazza Bondibene. 2015. "Raising the Standard: Minimum Wages and Firm Productivity." NIESR Discussion Paper No. 449. London: National Institute of Economic and Social Research. Retrieved February 10, 2017 from: www.niesr.ac.uk/sites/default/files/publications/Minimum%20wages%20and%20firm%20productivity%20NIESR%20DP%20449.pdf.

Stiglitz, Joseph. 2012. *The Price of Inequality: How Today's Divided Society Endangers Our Future*. New York: Norton.

U.S. Bureau of Labor Statistics. January 2017. "Current Population Survey (CPS)." Retrieved February 15, 2017 from: www.bls.gov/cps/tables.htm.

———. 1995. "Contingent and Alternative Employment Arrangements August 1995." Retrieved February 10, 2017 from: www.bls.gov/news.release/history/conemp_082595.txt.

———. 2005. "Contingent and Alternative Employment Arrangements February 2005." Retrieved February 10, 2017 from: www.bls.gov/news.release/pdf/conemp.pdf.

U.S. Census Bureau. 2016. "Income and Poverty in the United States: 2015." Report Number: P60-256. Retrieved March 1, 2017 from: www2.census.gov/programs-surveys/demo/visualizations/p60/256/figure4.pdf

U.S. Department of Commerce, Bureau of Economic Analysis. 2017. "National Economic Accounts Fourth Quarter 2016." Retrieved February 15, 2017 from: www.bea.gov/newsreleases/national/gdp/2017/pdf/gdp4q16_adv.pdf.

U.S. Department of Health and Human Services. 2016. "Marketplace Enrollment Report March 2016." Retrieved February 10, 2017 from: https://aspe.hhs.gov/health-insurance-marketplaces-2016-open-enrollment-period-final-enrollment-report.

U.S. Department of Labor Wage and Hour Division. 2015. "Administrator's Interpretation No. 2015–1." Retrieved February 10, 2017 from: www.dol.gov/whd/workers/Misclassification/AI-2015_1.pdf.

U.S. Department of the Treasury, Bureau of the Fiscal Service. 2016. "Final Monthly Treasury Statement September 2016." Retrieved February 15, 2017 from: www .fiscal.treasury.gov/fsreports/rpt/mthTreasStmt/mts0916.pdf.

U.S. Government Accountability Office (GAO). 2015. "Contingent Workforce: Size, Characteristics, Earnings, and Benefits." GAO-15-168R Contingent Workforce. Retrieved February 10, 2017 from: www.gao.gov/products/GAO-15-168R.

Weil, David. 2014. *The Fissured Workplace: Why Work Became So Bad for So Many and What Can Be Done to Improve It*. Cambridge: Harvard University Press.

CHAPTER 3

The Welfare State in the Twenty-First Century

LATEST TRENDS IN SOCIAL PROTECTION

Isabel Ortiz

This chapter presents a global consensus to expand social protection systems, mainly due to the significant impacts of social protection in reducing poverty and inequality. Social protection is the most redistributive public policy, as it entails (1) direct cash transfers from national budgets to citizens, (2) additional transfers from employers to workers in the case of contributory public schemes, and (3) transfers within the schemes that redistribute income from higher earners to lower earners. However, these redistributive components of social security systems were weakened in a number of countries with the introduction of individual accounts, pension privatization, and other reforms since the 1980s. Pressures continue, from austerity cuts to reductions in employer contributions: an attack on social security that would significantly increase inequality.

The chapter continues reviewing the divergent trends of 2010–2016: on the one hand, the great expansion of social protection in a majority of developing countries, and on the other, fiscal austerity measures undertaken in high-income as well as some middle-income countries that undermine progress in social protection. These short-term adjustments have high human costs, are bringing the global economy into further recession, and are eroding the achievements of the postwar welfare state model. Following this, the "aging crisis" is presented as an opportunity to generate jobs in the care and "silver" economy. The chapter closes with current debates on guaranteed minimum income and universal basic income and other areas of welfare, such as subsidized goods and services. The chapter concludes that reducing inequality will require adopting equitable macroeconomic and sector policies that generate jobs and strengthen public welfare systems, expanding social protection until universal coverage is achieved at adequate benefit levels.

A GLOBAL CONSENSUS TO EXPAND SOCIAL PROTECTION SYSTEMS

The case for social protection is compelling in our time. Social protection, or social security, is both a human right and a sound economic policy. Social protection powerfully contributes to reducing poverty and inequality while enhancing political stability and social cohesion. Social protection also contributes to economic growth by supporting household income and thus domestic consumption; this is particularly important during this time of slow growth and low global demand. Further, social protection enhances human capital and productivity, so it has become a critical policy for transformative national development.

Since the end of the nineteenth century, significant progress has been made in extending social security and building welfare systems. From early steps taken in a number of pioneering European countries, the scope of social security, measured by the number of areas covered by social protection systems,[1] was extended at an impressive pace (ILO 2014a). Today, the majority of countries have social security schemes established by law, albeit in many developing countries it is only for a minority within their populations.

Contributory social security systems were established around the world with the expectation that formal employment would keep expanding, and people would thus be able to contribute. However, since the 1980s, the majority of countries have experienced "jobless growth," and enrollments into social security did not expand as expected. This led to the significant expansion of noncontributory cash transfers, particularly in developing countries, to complement contributory schemes.

The strong positive impacts of social protection have brought social protection to the forefront of the development agenda. Social protection is a key element of national development strategies to reduce poverty and inequality and promote human capital, political stability, and inclusive growth.

The ILO Social Protection Floors Recommendation (No. 202), adopted in 2012, reflects a global consensus on the extension of social security reached among governments, employers' organizations, and workers' organizations from 185 countries at all levels of development. Further, the rollout of social protection floors has been endorsed by the G20 and is part of the UN SDGs, adopted by all countries in 2015, committing states to expand social protection systems and measures for all, including floors, by 2030.[2]

More than thirty developing countries have taken up the gauntlet and already made the vision of a world with universal social protection schemes a reality, including Argentina, Bolivia, Botswana, Brazil, Cabo Verde, Chile, China, Colombia, Kazakhstan, Kiribati, Kosovo, Kyrgyz Republic, Lesotho, Maldives, Mauritius, Mongolia, Namibia, Nepal, Samoa, Seychelles, South Africa, Swaziland, Zanzibar/Tanzania, Thailand, Timor-Leste, Trinidad and Tobago, Uruguay, Uzbekistan, and others. Further, main development agencies are working together to support universal social protection, social protection systems/floors, and SDG 1.3.

This global consensus is being challenged by short-term austerity pressures. Fiscal consolidation and adjustment measures threaten household living standards in a significant number of countries. Despite progress made in reducing levels of extreme poverty in some parts of the world, high levels of poverty and vulnerability persist; what is more, poverty is actually increasing in many high-income countries. In addition, high and still-rising levels of inequality in both advanced and developing economies are widely acknowledged as cause for great concern. Still grappling with the economic repercussions of the global financial crisis, the world is faced with a deep social crisis that is reflected in the loss of legitimacy of governments (Ortiz et al. 2013). Social protection measures are essential elements of a policy response that can address those challenges.

SOCIAL SECURITY REDUCES POVERTY

Contributory social security schemes were designed to prevent poverty in old age and in the event of disability, maternity, unemployment, and other life-cycle risks. Overall, social transfers and taxation reduce poverty by more than 50 percent in most European countries (see figure 3.1). Noncontributory cash transfer schemes have also successfully reduced poverty in Africa, Asia, Europe, and Latin America, delivering much faster results than those expected from the "trickle-down" effects of economic policies. Although benefits have tended to be lower than needed, a cash transfer at an adequate level can bring people out of poverty overnight. Equally importantly, cash transfers have had even larger effects on reducing the depth of poverty. For example, South Africa's noncontributory grants have reduced the poverty gap by more than one-third (Woolard, Harttgen, and Klasen 2010), the Oportunidades program in

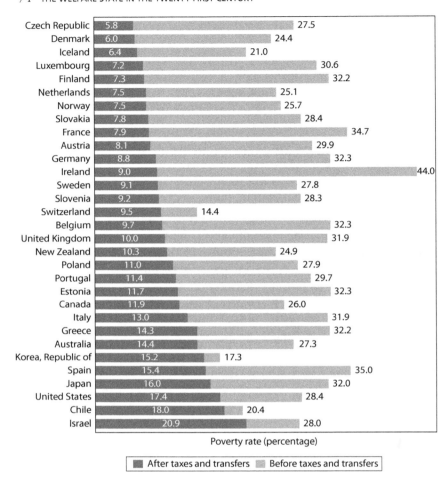

Figure 3.1 Poverty rates in OECD countries before and after taxes and social protection transfers.

Note: Relative poverty line defined as 50 percent of median equivalized household income.

Source: ILO 2014a, based on OECD Income Distribution Database.

Mexico has reduced the numbers living in poverty by 10 percent and the poverty gap by 30 percent (Skoufias and Parker 2001), and the expansion of food assistance in the United States is reported to have reduced the number of households in extreme poverty by half (Center on Budget and Policy Priorities 2014).

There is also strong evidence of the positive impacts of social protection on hunger and nutrition,[3] education,[4] and health outcomes,[5] as well

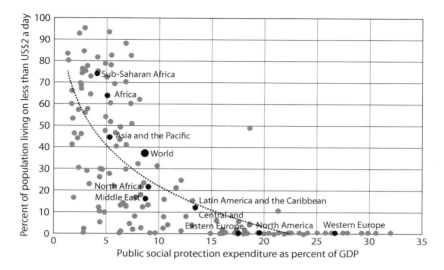

Figure 3.2 Public social expenditure (percentage of GDP) and proportion of the population in poverty, 2014.

Note: $R^2 = 0.5326$. The relationship between public social protection expenditure and poverty outcomes is complex, involving a variety of factors. It should be noted in particular that US$2 PPP per day does not represent a meaningful absolute poverty line in high-income countries; this cutoff point was selected for the purpose of the graph to ensure international comparability.

Sources: ILO 2014a, based on data from IMF, OECD, Eurostat, ILO, UN ECLAC, ADB, and national sources. Poverty headcount: World Development Indicators (World Bank).

as on employment.[6] It is therefore not surprising that higher levels of social protection expenditure are associated with lower levels of poverty (see figure 3.2).

SOCIAL SECURITY IS ALSO CRITICAL TO REDUCE INEQUALITY

By tackling poverty and improving human capacities, social protection is an effective instrument for narrowing development gaps and reducing inequality in all its forms. For example, a universal child allowance introduced in Argentina in 2009 is estimated to have reduced inequality by approximately 5 percent (Bertranou and Maurizio 2012; ILO 2015b). The Brazilian Bolsa Familia program is estimated to be responsible for 16 percent of income inequality reduction in the country between 1999 and 2009 (Soares et al. 2010). At more aggregate levels, Cornia (2014) estimates that social protection transfers have contributed 15 to 30 percent of the drop in inequality in Latin America between 2002 and 2012.[7]

Furthermore, social protection programs with gender-sensitive design features can be efficient mechanisms for empowering women, and cash transfers that focus on historically underprivileged groups can help mitigate horizontal inequalities.

The correlation between public social protection expenditure and inequality (as expressed by the Gini coefficient) is less strong than for poverty, but there is still a distinct relationship, suggesting that higher levels of social protection expenditure are associated with lower levels of inequality (see figure 3.3).

High expenditures on social protection reflect mostly contributory schemes, which provide higher and predictable benefits compared with noncontributory cash transfers, generally with low benefits targeted exclusively to the poor. The degree to which governments finance their social protection systems using employer and employee contributions can be substantial and varies widely (see figure 3.4). Some countries finance

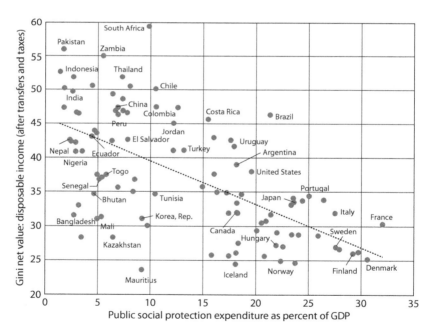

Figure 3.3   Public social protection expenditure (percent of GDP) and income in equality (Gini coefficient), 2014.

Note: R^2 = 0.3893.

Sources: ILO 2014a. Public social protection expenditure: based on data from IMF, OECD, Eurostat, ILO, UN ECLAC, ADB and national sources. Gini index: World Development Indicators (World Bank; Solt 2013).

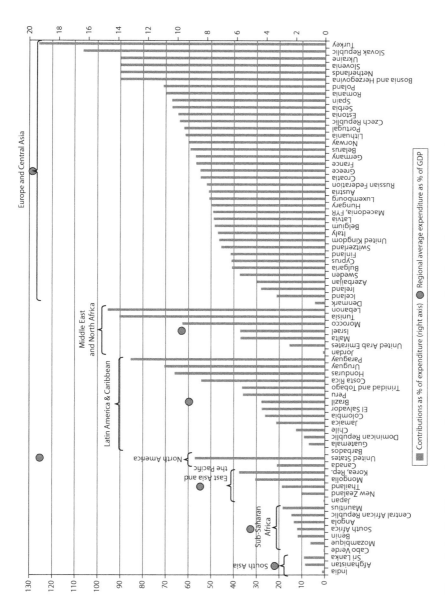

Figure 3.4 Social security contributions as a percentage of total social protection expenditure.

Source: Ortiz et al. 2017.

nearly all their social protection expenditures by contributions; others have larger public support.

The point is that both noncontributory and contributory public schemes are crucial to reduce inequality. Noncontributory schemes are a direct cash transfer from the national budget to a selected number of citizens (e.g., the poor, older persons) or to all citizens (universal basic income). Public contributory schemes are redistributive on two fronts: (1) they are transfers from employers to workers, and (2) they are traditionally designed to redistribute income from those with higher lifetime earnings to those with lower lifetime earnings.

Table 3.1 presents social security contributions around the world. Generally, employers' contributions are much larger than workers' contributions—as a world average, employers contribute 14 percent and workers 7 percent of covered earnings. Note that employers' social security contributions are a deferred wage.

Traditionally, public social security systems are also designed to redistribute income from those with higher lifetime earnings to those with lower lifetime earnings. The degree of redistribution from higher earners to lower earners varies country to country, but all contribute to reduce inequality.

However, the redistributive component of social security systems was broken in some countries with the introduction of individual accounts in the 1980s. The World Bank became a proponent of this approach, and was soon followed by the Inter-American Development Bank and the OECD. These institutions forcefully pressed for the introduction of individual accounts, defined contributions (instead of defined benefits), and other reforms, including full or partial privatization of the schemes, in a number of Eastern European and Latin American countries. While many of these countries have reversed this trend, these ideas remain in the policy discussions of the international financial institutions.

DIVERGENT TRENDS 2010–2016: EXPANSION VERSUS AUSTERITY

The global financial and economic crisis and the Great Recession have forcefully underlined the importance of social security as an economic and social necessity. In the first phase of the crisis (2008–2009), social protection played a strong role in the expansionary response. About fifty high- and middle-income countries announced fiscal stimulus packages totaling US$2.4 trillion, of which approximately a quarter was invested in countercyclical social protection measures (Ortiz and Cummins 2012).

Table 3.1   Social Security Contribution Rates, Circa 2015

Country	Workers	Employers	Total	Country	Workers	Employers	Total
Americas				Austria	17.20	25.15	42.35
Antigua and Barbuda	7.5	9.5	17	Belarus	7.0	34.3	41.3
Argentina	14	21.5[d]	35.5	Belgium	13.07	24.80	37.87
Bahamas	4.4	6.4[d]	10.8	Bulgaria	12.9	17.8	30.7
Barbados	9.18	10.43[d]	19.61	Croatia	20.0	15.2	35.2
Belize	e	e	e	Cyprus	7.8	7.8	15.6
Bermuda	5[f]	5[d,f]	10[f]	Czech Republic	11	34	45
Bolivia	12.71	27.71[d,g]	39.42	Denmark	8	0	8
Brazil	8	21[d,h]	29	Estonia	4	34	38
British Virgin Islands	4	4.5[d]	8.5	Finland	8.41	22.19	30.60
Canada	6.83	7.582[d,i,j]	14.412	France	13.2	37.5	50.7
Chile	17.65	4.61[d]	22.26	Germany	20.175	20.575	40.750
Colombia	8	28.848	37.848	Greece	12.05	23.60	35.65
Costa Rica	9.17	17.42[d]	26.59	Guernsey	6.0	6.5	12.5
Cuba	1	12.5	13.5	Hungary	16	27	43
Dominica	4.5	7.25[d]	11.75	Iceland	4.00	15.79	19.79
Dominican Republic	5.91	15.39[d]	21.3	Ireland	4.00	4.25	8.25
Ecuador	8.64	10.36	19	Isle of Man	11.0	12.8	23.8
El Salvador	9.25	12.05	21.3	Italy	9.19	33.68	42.87
Grenada	4	5[d]	9	Jersey	6.0	6.5	12.5
Guatemala	4.83	10.67	15.5	Latvia	10.50	23.59	34.09
Guyana	5.6	8.4	14	Liechtenstein	12.55	15.90	28.45
Haiti	6	8[d]	14	Lithuania	9.00	31.17	40.17
Honduras	3.5	7.2[d]	10.7	Luxembourg	12.70	11.95	24.65
Jamaica	2.5	2.5[d,j]	5	Malta	10	10	20
Mexico	2.4	31.3[d,j]	33.7	Moldova	6	23	29
Nicaragua	6.25	14.5[d]	20.75	Monaco	6.55	23.48	30.03
Panama	9.75	12.25[d]	22	Netherlands	22.70	19.07	41.77
Paraguay	9	14	23	Norway	8.2	14.1	22.3
Peru	13[m]	9.63[d]	22.63	Poland	22.71	19.38	42.09
Saint Kitts and Nevis	5	6[d]	11	Portugal	11.00	23.75	34.75
Europe				Romania	16.5	28	44.5
Albania	11.39	16.51	27.90	Russia	0	30.2	30.2
Andorra	5.5	14.5	20.0	San Marino	6.3	31.0	37.3

(continued)

Table 3.1 (continued)

Country	Workers	Employers	Total	Country	Workers	Employers	Total
Serbia	19.9	17.9	37.8	Liberia	3	4.75[e]	7.75
Slovak Republic	13.4	33.2	46.6	Libya	5.25	12.95	18.2
Slovenia	22.10	16.63	38.73	Madagascar[f]	1	13[e,g]	14
Spain	6.25	31.13	37.38	Malawi	0	0[e]	0
Sweden	7.00	31.42	38.42	Mali[f]	6.66	17.9[e,g]	24.56
Switzerland	13.25	13.35	26.60	Mauritania[f]	3	14[c,e,g]	17
Turkey	15.0	21.5	36.5	Mauritius[f]	4	6[e,k]	10
Ukraine	3.6	36.1	39.7	Morocco[f]	6.29	18.5[c,e]	24.79
United Kingdom	11.1	13.8	24.9	Namibia[f]	0.9	0.9[e,k]	1.8
Africa				Niger[f]	5.25	15.4[c,e,g]	20.65
Algeria	9	25	34	Nigeria	7.5	8.5[e]	16
Benin	3.6	16.4[c]	20	Rwanda[f]	3	5[e]	8
Botswana	0	0[e]	0	São Tomé and Principe.	4	6	10
Burkina Faso[f]	5.5	16[c,e]	21.5	Senegal[f]	11	23[e,g]	34
Burundi[f]	4	9[c,e]	13	Seychelles	1.5	1.5[l,m]	3
Cameroon[f]	2.8	12.95[c,e]	15.75	Sierra Leone	5	10[e]	15
Cape Verde[f]	8	17[c,e]	25	South Africa [f]	1	1[e,k]	2
Central African Republic[f]	3	19[c,e,g]	22	Sudan	8	19 [e]	27
Chad[f]	3.5	16.5[c,e,g]	20	Swaziland[f]	5	5[e]	10
Congo (Brazzaville)[f]	4	20.28[c,e,g]	24.28	Tanzania	10	10	20
Congo (Kinshasa)	3.5	9[c,e]	12.5	Togo	4	17.5[e,g]	21.5
Côte d'Ivoire[f]	6.3	15.45[c,e]	21.75	Tunisia	8.8	15.45[e,n]	24.25
Djibouti[f]	4	15.7	19.7	Uganda	5	10 [e]	15
Egypt[f]	14	26[e]	40	Zambia[f]	5	5 [e]	10
Equatorial Guinea[h]	4.5	21.5	26	Zimbabwe	3.5	3.5[e]	7
Ethiopia	7	11	18	**Asia-Pacific**			
Gabon [f]	5	20.1[c,e,g]	25.1	Armenia	8	0[b]	8[b]
Gambia[f]	5	30 [e]	35	Australia	0	9.5[b]	9.5[b]
Ghana	5.5	13[e]	18.5	Azerbaijan	3	22[c]	25[c]
Guinea[f]	5	20[c,e,g]	25	Bahrain	7	13	20
Kenya[f]	5	5[e]	10	Bangladesh	0[c]	0[c]	0[c]
Lesotho	0	0[e]	0	Brunei	8.5	8.5[b]	17[b]

Table 3.1 (continued)

Country	Workers	Employers	Total	Country	Workers	Employers	Total
Myanmar	6	7	13	Malaysia	12	14.75	26.75
China	9	24[c]	33[c]	Marshall Islands	7	7	14
Fiji	8	8[c]	16[c]	Micronesia	7.5	7.5	15
Georgia	0	0b[c]	0b,[c]	Nepal	10	10[c]	20[c]
Hong Kong	5	5[c]	10[c]	New Zealand	0	0[b]	0[b]
India	13.75	21.25	35	Oman	7	11.5	18.5
Indonesia	2.5	8[c]	10.5[c]	Pakistan	1	11	12[c]
Iran	7	23[c]	30[c]	Palau	6	6	12
Iraq	4.1	12.9	17	Papua New Guinea	6	8.4	14.4
Israel	0.39	3.43	3.82	Philippines	3.63	7.37[b]	11[b]
Japan	9.237[b]	9.987[b]	19.224[b]	Qatar	5	10[c]	15[c]
Jordan	6.5	12.25	18.75	Samoa	5	6[c]	11[c]
Kazakhstan	10	0[b]	10[b]	Saudi Arabia	10	12	22
Kiribati	7.5	7.5[c]	15[c]	Singapore	20	16[c]	36[c]
Kuwait	5.5	10.5	16	Solomon Islands	5	7.5[c]	12.5[c]
Kyrgyzstan	10	15.25	25.25	South Korea	5.195	6	11.195
Laos	4.75	5.25	10	Sri Lanka	8[b]	12[c]	20b[c]
Lebanon	0	14.5	14.5[c]	Syria	7	17.1[c]	24.1[c]

Note: This table provides an overview, and contribution rates are not directly comparable across programs and countries. Rates are in percent of covered earnings. For a full picture of the different contributions to old-age, disability, and survivors' schemes, sickness and maternity, work injury, unemployment benefits, and family allowances, see International Social Security Association (ISSA) and the ILO social protection platform.

[a] Includes old-age, disability, and survivors' schemes, sickness and maternity, work injury, unemployment benefits, and family allowances. In some countries, the rate may not cover all of these programs. In some cases, only certain groups, such as wage earners, are represented. When the contribution rate varies, either the average or the lowest rate in the range is used.

[b] Contributions finance old-age benefits only.

[c] Employers pay the total cost of family allowances.

[d] Government pays the total cost of the old-age, disability, and survivors' programs.

[e] Employers pay the total cost of work injury benefits.

[f] Contributions are submitted to a ceiling on some benefits.

[g] Employers pay the total cost of maternity benefits.

[h] Data are at least two years old.

[i] Also includes the contribution rates for other programs.

[j] There is no disability or survivors' program. An old-age program has yet to be implemented.

[k] Government pays the total cost of family allowances.

[l] Government pays the total cost of cash sickness and maternity benefits.

[m] Government pays the total cost of work injury benefits.

[n] National Social Security Fund pays the total cost of unemployment benefits.

Source: Ortiz et al. 2017, based on SSA (U.S. Social Security Administration), ISSA, and ILO.

In the second phase of the crisis (2010 onward), many governments embarked on fiscal consolidation and premature contraction of expenditures, despite an urgent need for public support among vulnerable populations. In 2016 the scope of public expenditure adjustment is expected to intensify significantly. According to IMF projections, 132 countries, of which 86 are developing, are contracting expenditures in terms of GDP. Further, worldwide 30 percent of countries are undergoing excessive fiscal contraction, defined as cutting public expenditures below precrisis levels (Ortiz et al. 2015).

High-income countries have reduced a range of social protection benefits and limited access to quality public services. Together with persistent unemployment, lower wages, and higher taxes, these measures have contributed to increases in poverty or social exclusion now affecting 123 million people in the European Union, 24 percent of the population, many of them children, women, and persons with disabilities. Future old-age pensioners will receive lower pensions in at least fourteen European countries. Several European courts have found the cuts unconstitutional. The cost of adjustment has been passed on to populations that have been coping with fewer jobs and lower income for more than five years. Depressed household income levels are leading to lower domestic consumption and lower demand, slowing down recovery. The achievements of the European social model, which dramatically reduced poverty and promoted prosperity and social cohesion in the period following the Second World War, have been eroded by short-term adjustment reforms (ILO 2014b; Vaughan-Whitehead 2014).

Most middle-income countries are boldly expanding their social protection systems, thereby contributing to their domestic demand–led growth strategies: this presents a powerful development lesson. China, for instance, has achieved nearly universal coverage of pensions and increased wages (ILO 2015a); Brazil has accelerated the expansion of social protection coverage and minimum wages since 2009. An ILO analysis of announced social protection policies/reforms worldwide from January 2010 to December 2015 reflects that, of 704 measures, the majority were on expansion of coverage (212), followed by increasing benefits (58), mostly in middle-income countries (ILO 2016b).

Some lower-income countries have extended social protection mainly through narrowly targeted temporary safety nets with very low benefit levels. However, in many of these countries, debates are under way on building social protection floors as part of comprehensive social protection systems.

This positive expansionary trend, however, is being countered by short-term adjustment pressures—mostly stemming from IMF policy advice, but some driven by a number of newly conservative governments, such as Brazil, the United States, and the United Kingdom, supporting welfare cuts. Contrary to public perception, austerity measures are not limited to Europe; a significant number of developing countries have also adopted fiscal consolidation measures, including the elimination or reduction of food and fuel subsidies; cuts or caps on the wage bill, including for teachers and health and social workers; more narrow targeting of social protection benefits (a de facto contraction of social protection, at a time of recession when social support is most needed); and reforms of contributory pension and health-care systems, among other reforms (see table 3.2). All these measures are detrimental to social welfare. Since 2010 the cost of adjustment has been passed on to populations, many of whom have been coping with fewer jobs, lower income, and reduced access to public goods and services for more than six years. In short, vulnerable households are most impacted by austerity measures and are bearing the costs of a "recovery" that has largely excluded them.

Table 3.2 Incidence of Austerity Measures in 183 Countries, 2010–2015 (Number of Countries)

Region/income	Subsidy reduction	Wage bill cuts/caps	Safety net targeting	Pension reforms	Labor reforms	Health reforms	Consumption tax increases	Privatization
East Asia and Pacific	15	18	10	6	9	2	18	8
Eastern Europe/ Central Asia	14	17	18	18	12	9	14	11
Latin America/ Caribbean	14	14	13	17	11	2	18	3
Middle East and North Africa	10	8	7	5	6	3	9	2
South Asia	6	7	5	2	3	0	7	3
Sub-Saharan Africa	38	32	15	12	8	6	27	13
Developing countries	97	96	68	60	49	22	93	40
High-income countries	35	34	39	45	40	34	45	15
All countries	132	130	107	105	89	56	138	55

Source: Ortiz et al. 2015, based on analysis of 616 IMF country reports published from February 2010 to February 2015.

Furthermore, while cost savings from fiscal consolidation measures may have assisted in servicing debt and/or keeping macroeconomic balances, they have not supported economic growth. Social protection supports household income and is essential to sustain consumption and domestic demand—adequate levels of social protection are an important element of an inclusive growth and recovery strategy. However, in most of Europe, and particularly in countries with structural programs, disposable household incomes have declined as a result of high unemployment, lower wages, and social protection expenditure cuts, and this in turn has led to lower consumption and low growth (ILO 2014a).

The UN has repeatedly warned that austerity is likely to bring the global economy into further recession and increase inequality (UN 2012; Ortiz et al. 2015). Policy makers must recognize the high human and developmental costs of poorly designed adjustment strategies and consider alternative policies that support socioeconomic recovery and the achievement of the SDGs.

DEBATES ON PENSION ADEQUACY AND SUSTAINABILITY: AN ATTACK ON PUBLIC SOCIAL SECURITY SYSTEMS

There is strong evidence about the key role of public pensions in reducing inequality—with public pensions having less effect than wages, the main source of household income, but much more than taxes and noncontributory cash transfers in countries where social protection systems are well developed (Behrendt and Woodall 2015) (see figure 3.5).

However, only half of the world's older persons receive a pension due to persistent gaps in coverage in many low- and middle-income countries. To address this, there has been impressive progress in a significant number of developing countries through the creation of universal noncontributory social pensions that provide at least a basic level of protection (e.g., Bolivia, Botswana, Lesotho, Namibia, Nepal, Swaziland, Timor Leste). Other countries (e.g., Brazil, Cabo Verde, China, Thailand, South Africa) have achieved universal coverage by expanding contributory schemes to previously uncovered groups of the population, in combination with an extension of noncontributory pensions (ILO 2014b, 2015a, 2016a).

Yet ensuring the adequacy of pensions remains a considerable challenge in both North and South, particularly as many countries seek to find cost savings in public pension schemes as part of the austerity drive. Governments (and the IMF) in search of fiscal savings are looking at

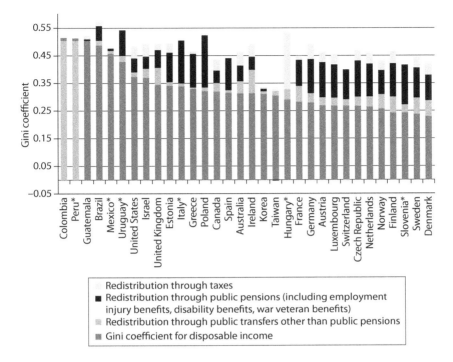

Figure 3.5   Public pensions reduce inequality.

Source: Behrendt and Woodall 2015.

reforming pensions, as these are generally the largest social protection expenditure.[8] Approximately 105 governments in 60 developing and 45 high-income countries are considering changes to their pension systems, including raising the retirement age, making eligibility conditions stricter, lowering replacement rates, eliminating minimum guarantees, stopping indexation to wages or prices, and (sometimes) instituting structural reforms such as changes to individual accounts and defined contributions (Ortiz et al. 2015). These adjustments are undermining the adequacy of pension systems and reducing their ability to prevent poverty in old age. It is alarming that future pensioners will receive lower pensions in at least fourteen countries of Europe (ILO 2014a). Several European courts have found cuts and reforms unconstitutional.[9]

In view of these recent trends, ensuring the adequacy of pensions is a key challenge after past pension reforms have prioritized financial sustainability over adequacy considerations (ILO 2014b; OECD 2015). In many countries, there is a clear trend toward lower-income replacement rates that will provide only a minimum level of protection. Long-term projections of pension levels for the EU show a marked decline of pension levels in the future (European Commission 2015). Inadequate pension benefits negatively affect household incomes and aggregate consumption and will increase inequality.

As mentioned earlier, pension reforms are not new. Since the 1980s, claims of a "social security crisis" or "old-age crisis" have been used as justification to introduce reforms and have led to large-scale privatizations of social security pensions. Reforms were contested at the time by the ILO and by many others, including Joseph Stiglitz (Stiglitz and Orzag 1999). Despite the arguments, reforms were implemented in twenty-three Latin American and Eastern European countries.

However, in recent years, a number of countries have reversed their earlier privatization programs (ILO 2014a; Mesa-Lago 2014). In several Latin American countries, reforms were declared unconstitutional or annulled before implementation (e.g., Ecuador and Nicaragua), and countries kept their public pension systems. A full or partial renationalization of assets accumulated in mandatory private systems has occurred in Argentina (2008), Bolivia (2010), Poland (2013), Hungary (2010), and Kazakhstan (2013). Some lessons include:

- Private systems based on individual accounts recorded poor performance in terms of coverage and the level of benefits for members; in general, individual account systems have not enjoyed a good reputation and became quite unpopular.
- Privatization did not reduce fiscal pressures; on the contrary, the transition from a public to a funded pension system was seriously underestimated and created new and strong fiscal pressures (e.g., in Poland and Hungary privatizations added 1.5 percent GDP yearly to national deficits), which proved difficult for most governments to afford.
- High administrative costs (which include high administration fees paid to private pension funds) also contributed to lower replacement rates.
- The risk of financial market fluctuations was left to pensioners, who risked losing their life savings if financial markets collapsed, as happened during the global financial crisis; in some cases, such as Chile, the state (the taxpayer) had to pay twice and act as a guarantor of last resort, providing a basic pension for citizens and topping up low pension benefits.
- Individual accounts have exacerbated gender inequalities.

- The privatization of pensions also contributed to increasing inequality by generating very high levels of profit for pension fund administrators and positioning a high concentration of the investment portfolio in favor of a few business groups and large banks.

AGING IS NOT A CRISIS, BUT AN OPPORTUNITY TO GENERATE JOBS IN THE CARE AND "SILVER" ECONOMY

Aging has become a global phenomenon, a positive result of improvements in health, nutrition, and welfare. While high-income countries continue to have the highest share of older persons, developing countries see the most rapid rates of population aging.

Some have presented aging as a crisis, focusing exclusively on the costs to societies and thus precipitating pension reforms, an inadequate policy response. On the contrary, it is necessary to expand coverage and benefits for pensions and health care, including long-term care. Across the world, only 50 percent of old-age persons have some type of pension, and at present old-age care is predominantly provided by relatives, mainly women; however, this work is often not sufficiently valued and not remunerated adequately, if at all.

The lack of nurses and other care professionals to meet the growing need has resulted in an ever-increasing pull of labor from developing countries into developed countries. It is based on an international "labor supply chain" involving mostly female migrant workers from poor families who provide care services to meet the physical and emotional needs of older persons in higher-income economies—for those who have sufficient income. The potential to expand the quality and quantity of old-age care services is large, and the care economy is expected to become a main area of job creation in future years (ILO 2014b; Scheil-Adlung 2015; WHO 2015).

The discussion of population aging has focused on economic challenges—mounting pressures on pension systems, rising costs of health care, and a potential decline in the active labor force—and has largely ignored the economic opportunities. According to the OECD (2014) and WEF (2016), more and more businesses today are awakening to opportunities in serving "the silver economy" in the following core areas: medical and long-term care goods and services (care for older persons, hearing aids, pharmaceuticals, home-based dialysis technology, and smart homes integrating assisted-living systems); leisure, lifestyle, and living support for consumers aged 60+ (specific holiday arrangements such as cruises with doctors on board, age-specific cosmetics, driverless vehicles, age-adjusted phones/TVs, etc.); food industry (enhanced flavor and soft food); and new emphasis on age-friendly design in the construction and transport industries (accessible universal design).

Investing in the care economy will generate millions of jobs in long-term, old-age care and childcare. Additionally, this will increase female labor force participation, liberating women from their traditional role in unpaid household care.

GUARANTEED MINIMUM INCOME VERSUS UNIVERSAL BASIC INCOME

A main driver of inequality is the decline of the labor shares in recent decades. With the exception of Asia, all other regions of the world had significant reductions since the neoliberal reforms of the 1980s; further, projections using the UN Global Policy Model indicate that unless active policies are made to promote higher wages and social security contributions (a deferred wage), the labor shares will not improve (see figure 3.6).

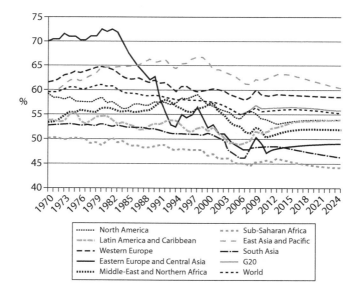

Figure 3.6   Labor shares: historical data and projections.

Note: Labor share is defined as sum of wages, social security contributions, and other mixed income in percent of GDP.

Source: Projections based on the UN Global Policy Model, 2015 baseline.

This forces a critical look at policies advising further labor and social security reforms, as proposed by international financial institutions, the OECD, and newly conservative governments. These have been intensified since the global financial crisis, first with a focus on labor flexibility and weakening collective bargaining (revising minimum wages, limiting salary adjustments to cost of living standards, decentralizing collective bargaining, increasing the ability of enterprises to fire employees) and recently with a focus on reducing social security contributions.

The IMF (2016) advises cuts on the so-called labor taxes[10] (which include employers' social security contributions) as a stimulus to enterprises in a desperate attempt to support the private sector in generating economic activity, rather than changing the current inadequate macroeconomic framework. Add to this the pension reforms suggested to 105 governments in 60 developing and 45 high-income countries, such as raising workers' contribution rates, increasing eligibility periods, raising the retirement age, and/or lowering benefits, among other reforms presented earlier. These policies are prone to increase poverty and inequality and erode welfare systems at a time when they are most needed to support populations during the Great Recession.

In its most radical version, the "neoliberal model of welfare" is based on privately provided insurance for those who can acquire it and a very basic level of public support for those unable to contribute to it. The latter is the trend of the European Troika policies on guaranteed minimum income (GMI); despite its attractive name, GMI is a de facto rationalization of social security benefits, often ending rights-based universal benefits (such as to persons with disabilities), turning them into a targeted benefit to the poorest only.

On the other hand, the most radical opposition to these conservative policies is found in the popular proposal of universal basic income (UBI). UBI aims to provide a universal and nonconditional cash transfer to all citizens. Pilot initiatives have been introduced in Canada, Finland, India, Namibia, and the Netherlands. Some key issues are:

- *UBI benefit level*: If set at an adequate level, such as a relative poverty line, basic income would be a very important redistributive mechanism and an important tool to reduce inequality and create societies free of exploitation. A lower benefit than the poverty line would be only an income supplement, as in Alaska, where all residents receive a yearly dividend from oil extraction (in 2015, it was set at $2,000 per annum for each resident).[11] However, even if the UBI benefit was set at the poverty line, it would be too low for pensioners, particularly those who have been contributing to social security for life, and would also be very low for persons with disabilities and others who may need further support.

- *UBI low administrative costs*: An advantage of replacing a number of current schemes with a universal transfer is that the administrative structure and costs necessary to provide income security would be much smaller.
- *UBI high fiscal costs*: However, fiscal costs would be very high (figure 3.7) compared with the lower costs of current social security systems (figure 3.4), and in the current context of fiscal austerity, UBI is unlikely to be implemented.[12]
- *New national laws regulating future UBI increases/indexation*: A number of trade unions have expressed reservations about UBI if it comes at the cost of dismantling existing social security systems, as social security is regulated and UBI is not, creating the risk that benefits could be slowly reduced over the years without adequate indexation to inflation.

For UBI to be successful, it must: (1) be agreed upon through legitimate national dialogue, including government, employers, trade unions, and civil society; (2) be set at an adequate level, at least the poverty line, for all working-age persons, ideally double for older persons, which can be compensated by providing a half benefit for children; (3) be adequately funded; (4) be regulated, having legislation enacted to ensure adequate transfers in the future; and (5) have a transition period for current pensioners and additional support for persons with disabilities.

DEVELOPMENT POLICIES, REDISTRIBUTION, AND THE WELFARE STATE

At the core of this debate is the issue of employment. For some, the pattern of "jobless growth," the declining trend in formal jobs, is going to increase in the future with technological advancement and the so-called "fourth industrial revolution"; therefore, societies will need to provide some social protection transfers to the large number of citizens who will be unable to find a decent job, unemployed, or working in precarious conditions (e.g., digital employment, Uber).

For others, the pattern of "jobless growth" could be reversed if policy makers would abandon short-term adjustment policies and instead prioritize macroeconomic and sector policies to boost demand and

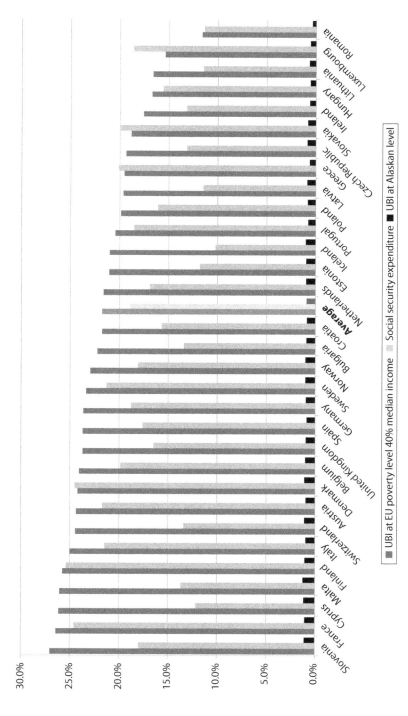

Figure 3.7   Cost of universal basic income compared with cost of social security in percentage of GDP; selected countries.

Note. Assumptions: basic income consisting of a universal transfer, 100 percent value for population aged 15–65, 50 percent value for children (<15), and 200 percent for older persons (>65), includes 1 percent administrative costs.

Source: Author's calculations based on Eurostat, UN World Population Prospects.

promote employment and socioeconomic recovery (UN 2008, 2012; UN Conference on Trade and Development 2011; Ortiz and Cummins 2012; Cornia 2014; ILO 2015c; Ortiz et al. 2015). This line of argument, defended by the UN, supports countercyclical policies and higher public spending to avert recession, revitalize the economy, generate productive employment, and repair the social contract. This would allow millions of formal jobs to be created, for youth and for those in the informal sector, including millions of jobs to be generated in the care and silver economy. These new jobs should be adequately regulated, together with those in digital employment and other precarious forms of work.

Social protection is the most redistributive public policy, as it entails (1) direct cash transfers from national budgets to a number of citizens, (2) additional transfers from employers to workers in the case of contributory public schemes, and (3) transfers within schemes, as public social security systems are designed to redistribute income from those with higher lifetime earnings to those with lower lifetime earnings. However, for inequality to be significantly reduced, it will also require redistributive policies in other sectors (table 3.3. In many countries, subsidized goods and services are part of the welfare state, such as free or subsidized services in health and education, scholarships and textbooks for students, free school meals, public transport subsidies, energy subsidies to consumers (e.g., kerosene,

Table 3.3   Social Protection and Welfare: Subsidizing Goods and Services to Citizens

Agriculture	Food security; food subsidies; livestock and credit for smallholders
Education	Universal free education; scholarships; support for textbooks and uniforms; programs to retain students (e.g., free school meals)
Energy	Subsidies to consumers (e.g., kerosene for cooking); lifeline tariffs
Health	Universal free health services; subsidized insurance contributions
Housing	Subsidized housing for lower-income groups; housing support
Transport and infrastructure	Public transport subsidies, provision of nonmotorized transport for households (bicycles, buffaloes, etc.)
Water	Subsidies for water supply and sanitation

Source: Ortiz and Cummins 2011.

gas, electricity lifeline tariffs), and so forth. Many governments consider food security, food subsidies, and the distribution of livestock in poor rural areas to be social protection.

These policies typically contribute to reducing inequality and should be an important component of welfare states. Above all, reducing inequality would require avoiding typically regressive interventions, many of which have been at the center of policy agenda during the global crisis and Great Recession, from bank bailouts to eliminating subsidies, cutting/capping the wage bill, and backtracking on labor and social security reforms.

In conclusion, reducing inequality will involve strengthening, not weakening, welfare systems in the twenty-first century, including: (1) expanding social protection until universal coverage is achieved at adequate benefit levels; (2) abandoning austerity policies and instead prioritizing macroeconomic and sector policies to boost demand and promote employment and socioeconomic recovery; (3) investing in the care economy, creating millions of jobs in long-term, old-age care and childcare (this will additionally increase female labor force participation); (4) re-reforming pensions to ensure pension adequacy and old-age income security; (5) reducing informality, incorporating youth and informal workers into the labor market, and regulating precarious forms of work (e.g., digital employment); (6) enhancing labor standards and social rights, strengthening collective bargaining and social dialogue; and (7) supporting other redistributive policies outside social protection, from agriculture to water.

It is time for global leaders to think about the longer term and to turn the current vicious circle of "jobless growth" and inequality into a virtuous circle that effectively links economic and human development. Today, another New Deal is warranted, a fair social contract for the twenty-first century through increased public investments to boost aggregate demand, promote sustainable development, protect populations, and achieve global prosperity for all.

NOTES

1. Countries tend to extend their national social security systems in a sequence of steps, depending on their national circumstances and priorities. In many cases, when building social security systems, countries first addressed the area of employment injury and then introduced old-age pensions, disability, and survivors' benefits, followed by sickness, health, and maternity coverage. Benefits for children and families and unemployment benefits typically came last (ILO 2014a).

2. Sustainable Development Goal 1.3.

3. In Africa, Asia, and Latin America, cash transfers have been shown to improve both the quantity and the diversity of food consumption and to protect food consumption during shocks; programs in Mexico, Malawi, and Colombia all demonstrate reductions in the numbers of children with stunted growth (Yablonski and O'Donnell 2009; Tirivayi, Knowles, and Davis 2013), while children in South African households receiving a pension grow an average 5 centimeters taller than those in households without a pension (Case 2001).

4. Transfer programs in Bangladesh, Brazil, Cambodia, Ecuador, Ethiopia, Malawi, Mexico, Nicaragua, Pakistan, South Africa, and Turkey have all demonstrated significant increases in children's school enrollment and/or attendance (Adato and Bassett 2008).

5. Financial support is needed to prevent families from falling into poverty because of heavy OOP health expenditures. A WHO cross-country study showed this can be done by reducing the health system's reliance on OOP (Xu, Evans, and Kawabata 2003).

6. Social protection plays a major role in creating access to full and productive employment and decent work for all, including women and young people, through cash transfers, active labor market measures, health insurance, and family support policies, and by covering the costs of job seeking and supporting those with childcare responsibilities—with particularly strong effects for women. In South Africa, labor market participation among those receiving cash transfers was 13–17 percent higher than in similar nonrecipient households, with the greatest difference among women (Economic Policy Research Institute 2004). A recent study from the United States indicates that giving food assistance to the children of poor families increases their average annual earnings in the long run by as much as US$3,000 and their average annual number of hours of work by 150 (Center on Budget and Policy Priorities 2014).

7. For a recent description of the social protection systems of Latin America, see Ocampo and Gomez-Arteaga (2016).

8. Globally, more than half of total public nonhealth social security expenditure, amounting to 3.3 percent of global GDP, is allocated to old-age pensions. Social protection expenditure for older persons range from 0 to 2 percent of GDP in low-income countries to 11 percent of GDP in higher-income Western Europe (ILO 2014a).

9. In some European countries, courts have reviewed the constitutional validity of fiscal consolidation or austerity measures. In 2013 the Portuguese constitutional court ruled that four fiscal consolidation measures in the budget, mainly affecting civil servants and pensioners, were unlawful and in breach of the country's constitution. In Latvia the 2010 budget proposed new spending cuts and tax increases, including a 10 percent cut in pensions and a 70 percent decrease for working pensioners; the constitutional court ruled that the pension cuts were unconstitutional on the grounds that they violated the right to social security, and the cuts had to be reversed. In Romania 15 percent pension cuts proposed in May 2010 were also declared unconstitutional (OHCHR 2013; ILO 2014a).

10. The so-called labor tax is a microeconomic concept from an enterprise perspective that includes taxes and employers' social security contributions. ILO opposes this concept; these different elements should not be mixed, given that social security contributions are a deferred wage, not a tax.

11. For reference, the EU's lowest poverty threshold (40 percent of median income) in 2015 was €77 per person month in Romania, €185 in Poland, €251 in Greece, €445 in Spain, €689 in Germany, €714 in France, £698 in the United Kingdom, and €792 in Finland. These are very low levels for a contributory pension; people who have been contributing for life expect and deserve a higher benefit. Therefore, if UBI were enacted, it would need (1) a higher benefit for older persons (e.g., 200 percent), compensated for by (2) a lower benefit for children (e.g., 50 percent, which was the level used in the UNICEF UBI pilot in India), and (3) a transition program for current pensioners and contributors. For future pensioners, a public voluntary pension system could be enacted to allow people to save for their pensions.

12. From the total cost, one needs to subtract contributions, which cuts the cost by more than half; for example, as an average in Europe, the total cost of social security is 19 percent (including contributions), but 9 percent when employers' and workers' contributions are subtracted (ILO calculations).

REFERENCES

Adato, M., and L. Bassett. 2008. "What Is the Potential of Cash Transfers to Strengthen Families Affected by HIV and AIDS? A Review of the Evidence on Impacts and Key Policy Debates." In *HIV, Livelihoods, Food and Nutrition Security: Findings from Renewal Research*, IFPRI Brief 10. Washington, D.C.: International Food Policy Research Institute.

Behrendt, C., and J. Woodall. 2015. "Pensions and Other Social Security Income Transfer Systems." In J. Berg, ed., *Labour Market Institutions and Inequality: Building Just Societies in the 21st Century*. Cheltenham: Elgar.

Bertranou, F., and R. Maurizio. 2012. "Semi-conditional Cash Transfers in the Form of Family Allowances for Children and Adolescents in the Informal Economy in Argentina." *International Social Security Review* 65(1):53–72.

Case, A. 2001. "Does Money Protect Health Status? Evidence from South African Pensions." NBER Working Paper No. 8495. National Bureau of Economic Research, Cambridge, Mass.

Center on Budget and Policy Priorities. 2014. "Today's Safety Net Cuts Poverty Nearly in Half, Provides Health Care to Millions, and Has Long-Term Benefits for Children." In *Chart Book: The War on Poverty at 50*. Washington, D.C.: Center on Budget and Policy Priorities.

Cornia, G. A., ed. 2014. *Falling Inequality in Latin America: Policy Changes and Lessons*. Oxford: Oxford University Press and United Nations University.

Economic Policy Research Institute. 2004. *The Social and Economic Impact of South Africa's Social Security System*. Cape Town: South Africa Department of Social Development.

European Commission. 2015. *The 2015 Pension Adequacy Report: Current and Future Income Adequacy in Old Age in the EU*. Brussels: European Commission.

ILO. 2014a. *World Social Protection Report 2014/15: Building Economic Recovery, Inclusive Development and Social Justice*. Geneva: ILO.

——. 2014b. *Social Protection for Older Persons: Key Policy Trends and Statistics*. Geneva: ILO.

——. 2015a. *Country Briefs: Bolivia, Cabo Verde, China, Lesotho Universal Pensions*. Geneva: ILO.

——. 2015b. *Social Protection for Children: Key Policy Trends and Statistics*. Geneva: ILO.

——. 2015c. *World Employment and Social Outlook—Trends 2015*. Geneva: ILO.

——. 2016a. *Country Briefs: South Africa, Thailand, Timor Leste Universal Pensions*. Geneva: ILO.

——. 2016b. *Social Protection Monitor*. January 2010 to December 2015. Available at: www.social-protection.org/gimi/gess/ShowWiki.action?wiki.wikiId=3068; accessed May 24, 2016.

IMF. 2016. *World Economic Outlook: Too Slow for Too Long*. Washington, D.C.: IMF.

Mesa-Lago, C. 2014. *Reversing Pension Privatization: The Experience of Argentina, Bolivia, Chile and Hungary*. Geneva: ILO.

Ocampo, J. A., and N. Gomez-Arteaga. 2016. *Social Protection Systems in Latin America: An Assessment*. Geneva: ILO.

OECD. 2014. *The Silver Economy as a Pathway for Growth*. Paris: OECD.

——. 2015. *Pensions at a Glance: OECD and G20 Indicators*. Paris: OECD.

OHCHR. 2013. *Report on Austerity Measures and Economic, Social and Cultural Rights, Presented to ECOSOC, Substantive Session of 2013, Geneva, 1–26 July, E/2013/82*. Geneva: OHCHR.

Ortiz, I., and M. Cummins. 2011. *Global Inequality: A Rapid Review of Income Distribution in 141 Countries*. New York: UNICEF.

——. 2012. *A Recovery for All*. New York: UNICEF.

Ortiz, I., S. Burke, M. Berrada, and H. Cortes. 2013. *World Protests 2006–2013*. New York: Initiative for Policy Dialogue and Friedrich-Ebert-Stiftung.

Ortiz, I., M. Cummins, J. Capaldo, and K. Karunanethy. 2015. *The Decade of Adjustment: A Review of Austerity Trends 2010–2020 in 187 Countries*. Geneva: ILO, Initiative for Policy Dialogue, and the South Centre.

Ortiz, I., M. Cummins, and K. Karunanethy. 2017. *Fiscal Space for Social Protection Options to Expand Social Investments in 187 Countries*. Geneva: ILO.

Scheil-Adlung, X. 2015. *Long-Term Care for Older Persons. A Review of Coverage Deficits in 46 Countries*. Geneva: ILO.

Skoufias, E., and S. Parker. 2001. "Conditional Cash Transfers and Their Impact on Child Work and Schooling: Evidence from PROGRESA Program in Mexico." FCND Discussion Paper No. 123. International Food Policy Research Institute, Washington, D.C.

Soares, F., E. Perez Ribas, and R. Osorio. 2010. "Evaluating the Impact of Brazil's Bolsa Familia: Cash Transfer Programs in Comparative Perspectives." *Latin America Research Review* 45(2):173–90.

Solt, F. 2013: *Standardized World Income Inequality Database* (SWIID, version 4.0). Available at: http://myweb.uiowa.edu/fsolt/swiid/swiid.html.

Stiglitz, J., and P. Orzag. 1999. *Rethinking Pension Reform: Ten Myths About Social Security Systems*. Washington, D.C.: World Bank.

Tirivayi, N., M. Knowles, and B. Davis, B. 2013. *The Interaction Between Social Protection and Agriculture: A Review of Evidence.* Rome: Food and Agriculture Organization.

UN. 2008. *United Nations Policy Notes for National Development Strategies.* New York: UN Department of Economic and Social Affairs.

———. 2012. *The World Economic Situation and Prospects 2012.* New York: UN Department of Economic and Social Affairs.

UN Conference on Trade and Development. 2011. *Development-Led Globalization: Towards Sustainable and Inclusive Development Paths.* Geneva: UNCTAD.

Vaughan-Whitehead, D., ed. 2014. *The European Social Model in Times of Economic Crisis and Austerity Policies.* Geneva: ILO.

WEF Global Agenda Council on Ageing. 2016. *The Silver Economy: How 21st-Century Longevity Can Create Markets, Jobs and Drive Economic Growth. Proposal for the B20.* Geneva: WEF.

WHO. 2015. *World Report on Ageing and Health.* Geneva: WHO.

Woolard, I., K. Harttgen, and S. Klasen. 2010. "The Evolution and Impact of Social Security in South Africa." Background Paper to the European Development Report 2010. Robert Schumann Centre for Advanced Studies, Florence.

Xu, K., D. Evans, and K. Kawabata. 2003. "Household Catastrophic Health Expenditure: A Multicountry Analysis." *Lancet* 362(9378):111–17.

Yablonski, J., and M. O'Donnell. 2009. *Lasting Benefits: The Role of Cash Transfers in Tackling Child Mortality.* London: Save the Children.

CHAPTER 4

Supporting Equal Opportunities Through Laws and Policies

GLOBAL PROGRESS AND PERSISTING CHALLENGES

Jody Heymann and Aleta Sprague

Despite recent rhetoric suggesting otherwise, there has long been broad political and popular support for equality of opportunity—the idea that all people should have equal chances to fulfill their potential regardless of class, race/ethnicity, gender, or other circumstances of birth. In practice, though, we have yet to achieve this ideal. Around the world, millions of children continue to miss out on a basic education, with some forgoing school due to child labor or early marriage. Discrimination in the economy continues to exclude people with much to contribute from positions of leadership and influence. Many others face barriers to fully participating in their societies due to insufficient income and resources to meet their basic needs.

Laws and policies have a critical role to play in creating equality of opportunity, which is in turn a precondition for more equitable economic and social outcomes. In recent decades, many national governments have enacted important legal reforms to advance equal rights and increase social and economic inclusion. Yet in many countries, these developments were preceded by a long history of embedding inequality in the law, which laid a foundation for much of the inequality that persists across both opportunities and outcomes today. Moreover, in some areas, such as gender, explicit legal inequalities remain commonplace, while in others we have recently seen policy retrenchment.

To produce a more level playing field, laws and policies must enshrine strong commitments to equal rights and nondiscrimination and guarantee universal access to the basics: a healthy childhood, economic opportunities, and a safety net that supports resilience in the face of hardship. Laws and social policies can also begin to dismantle broader systemic inequalities, including the deepening income and wealth inequality discussed elsewhere in this volume, which prior policies helped put in place. For example, the provision of free university education can increase economic mobility and reduce disparities in educational attainment linked to socioeconomic status. Altogether, laws and policies structured to truly uphold equal opportunities provide a mechanism for narrowing the persisting gaps in outcomes that bear no relationship to ability or effort.

This chapter will examine the extent to which countries' laws and policies support equal opportunity or leave barriers in the way. Using globally comparative legal data, we will assess global progress in the areas of healthy development, economic opportunity, foundations for resilience, and discrimination and equality over the past two decades and offer recommendations for building a stronger legal foundation for equality.

1. THE FOUNDATIONS OF EQUAL OPPORTUNITY: THE ROLE OF LAWS AND POLICIES IN FOUR AREAS

Experiences from around the world illustrate why policy solutions are critical for equity. For example, government guarantees that education will be free have had a particularly significant impact on girls and students living in poverty, for whom cost is most likely to be a barrier to attending school (World Bank and UN Children's Fund [UNICEF] 2009). After Malawi introduced a new policy that eliminated school fees in 1994, the rates of primary school completion improved markedly for all children, and the nearly 10-point gender gap observed in 1993 completely disappeared by 2006 (Heymann and McNeill 2013; UN Statistics Division 2016).

In terms of equal opportunities in the workplace, crucial supports like paid sick leave and parental leave achieve broadest coverage when they are implemented via a national policy, rather than left to the discretion of individual employers. For example, in the United States, one of only eight countries worldwide that has yet to enact paid maternal leave, only 12 percent of private sector employees have access to leave through their employers, and there are significant disparities between the lowest and highest earners: only 5 percent of workers in the lowest income quartile have access to leave, compared with 22 percent in the top quartile (U.S. Department of Labor 2015, 2016). Given the well-documented impacts of paid leave on both infant health and women's employment, a national policy that provides universal coverage is critical for allowing equal chances at health, development, and economic opportunities. Paid paternity leave markedly increases fathers' uptake and supports greater gender equality at home and work (Nepomnyaschy and Waldfogel 2007; Haas and Hwang 2008; Moss 2015).

As far as providing the foundation for resilience, policies can shape whether all people have the opportunity to build assets and own land. In Nepal, while men have historically been the primary landowners, a new tax exemption for land titled in women's names has succeeded in creating more gender-equitable access to resources (UN Women 2011). These approaches can be important in settings where there is a long history of cultural and legal barriers preventing women's ownership of property. While tackling inequality will require efforts in many sectors, a legal and policy approach by government has a number of unique and compelling strengths. Most critically, national laws and policies can bring effective solutions to scale, while bolstering other programmatic or smaller-scale efforts to reduce inequality.

Yet while the extensive reach of a legal and policy approach underlies its potential to create a more equitable playing field, both historic and contemporary examples reveal how inequality can also be embedded in the law, with similarly large-scale impacts. For example, in the United States, African-American families were systematically shut out of opportunities to build wealth through homeownership by policies like restrictive covenants and exclusionary zoning, as well as redlining and discriminatory implementation of the G.I. Bill. These policies and practices laid the groundwork for the massive racial wealth disparities we see today (Shapiro 2006).

Further, discrimination within the law is not just a relic of the past, as made clear by current laws and policies relating to sexual orientation and gender identity. Both the presence of discriminatory legal provisions, such as prohibitions of same-sex marriage, and the absence of essential protections, such as prohibitions of employment discrimination based on sexual orientation and gender identity, put the LGBT population at greater risk of economic insecurity and poor health in many parts of the world (Raub et al. 2016a). These examples underscore why a cross-cutting commitment to nondiscrimination is paramount in all efforts to promote opportunities for economic advancement. As these examples make clear that laws and policies govern whether all people have equal access to opportunities. Yet, although nearly every country around the world has committed to advancing equal rights for all through global agreements, such as the Universal Declaration on Human Rights and the Convention on the Rights of the Child, far fewer have fully aligned their domestic legal frameworks with these objectives.

Quantitative, globally comparative data on national laws and policies can help translate countries' commitments to reduce inequality into action, while providing a tool for quickly understanding where the world stands on a particular issue. Most fundamentally, these data can help evaluate the extent to which countries' legal frameworks currently support four of the pillars of equal opportunity: healthy development in childhood, economic opportunities, equal rights and nondiscrimination, and a foundation for resilience (see figure 4.1). Further, longitudinal legal and policy data enable the measurement of progress in strengthening legal protections and filling critical gaps over time. Finally, by linking globally comparative policy data with household survey data on economic, health, and well-being outcomes, researchers can rigorously evaluate the impact and effectiveness of legal reforms designed to increase equality. The next section will provide an overview of the extent to which legal frameworks globally support equal opportunities, and how the prevalence of key laws and policies across these four pillars has evolved over time.

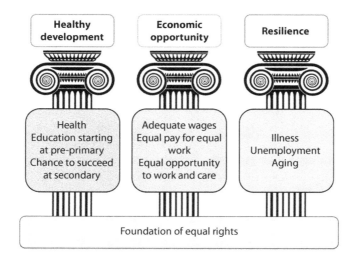

Figure 4.1   Pillars of equal opportunity.

2. EXAMINING GLOBAL PROGRESS IN LAWS AND POLICIES

Over the past several decades, the world has made significant progress in a range of areas critical to equal chances. For example, the number of children of primary school age who are not attending school has dropped by over 40 million since 2000 (UN 2015). While this success resulted from a wide range of coordinated efforts, changes in laws and policies played an instrumental role. For example, since 1990, the provision of free primary education has become nearly universal: by 2014, 89 percent of low-income countries, 97 percent of middle-income countries, and 100 percent of high-income countries had made primary school tuition-free, demonstrating the power of policy to remove a significant barrier to equal chances in education (Heymann and McNeill 2013; De Guzman Chorny et al. 2014; Heymann, Raub, and Cassola 2014). Equal opportunities for adults have grown as legal guarantees of equality, legal protections that support the ability of youth to finish school instead of labor, and policies that enable women and men to care for families while working have all become more common globally (Heymann and McNeill 2013; Heymann, McNeill, and Raub 2014, 2015; Waisath et al. 2014).

Nevertheless, inequalities persist across many areas vital to opportunity. Although primary enrollment rates have significantly increased, as of 2013, approximately 65 million children of lower secondary age were not attending school (UNICEF 2016). In developing countries, nearly one in three girls are married before their eighteenth birthday, while nearly one-third of the world's countries permit girls to be married at younger ages than boys (UN Population Fund 2012; Arthur et al. 2014), lowering the likelihood of completing secondary school and markedly increasing the risk of maternal and infant mortality. While maternal leave has become nearly universal, only a fraction of countries provide any leave to new fathers, creating a barrier to equal chances at home and at work (Heymann and McNeill 2013; Raub et al. 2014). Although guarantees of equal rights in constitutions have generally become more common, inadequate protections on the basis of disability and sexual orientation and gender identity are having tangible impacts on equal opportunities worldwide. Laws and policies can play a critical role in filling these remaining gaps and supporting further progress in the decades to come.

HEALTHY DEVELOPMENT

There has long been widespread agreement that healthy early development forms the foundation of long-term equal opportunities (Shonkoff and Phillips 2000). Creating the conditions for all children to have a healthy childhood starts with supporting parents.

Studies across low- and middle-income countries have found that longer maternal leave policies are associated with higher vaccination rates (Hajizadeh et al. 2015) and lower infant mortality (Nandi et al. 2016). Paid leave for mothers allows women to recover from birth, bond with their babies, and more easily access postnatal care.

Lower mortality rates also result from paid leave supporting mothers' ability to initiate and continue breastfeeding, one of the most effective child health interventions. A child who is exclusively breastfed is fourteen times less likely to die within the first six months than a nonbreastfed child, and breastfeeding has also been associated with improved neurocognitive development and lower rates of chronic diseases like diabetes (Jones et al. 1998; Eidelman and Feldma 2004; Black et al. 2008). While the World Health Organization recommends six months of exclusive breastfeeding for all infants, mothers who must return to work shortly after giving birth often face nearly insurmountable obstacles to following this recommendation. This helps explain why rates of exclusive breastfeeding for babies under six months vary markedly around the world, ranging from 1 percent to 89 percent (World Bank 2016). In recent decades, the global availability and average duration of paid maternal leave have both increased, with 55 percent of countries providing at least fourteen weeks, which is the minimum standard established by the International Labor Organization (ILO) (see figure 4.2).

For mothers who want or need to return to work within six months of giving birth, paid breastfeeding breaks offer a cost-effective and complementary policy approach to facilitating exclusive breastfeeding, provided that women have sufficient time to breastfeed or pump and access to adequate refrigeration for pumped milk. The positive relationship between breaks and breastfeeding is intuitive, but also supported by research: in an initial cross-sectional study of 182 countries, a guarantee of paid breastfeeding breaks for at least six months was associated with an 8.86 percentage point higher rate of exclusive breastfeeding for infants six months and younger (Heymann, Raub, and Earle 2013). As of 2014, 71 percent of

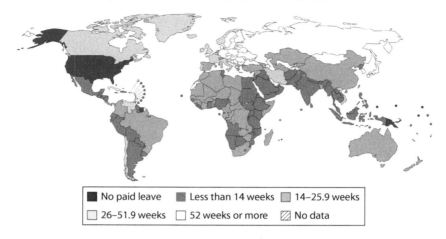

Figure 4.2   Is paid leave available for mothers of infants?

Source: WORLD Policy Analysis Center, Adult Labor Database, 2014.

countries provide paid breastfeeding breaks for at least six months, while 1 percent guarantee unpaid breaks (see figure 4.3). Strengthening these policies could give more infants worldwide a healthy start, while supporting their mothers' participation in the workforce (Atabay et al. 2015).

Parents play an essential role in the health of children far beyond infancy. Yet without being allowed to take leave from work to care for

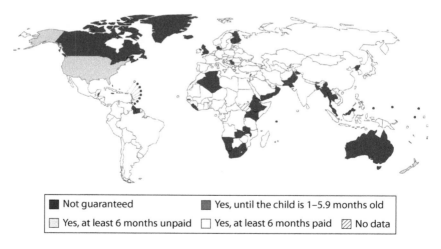

Figure 4.3   Are mothers of infants guaranteed breastfeeding breaks at work?

Source: WORLD Policy Analysis Center, Adult Labor Database, 2014.

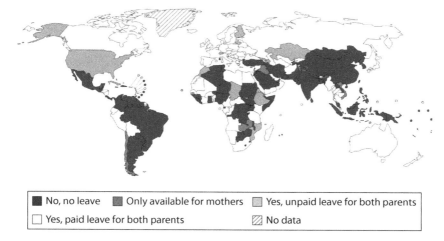

Figure 4.4   **Are working women and men guaranteed any leave for children's health needs?**

Source: WORLD Policy Analysis Center, Adult Labor Database, 2014.

children's health, working parents are often unable to get their children to needed care or must risk income or jobs to do so. As of 2014, only 40 percent of countries provided leave for both parents specifically for children's health needs, while barely half, 56 percent, provide some type of leave that parents can use for this purpose (see figure 4.4).

Policies that support children's access to education lay the foundation for economic opportunities throughout the life course. The connection between higher educational attainment and success in the labor market is well documented. Moreover, education also directly influences health and the well-being of the next generation. In a study across 175 countries over forty years, increases in women's education were found to account for half of the decrease in child mortality (Gakidou et al. 2010). Secondary education is especially critical. Beyond increasing women's earnings by up to 25 percent, studies have found that secondary education is associated with significant decreases in maternal mortality, lower fertility rates, and better health and nutritional outcomes for children (Schultz 2002; Abuya, Ciera, and Kimani-Murage 2012; Klugman et al. 2014; UN Educational, Scientific and Cultural Organization 2014).

Ensuring that education is accessible for all children requires policies that mitigate or remove financial barriers to attending school, including

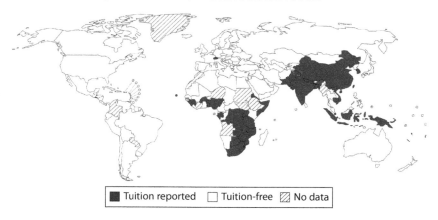

■ Tuition reported □ Tuition-free ▨ No data

Figure 4.5—Is completing secondary education tuition-free?

Source: WORLD Policy Analysis Center, Education Database, 2014.

direct costs such as tuition. While the overwhelming majority of countries have removed the tuition barrier at the primary level, tuition at the secondary level is a far more common barrier: in 86 percent of countries, it is free to begin secondary school, but only 75 percent make it free through completion (see figure 4.5). At the tertiary level, among the 150 countries for which we have data, 81 (54 percent) make education tuition-free.

Guaranteeing free schooling requires resources and government investment. Recognition of the range of resources countries have explains why global agreements commit countries only to "progressively realizing" free secondary and higher education. Yet incomplete progress in this area reflects lack of commitment as well as resource constraints. Nearly half of the countries that have yet to guarantee free secondary education invest less than 4 percent of their GDP in education, which suggests that lack of commitment by policy makers, as well as resource constraints, are limiting youth access to school (Heymann and McNeill 2013). Solutions will require both countries investing a sufficient amount of their own resources and global aid to the poorest countries until their economies strengthen.

Moreover, many countries do not include adequate legal provisions for protecting the educational rights of children with disabilities, who are far more likely to be out of school than their peers without disabilities, and girls with disabilities face even greater barriers. According to a study across thirteen developing countries, the gap in school attendance between six- to eleven-year-olds with disabilities and children in the same age group without disabilities ranges from 10 percentage points in India to nearly 60 percentage points in Indonesia, with even wider disparities among older children (Filmer 2008).

A range of studies have found that inclusive education leads to better outcomes for students with disabilities than education in separate settings (Ruijs and Peetsma 2009; Ruijs, Peetsma, and van der Veen 2010). As of 2014, 44 percent of countries have policies in place to provide education to students with disabilities in the same classrooms as other students, while 39 percent provide for education at least within the same school. However, 13 percent only provide for students with disabilities' needs in separate schools, while 5 percent provide no additional support to students with disabilities within the public school system (see figure 4.6).

Finally, there is widespread agreement that child labor and child marriage continue to put the educational opportunities of many children at risk. Child labor is driven in large part by underlying economic circumstances, and thus policies aimed at ensuring families can meet their basic needs, including policies that support parents' ability to find work and earn a decent wage, are essential to long-term change.

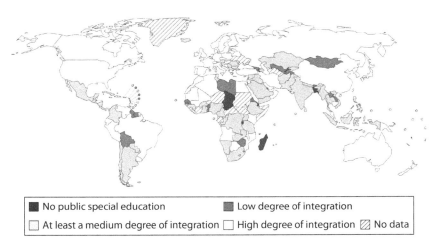

No public special education   Low degree of integration
At least a medium degree of integration   High degree of integration   No data

Figure 4.6   Is inclusive education available for students with disabilities?

Source: WORLD Policy Analysis Center, Education Database, 2014.

However, laws that prohibit child labor and early marriage, particularly when coupled with free and compulsory education, can shift norms and opportunities for universal school attendance. Although child labor has declined in recent years, according to the ILO, over 168 million children ages 5–17 were still involved in labor as of 2012, including over 85 million children engaged in hazardous work (ILO 2013). Studies from a wide range of countries, such as Nepal, Bolivia, Venezuela, and Ghana, have found that child laborers generally complete fewer years of school compared with their peers who are not engaged in labor (Psacharopoulos 1997; Ray 2000; Doocy et al. 2007). While ending child labor is complex, evidence suggests laws make a difference. A 2013 study using globally comparative data on child labor laws from 185 countries found that a minimum age of employment of 15 or higher was associated with net secondary enrollment rates that were 9.5 percentage points higher for girls and 7.8 percentage points higher for boys (Heymann, Raub, and Cassola 2013).

As of 2012, 43 percent of countries protect children from full-time work until at least age 16, and 74 percent protect children from hazardous work until age 18 (see figure 4.7). However, taking into account legal loopholes, including for work done for vocational purposes or in the company of family members, only 53 percent of countries protect children under 18 from hazardous work in all circumstances (see figure 4.8).

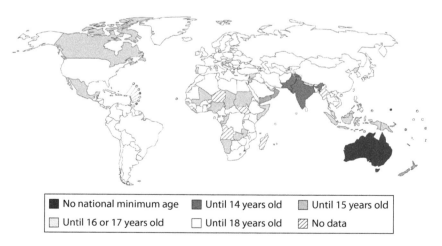

No national minimum age   Until 14 years old   Until 15 years old
Until 16 or 17 years old   Until 18 years old   No data

Figure 4.7   How long are children protected from hazardous work without taking legal loopholes into account?

Source: WORLD Policy Analysis Center, Child Labor Database, 2012.

Figure 4.8   How long are children protected from hazardous work when legal loopholes are considered?

Source: WORLD Policy Analysis Center, Child Labor Database, 2012.

Similarly, while rates of child marriage have significantly dropped in recent years and legal protections have improved, gaps within countries' legal frameworks and inadequate implementation of existing laws continue to pose significant challenges to ensuring all children, and in particular all girls, have the chance to complete their education. For example, across Africa, each additional year of early marriage reduces the probability of literacy by 7.5 percentage points, the probability of having some secondary education by 9.6 points, and the probability of completing secondary education by 7.5 points (Nguyen and Wodon 2014).

As of 2013, 88 percent of countries set the minimum age of marriage for girls at 18 or older (see figure 4.9). Critically, however, child marriage legislation commonly includes loopholes that allow for marriage at younger ages with parental consent or under customary or religious law. Given that most child marriages occur with parental consent or involvement, these exceptions seriously undermine protections in the law; 52 percent of countries permit girls to be married before the age of 18 with parental consent, while 22 percent allow marriage at age 15 or below (see figure 4.10). While there has been progress over the past two decades, closing these remaining gaps in the law will be critical to strengthening equal chances at education.

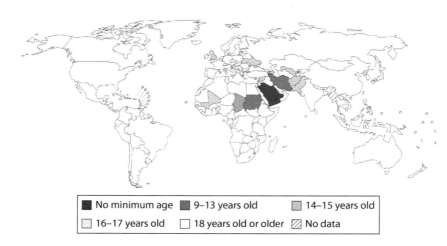

Figure 4.9   What is the minimum legal age of marriage for girls?

Source: WORLD Policy Analysis Center, Marriage Database, 2013.

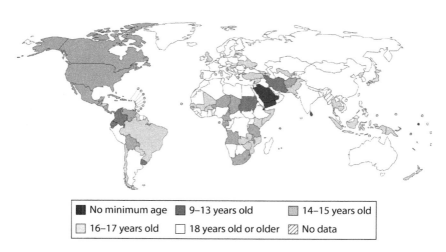

Figure 4.10   What is the minimum legal age of marriage for girls with parental consent?

Source: WORLD Policy Analysis Center, Marriage Database, 2013.

ECONOMIC OPPORTUNITY

At its core, economic opportunity is about access to a good job, which has long been understood as the key pathway out of poverty. Yet for this to remain true, countries have a role to play in creating an equal playing field in the labor market by ensuring nondiscrimination at work, that all workers earn an adequate wage, and that all workers have the opportunity to balance work and caregiving across the life course.

Political debates around the minimum wage have argued on the one side that it is a powerful tool for ensuring all families can meet their basic needs, and on the other side that raising the minimum wage may lead to job loss by the poor if the higher cost of labor leads to lower demand. The question is an empirical one, as the higher wages will also raise demand for goods. Research from developing countries has generally found that raising the minimum wage lowers national poverty rates (Lustig and McLeod 1997; Saget 2001), and further studies have shown that even modest increases to the minimum wage can have significant implications for families' health and well-being. Importantly, increases in the formal sector minimum wage can also have a "shadow effect" on average earnings in the informal economy (Maloney and Mendez 2004; Khamis 2008; Biero, Garibaldi, and Ribeiro 2010), making an adequate minimum wage an important priority even within economies where the majority of workers are in informal employment. Notably, a range of countries have demonstrated that for typical increases in the minimum wage, there was little to no loss of jobs (Rama 2001; Betcherman 2015; Bhorat, Kanbur, and Stanwix 2015; Hohberg and Lay 2015). As of 2012, 65 percent of countries had established a minimum wage that was sufficient to lift a parent with one dependent child above the global poverty line of US$2 per day, adjusted for purchasing power parity (PPP). However, 23 percent of countries have a minimum wage that is below even this low global poverty threshold, while 12 percent of countries have not legislated a minimum wage (see figure 4.11).

Without guarantees of equal pay, many workers will not earn what they deserve. The wage gap between men and women is particularly well documented, and discrimination based on race and other characteristics can widen the gap even further. While some portion of the gender wage gap is explained by occupational segregation and women's overrepresentation in low-wage work, research suggests that discrimination is still a significant factor shaping pay disparities. For example, in a study of

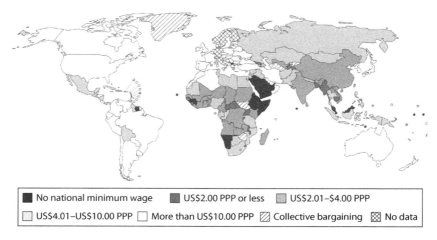

Figure 4.11   At what level are minimum wages set per day?

Source: WORLD Policy Analysis Center, Poverty Reduction Database, 2012.

wages across 38 economies, the ILO found that "unexplained factors"—beyond differences in educational attainment, experience, location, and other observable labor market characteristics—were responsible for some portion of the wage gap in every country studied (ILO 2015). Similarly, research from the Institute for Women's Policy Research shows that women's median earnings are below men's in all but four of 108 common occupations in the United States, suggesting that pay discrimination is still an influential factor (Hegewisch and DuMonthier 2016).

Constitutions, which typically take precedence over other forms of law, can be particularly powerful instruments for enshrining the right to equal pay for equal work, although many countries without constitutional protections take a legislative approach. Beyond establishing a norm of equal pay, these guarantees can have practical impact. For example, as part of austerity reforms in Greece, legislators reduced the minimum wage for workers over 25 by 22 percent, and reduced wages for those under 25 by 32 percent. A young worker who experienced a pay cut as a result challenged the disparate treatment in court, and succeeded in having the 32 percent cut struck down as a violation of the constitution's guarantee of equal pay (Theodoridis 2015). As of 2014, 21 percent of constitutions guarantee the right to equal pay based on gender, and 10 percent do so based on ethnicity.[1]

Beyond equal and adequate pay, substantive equality in the workplace requires that all workers can balance their work and caregiving obligations. As previously noted, paid maternal leave has become nearly universal; however, far fewer countries provide paid leave for fathers. Ensuring both parents have access to leave is essential to men's equal chances at home and women's equal chances at work.

Though research has shown that men are more likely to take parental leave when it is specifically allocated to them, only 40 percent of countries provide leave explicitly for fathers or incentives for fathers to take leave, while 8 percent of countries provide parental leave that can be shared between parents (see figure 4.12). The incentive approach, found in 4 percent of countries, encourages men to take leave by reserving some portion of the leave exclusively for men or offering "bonus" leave if leave is shared between parents. These targeted approaches have been found to be effective in increasing men's take-up of leave, which in turn is associated with more equitable sharing of childcare and household work between parents (Tanaka and Waldfogel 2007).

Globally, women are disproportionately represented in the informal sector, making adequate coverage of the informal economy especially consequential for gender equity. In areas like paid parental leave, governments can design policies to reach all people regardless of their attachment to a formal employer, generally by structuring these benefits as social insurance.

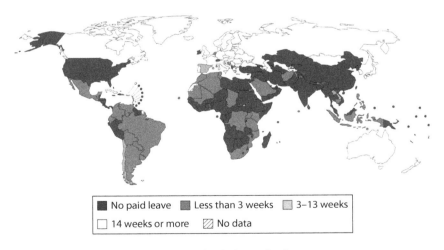

Figure 4.12   Is paid leave available for fathers of infants?

Source: WORLD Policy Analysis Center, Adult Labor Database, 2014.

FOUNDATIONS FOR RESILIENCE

For economies to remain strong and all people to have equal chances to contribute, households must be able to rebound from temporary setbacks and meet their basic needs during periods of vulnerability. Providing basic support during illness, unemployment, and old age can make a critical difference in enabling families to get back on their feet while promoting broader economic stability.

One key policy that supports workers' capacity for resilience is paid sick leave. Going to work while sick reduces productivity, increases the chances of work accidents, and can result in the spread of infections to coworkers, while paid leave enables workers to stay home and recover with job protection and at least partial wages.

As of 2012, 90 percent of countries provide paid sick leave, and 70 percent allow workers to take leave beginning on the first day of illness (see figure 4.13). Making leave available as of the first day of illness is critical for reducing the risk of spreading infections to other workers, clients, or customers. Beyond those countries that guarantee paid leave, 2 percent provide unpaid leave. While the provision of unpaid leave offers much-needed job security, workers in low-wage jobs may be unable to take advantage given other economic pressures. For example, a recent study in the United States found that workers without paid sick leave were three times more likely to

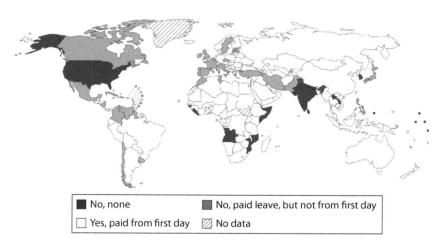

Figure 4.13   **Are workers entitled to sick leave from the first day of illness?**

Source: WORLD Policy Analysis Center, Adult Labor Database, 2012.

delay or completely forgo needed medical care compared with those with paid sick leave (DeRigne, Stoddard-Dare, and Quinn 2016).

A second policy that is critical for withstanding setbacks is unemployment insurance, particularly when shifts in the global economy result in widespread job loss. Ensuring that laid-off workers can continue to meet their basic needs becomes essential not only for individual families, but also for national economies. In the United States, for instance, unemployment insurance played a crucial role in keeping families out of poverty following the global recession. In 2009 alone, 3.3 million Americans, including 1 million children, were lifted above the poverty line by unemployment benefits (Sherman 2010).

Globally, 90 percent of countries guarantee some form of income protection during unemployment. However, 29 percent exclude the self-employed, and 45 percent only provide severance pay (see figure 4.14). Thirty-eight percent of countries provide at least 26 weeks of unemployment benefits, consistent with the minimum standard recommended by the ILO (ILO 1988). In 31 percent of countries, a minimum wage worker would receive over US$2 per day (the global poverty line used by the UN) to provide for themselves and one dependent, in PPP-adjusted dollars.

Finally, well-designed pension programs have an important role to play in ensuring an adequate income floor to keep households out of poverty in old age. Income protection during retirement is also particularly

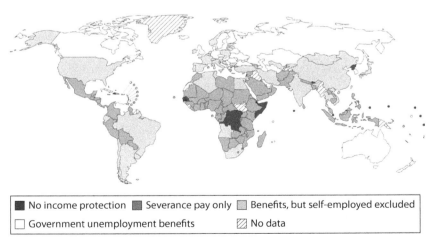

■ No income protection   ■ Severance pay only   ▨ Benefits, but self-employed excluded
□ Government unemployment benefits   ▨ No data

Figure 4.14   Is income protection during unemployment available?

Source: WORLD Policy Analysis Center, Poverty Reduction Database, 2012.

critical for women, who have historically faced a disproportionate risk of poverty in old age and lower savings due to lower wages and greater time out of the workforce for raising children. Similarly, workers in the informal economy, who rarely have access to retirement savings opportunities through their employers, are at greater risk of being unable to meet their basic needs in old age. The provision of noncontributory pensions can help mitigate gender disparities and other prior disadvantages in the labor market by ensuring all retirees have access to income during old age regardless of prior earnings or time in the formal workforce.

As of 2012, 4 percent of countries only provide noncontributory pensions, while 43 percent provide both noncontributory and contributory pensions (see figure 4.15). Ensuring that noncontributory pensions are more widely available would provide a broader foundation for security in retirement. Additional considerations that are important for equity in old age include whether contributory pensions are available with shorter vesting periods and lower minimum employment and contribution requirements, whether countries provide survivor or widower pensions at adequate levels, and whether older adults have the option to continue engaging in paid work while receiving their pensions.

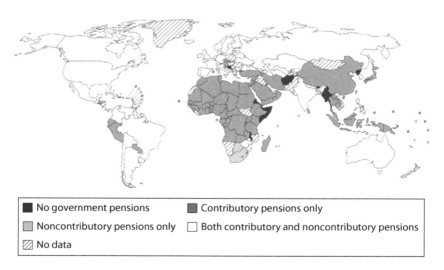

Figure 4.15　Are there income protections for the elderly?

Source: WORLD Policy Analysis Center, Poverty Reduction Database, 2012.

DISCRIMINATION AND EQUALITY

Across all areas, a fundamental commitment to equality and nondiscrimination is critical for ensuring that opportunities, services, and institutions are equally accessible to all people, regardless of gender, race or ethnicity, class, religion, sexual orientation or gender identity, migration status, or other common bases of discrimination. While legislative protections are also necessary, constitutions are ideal instruments for enshrining protections against discrimination: constitutions are often the key mechanism by which countries establish equal rights, provide a basis for challenging discriminatory practices or legislation, and have an important expressive function that communicates values on behalf of the state.

Further, constitutional protections of equality and nondiscrimination have had meaningful impacts on equal opportunities in many settings worldwide. In the first half of 2016 alone, constitutional protections of equality were leveraged to extend the right to marriage to same-sex couples in Colombia (Brodzinsky 2016); to clarify that abandoned babies whose parents cannot be identified are "natural born citizens" eligible to run for office in the Philippines (Gatmaytan 2016); and to newly permit women to enter temples in India that had long been restricted to men (Kapur 2016). Globally, nearly all constitutions provide some guarantee of gender equality in their constitutions. The proportion of constitutions that explicitly reference gender equality or women's rights has notably increased over time, aligning with developments in international law (Cassola et al. 2014). However, 16 percent of constitutions do not explicitly guarantee gender equality or nondiscrimination, while 8 percent include a gender equality provision but allow customary or religious law to take precedence over the constitution, potentially putting women's and girls' rights at risk (see figure 4.16).

Somewhat fewer countries include explicit protections against discrimination based on race or ethnicity within their constitutions, though these protections are also more prevalent in more recently adopted constitutions (Heymann, McNeill, and Raub 2015). Seventy-six percent guarantee equality or prohibit discrimination specifically on the basis of race or ethnicity, while 21 percent aspire to equality based on race or ethnicity or include a general guarantee of equality but make no explicit reference to race or ethnicity (see figure 4.17).

In contrast to race and gender protections, far fewer countries explicitly protect equality or prohibit discrimination on the basis of disability. Only 22 percent of countries include an explicit guarantee,

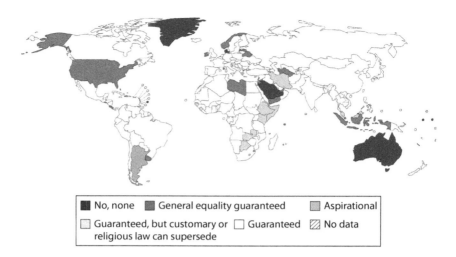

Figure 4.16 **Does the constitution take at least one approach to gender equality?**

Source: WORLD Policy Analysis Center, Constitution Database, 2014.

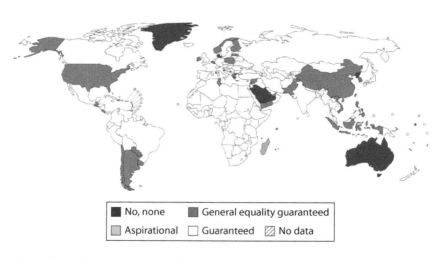

Figure 4.17 **Does the constitution take at least one approach to equality across ethnicity?**

Source: WORLD Policy Analysis Center, Constitution Database, 2014.

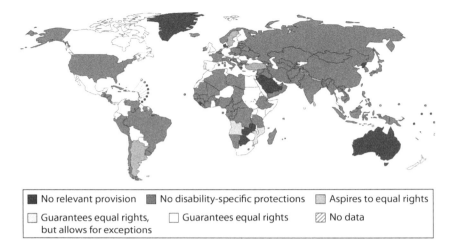

| No relevant provision | No disability-specific protections | Aspires to equal rights |
| Guarantees equal rights, but allows for exceptions | Guarantees equal rights | No data |

Figure 4.18 Does the constitution take at least one approach to equality across disability?

Source: WORLD Policy Analysis Center, Constitution Database, 2014.

while 2 percent guarantee equality subject to certain exceptions (see figure 4.18). However, as with protections based on race and gender, constitutional protections against discrimination based on disability have become more common over time. Protections of equal rights for persons with disabilities are found in 68 percent of constitutions adopted between 2000 and May 2014, compared with 43 percent of constitutions adopted in the 2000s, 23 percent adopted in the 1990s, and 11 percent adopted prior to 1990 (Raub et al. 2016b). With disability in particular, the shift from the "medical model," which frames disability as intrinsic to the individual, to the "social model," which focuses on socially constructed barriers to the full participation of people with disabilities in society, has influenced both constitutions and key pieces of legislation over the past several decades. This evolution speaks to the role of constitutions in both reflecting and shaping cultural norms about equality and inclusion.

A small number of constitutions include explicit protections against employment discrimination, including 25 percent that do so specifically on the basis of gender, 13 percent on the basis of race/ethnicity, and 10 percent on the basis of disability. These setting-specific protections can bolster other constitutional guarantees of equal rights and provide a powerful legal foundation for equal chances in the workplace.

3. AREAS FOR FURTHER RESEARCH AND ACTION

The past several decades have yielded remarkable progress across laws and policies that shape equal opportunity and across outcomes, though both low- and high-income countries alike have critical areas for improvement. Globally, numerous countries have reduced financial barriers to school, expanded workers' opportunities to balance work and care, and enacted new constitutional protections against discrimination. However, every country still has challenges to overcome. For many, this means reducing persisting barriers to secondary school, including child marriage and school fees. For others, this means better supporting children's health by ensuring working parents have the capacity to meet their health needs. Globally comparative legal and policy data allow for the quick identification of gaps and omissions in countries' legal frameworks, and key opportunities for enacting reforms that would better support equal chances for all.

Still, while every country has room for improvement, recent efforts and policy reforms have facilitated real progress across the four pillars of equal opportunity discussed in this chapter. Compared with two decades ago, far more children are surviving and receiving an education. Far more families are exiting poverty. Ending discrimination in all its forms may be a continuous pursuit, but courts around the world have handed down momentous victories for equal rights in recent years, grounded in increasingly inclusive constitutional protections.

Yet there is much more left to learn about which policies are most effective at supporting equal opportunities, and quantitative assessments of how specific policies influence outcomes will generate further insights into what works to address persisting challenges in different contexts. For example, within education, many studies have established that ensuring that secondary school is tuition-free has a positive impact on enrollment. However, less is known about how to design education policies to ensure that teachers are sufficiently qualified to provide a high-quality education, which is key for adequately preparing students for the workforce.

Within economic opportunity, although we know that both maternal and paternal leave have positive benefits for workers and families, less is known about what precise formulation of parental leave truly supports gender equality at work and at home. Furthermore, in terms of extending parental leave, pensions, and similar fundamental protections to the informal economy, more research is needed to identify the most effective approaches for supporting equal opportunities for workers in both the formal and informal sectors.

When it comes to discrimination and equal rights, the evidence is clear that all countries should have legislation prohibiting discrimination overall and in the key spheres that govern access to opportunities and advancement: education, the family, and work, including hiring, pay, and promotions. These basic guarantees are prerequisites for giving everyone an equal shot at health, mobility, and success. However, identifying the most effective additional policies to help countries create a more egalitarian society following a long legacy of discrimination remains an important challenge for policy makers. Further work is needed to understand how to design affirmative policy approaches that effectively remedy past discrimination without stigmatizing the groups these policies intend to help or creating other inequities.

Finally, equivalent data on implementation will be critical for assessing both whether countries have the laws and policies in place to support equal chances, and whether the potential of those policies is being fully realized. Effective implementation requires both that governments invest sufficient resources in rolling out and enforcing policies and that individuals have the means, ability, and knowledge to claim their rights. To that end, to have the greatest impact, this information must be widely disseminated in a clear, transparent way to ensure that it is accessible to all stakeholders. The maps presented throughout this chapter provide an illustrative example of this approach. A more comprehensive version would include regularly updated maps, readily available to anyone with an Internet connection, that would allow users to input their experiences and link national policies and implementation data.

4. CONCLUSION

Countries' laws and policies can play a pivotal role in laying the foundation for equal opportunities across health, education, work, and well-being from birth to old age. Globally comparative policy data can provide a powerful tool for assessing different approaches to reducing inequality and identifying what works. While the world has made important strides toward strengthening equal opportunities over the past several decades, every country still faces challenges, and much remains to be done. Quantitatively assessing the impact of social policies on economic, health, and well-being outcomes can accelerate progress toward ensuring all people can meet their basic needs and fulfill their potential.

NOTE

1. Constitutional rights are classified as "guaranteed" when constitutional articles unambiguously grant a right or phrase it as a duty or obligation of the state. Aspirational rights are phrased in nonauthoritative language (for example, "promotes," "endeavors to") or are listed as nonenforceable goals (for example, "subject to available resources").

REFERENCES

Abuya, B., J. Ciera, and E. Kimani-Murage. 2012. "Effect of Mother's Education on Child's Nutritional Status in the Slums of Nairobi." *BMC Pediatrics* 12:80.

Arthur, M., E. Atabay, A. Raub, I. K. Latz, N. De Guzman Chorny, M. Barrera, I. Vincent, A. Nandi, and S. J. Heymann. 2014. *CEDAW & Beijing+20—Legal protections against child marriage around the world.* Los Angeles, Calif.: UCLA WORLD Policy Analysis Center.

Atabay, E., G. Moreno, A. Nandi, G. Kranz, I. Vincent, T. M. Assi, E. M. Vaughan Winfrey, A. Earle, A. Raub, and S. J. Heymann. 2015. "Facilitating Working Mothers' Ability to Breastfeed Global Trends in Guaranteeing Breastfeeding Breaks at Work, 1995–2014." *Journal of Human Lactation* 31(1):80–88.

Betcherman, G. 2015. "Labor Market Regulations: What Do We Know About Their Impacts in Developing Countries?" *World Bank Research Observer* 30(1):124–153

Biero, T., P. Garibaldi, and M. Ribeiro. 2010. "Behind the Lighthouse Effect." Bonn, Germany: Institute for the Study of Labor (IZA) Working Paper 4890.

Bhorat, H., R. Kanbur, and B. Stanwix. 2015. "Minimum Wages in Sub-Saharan Africa: A Primer." IZA Discussion Paper 9204.

Black, R., L. Allen, Z. Bhutta, L. Caulfield, M. de Onis, M. Ezzati, C. Mathers, and J. Rivera. 2008. "Maternal and Child Undernutrition: Global and Regional Exposures and Health Consequences." *Lancet* 371(9608):243–60.

Brodzinsky, S. 2016. "Colombia's Highest Court Paves Way for Marriage Equality in Surprise Ruling." *Guardian.* Retrieved 7 April 2016 from: www.theguardian.com/world/2016/apr/07/colombia-court-gay-marriage-ruling.

Cassola, A., A. Raub, D. Foley, and S. J. Heymann. 2014. "Where Do Women Stand? New Evidence on the Presence and Absence of Gender Equality in the World's Constitutions." *Politics & Gender* 10(2):200–235.

De Guzman Chorny, M. N., A. Raub, N. Perry, E. Vaughan Winfrey, J. Looze, K. Savage, W. Waisath, T. M. Assi, and S. J. Heymann. 2014. *CEDAW & Beijing+20—Facilitating Girls' Access to Quality Education: Global Findings on Tuition-Free and Compulsory Education.* Los Angeles, Calif.: UCLA WORLD Policy Analysis Center.

DeRigne, L., P. Stoddard-Dare, and L. Quinn. 2016. "Workers Without Paid Sick Leave Less Likely to Take Time Off for Illness or Injury Compared to Those with Paid Sick Leave." *Health Affairs* 35(3):520.

Diallo, Y., A. Etienne, and F. Mehran. 2013. *Global Child Labour Trends 2008 to 2012.* Geneva: ILO.

Doocy, S., B. Crawford, C. Boudreaux, and E. Wall. 2007. "The Risks and Impacts of Portering on the Well-Being of Children in Nepal." *Journal of Tropical Pediatrics* 53(3):165–70.

Eidelman, A. I., and R. Feldma. 2004. "Positive Effect of Human Milk on Neurobehavioral and Cognitive Development of Premature Infants." In *Protecting Infants Through Human Milk: Advancing the scientific Evidence*, ed. L. Pickering, A. L. Morrow, G. M. Ruiz-Palacios, R. Schanler, 359–64. New York: Kluwer Academic /Plenum.

Filmer, D. 2008. "Disability, Poverty, and Schooling in Developing Countries: Results from 14 Household Surveys." *World Bank Economic Review* 22:141–63.

Gakidou, E., K. Cowling, R. Lozano, and C. Murray. 2010. "Increased Educational Attainment and Its Effect on Child Mortality in 175 Countries Between 1970 and 2009: A Systematic Analysis." *Lancet* 376(9745):959–74.

Gatmaytan, D. 2016. "Philippine Supreme Court: Foundlings Are Natural Born Citizens; May Run for President." *I-Connect* (blog). Retrieved 13 May 2016 from: www.iconnectblog.com/2016/03/philippine-supreme-court-foundlings-are-natural-born-citizens-may-run-for-president/.

Haas, L., and C. P. Hwang. 2008. "The Impact of Taking Parental Leave on Fathers' Participation in Childcare and Relationships with Children: Lessons from Sweden." *Community, Work and Family* 11(1):85–104.

Hajizadeh, M., J. Heymann, E. Strumpf, S. Harper, and A. Nandi. 2015. "Paid Maternity Leave and Childhood Vaccination Uptake: Longitudinal Evidence from 20 Low-and-Middle-Income Countries." *Social Science and Medicine* 140:104–17.

Hegewisch, A., and A. DuMonthier. 2016. "The Gender Wage Gap by Occupation 2015 and by Race and Ethnicity." Washington, DC: Institute for Women's Policy Research. Fact Sheet #C440.

Heymann, J., A. Raub, and A. Cassola. 2013. "Does Prohibiting Child Labor Increase Secondary School Enrolment? Insights from a New Global Dataset." *International Journal of Educational Research* 60:38–45.

Heymann, J., A. Raub, and A. Earle. 2013. "Breastfeeding Policy: A Globally Comparative Analysis." *Bulletin of the World Health Organization* 91(6):398–406.

Heymann, J., and K. McNeill. 2013. *Children's Chances: How Countries Can Move from Surviving to Thriving.* Cambridge: Harvard University Press.

Heymann, J., K. McNeill, and A. Raub. 2015. "Rights Monitoring and Assessment Using Quantitative Indicators of Law and Policy: International Covenant on Economic, Social and Cultural Rights." *Human Rights Quarterly* 37(4):1071–1100.

Heymann, S. J., K. McNeill, and A. Raub. 2014. "Assessing Compliance with the CRC: Indicators of Law and Policy in 191 Countries." *International Journal of Children's Rights* 22(3):425–45.

Heymann, S. J., A. Raub, and A. Cassola. 2014. "Constitutional Rights to Education and their Relationship to National Policy and School Enrolment Insights from a New Global Dataset." *International Journal of Educational Development* 39:131–41.

Hohberg, M., and J. Lay. 2015. "The Impact of Minimum Wages on Formal and Informal Labor Market Outcomes: Evidence from Indonesia." *IZA Journal of Labor & Development* 4:14.

International Labour Organization (ILO). 1988. *Employment Promotion and Protections Against Unemployment Convention, 1988* (No. 168). Adopted: Geneva, 75th ILC session (21 Jun 1988).

———. 2015. *Global Wage Report 2014/15: Wages and Income Inequality*. Report. Geneva: International Labor Office.

Jones, M. E., A. J. Swerdlow, L. E. Gill, and M. J. Goldacre. 1998. "Pre-natal and Early Life Risk Factors for Childhood Onset Diabetes Mellitus: A Record Linkage Study." *International Journal of Epidemiology* 27:444–49.

Kapur, R. 2016. "Supreme Court: Indian Temple Can't Stop Women from Entering." *The Diplomat.* Retrieved from: http://thediplomat.com/2016/05/supreme-court-indian-temple-cant-stop-women-from-entering.

Khamis, M. 2008. "Does the Minimum Wage Have a Higher Impact on the Informal than on the Formal Labor Market? Evidence from Quasi-Experiments." IZA Discussion Paper 3911.

Klugman, J., L. Hanmer, S. Twigg, T. Hasan, J. McCleary-Sills, and J. Santamaria. 2014. *Voice and Agency: Empowering Women and Girls for Shared Prosperity*. Washington, D.C.: World Bank.

Lustig, N., and D. McLeod. 1997. "Minimum Wages and Poverty in Developing Countries: Some Empirical Evidence." In *Labor Markets in Latin America: Combining Social Protection with Market Flexibility*, ed. N. Lustig and S. Edwards, 62–103. Washington, D.C.: Brookings Institution.

Maloney, W., and J. Mendez. 2004. "Measuring the Impact of Minimum Wages. Evidence from Latin America." In *Law and Employment: Lessons from Latin America and the Caribbean*, ed. J. J. Heckman and C. Pagés, 109–130. Chicago: University of Chicago Press.

Moss, P. ed. 2015. "Take-up of Leave." In *11th International Review of Leave Policies and Related Research 2015*, vol. 11. London: Institute of Education, University of London. Retrieved from: www.leavenetwork.org/fileadmin/Leavenetwork/overviews_2015/final.take-up.pdf.

Nandi, A., M. Hajizadeh, S. Harper, A. Koski, E. C. Strumpf, and S. J. Heymann. 2016. "Increased Duration of Paid Maternity Leave Lowers Infant Mortality in Low- and Middle-Income Countries: A Quasi-experimental Study." *PLoS Medicine*. Published online before print March 2016.

Nepomnyaschy, L., and J. Waldfogel. 2007. "Paternity Leave and Fathers' Involvement with Their Young Children: Evidence from the American Ecls–B." *Community, Work and Family* 10(4):427–53.

Nguyen, M. C., and Q. Wodon. 2014. "Impact of Child Marriage on Literacy and Education Attainment in Africa." UNICEF and UNESCO Institute for Statistics. Background Paper for "Fixing the Broken Promise of Education for All." Available at: http://allinschool.org/wp-content/uploads/2015/02/OOSC-2014-QW-Child-Marriage-final.pdf.

Psacharopoulos, G. 1997. "Child Labor Versus Educational Attainment—Some Evidence from Latin America." *Journal of Population Economics* 10(4):377–86.

Rama, M. 2001. "The Consequences of Doubling the Minimum Wage: The Case of Indonesia." *Industrial and Labor Relations Review* 54(4):864–81.

Raub, A., A. Cassola, I. Latz, and J. Heymann. 2016a. "Protections of Equal Rights Across Sexual Orientation and Gender Identity: An Analysis of 193 National Constitutions." *Yale Journal of Law & Feminism* 28:149–69.

Raub, A., I. Latz, A. Sprague, M. Stein, and J. Heymann. 2016b. "Constitutional Rights of Persons with Disabilities." *Harvard Human Rights Journal* 29:203–40.

Raub, A., T. M. Assi, E. Vaughan Winfrey, A. Earle, G. Moreno, G. Kranz, I. Vincent, A. Nandi, and S. J. Heymann. 2014. *CEDAW & Beijing+20—Labor Policies to Promote Equity at Work and at Home: Findings from 197 Countries and Beijing Platform Signatories*. Los Angeles, Calif.: UCLA WORLD Policy Analysis Center.

Ray, R. 2002. "The Determinants of Child Labor and Child Schooling in Ghana." *Journal of African Economies* 11:4:561–90.

Ruijs, N. M., and Thea T. D. Peetsma. 2009. "Effects of Inclusion on Students with and without Special Educational Needs Reviewed." *Educational Research Review* 4(2):67–79.

Ruijs, N., T. Peetsma, and I. van der Veen. 2010. "The Presence of Several Students with Special Educational Needs in Inclusive Education and the Functioning of Students with Special Educational Needs." *Educational Review* 62(1):1–37.

Saget, C. 2001. "Is the Minimum Wage an Effective Tool to Promote Decent Work and Reduce Poverty? The Experience of Selected Developing Countries." Geneva: Employment Sector, International Labor Office. Working Paper 2001/13.

Schultz, P. 2002. "Why Governments Should Invest More to Educate Girls." *World Development* 30(2):207–25.

Shapiro, T. 2006. "Race, Homeownership and Wealth." *Journal of Law and Policy* 20:53–74.

Sherman, A. 2010. "Looking at Today's Poverty Numbers." Center on Budget and Policy Priorities. Retrieved 16 September 2010 from: www.cbpp.org/blog/looking -at-todays-poverty-numbers.

Shonkoff, J., and D. Phillips, eds. 2000. *From Neurons to Neighborhoods: The Science of Early Child Development*. Washington, D.C.: National Academies Press.

Tanaka, S., and J. Waldfogel. 2007. "Effects of Parental Leave and Work Hours on Fathers' Involvement with Their Babies: Evidence from the Millennium Cohort Study." *Community, Work and Family* 10(4):409–26.

Theodoridis, A. 2015. "National Court Declared Unconstitutional the Reduction of the Minimum Wage for Employees Under the Age of 25." Retrieved from: www .equalitylaw.eu/downloads/2758-54-el-nd-court-decision-on-age-discrimination- in-the-field-of-employment.

UN. 2015. *The Millennium Development Goals Report 2015*. New York: United Nations.

UN Women. 2011. *Progress of the World's Women 2011–2012: In Pursuit of Justice*. New York: UN Women.

UN Educational, Scientific and Cultural Organization. 2014. *Teaching and Learning: Achieving Quality for All—EFA Global Monitoring Report 2013/4*. Paris: UNESCO.

UN Population Fund. 2012. *Marrying Too Young*. New York: UNFPA.

UNICEF. 2016. "Globally, Four Out of Five Children of Lower Secondary School Age Are Enrolled in School." Last updated April 2016. Retrieved from: http://data .unicef.org/education/secondary.html#sthash.ipYzUE7N.dpuf.

United Nations Statistics Division. 2016. "2.2 Proportion of Pupils Starting Grade 1 Who Reach Last Grade of Primary." Millennium Development Goals Indicators. Accessed 18 May 2016. http://mdgs.un.org/unsd/mdg/data.aspx.

U.S. Department of Labor. 2015. *The Cost of Doing Nothing: The Price We All Pay Without Paid Leave Policies to Support America's 21st Century Working Families*. Retrieved from: https://archive.org/details/TheCostOfDoingNothing.

——. 2016. "DOL Factsheet: Paid Family and Medical Leave." Retrieved 2 June 2016 from: www.dol.gov/wb/PaidLeave/PaidLeave.htm.

Waisath, W., N. Perry, I. K. Latz, A. Raub, A. Sprague, T. M. Assi, and S. J. Heymann. 2014. *CEDAW & Beijing+20—Closing the Gender Gap: A Summary of Findings and Policy Recommendations*. Los Angeles, Calif.: UCLA WORLD Policy Analysis Center.

World Bank. 2016. Exclusive Breastfeeding (percent of children under 6 months). Last accessed 6 May 2016. http://data.worldbank.org/indicator/SH.STA.BFED.ZS (.

World Bank and UNICEF. 2009. *Abolishing School Fees in Africa: Lessons from Ethiopia, Ghana, Kenya, Malawi, and Mozambique*. Development Practice in Education. Washington, D.C.: World Bank.

WORLD Policy Analysis Center. Adult Labor Database. 2014. Last accessed 17 Aug 2017. https://www.worldpolicycenter.org/maps-data/data-download.

WORLD Policy Analysis Center. Child Labor Database. 2012. Last accessed 17 Aug 2017. https://www.worldpolicycenter.org/maps-data/data-download.

WORLD Policy Analysis Center. Constitutions Database. 2014. Last accessed 17 Aug 2017. https://www.worldpolicycenter.org/maps-data/data-download.

WORLD Policy Analysis Center. Education Database. 2012. Last accessed 17 Aug 2017. https://www.worldpolicycenter.org/maps-data/data-download.

WORLD Policy Analysis Center. Marriage Database. 2013. Last accessed 17 Aug 2017. https://www.worldpolicycenter.org/maps-data/data-download.

CHAPTER 5

The Sustainable Development Goals, Domestic Resource Mobilization, and the Poor

Nora Lustig

At the UN General Assembly of September 2015, countries around the world committed to the Sustainable Development Goals (SDGs).[1] Countries committed to attaining poverty and hunger eradication, healthy lives, quality education, gender equality, and sustainable development by 2030. Countries also committed to promoting full-employment growth, decent work, peaceful societies, and accountable institutions and to reducing inequality and strengthening global partnerships for sustainable development. One key factor to achieving the SDGs will be the availability of fiscal resources to deliver the floors in social protection, social services, and infrastructure embedded in the SDGs. A significant portion of these resources is expected to come from domestic sources in developing countries themselves, complemented by transfers from wealthier countries. The conference on financing for development in July 2015,[2] for example, set the framework for obtaining the resources to achieve the SDGs and other commitments endorsed in the numerous global and regional compacts. Moreover, countries will be expected to set both spending targets to deliver social protection and essential public services for all and nationally defined domestic revenue targets.

As is typical with these exercises designed to identify priorities and commitments, which the great majority of countries endorse, the proposals shy away from acknowledging that goals have trade-offs. In particular, that raising additional revenues domestically for infrastructure, protecting the environment, or social services may leave a significant portion of the poor with less cash to buy food and other essential goods. It is not uncommon that the net effect of all government taxing and spending is to leave the poor worse off in terms of actual consumption of private goods and services. Achieving the new SDGs will depend in part on the ability of governments to improve their tax collection and enforcement systems. However, demand for investments into infrastructure and public services must be balanced against the competing need to protect low-income households that may otherwise be made worse off from misaligned tax and transfer policies.

Based on the fiscal incidence studies by the Commitment to Equity (CEQ) Institute at Tulane University, this document addresses three questions:

1. To what extent do fiscal systems leave the poor worse off in terms of consumption of private goods and services?
2. How frequently do fiscal systems reduce inequality but at the same time leave the poor worse off in terms of their purchasing power of private goods and services?
3. In what countries are the poor and the vulnerable net payers of the fiscal system?

The data used for the analysis are based on household surveys for the following twenty-five countries: Argentina (Rossignolo 2018), Armenia (Younger and Khachatryan 2017), Bolivia (Paz Arauco et al. 2014), Brazil (Higgins and Pereira 2014), Chile (Martinez-Aguilar et al. 2018), Colombia (Melendez and Martinez 2015), Costa Rica (Sauma and Trejos 2014), Dominican Republic (Aristy-Escuder et al. 2018), Ecuador (Llerena et al. 2015), El Salvador (Beneke et al. 2018), Ethiopia (Hill et al. 2017), Georgia (Cancho and Bondarenko 2017), Ghana (Younger, Osei-Assibey, and Oppong 2017), Guatemala (Cabrera, Lustig, and Moran 2015), Honduras (Icefi 2017), Indonesia (Afkar, Jellema, and Wai-Poi 2017), Jordan (Alam, Inchauste, and Serajuddin 2017), Mexico (Scott 2014), Peru (Jaramillo 2014), Russia (Lopez-Calva et al. 2017), South Africa (Inchauste et al. 2017), Sri Lanka (Arunatilake, Inchauste, and Lustig 2017), Tanzania (Younger, Myamba, and Mdadila 2016), Tunisia (Jouini et al. 2018), and Uruguay (Bucheli et al. 2014).

In table 5.1, one can observe the change in head-count ratio from market income to consumable income (income after net direct and indirect taxes) for three poverty lines: US$1.25, US$2.50, and US$4 dollars per day (2005 PPP), lines that the World Bank has used to measure global poverty and extreme and moderate poverty in middle-income countries, respectively.[3] These results are for twenty-five countries for which CEQ

Table 5.1a   Fiscal Policy and Poverty Reduction: Effect of Direct and Indirect Taxes, Direct Transfers and Indirect Subsidies (ca. 2010), With Poverty Line at US$1.25 2005 PPP Per Day

Country	Market income plus pensions	Disposable income	Consumable income	Disposable income: change in %	Consumable income: change in %
			Contributory pensions as deferred income		
Argentina (2012)	1.3%	0.3%	0.5%	−78.7%	−65.4%
Armenia (2011)	12.8%	9.6%	11.9%	−24.9%	−7.5%
Bolivia (2009)	10.0%	8.4%	9.7%	−16.1%	−2.3%
Brazil (2009)	6.5%	3.2%	4.2%	−50.6%	−36.2%
Chile (2013)	0.8%	0.2%	0.3%	−69.8%	−66.2%
Colombia (2010)	7.0%	5.7%	5.3%	−18.5%	−24.6%
Costa Rica (2010)	2.2%	1.2%	1.7%	−45.5%	−22.7%
Dominican Republic (2013)	5.7%	4.7%	4.9%	−18.0%	−14.1%
Ecuador (2011)	3.4%	1.9%	1.6%	−46.0%	−54.1%
El Salvador (2011)	4.3%	2.9%	3.6%	−31.8%	−15.7%
Ethiopia (2011)	31.9%	30.9%	33.2%	−3.3%	**4.2%**
Georgia (2013)	20.5%	6.0%	9.4%	−70.7%	−54.2%
Ghana (2013)	6.0%	5.9%	6.7%	−1.8%	**12.0%**
Guatemala (2011)	5.6%	5.2%	5.8%	−8.3%	**2.4%**
Honduras (2011)	10.2%	9.1%	9.3%	−11.5%	−8.8%
Indonesia (2012)	12.1%	10.8%	10.5%	−10.3%	−12.7%
Jordan (2010)	0.5%	0.1%	0.1%	−69.6%	−76.4%
Mexico (2010)	5.0%	3.3%	3.2%	−33.9%	−35.0%
Peru (2009)	n.c.	n.c.	n.c.	n.c.	n.c.
Russia (2010)	2.6%	1.4%	1.6%	−44.9%	−37.8%
South Africa (2010)	37.0%	16.1%	21.2%	−56.4%	−42.7%
Sri Lanka (2010)	5.0%	4.2%	4.3%	−16.5%	−14.1%
Tanzania (2011)	43.7%	43.6%	51.5%	−0.2%	**17.8%**
Tunisia (2010)	0.5%	0.3%	0.2%	−34.6%	−53.8%
Uruguay (2009)	1.3%	0.0%	0.2%	−97.0%	−82.6%

Note: Boldface means that, in these countries, the headcount poverty ratio after taxes and transfers is higher than the prefiscal headcount ratio with the international $1.25/day (in 2005 PPP dollars).

See endnote 4 to this chapter for notes and source lines for table 5.1.

Table 5.1b Fiscal Policy and Poverty Reduction: Effect of Direct and Indirect Taxes, Direct Transfers and Indirect Subsidies (ca. 2010), With Poverty Line at US$2.50 2005 PPP Per Day

| Country | Contributory pensions as deferred income | | | | |
	Market income plus pensions	Disposable income	Consumable income	Disposable income: change in %	Consumable income: change in %
Argentina (2012)	4.7%	1.8%	3.0%	−61.0%	−35.4%
Armenia (2011)	31.3%	28.9%	34.9%	−7.7%	**11.4%**
Bolivia (2009)	19.6%	17.6%	20.2%	−10.4%	**3.3%**
Brazil (2009)	16.8%	13.1%	16.0%	−22.0%	−4.7%
Chile (2013)	2.8%	1.2%	1.3%	−58.4%	−51.8%
Colombia (2010)	20.3%	18.9%	18.5%	−7.0%	−9.0%
Costa Rica (2010)	5.4%	3.9%	4.2%	−27.8%	−22.2%
Dominican Republic (2013)	19.5%	18.2%	19.5%	−6.5%	−0.2%
Ecuador (2011)	10.8%	7.7%	7.0%	−28.7%	−35.0%
El Salvador (2011)	19.2%	17.3%	19.1%	−10.1%	−0.8%
Ethiopia (2011)	81.7%	82.4%	84.2%	**0.9%**	**3.1%**
Georgia (2013)	39.2%	23.3%	30.0%	−40.6%	−23.3%
Ghana (2013)	26.4%	26.8%	28.8%	**1.5%**	**9.1%**
Guatemala (2011)	33.3%	32.3%	35.1%	−2.8%	**5.4%**
Honduras (2011)	25.1%	24.2%	25.2%	−3.3%	**0.5%**
Indonesia (2012)	56.4%	55.9%	54.8%	−1.0%	−2.9%
Jordan (2010)	5.2%	4.0%	3.4%	−24.0%	−34.8%
Mexico (2010)	12.6%	10.7%	10.7%	−14.9%	−15.1%
Peru (2009)	15.2%	14.0%	14.5%	−7.3%	−4.4%
Russia (2010)	4.0%	2.6%	2.8%	−35.9%	−29.1%
South Africa (2010)	49.3%	38.7%	44.1%	−21.4%	−10.6%
Sri Lanka (2010)	38.9%	38.2%	39.4%	−1.8%	**1.1%**
Tanzania (2011)	83.5%	84.4%	88.4%	**1.1%**	**5.9%**
Tunisia (2010)	5.0%	4.6%	3.8%	−8.3%	−25.2%
Uruguay (2009)	5.0%	1.4%	2.5%	−71.4%	−51.1%

Note: Boldface means that, in these countries, the headcount poverty ratio after taxes and transfers is higher than the prefiscal headcount ratio with the international $1.25/day (in 2005 PPP dollars).

Table 5.1c   Fiscal Policy and Poverty Reduction: Effect of Direct and Indirect Taxes, Direct Transfers and Indirect Subsidies (ca. 2010), With Poverty Line at US$4.00 2005 PPP Per Day

Country	Contributory pensions as deferred income				
	Market income plus pensions	Disposable income	Consumable income	Disposable income: change in %	Consumable income: change in %
Argentina (2012)	12.3%	7.3%	12.5%	–41.0%	**1.6%**
Armenia (2011)	55.1%	55.5%	62.7%	**0.7%**	**13.7%**
Bolivia (2009)	32.5%	30.7%	33.9%	–5.6%	**4.4%**
Brazil (2009)	28.8%	26.3%	31.1%	–8.5%	**8.1%**
Chile (2013)	7.5%	4.4%	5.7%	–41.2%	–24.2%
Colombia (2010)	36.3%	35.5%	35.5%	–2.1%	–2.3%
Costa Rica (2010)	10.8%	9.3%	11.1%	–13.9%	**2.8%**
Dominican Republic (2013)	37.0%	35.9%	37.7%	–2.9%	**1.9%**
Ecuador (2011)	24.2%	21.1%	20.4%	–13.0%	–15.7%
El Salvador (2011)	39.3%	38.3%	40.8%	–2.7%	**3.8%**
Ethiopia (2011)	95.2%	95.6%	96.1%	**0.4%**	**1.0%**
Georgia (2013)	n.c.	n.c.	n.c.	n.c.	n.c.
Ghana (2013)	48.9%	49.9%	52.1%	**2.0%**	**6.6%**
Guatemala (2011)	58.5%	58.3%	60.9%	–0.4%	**4.1%**
Honduras (2011)	39.7%	39.0%	41.6%	–1.7%	**4.9%**
Indonesia (2012)	78.4%	78.3%	77.8%	–0.2%	–0.8%
Jordan (2010)	25.8%	24.6%	23.6%	–4.7%	–8.4%
Mexico (2010)	24.7%	23.1%	23.8%	–6.2%	–3.5%
Peru (2009)	28.6%	27.8%	28.7%	–2.7%	**0.4%**
Russia (2010)	6.3%	4.6%	5.5%	–26.8%	–12.5%
South Africa (2010)	57.5%	52.9%	57.3%	–8.0%	–0.3%
Sri Lanka (2010)	69.8%	69.7%	71.2%	–0.1%	**1.9%**
Tanzania (2011)	93.7%	94.6%	96.5%	**1.0%**	**3.0%**
Tunisia (2010)	14.3%	14.9%	14.7%	**4.3%**	**2.7%**
Uruguay (2009)	11.4%	6.6%	8.9%	–42.0%	–21.8%

Note: Boldface means that, in these countries, the headcount poverty ratio after taxes and transfers is higher than the prefiscal headcount ratio with the international $1.25/day (in 2005 PPP dollars).

Assessments are available. Using the US$1.25 poverty line, fiscal policy increases the head-count ratio in Ethiopia, Ghana, Guatemala, and Tanzania. That is, in these countries the number of poor people who are made poorer through the taxing and spending activities of governments exceeds the number who actually benefit from those activities. When using the US$2.50 poverty line, the head-count ratio increases in Armenia, Bolivia, Ethiopia, Ghana, Guatemala, Honduras, Sri Lanka, and Tanzania. And the same countries experience an increase in the head-count ratio with the US$4 line.[4]

As shown by Higgins and Lustig (2016), conventional measures of poverty such as the head-count ratio can fail to capture whether the poor are made worse off (and the non-poor made poor) by fiscal interventions. A stylized illustration of fiscal impoverishment can be seen in figure 5.1. The areas in dark gray indicate the order of magnitude of fiscal impoverishment and the areas in light gray show the extent of fiscal gains to the poor.

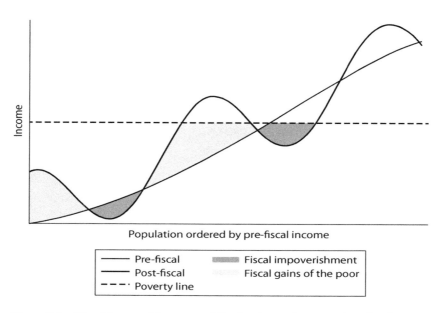

Figure 5.1   Fiscal impoverishment and fiscal gains to the poor: A stylized illustration.

Source: Higgins and Lustig (2016).

Table 5.2 presents the proportion of individuals who are fiscally impoverished (i.e., the equivalent of those for whom the wavy line falls below the line in the stylized figure, represented by the dark shaded area under the curve) as a share of the total population (column 6) and of the population classified as poor with consumable income (column 7) for the eighteen countries for which these calculations were available. To measure fiscal impoverishment, table 5.2 shows indicators for consumable income[5] as the relevant after taxes and transfers income concept, even though taxes are used to fund more than just direct cash and food transfers and indirect subsidies from the government (e.g., they are used to fund public goods and services, many of which also reach the poor), because this is the income concept relevant for measuring poverty: it is "disposable money and near-money income" that should be compared to the poverty line when the latter is based on "a poverty budget for food, clothing, shelter, and similar items" (Citro and Robert 1995, 212, 237). For low- and lower-middle-income countries, a poverty line of $1.25 per person per day is used; for upper-middle-income countries, $2.50 per day is used. Table 5.2 column 1 shows the market income poverty head count, and column 2 shows the change in poverty from market to consumable income. Moving to the progressivity of the tax and transfer system and change in inequality in each country, column 3 shows the market income Gini coefficient, and column 4 shows the Reynolds and Smolensky (1977) index of global progressivity (the Reynolds-Smolensky equals the market income Gini minus the concentration coefficient of consumable income with respect to market income, and thus globally progressive systems have a positive Reynolds-Smolensky index). Column 5 shows the change in inequality, with negative numbers indicating that inequality declined because of the tax and transfer system.

Note that although fifteen of the eighteen countries in table 5.2 experienced a *reduction* in poverty and inequality due to the tax and transfer system, they experienced various degrees of fiscal impoverishment.[6] In ten countries—Armenia, Bolivia, Brazil, El Salvador, Guatemala, Indonesia, Mexico, Russia, Sri Lanka, and Tunisia—between one-quarter and two-thirds of the post-fisc poor lost income to the fiscal system (see appendix). In other countries, this figure is much lower, at 13.3 percent of the post-fisc poor in South Africa (but, due to the high proportion of the total population that is poor, this implies that 5.9 percent of the total population was impoverished by the fiscal system) and 3.2 percent

Table 5.2 Fiscal Impoverishment (Market Income Plus Pensions to Consumable Income, ca. 2010)

Country (survey year)	1. Market income plus pensions poverty headcount (%)	2. Change in poverty headcount (p.I.)	3. Market income plus pensions inequality (gini)	4. Reynolds-smolensky	5. Change in inequality (Δ Gini)	6. Fiscally impoverished as % of population	7. Fiscally impoverished as % of consumable income poor
A. Upper-middle-income countries, using a poverty line of $2.50 PPP 2005 per day							
Brazil (2009)	16.8	-0.8	57.5	4.6	-3.5	5.6	34.9
Chile (2013)	2.8	-1.4	49.4	3.2	-3.0	0.3	19.2
Ecuador (2011)	10.8	-3.8	47.8	3.5	-3.3	0.2	3.2
Mexico (2012)	13.3	-1.2	54.4	3.8	-2.5	4.0	32.7
Peru (2011)	13.8	-0.2	45.9	0.9	-0.8	3.2	23.8
Russia (2010)	4.3	-1.3	39.7	3.9	-2.6	1.1	34.4
South Africa (2010)	49.3	-5.2	77.1	8.3	-7.7	5.9	13.3
Tunisia (2010)	7.8	-0.1	44.7	8.0	-6.9	3.0	38.5
B. Lower-middle-income countries, using a poverty line of $1.25 2005 PPP per day							
Armenia (2011)	21.4	-9.6	47.4	12.9	-9.3	6.2	52.3
Bolivia (2009)	10.9	-0.5	50.3	0.6	-0.3	6.6	63.2
Dominican Republic (2013)	6.8	-0.9	50.2	2.2	-2.2	1.0	16.3
El Salvador IDB (2011)	4.3	-0.7	44.0	2.2	-2.1	1.0	27.0
Ethiopia (2011)	31.9	2.3	32.2	2.3	-2.0	28.5	83.2
Ghana (2013)	6.0	0.7	43.7	1.6	-1.4	5.1	76.6
Guatemala (2010)	12.0	-0.8	49.0	1.4	-1.2	7.0	62.2
Indonesia (2012)	12.0	-1.5	39.8	1.1	-0.8	4.1	39.2
Sri Lanka (2010)	5.0	-0.7	37.1	1.3	-1.1	1.6	36.4
Tanzania (2011)	43.7	7.9	38.2	4.1	-3.8	50.9	98.6

Note: Year of data in fiscal incidence analysis in parenthesis. For definitions of income concepts, see appendix.

Source: Higgins and Lustig (2016).

of the post-fisc poor in Ecuador. In the three countries where the head-count ratio rose (Ethiopia, Ghana, and Tanzania), the proportion of the poor who were impoverished by the fiscal system is staggering (above 75 percent).

It should also be noted that "even if we add the value of public spending on education and health (imputed at their government cost to families who report a child attending public school or who report using public health facilities), fiscal impoverishment is still high in several countries: in Armenia, Ethiopia, Indonesia, Tunisia, and Russia, between 25 and 50 percent of those who are fiscally impoverished before adding in benefits from public spending on health and education are still fiscally impoverished when these benefits are included as transfers" (Higgins and Lustig 2016, 8).

This undesirable outcome of the poor being made worse off by the combination of taxes and transfers is the consequence of primarily consumption taxes—for example, value-added or excise taxes. For example, the Brazilian tax system results in heavy taxes on such basic staples as rice and beans. For many households, transfers from Bolsa Familia are not there or are not large enough to compensate what they pay in consumption taxes (Higgins and Pereira 2014). This is not the result of a "diabolical" plan: it is the outcome of targeting schemes that select households on their characteristics (poor with school-age children), a very complex cascading tax system, and consumption patterns of the poor. In the case of Ethiopia, it is mainly the result of taxes on agriculture, even smallholder agriculture.

In figure 5.2, one can observe which deciles, on average, are net receives or net payers (in light gray) to the fisc in cash terms (that is, excluding benefits derived from public goods and services such as public education and health). In the twenty-five countries analyzed here, on average, all deciles are net payers in Ghana and Tanzania, whereas at the other end of the spectrum is Indonesia, in which all deciles are net receivers, on average.

The big risk in setting an ambitious domestic resource-mobilization agenda is that governments will impoverish poor people even further. As it stands, the SDGs list of targets would not alert us of such a perverse outcome. Under goal one on poverty reduction, there should be a target 1.6: "By 2030 to ensure that the fiscal system does not reduce the income of the poor."

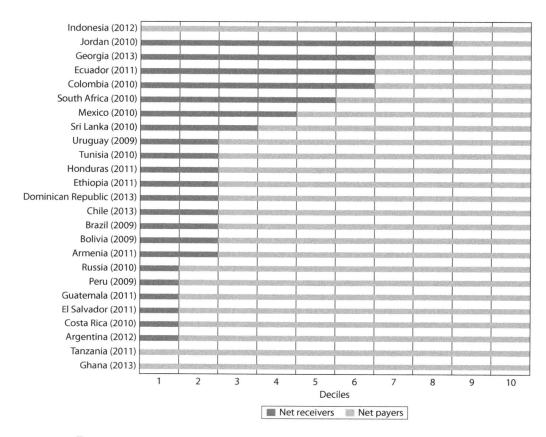

Figure 5.2   Net payers and receivers in the fiscal system by decile (ca. 2010).

Note: Year of data in fiscal incidence analysis in parenthesis. For definitions of income concepts see Appendix.

Sources: Based on Argentina (Rossignolo 2018); Armenia (Younger and Khachatryan 2017); Bolivia (Paz-Arauco et al. 2014); Brazil (Higgins and Pereira 2014); Chile (Martinez-Aguilar et al. 2018); Colombia (Melendez and Martinez 2015); Costa Rica (Sauma and Trejos 2014); Dominican Republic (Aristy-Escuder et al. 2018); Ecuador (Llerena et al. 2015); El Salvador (Beneke, Lustig, and Oliva 2018); Ethiopia (Hill et al. 2017); Georgia (Cancho and Bondarenko 2017); Ghana (Younger, Osei-Assibey, and Oppong 2017); Guatemala (Cabrera, Lustig, and Moran 2015); Honduras (Icefi 2017); Indonesia (Afkar, Jellema, and Wai-Poi 2017); Jordan (Alam, Inchauste, and Serajuddin 2017); Mexico (Scott 2014); Peru (Jaramillo 2014); Russia (Lopez-Calva et al. 2017), South Africa (Inchauste et al. 2017); Sri Lanka (Arunatilake, Inchauste, and Lustig 2017); Tanzania (Younger, Myamba, and Mdadila 2016); Tunisia (Jouini et al. 2018); and Uruguay (Bucheli et al. 2014).

APPENDIX

FISCAL INCIDENCE ANALYSIS: METHODOLOGICAL HIGHLIGHTS[7]

Fiscal incidence analysis is used to assess the distributional impacts of a country's taxes and transfers. Essentially, fiscal incidence analysis consists of allocating taxes (personal income tax and consumption taxes, in particular) and public spending (social spending in particular) to households or individuals so that one can compare incomes before taxes and transfers with incomes after taxes and transfers. Transfers include both cash transfers and benefits in kind such as free government services like education and health care. Transfers also include consumption subsidies such as food, electric, and fuel subsidies.

As with any fiscal incidence study, let's start by defining the basic income concepts. Here there are four: market, disposable, post-fiscal, and final income. These income concepts are described below and summarized in figure 5.3.

Market income[8] is total current income before direct taxes, equal to the sum of gross (pretax) wages and salaries in the formal and informal sectors (also known as earned income), income from capital (dividends, interest, profits, rents, etc.) in the formal and informal sectors (excludes capital gains and gifts), consumption of own production,[9] imputed rent for owner-occupied housing, and private transfers (remittances, pensions from private schemes, and other private transfers such as alimony).

Disposable income is defined as market income minus direct personal income taxes on all income sources (included in market income) that are subject to taxation plus direct government transfers (mainly cash transfers but can include near-cash transfers such as food transfers, free textbooks, and school uniforms).

Post-fiscal (also called consumable) income is defined as disposable income plus indirect subsidies (e.g., food and energy price subsidies) minus indirect taxes (e.g., value-added taxes, excise taxes, sales taxes, etc.).

Final income is defined as post-fiscal income plus government transfers in the form of free or subsidized services in education and health valued at average cost of provision[10] (minus copayments or user fees, when they exist).

One area in which there is no clear consensus is how pensions from a pay-as-you-go contributory system should be treated. Arguments exist in favor of both treating contributory pensions as deferred income[11] or as a government transfer, especially in systems with a large subsidized

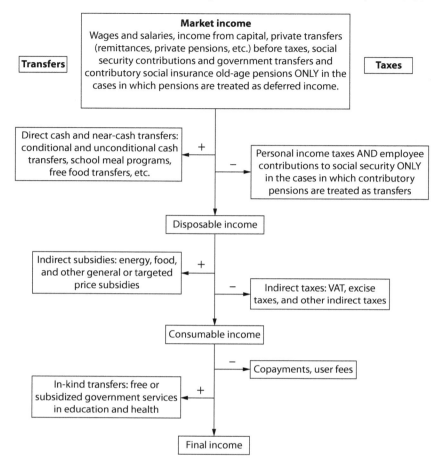

Figure 5.3   Income concepts: From market income to final income.

Source: Lustig (2018).

component.[12] Since this is an unresolved issue, CEQ studies present results for both methods. One scenario treats social insurance contributory pensions (herewith called contributory pensions) as deferred income (which in practice means that they are added to market income to generate the original or pre-fisc income). The other scenario treats these pensions as any other cash transfer from the government.[13] The studies analyzed here present results considering contributory pensions as deferred income. For consistency, when pensions are treated as deferred income, the contributions by individuals are included under savings (they are mandatory savings); when they are treated as government transfers, the contributions are considered a direct tax.

It is important to note that the treatment of contributory pensions not only affects the amount of redistributive spending and how it gets redistributed but also the ranking of households by original income or pre-fiscal income. For example, in the scenario in which contributory pensions are considered a government transfer, households whose main (or sole) source of income is pensions will have close to (or just) zero income before taxes and transfers and hence will be ranked at the bottom of the income scale. When contributory pensions are treated as deferred income, in contrast, households who receive contributory pensions will be placed at a (sometimes considerably) higher position in the income scale. Thus, the treatment of contributory pensions in the incidence exercise could have significant implications for the order of magnitude of the pre-fisc and post-fisc inequality and poverty indicators.

In the construction of final income, the method for education spending consists of imputing a value to the benefit accrued to an individual of going to public school, which is equal to the per beneficiary input costs obtained from administrative data: for example, the average government expenditure per primary school student obtained from administrative data is allocated to the households based on how many children are reported attending public school at the primary level. In the case of health care, the approach was analogous: the benefit of receiving health care in a public facility is equal to the average cost to the government of delivering health-care services to the beneficiaries. In the case of Colombia, however, the method used was to impute the insurance value to beneficiary households rather than base the valuation on use of health-care services.

This approach to valuing education and health-care services amounts to asking the following question: How much would the income of a household have to be increased if it had to pay for the free or subsidized public service (or the insurance value in the cases in which this applies to health-care benefits) at the full cost to the government? Such an approach ignores the fact that consumers may value services quite differently from what they cost. Given the limitations of available data, however, the cost of provision method is the best one can do for now.[14] For the readers who think that attaching a value to education and health services based on government costs is not accurate, the method applied here is equivalent to using a simple binary indicator of whether or not the individual uses the government service.[15]

The welfare indicator used in the fiscal incidence analysis is income per capita.

The fiscal incidence analysis used here is point in time and does not incorporate behavioral or general equilibrium effects. That is, no claim is made that the original or market income equals the true counter-factual income in the absence of taxes and transfers. It is a first-order approximation that measures the average incidence of fiscal interventions. However, the analysis is not a mechanically applied accounting exercise. The incidence of taxes is the economic rather than statutory incidence. It is assumed that individual income taxes and contributions both by employees and employers, for instance, are borne by labor in the for-mal sector. Individuals who are not contributing to social security are assumed to pay neither direct taxes nor contributions. Consumption taxes are fully shifted forward to consumers. In the case of consumption taxes, the analyses take into account the lower incidence associated with own consumption, rural markets, and informality.

In general, fiscal incidence exercises are carried out using household surveys, and this is what was done here. The surveys used in the coun-try studies are the following: Argentina: Encuesta Nacional de Gasto de los Hogares 2012–2013; Armenia: Integrated Living Conditions Survey 2011; Bolivia: Encuesta de Hogares 2009; Brazil: Pesquisa de Orçamentos Familiares 2008–2009; Chile: Encuesta de Caracterizacion Social 2013; Colombia: Encuesta Nacional de Calidad de Vida 2010; Costa Rica: Encuesta Nacional de Hogares 2010; Dominican Republic: Encuesta Nacional de Ingresos y Gastos de los Hogares 2006–2007; Ecuador: Encuesta Nacional de Ingresos y Gastos de los Hogares Urbano y Rural 2011–2012; El Salvador: Encuesta de Hogares de Propositos Multiples 2011; Ethiopia: Household Consumption Expenditure Survey 2010–2011 and Welfare Monitoring Survey 2011; Georgia: Integrated Household Survey 2013; Ghana: Living Standards Survey 2012–2013; Guatemala: Encuesta Nacional de Ingresos y Gastos Familiares 2009–2010 and Encuesta Nacional de Condiciones de Vida 2011; Honduras: Encuesta Permanente de Hogares de Propositos Multiples 2011; Indonesia: Survei Sosial-Ekonomi Nasional 2012; Jordan: Household Expenditure and Income Survey 2010–2011; Mexico: Encuesta Nacional de Ingresos y Gastos de los Hogares 2010; Peru: Encuesta Nacional de Hogares 2009; Russia: Russian Longitudinal Monitoring Survey of Higher School of Economics 2010; South Africa: Income and Expenditure Survey 2010–2011; Sri Lanka: Household Income and Expenditure Survey 2009–2010;

Tanzania: Household Budget Survey 2011–2012; Tunisia: National Survey of Consumption and Household Living Standards 2010; Uruguay: Encuesta Continua de Hogares 2009.

NOTES

This chapter was originally prepared as a background document for the World Bank's World Development Report 2017 *Governance and the Law*. The author is very grateful to Sandra Martinez, Israel Martinez, and Cristina Carrera for their excellent assistance in the preparation of tables and graphs. She also wants to thank Ruoxi Li and Xavi Recchi for their excellent research assistance.

1. For the document endorsed by the General Assembly in September 2015, see UN General Assembly (2015a). The Sustainable Development Goals and their targets can be found at: https://sustainabledevelopment.un.org/?menu=1300.

2. Document endorsed by the General Assembly on July 27, 2015 (UN General Assembly 2015b).

3. All the CEQ studies applied the common fiscal incidence methodological framework discussed in Lustig and Higgins (2013) and Lustig (forthcoming). Results presented here consider contributory pensions as deferred income. The definition of income concepts and a brief methodological overview are in the appendix.

4. Notes and sources for table 5.1 (results not shown in table 5.1 are available upon request):

n.c.: not calculated

Percentage of poverty reduction is defined as percentage change in head-count ratio from market income plus contributory pensions to consumable income.

In Ethiopia, Ghana, Indonesia, Jordan, Sri Lanka, Tanzania, and Tunisia, consumption expenditure is the primary income measure; all other income concepts, including market income, are derived assuming that consumption expenditure is equal to disposable income.

For Argentina, Ethiopia, Ghana, Indonesia, Jordan, Russia, South Africa, and Tanzania, the study includes indirect effects of indirect taxes and subsidies.

Bolivia does not have personal income taxes.

In Bolivia, Costa Rica, Ecuador, Honduras, South Africa, and Sri Lanka, market income does not include consumption of own production, because the data was either not available or not reliable.

For Brazil, the results for the analysis presented here differ from the results published in Higgins and Pereira (2014), because the latter includes taxes on services (ISS), on goods and services to finance pensions (CONFINS), and to finance social workers (PIS), while the results presented here do not include them. The authors concluded that the source for these taxes was not reliable after the paper was published.

Gini coefficients for Chile are estimated here using total income and therefore differ from official figures of inequality, which are estimated using monetary income (i.e., official figures exclude owner-occupied imputed rent).

In South Africa, the results presented here assume that free basic services are a direct transfer.

In Armenia, Costa Rica, Peru, South Africa, and Uruguay, there are no indirect subsidies.

For the Dominican Republic, the study analyzes the effects of fiscal policy in 2013, but the household income and expenditure survey dates back to 2006–2007.

For Indonesia, the fiscal incidence analysis was carried out by adjusting for spatial price differences.

Personal income taxes are assumed to be zero, because the vast majority of households have implied market incomes below the tax threshold.

The only contributory pensions in South Africa are for public servants who must belong to the GEPF.

The only contributory pensions in Sri Lanka are for public servants, and income from pensions has been considered as part of the public employees' labor contract, rather than a transfer, in spite of the fact that the funding comes from general revenues.

Georgia has a noncontributory public pension scheme only, which is treated as a transfer.

Source: CEQ Data Center on Fiscal Redistribution. Based on Argentina (Rossignolo 2017); Armenia (Younger and Khachatryan 2017); Bolivia (Paz-Arauco et al. 2014); Brazil (Higgins and Pereira 2014); Chile (Martinez-Aguilar et al. 2017); Colombia (Melendez and Martinez 2015); Costa Rica (Sauma and Trejos 2014); Dominican Republic (Aristy-Escuder et al. 2017); Ecuador (Llerena et al. 2015); El Salvador (Beneke, Lustig, and Oliva 2017); Ethiopia (Hill et al. 2017); Georgia (Cancho and Bondarenko 2017); Ghana (Younger, Osei-Assibey, and Oppong 2017); Guatemala (Cabrera, Lustig, and Moran 2015); Honduras (Icefi 2017); Indonesia (Afkar, Jellema, and Wai-Poi 2017); Jordan (Alam, Inchauste, and Serajuddin 2017); Mexico (Scott 2014); Peru (Jaramillo 2014); Russia (Lopez-Calva et al. 2017), South Africa (Inchauste et al. 2017); Sri Lanka (Arunatilake, Inchauste, and Lustig 2017); Tanzania (Younger, Myamba, and Mdadila 2016); Tunisia (Jouini et al. 2018); and Uruguay (Bucheli et al. 2014).

5. As indicated in figure 5.3 in the appendix, consumable income equals market income plus direct transfers and indirect subsidies minus direct and indirect taxes.

6. Note that Brazil here appears with a reduction in the head-count ratio because poverty was measured differently than for the results shown in table 5.1.

7. This appendix is based on Lustig and Higgins (2013) and Lustig (forthcoming).

8. Market income is sometimes called primary or original income.

9. Except in the case of South Africa, whose data on autoconsumption (also called own-production or self-consumption) was not considered reliable.

10. See, for example, Sahn and Younger (2000).

11. Breceda, Rigolini, and Saavedra (2008); Immervoll et al. (2009).

12. Goñi, Lopez, and Serven (2011); Immervoll et al. (2009); Lindert, Skoufias, and Shapiro (2006).

13. Immervoll et al. (2009) did the analysis under these two scenarios as well.

14. By using averages, it also ignores differences across income groups and regions: for example, governments may spend less (or more) per pupil or patient in poorer areas of a country. Some studies in the CEQ project adjusted for regional differences. For example, Brazil's health spending was based on regional specific averages.

15. This is, of course, only true within a level of education. A concentration coefficient for total nontertiary education, for example, where the latter is calculated as the sum of the different spending amounts by level, is not equivalent to the binary indicator method.

In order to avoid exaggerating the effect of government services on inequality, the totals for education and health spending in the studies reported here were scaled down so that their proportion to disposable income in the national accounts are the same as those observed using data from the household surveys.

REFERENCES

Afkar, Rythia, Jon Jellema, and Matthew Wai-Poi. 2017. "The Distributional Impact of Fiscal Policy in Indonesia." In *The Distributional Impact of Fiscal Policy: Experience from Developing Countries*, ed. Gabriela Inchauste and Nora Lustig, 149–80. Washington, D.C.: World Bank.

Alam, Shamma Adeeb, Gabriela Inchauste, and Umar Serajuddin. 2017. "The Distributional Impact of Fiscal Policy in Jordan." In *The Distributional Impact of Fiscal Policy: Experience from Developing Countries*, ed. Gabriela Inchauste and Nora Lustig. Washington, D.C.: World Bank.

Aristy-Escuder, Jaime, Maynor Cabrera, Blanca Moreno-Dodson, and Miguel Eduardo Sanchez-Martin. 2018. "Fiscal Policy and Redistribution in the Dominican Republic." In *Commitment to Equity Handbook. Estimating the Impact of Fiscal Policy on Inequality and Poverty*, ed. Nora Lustig. Washington, D.C.: Brookings Institution Press and New Orleans, La.: CEQ Institute, Tulane University. Advance online version available at: http://www.commitmentoequity.org/publications/handbook.php.

Arunatilake, Nisha, Gabriela Inchauste, and Nora Lustig. 2017. "The Incidence of Taxes and Spending in Sri Lanka." In *The Distributional Impact of Fiscal Policy: Experience from Developing Countries*, ed. Gabriela Inchauste and Nora Lustig, 269–95. Washington, D.C.: World Bank.

Beneke, Margarita, Nora Lustig, and Jose Andres Oliva. 2018. "The Impact of Taxes and Social Spending on Inequality and Poverty in El Salvador." In *Commitment to Equity Handbook. Estimating the Impact of Fiscal Policy on Inequality and Poverty*, ed. Nora Lustig. Washington, D.C.: Brookings Institution Press and New Orleans, La.: CEQ Institute, Tulane University. Advance online version available at: http://www.commitmentoequity.org/publications/handbook.php.

Breceda, Karla, Jamele Rigolini, and Jaime Saavedra. 2008. "Latin America and the Social Contract: Patterns of Social Spending and Taxation." Policy Research Working Paper 4604. Washington, D.C.: World Bank Latin American and Caribbean Region Poverty Department Poverty Reduction and Economic Management Division.

Bucheli, Marisa, Nora Lustig, Maximo Rossi, and Florencia Amabile. 2014. "Social Spending, Taxes and Income Redistribution in Uruguay." In *The Redistributive Impact of Taxes and Social Spending in Latin America*, ed. Nora Lustig, Carola Pessino, and John Scott. Special issue, *Public Finance Review* 42(3):413–33.

Cabrera, Maynor, Nora Lustig, and Hilcias Moran. 2015. "Fiscal Policy, Inequality and the Ethnic Divide in Guatemala." *World Development* 76:263–79.

Cancho, Cesar, and Elena Bondarenko. 2017. "The Distributional Impact of Fiscal Policy in Georgia." In *The Distributional Impact of Fiscal Policy: Experience from Developing Countries*, ed. Gabriela Inchauste and Nora Lustig, 113–48. Washington, D.C.: World Bank.

Citro, Constance F., and Michael T. Robert. 1995. *Measuring Poverty: A New Approach.* Washington, D.C.: National Academies Press.

Goñi, Edwin, J. Humberto Lopez, and Luis Serven. 2011. "Fiscal Redistribution and Income Inequality in Latin America." *World Development* 39:1558–69.

Higgins, Sean, and Claudiney Pereira. 2014. "The Effects of Brazil's Taxation and Social Spending on the Distribution of Household Income." In *The Redistributive Impact of Taxes and Social Spending in Latin America*, ed. Nora Lustig, Carola Pessino, and John Scott. Special issue, *Public Finance Review* 42(3):346–67.

Higgins, Sean, and Nora Lustig. 2016. "Can a Poverty-Reducing and Progressive Tax and Transfer System Hurt the Poor?" *Journal of Development Economics*, September: 63–75.

Hill, Ruth, Gabriela Inchauste, Nora Lustig, Eyasu Tsehaye, and Tassew Woldehanna. 2017. "A Fiscal Incidence Analysis for Ethiopia." In *The Distributional Impact of Fiscal Policy: Experience from Developing Countries*, ed. Gabriela Inchauste, and Nora Lustig, 79–112. Washington, D.C.: World Bank.

Icefi. 2017. "Incidencia de la politica fiscal en el ambito rural de Centro America: el caso de Honduras." CEQ Working Paper 51. New Orleans, La.: CEQ Institute, Tulane University, IFAD and Instituto Centroamericano de Estudios Fiscales.

Immervoll, Herwig, Horacio Levy, Jose Ricardo Nogueira, Cathal O'Donoghue, and Rozane Bezerra de Siqueira. 2009. "The Impact of Brazil's Tax-Benefit System on Inequality and Poverty." In *Poverty, Inequality, and Policy in Latin America*, ed. Stephan Klasen and Felicitas Nowak Lehmann, 271–302. Cambridge: MIT Press.

Inchauste, Gabriela, Nora Lustig, Mashekwa Maboshe, Catriona Purfield, and Ingrid Wollard. 2017. "The Distributional Impact of Fiscal Policy in South Africa." In *The Distributional Impact of Fiscal Policy: Experience from Developing Countries*, ed. Gabriela Inchauste and Nora Lustig, 235–68. Washington, D.C.: World Bank.

Jaramillo, Miguel. 2014. "The Incidence of Social Spending and Taxes in Peru." In *The Redistributive Impact of Taxes and Social Spending in Latin America*, ed. Nora Lustig, Carola Pessino, and John Scott. Special issue, *Public Finance Review* 42(3):391–412.

Jouini, Nizar, Nora Lustig, Ahmed Moummi, and Abebe Shimeles. 2018. "Fiscal Incidence and Poverty Reduction: Evidence from Tunisia." In *Commitment to Equity Handbook. Estimating the Impact of Fiscal Policy on Inequality and Poverty*, ed. Nora Lustig. Washington, D.C.: Brookings Institution Press and New Orleans, La.: CEQ Institute, Tulane University. Advance online version available at: http://www.commitmentoequity.org/publications/handbook.php.

Lindert, Kathy, Emmanuel Skoufias, and Joseph Shapiro. 2006. "Redistributing Income to the Poor and Rich: Public Transfers in Latin America and the Caribbean." Social Protection Discussion Paper 0605. Washington, D.C.: World Bank.

Llerena, Freddy, Christina Llerena, Roberto Saa, and Maria Andrea Llerena. 2015. "Social Spending, Taxes and Income Redistribution in Ecuador." CEQ Working Paper 28. New Orleans, La.: Center for Inter-American Policy and Research and Department of Economics, Tulane University, and Inter-American Dialogue.

Lopez-Calva, Luis F., Nora Lustig, Mikhail Matytsin, and Daria Popova. 2017. "Who Benefits from Fiscal Redistribution in the Russian Federation?" In *The Distributional Impact of Fiscal Policy: Experience from Developing Countries*, ed. Gabriela Inchauste and Nora Lustig, 201–34. Washington, D.C.: World Bank.

Lustig, Nora, and Sean Higgins. 2013. "Commitment to Equity Assessment (CEQ): Estimating the Incidence of Social Spending, Subsidies and Taxes. Handbook." CEQ Working Paper 1. New Orleans, La.: Center for Inter-American Policy and Research and Department of Economics, Tulane University, and Inter-American Dialogue, September. [Version replaced by Lustig, editor, 2018; available upon request]

Lustig, Nora, ed. 2018. *Commitment to Equity Handbook. Estimating the Impact of Fiscal Policy on Inequality and Poverty*. Washington, D.C.: Brookings Institution Press and New Orleans, La.: CEQ Institute, Tulane University. Advance online version available at: http://www.commitmentoequity.org/publications/handbook.php.

Martinez-Aguilar, Sandra, Alan Fuchs, Eduardo Ortiz-Juarez, and Giselle del Carmen. 2018. "The Impact of Fiscal Policy on Inequality and Poverty in Chile." In *Commitment to Equity Handbook. Estimating the Impact of Fiscal Policy on Inequality and Poverty*, ed. Nora Lustig. Washington, D.C.: Brookings Institution Press and New Orleans, La.: CEQ Institute, Tulane University. Advance online version available at: http://www.commitmentoequity.org/publications/handbook.php.

Melendez, Marcela, and Valentina Martinez. 2015. "CEQ Master Workbook: Colombia. Version: December 17, 2015." New Orleans, La.: CEQ Data Center, CEQ Institute, Tulane University and Inter-American Development Bank.

Paz Arauco, Veronica, George Gray Molina, Wilson Jimenez Pozo, and Ernesto Yañez Aguilar. 2014. "Explaining Low Redistributive Impact in Bolivia." In *The Redistributive Impact of Taxes and Social Spending in Latin America*, ed. Nora Lustig, Carola Pessino, and John Scott. Special issue, *Public Finance Review* 42(3):326–45.

Reynolds, Morgan, and Eugene Smolensky. 1977. *Public Expenditures, Taxes and the Distribution of Income: The United States, 1950, 1961, 1970*. New York: Academic.

Rossignolo, Dario. 2018. "Taxes, Expenditures, Poverty, and Income Distribution in Argentina." In *Commitment to Equity Handbook. Estimating the Impact of Fiscal Policy on Inequality and Poverty*, ed. Nora Lustig. Washington, D.C.: Brookings Institution Press and New Orleans, La.: CEQ Institute, Tulane University. Advance online version available at: http://www.commitmentoequity.org/publications/handbook.php.

Sahn, David E., and Stephen D. Younger. 2000. "Expenditure Incidence in Africa: Microeconomic Evidence." *Fiscal Studies* 21:329–47.

Sauma, Pablo, and Juan Diego Trejos. 2014. "Gasto publico social, impuestos, redistribucion del ingreso y pobreza en Costa Rica." CEQ Working Paper 18. New Orleans, La.: Center for Inter-American Policy and Research and Department of Economics, Tulane University, and Inter-American Dialogue.

Scott, John. 2014. "Redistributive Impact and Efficiency of Mexico's Fiscal System." In *The Redistributive Impact of Taxes and Social Spending in Latin America*, ed. Nora Lustig, Carola Pessino, and John Scott. Special issue, *Public Finance Review* 42(3):368–90.

UN General Assembly. 2015a. "Transforming Our World: The 2030 Agenda for Sustainable Development." Resolution adopted by the General Assembly on September 25, 2015. Available online at: www.un.org/ga/search/ view_doc.asp? symbol=A/RES/70/1&Lang=E.

——. 2015b. "Addis Ababa Action Agenda of the Third International Conference on Financing for Development." Available online at: www.un.org/esa/ffd/wp-content/ uploads/2015/08/AAAA_Outcome.pdf.

Younger, Stephen D., and Artsvi Khachatryan. 2017. "Fiscal Incidence in Armenia." In *The Distributional Impact of Fiscal Policy: Experience from Developing Countries*, ed. Gabriela Inchauste and Nora Lustig, 43–78. Washington, D.C.: World Bank.

Younger, Stephen, Flora Myamba, and Kenneth Mdadila. 2016. "Fiscal Incidence in Tanzania." *African Development Review* 28(3):264–76.

Younger, Stephen, Eric Osei-Assibey, and Felix Oppong. 2017. "Fiscal Incidence in Ghana." *Review of Development Economics*. Published electronically January 11. doi:10.1111/rode.12299.

CHAPTER 6

Intrahousehold Inequality and Overall Inequality

Ravi Kanbur

The discourse on inequality in the welfare state and more generally has two strands. One strand focuses on inequality between individuals and the poverty of individuals. This is perhaps the fundamental orientation. The standard measures of inequality and poverty are built up from information on well-being at the individual level. The second strand looks at inequality across broadly defined salient groups. For example, total inequality among individuals is often decomposed into "between-group" and "within-group" components. In this second strand, the grouping is sometimes envisaged as merely instrumental for policy, providing a point of intervention, but the objective is still inequality between individuals. At other times, however, the group is seen as having normative significance. Now the inequality decomposition has ethical significance over and above the instrumental.

Consider the decomposition of inequality across groupings defined by race, gender, ethnicity, or caste. Such a decomposition can be used in myriad ways (Kanbur 2006). In terms of positive analysis, a decomposition is the start of a causal analysis, identifying the key determinants of variation in income among individuals. In effect, it is the nonparametric analog of running a parametric regression with dummy variables for the different groupings and with interaction terms across the groupings.

However, the same decomposition can be turned to normative use. Thus one can develop rules for intervention across groups, even if the objective is overall inequality or poverty, if fine differentiation of individuals within a group is very costly. In effect, one is using the group identifier as a targeting device (Kanbur and Tuomala 2016). But one can go further. Following Roemer's (1998) framework, and as implemented by Paes de Barros et al. (2009), one can imbue the inequality accounted for by differences across groups with an ethical significance—it can be identified with "inequality of opportunity."

One grouping that is not usually thought of as such is grouping by household. Each household is a group unto itself, and inequality (and poverty) can be decomposed across these "groups." There are, of course, many more groups now than in the case of gender, say, but the basic analytical structure remains the same. We can develop between-group and within-group decompositions, and we can discuss the consequences of policy across and within groups. Policy, in turn, can treat the household grouping as purely instrumental, the ultimate objective being inequality or poverty across individuals, or it can imbue the household per se with special normative significance.

It is this relationship between inequality within and between households, and overall inequality, that is explored in this paper. I hope to show that this approach provides interesting perspectives on inequality and policy, and indeed raises some difficult questions for policy. Section 1 begins with some analytical preliminaries on inequality and poverty decomposition. Section 2 asks how much we know about within-household and between-household inequality. Section 3 is the first of three sections that conduct exercises to illustrate the significance of the intrahousehold inequality issue. It considers the relationship between growth and poverty reduction through the intrahousehold lens. Section 4 does the same for the debate on minimum wages, and section 5 takes up targeting of public expenditure for poverty reduction. Section 6 presents my conclusions.

1. SOME BASIC ANALYTICS

Before proceeding to empirical and policy discussion, I begin with some basic analytics that will be referred to in the rest of the paper. Let there be n individuals, each of whom can be allocated to G mutually exclusive and exhaustive groups. Let income or consumption be denoted y_{ig} for individual $i = 1, 2, \ldots, n_g$ in group $g = 1, 2, \ldots G$. The population share of group g is written x_g, where the shares obviously sum to 1, and the mean income of group g is written m_g. Overall mean income for the whole population is m. Let overall inequality, a function of all n incomes, be written I. Consider now the case where each individual in a group is given the mean income of that group. We thus have an income distribution with G mass points with income and populations shares given by the

G pairs (m_g, x_g) for $g = 1,2, \ldots G$. This is a distribution in which there is no inequality within each group. What is left is variation due to differences in mean income group across groups. Denote the inequality of this distribution as I_B, the between-group component of overall inequality. Thus the difference between overall inequality and I_B can be called the within-group component of overall inequality, denoted $I_W = I - I_B$.

Obviously, between-group inequality is less than overall inequality. In fact, the distribution where inequality within each group is suppressed by giving each person in a group the mean income of that group is a mean preserving contraction of the overall distribution. Put another way, the overall distribution is a mean preserving spread of the distribution, which only reflects between-group variation. For specific inequality indices, expressions can be derived and amounts calculated for I_W and I_B. A commonly used measure of inequality is the mean log deviation (MLD), which we denote by L. Let MLD within group g be L_g. In this case,

$$L = (1/n) \sum \sum \log(y_{ij}/m)$$
$$= L_W + L_B$$
$$= \sum_g x_g L_g + \sum_g x_g \log(m_g/m) \tag{1}$$

Thus the within-group component of the MLD is simply a weighted sum of the group MLDs. For poverty, a group decomposition can also be carried out for the FGT class of poverty indices P_α (Foster, Greer, and Thorbecke 1984). Let the poverty line be z and the poverty in group g be written $P_{\alpha,g}$

$$P_\alpha = (1/n) \sum \sum [(z - y_{ij})/z]^\alpha \text{ for } z \geq y_{ij}$$
$$= \sum_g x_g P_{\alpha,g} \tag{2}$$

Thus national poverty is a weighted sum of group poverty, the weights being group population shares. The decomposition holds for all values of α. Of particular interest are the cases of $\alpha = 0$, which is the head-count ratio measure of poverty; $\alpha = 1$, which is the income gap measure; and $\alpha = 2$, which is the squared gap measure of poverty.

Notice that P_α is nothing other than the expectation of the function

$$h(y) = [(z - y_{ij})/z]^\alpha \text{ for } z \geq y_{ij}; \text{ 0 otherwise} \tag{3}$$

For $\alpha \geq 1$, $h(y)$ is a convex function of y. But since the distribution with inequality within each group suppressed is a mean preserving contraction of the overall distribution, not only inequality but poverty in the overall distribution will be greater than in the between-group distribution (where every member of a group is given the mean income of that group). When $\alpha = 0$, the function is nether convex not concave, so whether poverty is overstated or understated in this way will depend on the detail of the distribution and the location of the poverty line (Haddad and Kanbur 1990)

The groupings used in the expressions above can be anything, provided they are mutually exclusive and exhaustive. As noted in the introduction, the use of groupings by gender, ethnicity, place of birth, and so on, is quite common in the literature. In this chapter, however, we focus on each household as a group and consider the inequality and poverty consequences of inequality within the household.

2. HOW MUCH INTRAHOUSEHOLD INEQUALITY?

A large literature has developed in the last three decades on intrahousehold allocation of resources. This literature has moved in a mutually supportive parallel fashion with a corresponding literature on alternative models of household decision making. The dominant model of household decision making was, and to some extent still is, the unitary model, where household behavior is represented by the maximization of a single utility function. The household acts as though it had a single budget constraint. Observed variations in consumption across members of the household are then attributed to the budget constraint and the household utility function. Alternatives to the unitary approach include noncooperative models, and cooperative models in which individuals cooperate but bargain over the gains from cooperation. A recent review of this literature is provided in Browning, Chiappori, and Weiss (2014).

In all of the models described earlier, there can be inequality within the household. In the unitary model, this can be attributed to the degree of inequality aversion in the household utility function. In cooperative models, on the other hand, inequality can be attributed to differences in the fallback options in a Nash bargaining game. And there are many variations on these themes. But a central question is the empirical one of how much intrahousehold inequality actually exists within a society, and how do we find this out?

Inequality is the variation of some valued attribute across individuals, as in equation 1. Thus we need to be able to measure this attribute across all individuals, including within a household. The standard instrument for collecting such information is the household survey. As the name suggests, the survey is administered to households who have been selected through appropriate stratified random-sampling methods, usually drawn from census lists. The survey questionnaire consists of various modules, including those that collect information on household-level consumption expenditures, and at the individual level with questions on demographic attributes, health, education, anthropometric variables, and so on. Some of these variables can then be analyzed for inequality.

The standard headline measures of money metric inequality and poverty are very important in our analytical and policy discourse. They are based on the consumption/expenditure modules of the household survey. These modules give us a household-level total expenditure. But for inequality and poverty, we need individual-level information. How is this accomplished? For the most part, in official statistics and especially in developing countries, we generate individual-level distributions by assuming that household-level expenditure is equally divided among individuals in the household. Thus intrahousehold inequality is assumed to be zero. How robust are the poverty and inequality numbers to the assumption that expenditures are distributed equally within the household? The literature makes several, admittedly imperfect, attempts to answer this question, and these attempts (there are very few of them), from different angles and perspectives, are collected together here. They provide useful information and a useful corrective to the standard method, where the intrahousehold component of expenditure inequality is set to zero, not so much on the basis of argumentation or evidence, but as an assumption.

A leading example of the use of individual-level data from household surveys is the use of the body mass index (BMI) to assess intrahousehold inequality:

> This paper examines the relationship between level of well-being and inequality at inter-country and intra-household levels, using individuals' body mass index (BMI) rather than income as the indicator of well-being. BMI is useful for these purposes because (1) it is measured at the individual rather than household level; (2) it reflects command over food, but also non-food resources that affect health status like sanitary conditions and labor saving technologies; (3) it accounts for caloric consumption relative to needs; (4) it is easily measured; and (5) any measurement error is likely to be random. . . . Perhaps the most striking finding in the paper is that about half of total BMI inequality at the country level is within households. Thus, standard measures of inequality that use household-level data may drastically understate true inequality. (Sahn and Younger, 2009, S13)

For the mean log deviation measure of inequality in equation 1, Sahn and Younger (2009, S32) find that, for fourteen household surveys across seven countries, intrahousehold inequality accounts for between 55 percent and 66 percent of total inequality: "If we did not take into account the 'within' household component of total inequality in the seven countries examined, country inequality would have been reduced by more than half, and as much as two-thirds in the case of Cote d'Ivoire."

A similar point was made in an earlier paper by Haddad and Kanbur (1990), using data on individual-level food intake from a small purposely designed household survey in the Philippines. Here individual food intake was first converted to calories and then to a calorie adequacy ratio using individual-specific calorie requirements for the Philippines for different demographic groups. A synthetic distribution was then constructed in which the total caloric intake of a household was allocated pro rata per requirements within the household. This is, in fact, the distribution we would have if we only had food intake information at the household level, which is the case for most national-level household surveys. Haddad and Kanbur (1990) then compared actual inequality and poverty (using as the poverty line a calorie adequacy ratio of 1) with the inequality and poverty in the synthetic distribution:

> Our theoretical analysis suggested that potentially serious errors could be made so far as the *levels* of inequality . . . are concerned. Empirically, we showed that this is indeed the case—the errors are of the order of 30 percent or more. (Haddad and Kanbur 1990, 879)

In a similar vein, Malghan and Swaminathan (2016) use Luxembourg Income Study data for a range of countries and years, restricting the samples to "households where the head is living with a partner." They find that "for a wide range of countries and over four decades, we show that at least 30 per cent of total inequality is attributable to inequality within the household" (1).

Most recently, De Vreyer and Lambert (2016) have used a survey for Senegal that allows consumption expenditures to be collected within the household to investigate the extent of intrahousehold inequality. Their findings on inequality and poverty are instructive:

> We show that within household inequality accounts for as much as 15 percent of total inequality in Senegal. One of the consequences of such unequal repartition of resources within households is the potential

existence of "invisible poor" in households classified as non-poor. Our assessment is that as many as 12.5 percent of the poor individuals live in non-poor households. They are therefore ignored when the poverty status of the household is supposed to apply uniformly to all household members. This could have important consequences for the effectiveness of anti-poverty policies. (De Vreyer and Lambert 2016, 19)

A more recent approach to measurement of intrahousehold inequality is to estimate a collective model of intrahousehold resource allocation, to recover the relevant sharing parameters from the model, and thus get at intrahousehold inequality in consumption. Thus Lise and Seitz (2011, 352) conclude their investigation into UK data as follows:

> The large dispersion in incomes within the household are highly inconsistent with equal division of consumption. When equal division is relaxed, we estimate that there is substantial inequality within the household. This suggests previous work underestimates the level of individual consumption inequality by between 25 percent and 50 percent.

Overall, then, a picture emerges of significant understatement of inequality when intrahousehold inequality is ignored. But our standard household survey–based measures of consumption inequality do precisely that. All of the above are special exercises—using either an anthropometric measure of well-being, a detailed survey on individual food intake in a small number of households, or a full estimation of a household allocation model. However, our headline measures of inequality, especially in developing countries, are not the product of any of these types of exercises. The consumption or expenditure data they collect is at the household level only, and conversion to the individual level essentially involves dividing the household total by the number of (sometimes equivalized and sometimes not) individuals in the household. Intrahousehold inequality is thus suppressed, and overall inequality is understated by a significant but unknown amount.

Technically, the true distribution across individuals is a mean preserving spread of the distribution, where intrahousehold inequality is assumed to be zero. Using this, Haddad and Kanbur (1990) argue that the FGT class of poverty indices is also understated for $\alpha \geq 1$, since the poverty index is the expectation of a convex function. When $\alpha = 0$, the ranking is no longer unambiguous and depends on the shape of the distribution and the location of the poverty line; it is an empirical question.[1] Haddad and

Kanbur (1990) and De Vreyer and Lambert (2016) do find understatement of poverty.[2] Of course, intrahousehold inequality also means that poor individuals are found in non-poor households, the extent of which has been quantified most recently by Brown, Ravallion, and Van De Walle (2017, 22), who find that in a study of thirty countries in sub-Saharan Africa, "about three-quarters of underweight women and undernourished children are not found in the poorest 20 percent of households."

3. EXERCISE 1: GROWTH, POVERTY REDUCTION, AND INEQUALITY

How far wrong do we go by ignoring intrahousehold inequality in our standard national-level analysis of inequality? As noted earlier, in terms of levels, we can be off by at least 25 percent, and perhaps as much as 65 percent. But there is another error we can commit in a dynamic setting, which perhaps underlies a disconnect between the trends of official data on poverty and public sentiments on the perceived trend of poverty.

In the early 1990s, I was the director of the World Bank's field office in Ghana, having previously worked on and analyzed poverty and poverty trends in Ghana through the Ghana Living Standards Measurement Survey (Boateng et al. 1992). Throughout the late 1980s and the 1990s, official data showed that Ghana had seen poverty reduction since the start of the structural adjustment program in the mid-1980s. Yet this was not the perception on the ground, and I can attest to this, having presented the official statistical view multiple times in multiple venues in the country.

This led me to think about a range of reasons for the disconnect, which I set out in my paper on economic policy, distribution, and poverty (Kanbur 2001). These included, for example, the practice in official data and in economics more generally to present the number of poor divided by total population—the head-count ratio or the poverty rate or poverty incidence—rather than the absolute number of poor. I argued that the particularly axiom in Sen (1976) that led to normalization by population size was not necessarily appropriate. In societies with high population growth, the absolute number of poor could increase at the same time as the poverty incidence fell. Thus a civil society organization dealing with the poor would see an increase in its activities even as officials pronounced that poverty was falling! I argued for presentation of the absolute number of poor alongside the poverty rate, which is now much more common, and developed analysis of poverty measurement without the relevant Sen axiom (Chakravarty, Kanbur, and Mukherjee 2006).

But there was one reason for the disconnect that I did not fully appreciate at that time and set out in a later paper (Kanbur 2010). And this reason is related to a well-known construct in the literature—the growth elasticity of poverty reduction (Bourguignon 2003). This is the percentage change in poverty for each percent increase in mean income, this increase happening in distribution-neutral terms (i.e., each income increasing at the same rate as the mean). This distribution-neutral impact of growth on poverty is one component of decomposing poverty change into a part attributable to growth (change in mean) and a part attributable to distributional change. But what is interesting is that the (distribution-neutral) growth elasticity of poverty reduction depends on the *level* of inequality in the distribution. For the head-count ratio, and if the distribution is lognormal, then Bourguignon (2003) shows that the elasticity ε can be written as

$$\varepsilon = (1/\sigma)\ \lambda\{[\log(z/m)]/\sigma + \sigma/2\} \tag{4}$$

where z is the poverty line, m is mean income, σ is the standard deviation of log income, and $\lambda\{\ \}$ is the Mills ratio of the standard normal distribution. Bourguignon's (2003) figure 3 gives a feel for the quantitative magnitudes involved: "the growth elasticity is around 3 if inequality is low—i.e. a Gini coefficient around .3—but it is only 2 if the Gini coefficient is around the more common value of .4." That figure shows more generally that for a range of plausible parameter values, the growth elasticity is an increasing function of inequality measured by σ. Bourguignon (2003) derives similar expressions for other measures of poverty in the FGT class.

Equation 4 has been an entry point in the literature to discussions of why the impact of growth on poverty reduction varies across countries, which it does empirically. One explanation is that, as shown in the equation, the poverty reduction impact of distribution-neutral growth depends on the level of inequality, because greater inequality means that the incremental fruits of growth flow less to the lower tail of the distribution. Equation 4 formalizes the intuition for a particular distributional structure. A large empirical literature has thus grown up linking inequality to poverty reduction in this way.

But now consider the following argument. We know that the official method of calculating inequality, which ignores intrahousehold inequality, understates the level of inequality by at least a factor of a third, which means that it overstates the growth elasticity of poverty reduction by a factor of over a half, from the expression above and Bourguignon's (2003)

Figure 3. The variation in σ is not now one across countries, but one between the official distribution and the actual distribution of consumption. Thus the beneficial effects of growth for poverty reduction is overstated by our standard methods and our standard data by as much as 50 percent.

It is, of course, too much to ask that standard national-level household surveys collect individual-level consumption data and provide us with the "true" distribution of consumption, from which we can calculate actual inequality and poverty as our headline statistics. There are conceptual and empirical issues associated with allocating the consumption value of household public goods—How are we to discern the benefits of a bicycle to each different member of the household? This is in principle doable with a more detailed survey module, but outside the realm of practical feasibility. Even for private consumption items like food, for which there are no conceptual issues, it would require a much thicker questionnaire to get at individual-level data. It would seem that, for developing countries at least, we will have to make do with standard household surveys that collect consumption and expenditure data at the household level.

What is one to do? The answer is twofold. First, we should go on doing specialized analyses like the ones discussed at the start of this section, analyses involving nonconsumption measures of well-being, which are easily collected at the individual level, or small-scale specialized surveys that collect information on individual-level consumption, or estimates of structural models of intrahousehold allocation. These will continue to update the broad quantitative magnitude of the errors we make when we ignore intrahousehold inequality in estimating overall inequality and poverty. Second, however, we should carry around with us a rule of thumb correction for official inequality measures. We have seen that the error can range from one-third to two-thirds. We might, therefore, start by using a minimal correction factor of one-third for any official inequality measure to take account of intrahousehold inequality.

4. EXERCISE 2: MINIMUM WAGES AND POVERTY

On the face of it, the discourses on intrahousehold inequality and minimum wages seem to have no connection to each other. The minimum wage discourse is associated with labor markets, the elasticity of labor demand, whether the labor market is competitive or monopsonistic, enforcement of minimum wages, and so on (see, for example, Basu, Chau, and Kanbur 2010; Bhorat, Kanbur, and Mayet 2012). Typically, protagonists divide into camps that either support minimum wages because of their potential impact on the wages of the working poor or oppose them because of their possible effects in increasing unemployment. The first group argues for the poverty-reducing impact of minimum wages; the second group, of course, highlights the poverty-increasing consequences of higher unemployment.

But workers, whether employed or unemployed, do not in general live in isolation. Thus a wage (or lack of it) does not necessarily translate directly into individual consumption. When workers live in households, it is the intrahousehold allocation process that determines consumption outcomes for them and for nonearners within the household. Intrahousehold inequality thus plays a key role in determining the inequality and poverty impact of an increase in the minimum wage. The worker composition of households has been used in different ways in the minimum wage debate. In the United States, for example, it has been argued that those who would benefit from a minimum wage tend not to live in poverty households (Burkhauser 2015). Analysis for South Africa shows complex patterns of employment and unemployment:

> Only 16 percent of working age adults in quintile 1 are employed, while in quintile 5 this percentage rises to 75 percent. This suggests that high rates of unemployment and low rates of employment are at the core of the high levels of observed household poverty levels. . . . It is additionally clear that among poor households, the number of people reliant on each employed person is high. (Bhorat et al. 2016, 39–40)

The employment composition patterns across households have been prominent in policy debates in South Africa. The first part of the findings above is used in the usual way to suggest that raising the minimum wage will not necessarily have a big impact on poverty, since unemployment, not employment, is a key characteristic of the poor, and introducing or raising minimum wages may increase unemployment (whether it does so or not is an empirical question; see Bhorat, Kanbur, and Mayet 2013). But the second part has been used in policy debates, for example, by trade union organizations like COSATU in South Africa, to make the following informal argument: poor households depend on the earnings of a small number of workers, and raising the wage of the employed through minimum wage regulation will reduce poverty.

The second of these arguments can be developed as follows in intuitive fashion. Take a competitive labor market with homogeneous labor that initially clears at some low wage. A minimum wage is now introduced that raises the wage but lowers employment and creates unemployment. Suppose that all workers in the country form a giant national household and that all income is equally shared between employed and unemployed. For simplicity, think of the case where these are the only individuals in society. Then it should be clear that the consumption of each individual goes up when the total wage bill goes up, irrespective of the employment and unemployment levels associated with any wage rate. Further, if the elasticity of labor demand is less than one, which is empirically the case almost universally (in South Africa the conventional number referred to in debates is 0.7), then as the wage rises so does the total wage bill. In this case, therefore, raising the minimum wage will raise consumption of all workers and thus tend to reduce poverty if the previous consumption level was below the poverty line.

Of course if we take the other extreme and assume no income sharing at all between employed and unemployed, then introducing or raising the minimum wage will increase the number of people at very low consumption, and this is to be balanced against the higher consumption of the now smaller number of employed. The net effect on poverty will depend where exactly the poverty line lies in relation to the consumption of the unemployed and that of the employed. If it lies between the two, this will rationalize the view taken on one side of the debate, that higher minimum wages will increase poverty. But the central point is that the degree of income sharing between employed and unemployed turns out to be central to the debate. This point is developed formally in Fields and Kanbur (2007, using the FGT class of poverty indices in equation 2). For the case of the "national household," clearly the poverty impact of a minimum wage ranges from adverse when there is no income sharing to beneficial when there is perfect income sharing. The analysis is then extended to the case where there is not a national household, but the nation is made up of two-person households. Each member of a household can be employed or unemployed with probability given by the national employment and unemployment rates, e and $1 - e$, respectively. There are thus three types of households. A fraction e^2 of individuals are in households where both are employed; a fraction $(1 - e)^2$ of individuals are in households where both are unemployed; and a fraction $2e(1 - e)$ of individuals are in households where one person is employed and the other is unemployed. Given an income-sharing rule for members of the household, we can thus derive a national consumption distribution and, given a poverty line, the poverty index. Changes in poverty can then be tracked as the minimum wage changes and the associated national employment rate changes with it. The overall conclusion of the Fields and Kanbur (2007, 146) analysis is as follows:

> The results of this paper lead us to a more nuanced view about minimum wages than is commonly found in the literature. A higher minimum wage does not necessarily increase poverty because of the unemployment it creates. On the other hand, a higher minimum wage does not necessarily reduce poverty simply because it might increase total labor income, and some of this increased income is shared with the unemployed, either through family sharing or through social sharing. Thus the "standard labor economist's view" and the "standard trade unionist's view" are both simplistic. Not only does the truth lie somewhere in between, but it can be characterized precisely in terms of empirically observable parameters.

And a key parameter is the extent of income sharing within the household. Of course, if the labor market is not competitive but is monopsonistic, a minimum wage will increase employment, provided it is not set too high. Similarly, if the higher wage income as the result of the minimum wage has macroeconomic Keynesian beneficial effects, employment will increase. These beneficial impacts on employment will surely have beneficial impacts on poverty, but the detailed impacts will once again depend on the specifics of intrahousehold allocation of the gains from wage and from employment.

5. EXERCISE 3: TARGETING OF PUBLIC PROGRAMS

Intrahousehold issues are prominent in the design of transfer programs. The old argument in the United Kingdom between whether child benefit should be given through the tax system (essentially through the male paycheck) or through the benefit system (say picked up at the post office by the mother) reflects these concerns. This is the "wallet versus purse" choice faced by policy implementers. In the developing country context, and also in developed countries, the intrahousehold adjustment following on from nutritional supplements given at school are of great concern. What good is an extra glass of milk at school if the child gets one less glass of milk at home as a result? There is a large literature on intrahousehold "flypaper effects"—to what extent does the transfer given to an individual "stick" to that individual once intrahousehold (re)allocation processes have had their sway? Early contributions to the literature include Haddad and Kanbur (1992, 1993). Just two recent papers for developing countries in this spirit are Islam and Hoddinott (2009) and Shi (2012).

These policy issues are linked closely to the literature on unitary versus nonunitary models of the household. If households were unitary, with an integrated budget constraint, it would not matter to whom the resources from the public program were targeted. But there is now considerable evidence against the unitary model, with the implication that who has the transfer matters (see Alderman et al. 1995; Browning, Chiappori, and Weiss 2014). The detail of intrahousehold transfers and adjustments thus needs to be understood for a welfare state policy whose objective is to reduce inequality among individuals and the deprivation of individuals. This is not the place to delve into the intricacies of the targeting literature as applied to intrahousehold issues. Haddad and Kanbur (1993), for example, ask how far wrong we go in targeting for nutritional deficiency if we assume that the only inequality is that between household and assume (erroneously) that there is no intrahousehold inequality. Their numerical calculations show that there is considerable gain to be had by adding information on intrahousehold inequality.

Two questions have not, however, been fully explored in this literature. First, keeping the objective of maximizing social welfare defined on individual well-being, is intrahousehold redistribution a more potent instrument for achieving impact on social welfare than interhousehold redistribution? If we had costless redistribution instruments but could choose only one—intrahousehold or interhousehold—which would we choose? The answer depends on which of these two components makes the greater contribution to overall inequality between individuals. The empirical findings discussed in section 2 suggest a split ranging from one-third/two-thirds to two-thirds/one-third. It is, then, a country-specific empirical matter. But if we take the midpoint of this range, half/half, it would seem that focusing on and eliminating one or the other would make an equal contribution to reducing overall inequality.

However, our redistributive instruments are not perfect, nor are they costless. Direct redistribution within a household is not easy to effect. In developed countries, if husband and wife choose to elect for separate taxation, then income taxes could in principle be used to differentiate within a household. But if most households choose to elect household-level taxation, then this instrument is better at achieving between-household redistribution than within-household redistribution. Expenditure instruments such as free school meals could in principle be targeted differentially by age and gender and thus affect intrahousehold inequality, but (1) this effect will depend on intrahousehold reallocations after the transfer, and (2) these instruments will also have interhousehold effects. Thus, although we have indirect discussions of this question in the literature, in my view it remains an open area of research.

The second question is as follows: Moving beyond the instrumental, what is the normative legitimacy of a welfare state getting deep into intrahousehold redistribution issues? At what point should such intervention stop? Notice that similar questions arise in the context of global redistribution. If the objective is reducing global inequality (or poverty), there is clearly a possible instrumental role for transfers to, say, poorer countries. But there are deeper philosophical debates between, for example, global Rawlsians and Rawls himself, on the nature of moral responsibility toward the poor in non-poor nations (Kanbur and Sumner 2012).

The issue has a family resemblance to discussions of legitimate and illegitimate realms of redistribution. Thus the literature inspired by Roemer (1998) deems it legitimate to address inequality in outcomes attributable to circumstance—factors outside an individual's control—and effort—factors an individual controls. For within-household inequality of consumption, what is legitimate and what is not in the "equality of opportunity" frame depends on the specific model we have in mind for intrahousehold allocation. If it is a unitary model, then presumably it is all determined by the household utility function, which may be exogenous to everybody except perhaps the patriarch, who would have to be identified. If, on the other hand, it is a collective model, then how do we apply the frame? In the case of adults, on the one hand they choose to participate in the collective enterprise, but on the other hand the distribution of surplus from this enterprise is determined by their outside option, which may be thought of as exogenous to them. For children, of course, we would be right in specifying everything as exogenous.

In my view, progressives and egalitarians have not addressed the normative question of the legitimacy of intrahousehold interventions sufficiently. It is an area open for clarification and development.

6. CONCLUSION

To conclude briefly, assessing the specific contribution of intrahousehold inequality to standard measures of overall inequality and poverty is an underdeveloped area for research and policy analysis. However, intrahousehold inequality is clearly important. Neglecting it could lead to (1) an understatement of inequality and an overstatement of the impact of growth on poverty reduction; (2) a misstatement of the potential impact of minimum wage policies on poverty; and (3) misdesign of transfer policies to reduce inequality and poverty. Any discussion of the welfare state cannot afford to ignore intrahousehold inequality.

NOTES

This chapter is based on a presentation to the Conference on the Welfare State and the Fight Against Inequality, Columbia University, November 8–9, 2015.

1. A comprehensive analysis of the effect of "measurement error" on broad classes of social welfare functions is provided in Cheshire and Schluter (2002).

2. De Vreyer and Lambert (2016, 12) state: "The results show that the aggregated approach leads to an underestimation of poverty rates by 0.3 to 5.5 percentage points, depending on the poverty line and the residential area. This corresponds to an underestimation of the prevalence of poverty by 7.3 percent (national poverty line) and 10.4 percent (food poverty line) at the national level. The underestimation is particularly severe in Dakar (above 15 percent), as could have been expected given the especially high within household inequality in that area."

REFERENCES

Alderman, Harold, Pierre-Andre Chiappori, Lawrence Haddad, John Hoddinott, and Ravi Kanbur. 1995. "Unitary Versus Collective Models of the Household: Is It Time to Shift the Burden of Proof?" *World Bank Research Observer* 10(1):1–19.

Basu, Arnab, Nancy Chau, and Ravi Kanbur. 2010. "Turning a Blind Eye: Costly Enforcement, Credible Commitment and Minimum Wage Laws." *Economic Journal* 120(March):244–69.

Bhorat, Haroon, Tara Caetano, Benjamin Jourdan, Ravi Kanbur, Christopher Rooney, Benjamin Stanwix, and Ingrid Woolard. 2016. "Investigating the Feasibility of a Minimum Wage for South Africa." Development Policy Research Unit, School of Economics, University of Cape Town, Cape Town, South Africa. Retrieved from: www.dpru.uct.ac.za/sites/default/files/image_tool/images/36/News_articles /NMW%20Report_final.pdf.

Bhorat, Haroon, Ravi Kanbur, and Natasha Mayet. 2012. "Minimum Wage Violation in South Africa." *International Labour Review* 151(3):277–87.

———. 2013. "The Impact of Sectoral Minimum Wage Laws on Employment, Wages and Hours of Work in South Africa." *IZA Journal of Labor and Development* 2(1):1–27.

Boateng, E. Oti, K. Ewusi, R. Kanbur, and A. McKay. 1992. "A Poverty Profile for Ghana, 1987–88." *Journal of African Economies* 1(1):25–58.

Bourguignon, F. 2003. "The Growth Elasticity of Poverty Reduction: Explaining Heterogeneity Across Countries and Time Periods." In *Inequality and Growth: Theory and Policy Implications*, ed. T. S. Eicher and S. J. Turnovsky, chaps. 1, 3–27. Cambridge: MIT Press.

Brown, Caitlin, Martin Ravallion, and Dominique Van De Walle. 2017. "Are Poor Individuals Mainly Found in Poor Households? Evidence Using Nutrition Data for Africa." World Bank Policy Research Working Paper No. 8001. World Bank Group, Washington, D.C.

Browning, Martin, Pierre-Andre Chiappori, and Yoram Weiss. 2014. *Economics of the Family*. Cambridge: Cambridge University Press.

Burkhauser, Richard V. 2015. "The Minimum Wage Versus the Earned Income Tax Credit for Reducing Poverty." *IZA World of Labor: Evidence-Based Policy Making*, doi: 10.15185/izaw ol.153.

Chakravarty, S., R. Kanbur, and D. Mukherjee. 2006. "Population Growth and Poverty Measurement." *Social Choice and Welfare* 26(3):471–83.

Cheshire, Andrew, and Christian Schluter. 2002. "Welfare Measurement and Measurement Error." *Review of Economic Studies* 69:357–78.

De Vreyer, Philippe, and Sylvie Lambert. 2016. "Intrahousehold Inequalities and Poverty in Senegal." Mimeo, Paris School of Economics.

Fields, Gary, and Ravi Kanbur. 2007. "Minimum Wages and Poverty with Income Sharing." *Journal of Economic Inequality* 5(2):135–47.

Foster, J., J. Greer, and E. Thorbecke. 1984. "A Class of Decomposable Poverty Measures." *Econometrica* 52(3):761–76.

Haddad, Lawrence, and Ravi Kanbur. 1990. "How Serious Is the Neglect of Intra-Household Inequality?" *Economic Journal* 100(September):866–81.

———. 1992. "Intrahousehold Inequality and the Theory of Targeting." *European Economic Review* 36(2–3):372–78.

———. 1993. "The Value of Intrahousehold Survey Data for Age-Based Nutritional Targeting." *Annales d'Economie et de Statistique* 29:65–81.

Islam, Mahnaz, and John Hoddinott. 2009. "Evidence of Intrahousehold Flypaper Effects from a Nutrition Intervention in Rural Guatemala." *Economic Development and Cultural Change* 57(2):215–38.

Kanbur, Ravi. 2001. "Economic Policy, Distribution and Poverty: The Nature of Disagreements." *World Development* 29(6):1083–94.

———. 2006. "The Policy Significance of Inequality Decompositions." *Journal of Economic Inequality* 4(3):367–74.

———. 2010. "Globalization, Growth and Distribution: Framing the Questions." In *Equity in a Globalizing World*, eds. Ravi Kanbur and A. Michael Spence, 41–70. Washington, D.C.: World Bank.

Kanbur, Ravi, and Andy Sumner. 2012. "Poor Countries or Poor People? Development Assistance and the New Geography of Global Poverty." *Journal of International Development* 24(6):686–95.

Kanbur, Ravi, and Matti Tuomala. 2016. "Groupings and the Gains from Targeting." *Research in Economics* 70:53–63.

Lise, Jeremy, and Shannon Seitz. 2011. "Consumption Inequality and Intrahousehold Allocations." *Review of Economic Studies* 78(1):328–55.

Malghan, Deepak, and Hema Swaminathan. 2016. "What Is the Contribution of Intra-household Inequality to Overall Income Inequality? Evidence from Global Data, 1973–2013." LIS Working Paper Series, No. 679.

Paes de Barros, R., F. H. G. Ferreira, J. R. M. Vega, J. C. Saavedra, M. De Carvalho, S. Franco, S. Freije-Rodriguez, and J. Gignoux. 2009. *Measuring Inequality of Opportunities in Latin America and the Caribbean*. Washington, D.C.: World Bank.

Roemer J. E. 1998. *Equality of Opportunity*. Cambridge: Harvard University Press.

Sahn, David, and Stephen D. Younger. 2009. "Measuring Intra-Household Inequality: Explorations Using the Body Mass Index." *Health Economics* 18(S1):S13–S36.

Sen, Amartya K. 1976. "Poverty: An Ordinal Approach to Measurement." *Econometrica* 44:219–31.

Shi, Xinzheng. 2012. "Does an Intra-household Flypaper Effect Exist? Evidence from the Educational Fee Reduction Reform in Rural China." *Journal of Development Economics* 99(2):459–73.

CHAPTER 7

Human Capital, Inequality, and Growth

Torben M. Andersen

The income distribution may then be derived from the distribution of qualifications required and qualifications available. Income could become almost equal if there is no tension between the two distributions. People would not need to be of equal productive quality in order to attain this near-equality of incomes.

Tinbergen (1972, 256).

Inequality has displayed an increasing trend in many countries for some decades. Not only has the income distribution widened, but some groups have even experienced declining real incomes. Gains from growth became more unequally distributed in the period prior to the financial crisis, and the crisis has further increased inequality in a number of countries. These developments raise many questions surrounding both the causes and the policy implications.

Globalization and technological changes are frequently given as reasons for this trending increase in inequality. While both are usually associated with aggregate gains, their development clearly demonstrates that there are both winners and losers. Looking forward, it is crucial to consider the scope for a more equitable distribution of the net gains.

These developments also raise questions on policy. Have policies become less redistributive in recent years, implying that the difference between the winners and losers has widened? Structural reforms to improve the incentive structure and deregulation to strengthen competition have been a major focus. But has there been a bias in this process that disregards the implications in the equity dimension, or has the political weighting of equity relative to efficiency changed? It is also possible that policy outcomes have changed because the costs of redistributive policies have increased. This has ties to globalization, which is often taken to make it more difficult and costly to maintain tax-financed activities, particularly traditional redistribution policies. The constrained fiscal space (high debt and looming sustainability problems) is a further restraint in many countries.

These trends have raised concerns in many quarters (for example, the World Economic Forum, Organisation for Economic Co-operation and Development [OECD], International Monetary Fund, and EU Commission) that the social balance may be affected adversely, with both political and economic consequences.[1] Looking to the future, the question is what policy makers can do to turn the trend, especially if public finances are strained. This chapter discusses factors determining income distribution and considers policy options to counteract the tendency toward increasing inequality and its link to economic growth.

Much of the traditional policy discussion focuses on how to repair an unjust distribution of market incomes via taxes and transfers (passive redistribution). While important, this perspective is too narrow. First, countries with low levels of inequality in disposable incomes also tend to have low inequality in market incomes. Although they also redistribute, this is quantitatively not more important than the more equal distribution of market income in accounting for their low inequality. This points to the importance of considering the factors framing the distribution of market incomes and how it can be affected (active redistribution). Second, given strained public finances and the potential disincentive effects of passive forms of redistribution, there is a need to consider redistribution policies in a broader perspective. Finally, market inefficiencies should be considered carefully. It is a standard view that redistribution comes at the cost of distorted incentives having efficiency costs, implying a trade-off between efficiency and equity. In the presence of market imperfections, these issues become more nuanced, since there may be efficiency arguments for policies that also can be justified on equity grounds. It thus becomes important to consider market imperfections and their policy implications carefully.

This chapter focuses primarily on the distribution of labor income, and not on the functional distribution between labor and capital,[2] with a primary focus on the lower end of the income distribution, and what can be done to improve the position for this demographic. The chapter therefore takes a labor market perspective. The trends driven by globalization and technological changes may be interpreted as affecting both the level and composition of labor demand. For a given labor supply, this inevitably shows up in wages and employment, the exact division depending on labor market institutions. It follows that the consequences of these changes to labor demand can be counteracted by changes in labor supply. This is precisely the essence of the quote by Tinbergen at the beginning of the chapter. Labor supply depends on many factors, among which human capital, and consequently education, is crucial. This emphasizes that questions of inequality and policies to reduce it should not only be concerned with traditional redistribution policies (passive redistribution) but should also involve education and labor market policies determining the level and distribution of qualifications and skills (active redistribution). The distinction between passive versus active distribution policies is at the center of the following discussion.

The chapter is organized as follows. Section 1 presents a very stylized framework useful for a discussion of some key issues related to inequality and its driving forces. This framework provides a starting point for a brief overview of some important recent trends. Section 2 provides a critical discussion of the empirical evidence on inequality and growth and the possible causal links between the two. The subsequent discussion focuses on mechanisms through which inequality can influence growth due to market imperfections. Section 3 considers the role of capital market imperfections and social barriers for educational choices and outcomes, and section 4 offers some concluding remarks.

1. A SIMPLE FRAMEWORK AND SOME STYLIZED FACTS

There is a large empirical literature documenting the developments in inequality from both single-country and comparative perspectives; see, for example, Atkinson and Morelli (2011), OECD (2012a), and Roine and Waldenström (2015). It is beyond the scope of this chapter to present all this evidence; instead, some key stylized facts important to the following discussion are presented.

To organize the discussion, it is useful to think of a trinity linking the distribution of[3]

- qualifications
- market incomes
- disposable income

The distribution of qualifications is an important factor in determining the distribution of market incomes. The distribution of wages, and therefore market incomes, is formed via the interaction between labor demand

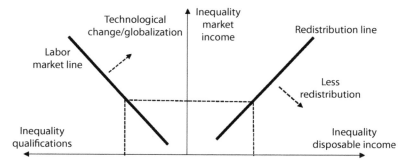

Figure 7.1   Linkage between the distribution of human capital, market incomes, and disposable incomes.

and supply. Via taxes and transfers, this determines the distribution of disposable incomes.

All theories of wage distribution attribute a role to relative supplies and demands. If labor demand increases (decreases) for a particular type of labor, its relative position will improve (deteriorate). For a given structure of labor demand, a more unequal distribution of qualifications will under general conditions lead to a more unequal distribution of market incomes (cf. the "labor market line" in figure 7.1.). Clearly, the precise relation depends on labor market institutions, and there are other reasons for wage differences than differences in qualifications, which are neglected here to simplify.

Disposable incomes are given as market incomes less taxes and plus transfers. For a given tax-transfer scheme, it follows that a more unequal distribution of market incomes will lead to a more unequal distribution of disposable incomes (cf. the "redistribution line" in figure 7.1). The less extensive the redistribution, the farther to the right the redistribution line will be positioned.

Relations like the ones depicted in figure 7.1 may be expected to hold for a given country, that is, for given structures, institutions, and policies. Figure 7.2 takes a very crude approach by plotting cross-country evidence on inequality in qualifications, market incomes, and disposable incomes. It is striking that even with such a bold approach, disregarding all sorts of control variables, a clear pattern appears in accordance with figure 7.1. The countries having the most equal distribution of qualifications tend to have the most equal distribution of market incomes, and the countries

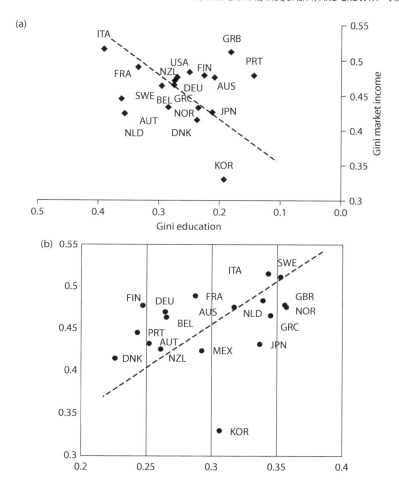

Figure 7.2   Inequality—education, market incomes (a); disposable incomes, OECD countries (b).

Note: Inequality in disposable income and market income measured by the Gini coefficient. Inequality in education measured by the coefficient of variation for test of literacy and numeracy. Data apply to 2012.

Source: Based on data from www.oecd-ilibrary.org and http://piaacdataexplorer.oecd.org.

with the most equal distribution of market incomes tend to have the most equal distribution of disposable incomes.

This basic reasoning based on the stylized facts leads to two key observations. First, from a policy perspective, low inequality in disposable income may be achieved either via traditional redistribution policies (passive redistribution), attempting to repair the inequality in market income, or via education and labor market policies ensuring a more equal distribution of qualifications (active redistribution). Second, the discussion about technological changes and globalization can be translated to a shift in the "labor market line" to the northwest; that is, for a given distribution of qualifications, inequality in market incomes, and therefore disposable incomes, increases for given redistribution policies. If redistribution policies at the same time become less generous, this will further increase income inequality.

The Nordic countries are often highlighted for having achieved both a high per capita income level and a relatively low inequality of income. This is usually attributed to the more generous welfare state, and it is a fact that the welfare state is extended in the Nordic countries (total public expenditure amounts to about 50 percent of GDP compared with the OECD average of about 40 percent). However, this does not imply that the low inequality in the Nordic countries is achieved solely via the classical passive form of redistribution policies considered in textbooks. To see this, we exploit the fact that the difference in the Gini coefficient from the OECD average can be decomposed,[4] in part due to inequality in market incomes and in part due to redistribution.[5]

Figure 7.3 reports the results of such a decomposition for a selection of OECD countries. It is seen that the lower inequality in disposable income in the Nordic countries included (Norway, Denmark, and Sweden) is attributable both to lower inequality in market incomes and more redistribution (roughly a 50–50 split). While redistribution is important in the Nordic countries, it is equally important that the distribution of market incomes displays comparatively low inequality.

Other countries, such as the United States, have more inequality in disposable incomes, due to both more unequally distributed market incomes and less redistributive policies. Some countries, such as Germany, France, and Italy, have more inequality in market incomes than the average, but redistribution counteracts the effect on disposable income. Conversely, Canada and New Zealand have less inequality in market incomes, but then tend to redistribute less than the average.

INEQUALITY IN MARKET INCOMES

Turning to inequality in market incomes, both the wage and the employment side are important. Various studies (see, for example, Atkinson and

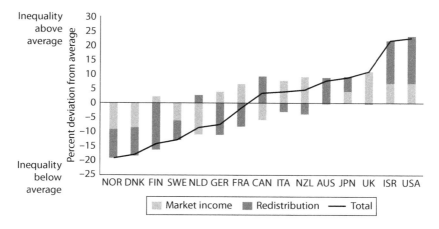

Figure 7.3   Decomposition of difference in inequality from OECD average.

Note: The graph shows how much the Gini coefficient deviates in percent from the OECD average (for countries included in the graph) and decomposes this into the part coming from inequality in market incomes deviating from the OECD average and the part coming from redistribution deviating from the OECD average. Redistribution is measured as the percent reduction in the Gini coefficient measured over market and disposable income, respectively. Negative values indicate contribution to inequality below average, and positive values indicate contribution to inequality above average. Data apply to 2014.

Source: Author's calculations based on data from www.oecd-ilibrary.org.

Morelli 2011; OECD 2012a) have documented a trend toward wider wage inequality. Figure 7.4 illustrates the trends by decile ratios, capturing both developments at the bottom and top of the wage distribution. While there are country differences, there is a trend increase in the D5/D1 and the D9/D1 ratios. The lower end of the wage distribution is losing ground to the middle, and the middle is losing ground to the top.

That labor market options are closely related to education is well documented (see, for example, OECD 2014).[6] There is a strong educational gradient in employment possibilities. Figure 7.5 displays average employment rates for low, medium, and high levels of education for OECD countries, as well as the maximum and minimum value observed in any country. While the overall level of employment in a particular country depends on various institutional policies, it is striking that the difference is coming out so clearly across all OECD countries.

A second and more striking observation is that the variation in the share of the less educated varies significantly across countries (since the share sums to 100, large variation in one category is correlated with large

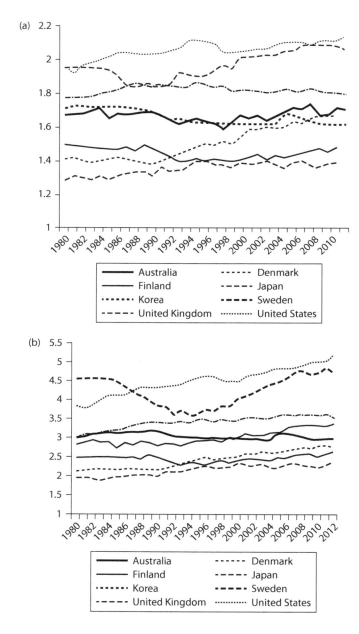

Figure 7.4 Wage inequalities, D5/D1 (a) and D9/D1 (b), selected OECD countries, 1980–2011.

Note: Gross earnings decile ratios.

Source: www.oecd-ilibrary.org.

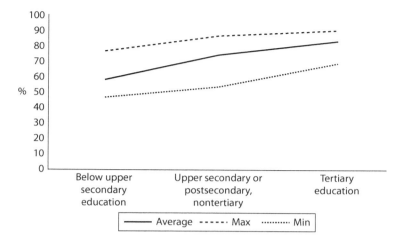

Figure 7.5   Employment rates conditional on level of education, OECD countries.

Note: Data for 22 OECD countries, 2014. Age group 25–64 years.

Source: Author's calculations based on data from www.OECD-ilbrary.org.

variation in other categories; see figure 7.6). The larger the share of less-educated people, the lower the average employment rate. As an example, the average OECD country can increase the aggregate employment rate by almost 2 percentage points from 73.4 percent to 75.2 percent by reducing the share of the less educated by 10 percentage points and increasing the share of those falling in the middle of the education spectrum by the same size.

It is widely agreed that both new technologies and globalization tend to induce a skill bias in labor demand; that is, job creation tends to be concentrated at the top of the qualification distribution, while job destruction is concentrated at the lower end. Demand for unskilled jobs falling either due to new technologies or competition from low-wage countries (classical Stolper-Samuelson theorem in trade theory) implies that the wage distribution shifts in favor of the more skilled at the cost of less skilled. The split of these changes between wages and employment depends critically on labor market structures and institutions. While there has been some controversy over the role of technology and globalization[7]—and the two are clearly interrelated—it is less important in the present context to separate the two, since it is the net consequences that matter from a distributional perspective.

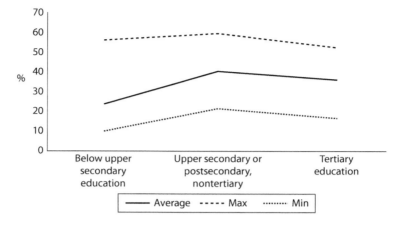

Figure 7.6 Share of population with given educational attainment.

Note: Data for 22 OECD countries, 2014. Age group 25–64 years.

Source: Author's calculations based on data from www.OECD-ilbrary.org.

This debate on skill bias is still ongoing and has recently been amended through discussion of tasks and its implications for labor demand; see for example, Autor and Acemoglu (2012). Lower transaction and information costs, seen most clearly for services that can be delivered electronically, lead to foreign competition in areas that previously have been considered "non-tradeables" and that often have a concentration of medium educated workers. The importance of globalization in terms of winners and losers therefore need not be monotonously related to the position in the qualification distribution. On the other hand, it may be argued that an aging population may increase labor demand in this medium educated segment via demand for care and services.

A number of empirical studies show that educational expansion during the 1950s, 1960s, and 1970s had an important effect on wage distributions. Despite a change in the composition of labor demand, there was a general increase in human capital and a larger supply of skilled and highly skilled labor. Following Tinbergen (1972), it may be interpreted as the distribution of qualifications kept up with changes in the distribution of the demanded qualifications, implying that the wage distribution was not much affected. As to the observed expansion of wage inequality, Goldin and Katz (2009, 291) conclude in a recent book that the "lion's share of rising wage inequality can be traced to an increasing educational wage differential." OECD (2011) also presents empirical evidence showing that the widening earnings inequality is driven by technological changes, but also by deregulation and less generous social transfers (see also Jaumotte, Lall, and Papageorgiou 2013).

Finally, there is the question of whether policies have become less redistributive in recent years. First, a remark on conventional measures of inequality like the Gini coefficient. Income distributions are compared on the basis of equivalized household incomes. That is, the income for the entire household is taken into account and adjusted for the size and composition of the household.[8] Both the income concept and the equivalence scale are of importance. On the income side, it is particularly important whether imputed rents for owner-occupied housing are included, since these rents tend to follow house prices and thus the business cycle. Changes in the family structure also matter. Changes in marriage pattern and assortative matching are of importance (see Salverda et al. 2014). Many countries are experiencing an increase in the number of single households because more young people are living as singles and populations are aging. This tends, other things being equal, to make the income distribution more unequal. Likewise, an increase in student enrollment may, in the short run, lead to more inequality. In short, inequality can be significantly affected by various factors on top of the direct effects of labor market conditions and public redistribution policies.

Policy reforms in a number of countries have focused primarily on incentive effects, which in turn may lead to less redistribution (see Knieser and Ziliak 2002; Andersen 2016a). This trend may reflect underestimation in the past of incentive effects or higher efficiency costs from redistribution due to globalization. Nevertheless, it may be argued that recent policy reforms have focused mostly on the incentive effects, paying little attention to the implications for insurance and redistribution.

2. INEQUALITY AND HUMAN CAPITAL

Empirical studies—both in the time and the cross-country dimension—have extensively explored the relation between income levels or growth and inequality. Typically, per capita income (GDP) and the Gini coefficient defined over equivalent household income are the measures used. Some studies focus on how inequality affects growth, while others consider the link from growth to inequality.

In a recent survey of some 20 studies, Neves and Silva (2014, 13) conclude: "To sum up, from all the studies reviewed we reach the conclusion that inequality is most likely to affect growth negatively in some cases and positively in others, depending on the specification for the growth regression, the initial level of inequality, the whole shape of the income distribution and the development level." In short, the empirical evidence does not lead to clear-cut conclusions. However, the evidence points in the direction that inequality is found to have a negative effect on growth in cross-section studies for low-income countries and when inequality is measured over some wealth variable.

These findings emphasize the importance of exploring the channels through which inequality may have a causal effect on growth; that is, can specific channels through which inequality affects growth be identified and what are the policy implications? This leads to a consideration of various forms of imperfections through which such a linkage may run.[9]

An important channel through which inequality may matter for growth is via initial conditions or stocks. That is, accumulation of various forms of capital constitutes the initial conditions that may differ across individuals and have implications for growth.

There is a fundamental difference between accumulation of real capital and human capital. While there may be diminishing returns in both forms of capital accumulation, for real capital accumulation it applies at the firm or aggregate level, and for human capital it applies at the individual level, since human capital is embodied in humans. Even though abilities matter and differ, diminishing returns to education imply that the distribution of human capital/education matters for the overall level of human capital. The social gains from human capital investments are larger if these investments are distributed across individuals.[10] The same does not apply to real capital. Diminishing returns do not apply at the individual level, and therefore the social gains from investments in real capital do not directly depend on the distribution across individuals. For real capital, it has been argued that inequality may strengthen capital accumulation and economic growth (per capita income). This is so if savings are increasing in income (see, for example, Lewis 1954; Kaldor 1957). This suggests that inequality is good for capital accumulation and bad for human capital accumulation.

The role of human capital in growth is well established. A rather large literature has explored the importance of education in increased productivity (see, for example, de la Fuente 2011; Hanushek and

Woessmann 2011). Early empirical studies measured education in the quantitative dimension, for example, as the share of the population having reached a level of education measured in years of study. These analyses tended to find a positive but not very large effect of education on productivity. More recent studies include both quantitative and qualitative measures of education, and education is generally found to have a significant importance for productivity growth. Education in the qualitative dimension (measured by various proficiency tests) is at least as important as education along the quantitative dimension (years of education/level of education). It is also found that the quality of education for broad groups in the labor market is at least as important as for education of the elite (see Hanushek and Woessmann 2011).

Another strand of empirical work has analyzed the role of the public sector (size and composition) for growth. These studies show that various government expenditures have different implications for growth.[11] The composition of expenditures matters, and so-called productive or active spending, like education, has positive effects on growth. In this sense, the balanced budget multiplier over the medium or long run is different for different types of expenditures.

This reasoning strongly suggests that acquisition of human capital is an area where equity and efficiency are intimately related. In the next section we turn to explanations stressing the effects running from inequality to growth via human capital accumulation. This points to the scope for what may be termed active redistribution policies, which affect both the level and distribution of income via education. The distributional issue pertains mainly to education along the extensive margin, that is, to an increase in the number of skilled/educated workers. Historically it has been a great achievement to increase the share of educated workers, but as discussed earlier, significant problems remain.

In the following section, we consider how capital market imperfections and social background factors can affect educational choices and create a link between income distribution, human capital formation, and growth.

3. CAPITAL MARKET IMPERFECTIONS

In the presence of capital market imperfections, the initial distribution of wealth may have critical importance for accumulation of human capital and therefore be a source of both inequality and persistence in the distribution of income across generations.[12] If families are not able to self-finance education for their children, education is reduced below the (social) optimal level. This implies a locking-in of talent in the sense that the level of education chosen for given abilities is lower than in a situation with a perfect capital market.

The implications of capital market imperfections for the interaction between income/wealth inequality and human capital accumulation are worked out in an important contribution by Galor and Zeira (1993). Becoming educated requires a fixed investment (extensive margin). They consider a setting where all have the same abilities, but families differ in initial financial wealth. Parents are altruistic and bequeath their children. The capital market is imperfect in the sense that the borrowing rate exceeds the lending rate, which in turn implies that the opportunity costs of education depend on the ability to self-finance education. As a consequence, some young receive so low a bequest that they abstain from education, implying that their own children also get a small bequest and refrain from investing in education. Galor and Zeira (1993) show that even when all have the same abilities, the outcome may be a stationary equilibrium with uneducated, low-income families and educated, high-income families. In this environment there is complete persistence (hysteresis) in the position in the income distribution. It is an implication that the stationary equilibrium depends on the initial distribution of wealth and that there may be multiple equilibria. If it has a large share of families with low wealth who abstain from education, the steady-state equilibrium will also have a high share of uneducated, and in this sense an unequal distribution of income/wealth and a lower level of capital.

The important insight is that the distribution of income/wealth matters for educational choices, and thus the total human capital stock. Inequality is an impediment to education, human capital, and therefore potentially growth. A more equal distribution of income/wealth may therefore be associated with more education leading to more human capital and higher income growth. In short, equity and efficiency are not necessarily in conflict. Equality may alleviate the consequences of capital market imperfections.

Galor and Moav (2004) develop an explanation as to why inequality in early phases of development may be conducive for growth, and with the opposite true at later stages of development. Their analysis combines the savings and the imperfect capital market arguments. At low income levels, capital accumulation is more important than human capital, and inequality induces a higher level of capital accumulation when savings rates are increasing in income/wealth. At later stages, human capital becomes more important, and capital market imperfections imply that inequality may be lowering capital accumulation and thus growth. Stated differently, the relation between inequality and growth is nonlinear, depending on the level of economic development.

Observe that in models stressing the importance of capital market imperfections, the issue of active and passive redistribution does not arise. A traditional redistribution policy will lead to more wealth for low-income families, increasing the likelihood that their children get education. There is no immediate conflict between traditional redistribution policies and the aim of boosting educational investments. The arguments here rely on parental altruism; in its absence, more targeted measures may be called for to ensure that educational choices are affected.

SOCIAL BARRIERS

The role of social gradients in educational options and choices is of particular policy concern, since it questions equality of opportunity in pursuing abilities and developing interests and motivations; an ethical value with wide support. Equality of opportunity concerns both the formal access and entry possibilities into the educational system as well as the outcomes. When social and cultural capital matters, a removal of economic and formal barriers to entry into the educational system is not sufficient to create equal opportunities in outcome possibilities for given talent and abilities. From an efficiency point of view, it implies that the human capital potential in the population is not exploited as best as possible, or, as phrased by Halsey (1961), that there is an unused "pool of ability."

The social gradient in education is strong. While the precise mechanisms are debated, there is ample empirical evidence that the social backgrounds of children and youth affect their educational attainment (entry and performance). The following is a list of a few key findings of importance for the following discussion:[13]

- The odds that young people will attain higher education are low if neither of the parents has completed higher education, and much higher if one of the parents has completed higher education (OECD 2012a).
- The barrier is not only economic, but cultural, and social capital matters critically (Holm and Jæger 2007). Even for children with comparable

performance in primary and lower secondary school in terms of grades, there is a social gradient in educational choices (OECD 2012a).

- Literacy and numeracy proficiency depend positively on parents' levels of education (OECD 2014).
- Previous schooling has a substantially larger impact on preparing students from less-educated families to enter higher education. There is a link between inequalities in early schooling and students from families with low levels of education enrolling in higher education (see Heckman and Mosso 2014).
- The advantage of having highly educated parents is smaller in countries with high educational levels, high overall quality of overall schooling, and large public involvement in education (smaller private costs) (see OECD 2012a).
- Social mobility is lower in countries with higher income inequality (cf. Björklund and Jäntti 2009; Corak 2013).

These findings suggest that education is not only constrained by financial factors (credit constraints), and this raises questions on the scope and effect of public intervention in education. The following considers this issue in some detail. To clarify, the mechanisms focus solely on social barriers to education. Clearly, personal characteristics and, in particular, abilities matter as well, but these aspects are disregarded to focus on the role of social barriers. The following is based on Andersen (2016b).

Consider a basic overlapping-generations setting in which individuals live for two periods (young and old). The young make educational efforts to become skilled when they are old. Individuals succeed in their educational endeavors and become skilled with a probability that is dependent on both their educational effort and their social background. Children with skilled parents have a higher chance of becoming skilled than children with unskilled parents. This captures key points on the role of social factors outlined earlier. While they are young, agents can spend time studying or working as unskilled laborers. When older, they become skilled workers if they succeeded in obtaining an education or unskilled workers if they were unable to acquire an education. Education has an opportunity cost in terms of reduced income in youth.[14] Since children with skilled parents, other things being equal, have a better chance of succeeding in the educational arena, they invest more in education, and this tends to reinforce their chance of succeeding in the educational system and becoming skilled. Similarly, children with unskilled parents are less inclined to pursue an education and less likely to succeed in the educational arena.

In equilibrium there is social mobility, but social status is still reproduced in the sense that children with skilled parents are more likely to become skilled than children with unskilled parents, and vice versa. Importantly, there is a dynamic effect of a change in the share of skilled workers. If more education inputs are invested, more workers will become skilled, which in turn affects future educational choices and therefore the share of skilled workers. In this sense, education produces education.

This raises questions on the rationale and form of public intervention. Assume for the sake of argument that the public sector can offer educational inputs that are perfect substitutes for private education inputs; that is, the public sector does not have any options that are not available in the market. In the same vein, it is assumed that public education is general and accessible to all at the same terms; that is, it is not targeted to specific groups.[15] To a first approximation, this may be said to characterize general public schooling, and serves the purpose of not biasing the analysis toward a favorable role for public education. Under these assumptions, public education will crowd out private education; however, crowding out is in general less than complete. Educational inputs will therefore, in net terms, increase. The reason for less than complete crowding out is that more public education releases an income effect for the young, which in turn lowers their marginal utility of consumption and thus the opportunity costs of private education.

In figure 7.7 the effect of an increase in public education is illustrated. The figure shows the effects on efficiency measured by aggregate living standards (consumption) and equity by its distribution for various levels of public education. An increase in public education traces out a hump-shaped pattern in the efficiency-equity space. Starting from the laissez-faire situation, an increase in public consumption increases aggregate living standards and reduces inequality, but at some point living standards start declining while inequality keeps declining. The hump shape implies that public intervention over some interval does not raise a conflict between efficiency and equity. However, continually increasing public education would imply that a turning point is reached, and a conflict or trade-off between income and inequality arises. Note also that if social preferences are increasing in living standards and equality, it is optimal to be on the segment of the locus that displays a trade-off.

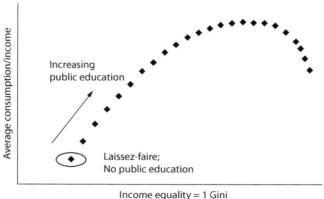

Figure 7.7   Income-equality locus—public investments in education.

Note: Income inequality is measured as 1 – Gini.

Source: Results from simulations reported in Andersen (2016b).

Any suboptimal educational choices in this setting are caused by social barriers. There are no differences in abilities or capital market imperfections or the like impeding education. This suggests a possibility that the pool of abilities in the population is not efficiently used. Is it possible that public intervention in a setting with social barriers to education can be Pareto-improving? In Andersen (2016b) it is shown that public intervention can be Pareto-improving. The condition is that public education increases total consumption possibilities in society. If this is the case, the winners are able to compensate the losers. On pure efficiency grounds, there may thus be an argument for public intervention. Social barriers are a market failure on par with capital market imperfections.

Inequality in consumption possibilities creates a motive for redistribution. The skilled (old) will have higher income than the unskilled (old). Consider a transfer scheme that provides income support to the unskilled, which is financed by a tax on the skilled. Compare the passive scheme to an active scheme providing education to the young, also financed by a tax on the skilled (old). The two forms of redistribution affect education differently. The active scheme increases education, while the passive scheme reduces education. On impact, the passive scheme benefits the unskilled old, but over time it implies that the number of unskilled increases. The passive scheme distorts educational choices by lowering the gain from education.

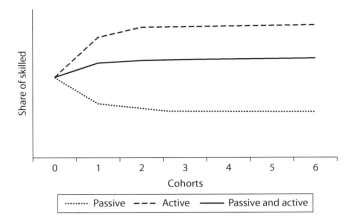

Figure 7.8   Dynamic adjustment of the share of skilled, active versus passive redistribution.

Source: Results from simulation reported in Andersen (2015).

Conversely, the active scheme does not immediately benefit the unskilled, but it reduces the share of unskilled workers over time.[16] These different dynamic implications are illustrated in figure 7.8, which considers three different policy scenarios all starting from an initial situation without any public intervention (laissez-faire): passive redistribution, active redistribution, and combining passive and active redistribution. It is seen that the share of skilled workers develops differently. Active redistribution has a tailwind by increasing the share of skilled workers by improving the social background of children, which further increases the number of skilled workers and reduces taxes, while passive transfers work in the opposite direction.

3. CONCLUDING REMARKS

Inequality is on the rise at the same time as the scope for traditional distribution policies via taxes and transfers is constrained by lack of fiscal space. Moreover, the distortionary effects and thus societal cost of redistribution may be increasing due to globalization. This presents a gloomy picture, but the traditional discussion on redistribution overlooks the basic fact that the foundation for income equality is created in the labor market. Ensuring a more equal distribution of education would lead to a more equal distribution of income. This points to the importance of an active distribution policy via education (level and distribution), which also requires more focus on ensuring de facto equal opportunities in educational choices and options—an ethical value that is widely supported.

Importantly, there is scope for improvement given the resources already allocated to education. More resources may be called for, but in the first place, it is an important policy challenge to exploit the room for improvement given the resources already provided. The most binding constraint for educational performance and achievement does not seem to be educational supply capacity in the quantitative dimension; most young people start on some postsecondary education. The problem is that a large share never complete their education. The reasons for this are many, including insufficient proficiency and motivation as well as social background factors that impede educational performance. There is therefore an urgent need for improvement in education in both the quantitative and qualitative dimensions to ensure that education is not lagging too far behind in the race against technology.

NOTES

1. As a notable example of a result of the so-called five presidents report, there is an ongoing process to develop a social pillar for Economic and Monetary Union countries (see Juncker et al. 2015), and the objective is stated as: "Europe's aim should be to earn a 'social triple A,' " and "I will want to develop a European Pillar of Social Rights, which takes account of the changing realities of the world of work and which can serve as a compass for the renewed convergence within the euro area" (President Juncker, State of the Union, 9 September 2015).

2. This discussion has recently been revived by Piketty (2014). It is beyond the scope of this chapter to discuss the functional distribution of income. It should be noted, though, that the text discuss human capital and its distribution, a form of capital that is important in accounting for wealth and its distribution and that is not featured in the discussion raised by Piketty (2014). Wages and salaries are quantitatively of much larger importance than capital income for the distribution of disposable income (see, for example, OECD 2012b).

3. Consider the following very stylized way of thinking of the problem. Disposable income for household i is given as $y_i^d = (1 - \tau(y_i)) y_i \equiv d(y_i)$, where $\tau(y_i)$ is the net tax payment made given market income y_i, $1 > \tau' > 0$, $\tau'' \geq 0$. Disposable income is given by $d(y_i)$, where $0 < d' = 1 - \tau - \tau' y_i < 1$, and $d'' = -2\tau' - \tau'' y_i < 0$. Let market income be given as $y_i = w(h_i)$, where h_i denotes human capital by type i and $w(h_i)$ gives the wage as a function of human capital, $w' > 0$. It follows that

$$Var(y^d) \cong (d')^2 \, Var(y)$$
$$Var(y) \cong (w')^2 \, Var(h)$$

That is, the dispersion in market income depends on the dispersion in human capital/qualification weighted by the sensitivity of wages to human capital. Likewise, the dispersion of disposable income depends on the dispersion of market income weighted by the sensitivity of disposable income to the market income.

4. Define the Gini measured over market income as G_M and over disposable income as G_D. The redistribution coefficient is defined as $R \equiv G_D/G_M$. Define the respective average value by an upper bar, implying $\bar{R} \equiv \dfrac{\bar{G}_D}{\bar{G}_M}$. The decomposition is based on the following formula:

$$\frac{G_D - \bar{G}_D}{\bar{G}_D} = \frac{G_M - \bar{G}_M}{\bar{G}_M} \frac{R}{\bar{R}} + \frac{R - \bar{R}}{\bar{R}}$$

where the first term on the right-hand side is the contribution from market income and the second term is the contribution from redistribution.

5. A relative measure is better than the absolute difference between the Gini for market incomes and disposable incomes, since the latter is not independent of the level of inequality. That is, the absolute difference can be small due to much redistribution or a high level of inequality in market incomes.

6. Note that education is also associated with better health, longer longevity, social outcomes, participation in social and political activities, etc. It is conceptually difficult to separate the causal links here, and there may be severe selection problems underlying the observed correlations. However, some studies do find a causal link between education and health; see Conti, Heckman, and Urzúa (2010). Heckman and Kautz (2013) find that cognitive and socioemotional skills explain labor market and social outcomes.

7. See, for example, Goldin and Katz (2009); Jaumotte, Lall, and Papageorgiou (2013).

8. The OECD equivalence scale gives the equivalence factor as the square root of the number of family members. The equivalized income is the total household income divided by the equivalence factor.

9. Alesina and Perotti (1996) present empirical evidence that inequality is associated with social discontent and sociopolitical instability, which reduce investment incentives; see also Venieris and Gupta (1996).

Inequality may also be a source of crises and thus macroeconomic stability. Discussion has been prompted by the increase in inequality (in particular at the top) prior to the financial crisis and the rising debt levels (for a survey, see van Treeck and Sturn 2012). Atkinson and Morelli (2011) do not find empirical evidence in support of increasing inequality leading to financial crises. Coibion et al. (2014) do not find support in U.S. data that low-income households accumulated more debt than high-income households.

10. Let human capital be given as $h = h(a_i, e_i)$, where a_i is ability, and e_i educational input. Assume that $h_a(.) > 0$ and $h_e(.) > 0$, $h_{ee}(.) < 0$ and $h_e \to \infty$ for $e \to 0$. If a given educational input $\Sigma e_i = e$ is to be allocated to maximize total human capital, the optimum would have $h_e(a_i, e_i) = h_e(a_j, e_j)$ for all i,j. Hence, $e_i > 0$ for all i. If abilities and

education are complements, $h_{ea}(.) > 0$, it follows that $e_i > e_j$ if $a_i > a_j$, i.e., there is a regressive bias, cf. Arrow (1971).

11. For an overview and discussion see Andersen (2015).

12. Becker and Tomes (1979) consider sources of persistence in human capital (via parental altruism there is investment in education and bequests) and income/wealth and show that there is path dependence but mean reversion in income/wealth positions if capital markets are complete and endowments (abilities, social capital, etc.) are exogenously given and display persistence but do not affect the marginal return to educational investments.

13. See, for example, Holmlund, Lindahl, and Plug (2011, 626) for an overview and discussion of various methods to separate the two. Among other things it is concluded that "we think that all these twin, adoption, and IV findings suggest that schooling is in part responsible for the intergenerational schooling link: more educated parents get more educated children because of more education." Heckman has in a number of studies analyzed the role of (early) intervention in overcoming social barriers to education; see, for example, Heckman and Mosso (2014) for an overview and references.

14. Hence, there is no upfront financing requirement to start education, and the capital market plays no role.

Note that the educational decision is entirely driven by economic conditions, the choice sets are the same for all youth, but the "productivity" of their educational efforts differ due to social factors.

15. There are de jure equal opportunities to undertake education, but de facto there are not, due to the role of social factors.

16. The present case assumes constant wages. If wages are endogenous, there is the additional effect that more skilled workers will tend to reduce the wages of skilled workers and increase the wages of unskilled workers, and therefore further reduce wage inequality.

REFERENCES

Alesina, A., and R. Perotti. 1996. "Income Distribution, Political Instability, and Investment." *European Economic Review* 40(6):1203–28.

Andersen, T. M. 2015. *The Welfare State and Economic Performance*. SOU (Statens Offentliga Utredningar) 2015:53. Stockholm: SOU.

———. 2016a. "Automatic Stabilizers—The Intersection of Labor Market and Fiscal Policies." *IZA Journal of European Labor Studies* 5:11.

———. 2016b. "Social Background, Education and Inequality." Centre for Economic Policy Research (CEPR) Discussion Paper.

Arrow, K. J. 1971. "A Utilitarian Approach to the Concept of Equality in Public Expenditures." *Quarterly Journal of Economics* 85(3):409–15.

Atkinson, A. B., and S. Morelli. 2011. "Economic Crisis and Inequality." United Nations Development Programme—Human Development Reports Occasional papers 2011/6.

Autor, D., and D. Acemoglu. 2012. "Skills, Tasks and Technologies: Implications for Employment and Earnings." In *Handbook of Labour Economics*, vol. 4b, ed. O. Ashenfelter and D. Card, chap. 12. New York: Elsevier.

Becker, G. S., and N. Tomes. 1979. "An Equilibrium Theory of the Distribution of Income and Intergenerational Mobility." *Journal of Political Economy* 87:1153–89.

Björklund, A., and M. Jäntti. 2009. "Intergenerational Income Mobility and the Role of Family Background." In *The Oxford Handbook of Income Inequality*, ed. W. Salverda, B. Noland, and T. M. Smeeding, chap. 20. Oxford: Oxford University Press.

Coibion, O., Y. Gorodnichenko, M. Kudlyak, and J. Mondragon. 2014. "Does Greater Inequality Lead to More Household Borrowing?" Institute of Labour Economics (IZA) Working Paper 7910.

Conti, G., J. J. Heckman, and S. Urzúa. 2010. "The Education-Health Gradient." *American Economic Review, Papers and Proceedings* 100:234–48.

Corak, M. 2013. "Income Inequality, Equality of Opportunity, and Intergenerational Mobility." *Journal of Economic Perspectives* 27(3):79–102.

de la Fuente, A. 2011. "Human Capital and Productivity." *Nordic Economic Policy Review* 2:103–31.

Galor, O., and O. Moav. 2004. "From Physical to Human Capital—Inequality and the Process of Development." *Review of Economic Studies* 71:1001–26.

Galor, O., and J. Zeira. 1993. "Income Distribution and Macroeconomics." *Review of Economic Studies* 60:35–52.

Goldin, C., and L. F. Katz. 2009. *The Race Between Education and Technology*. Cambridge: Harvard University Press.

Halsey, A. H. 1961. *Ability and Educational Opportunity*. Paris: OECD.

Hanushek, E. A., and L. Woessmann. 2011. "How Much Do Educational Outcomes Matter in OECD Countries?" *Economic Policy* 26(67):427–91.

Heckman, J. J., and S. Mosso. 2014. "The Economics of Human Development and Social Mobility." NBER Working Paper 19925. Cambridge, Mass.: National Bureau of Economic Research.

Heckman, J. J., and T. Kautz. 2013. "Fostering and Measuring Skills: Interventions That Improve Character and Cognition." NBER Working Paper No. 19656. Cambridge, Mass.: National Bureau of Economic Research.

Holm, A, and M. M. Jæger. 2007. "Does Parents Economic, Cultural, and Social Capital Explain the Social Class Effect on Educational Attainment in the Scandinavian Mobility Regime?" *Social Science Research* 36:719–44.

Holmlund, H., M. Lindahl, and E. Plug. 2011. "The Causal Effect of Parents' Schooling on Children's Schooling: A Comparison of Estimation Methods." *Journal of Economic Literature* 49(3):615–51.

Jaumotte, F., S. Lall, and C. Papageorgiou. 2013. "Rising Income Inequality: Technology, or Trade and Financial Globalization." *IMF Economic Review* 61(2):217–309.

Juncker, J. C., D. Tusk, J. Dijsselbloem, M. Draghi, and M. Schulz. 2015. *Completing Europe's Economic and Monetary Union*. Brussels: European Commission.

Kaldor, N. 1957. "A Model of Economic Growth." *Economic Journal* 67:591–624.

Knieser, T. J., and J. P. Ziliak. 2002. "Tax Reform and Automatic Stabilization." *American Economic Review* 92:590–621.

Lewis, A. W. 1954. "Economic Development with Unlimited Supplies of Labour." *Manchester School* 22(2):139–91.

Neves, P. C., and S. N. T. Silva. 2014. "Inequality and Growth: Uncovering the Main Conclusions from the Empirics." *Journal of Development Studies* 50(1):1–21.

OECD. 2011. *Divided we stand: Why Inequality Keeps Rising.* Paris: OECD.

———. 2012a. *Equity and Quality in Education—Supporting Disadvantaged Students and Schools.* Paris: OECD.

———. 2012b. *Going for Growth.* Paris: OECD.

———. 2014. *Education at a Glance.* Paris: OECD.

Piketty, T. 2014. *Capital in the Twenty-First Century.* Cambridge: Harvard University Press.

Roine, J., and D. Waldenström. 2015. "Long-Run Trends in the Distribution of Income and Wealth." Working Paper. University of Uppsala, Uppsala, Sweden.

Salverda, W., et al. (eds.). 2014. *Changing Inequalities in Rich Countries: Analytical and Comparative Perspectives.* Oxford: Oxford University Press.

Tinbergen, J. 1972. "The Impact of Education on Income Distribution." *Review of Income and Wealth* 18(3):255–65.

Van Treeck, T., and S. Sturn. 2012. *Inequality as a Cause of the Great Recession? A Survey of Current Debates.* ILO Series 39. Geneva: ILO.

Venieris, V., and D. Gupta. 1996. "Income Distribution and Socio-political Instability as Determinants of Savings." *Journal of Political Economy* 96:873–83.

PART II

CHAPTER 8

The EU Welfare State

PAST, PRESENT, AND FUTURE

Ernst Stetter

> The single greatest challenge we face today is how to rethink social policy so that, once again, labor markets and families are welfare optimizers and a good guarantee that tomorrow's adult workers will be as productive and resourceful as possible.
>
> Esping-Andersen et al. 2002, 25

The European welfare state has long been identified as a major pillar of the European socioeconomic identity. Along its multiple variants across EU regions, European welfare systems can generally be characterized by sizable spending on education, health, and social protection. Created during the 1950s and 1960s, these systems served well in addressing social risks of European economies at that time. Faced on the one side with the challenges posed by evolving economic forces and demographic trends, and on the other side with shifts in the economic-policy paradigm and further integration of the EU construct, these welfare states underwent major transformations. A first wave of changes took place in the 1990s as a reaction to the surge in unemployment triggered by the second oil shock and as a way to adapt the system to an aging population and a change in the gender roles within households. A second wave of changes occurred after 2008 during the global financial crisis and the ensuing austerity measures. While the changes of the 1990s mostly implied a transformation of the welfare state, resulting in a change in its *design* so as to better adapt it to the changing socioeconomic reality, the austerity measures entailed primarily a retrenchment (at times across the board) of welfare, affecting mostly its volume.

In both phases, changes in the welfare systems were flanked by labor market liberalization reforms and associated with a reduction in the power and role of collective bargaining. Further, in the ensemble, these social policy changes were part of the expansion of the neoclassical economic paradigm that implied a retrenchment of the role of the state, and consequently smaller budgets, a shift in the focus from the individual and household to the worker and firm, and the overall submission of social matters under the economic agenda. At time of increased international competitiveness, the goal of solidarity and protection has lost grounds to competitiveness goals.

In light of the well-known consequences of the recent austerity measures on social indicators in many European countries, the EU welfare system now faces the double challenge of ensuring adequate coverage of social protection by closing its many gaps (a change in volume) and adapting to new social risks (a change in design). With old risks remaining and new social risks emerging, this chapter argues in favor of reaffirming the EU social model and the importance of social policy for both economic growth and the EU integration process. To this end, the chapter first illustrates the main features of the EU welfare systems and highlights main differences between country groups. It then shows the transformation that the EU welfare system underwent around the 1990s and the choices made during the austerity period. Within this, we illustrate the shift toward a gradual submission of social issues under the new economic imperative of competitiveness. We finally argue that such shift from demand-side welfare to supply-side welfare further dampened aggregate demand in the EU, making the recovery from the crisis a much harder task.

This chapter is structured as follows. The first section will describe different social models in the EU as created in the 1950s. Section 2 will then discuss major transformations that took place during the 1990s, and section 3 will highlight the role played by the EU integration process in social policies in the member states. Section 4 presents evidence regarding the austerity measures and their toll on socioeconomic indicators. Section 5 concludes and proposes some new strategies to enhance and protect the social *aquis* of the EU.

1. ELEMENTS OF THE EUROPEAN WELFARE STATE

As expressed in Esping-Andersen (1990), the concept of welfare state regimes denotes institutional arrangements, rules, and understandings that guide and shape social policy decisions and the respond-and-demand structure of citizens and welfare consumers. Generally, welfare systems in the EU entail largely free health care and education, unemployment support, a broadly accessible social security system, and sound maternity and childcare benefits. As is well documented by the literature (Esping-Andersen 1990, 1996), key differences apply across countries, reflecting historical and cultural divergences. From a comparative perspective, welfare types or institutions are usually distinguished according to four parameters: (1) the criteria governing the eligibility and entitlement of the benefits (Who is entitled to benefit?); (2) the types of benefits provided; (3) the financing mechanism (Who pays, and how?); and (4) the organization and management of the scheme (Pallier 2010a).

Based on these criteria, four types of welfare regimes have been considered (Esping-Andersen 1990, 1996; Ferrera 1996; Seeleib-Kaiser 2013). These are the social democratic or Scandinavian model, the conservative or continental regime, the liberal or Anglo-Saxon model, and the Mediterranean or southern model (see table 8.1). The social democratic model, typical of Denmark, Finland, Norway, Sweden, and the Netherlands, places large emphasis on redistribution, social inclusion, and universality. Benefits are high and universal, and women are encouraged to work. The conservative or continental regime (such as Austria, Belgium, France, Germany, and Luxembourg) places less emphasis on the need to redistribute wealth, sees employment as the basis of social transfers, and links benefits to income. It protects the traditional role model (for instance, the role of men as the breadwinners) and maintains differences between social classes. The liberal or Anglo-Saxon regime

Table 8.1   Welfare Regimes

	Social democratic	Conservative	Liberal	Mediterranean
Aim	Social citizenship, equality, full employment	Social cohesion, social integration	Poverty reduction, poverty alleviation	Clientelism
Eligibility	Citizens/residents	Workers/insured/toward quasi-universalism	Poor	Insiders/very limited coverage
Financing	Taxation	Social insurance contributions	Taxation	Contributions plus taxes
Benefits	Flat and universal	Earnings/contributions related	Means tested	Earnings/contributions related

Source: Seeleib-Kaiser (2015).

(Ireland and United Kingdom) pivots around market-based social security schemes, with smaller social transfers, and targeted and means-tested benefits; it allows for complementary private schemes. The Mediterranean regime (Greece, Spain, Italy, and Portugal) features low social transfers, with social policies characterized by particularistic and clientelistic traits (Ferrera 1996).

This grouping of welfare regimes, as initially developed by the literature, does not encompass Eastern European countries. With the deepening of these countries' integration into the world economy and further to the European 2004 enlargement, Eastern European countries have been transitioning from systems with large social protection and benefits to hybrid welfare systems. These hybrid systems mix forms and features of the four traditional regimes in ways that are still evolving (Fenger 2007; Seeleib-Kaiser 2015). The Czech Republic, Poland, Hungary, and Slovakia, for example, developed welfare systems that mix components of the continental social insurance model (the unemployment and healthcare insurance systems), communist egalitarianism (extensive childcare provisions), and liberal market orientation (Cerami 2010).

Each regime bears implications regarding the economic and social outcome in an economy. For example, inequality and poverty rates tend to be the lowest in the Scandinavian countries and highest in the liberal welfare system (see table 8.2). Another crucial difference often mentioned by the literature is the adaptability of these systems to changes in the socioeconomic reality. It was in fact traditionally argued that the continental system, heavily hinged on full employment and traditional familistic views, in particular on the figure of the male breadwinner, was less prone to change. Yet, as put forward in Hemerijck and Marx (2010), the transformations this welfare state underwent during the 1990s prove the contrary.

Table 8.2   Inequality and Poverty by Regime

	Gini coefficient	Relative poverty rates (60% median)
Social democratic regime	0.247	12.615
Conservative regime	0.273	14.353
Liberal regime	0.332	21.110
Mediterranean regime	0.327	20.202

Source: Seeleib-Kaiser (2015) from Luxembourg income study.

2. CHANGES IN THE EU SOCIOECONOMIC FABRIC DURING THE 1990S

Designed in the era of industrial capitalism and reflecting household models, labor relations, and social risks specific to the 1960s, European welfare states underwent major changes in and around the 1990s,[1] in an attempt to adapt to new social realities. These changes took place at different times, earlier for some countries (like Sweden) and later for others (like Greece). As expressed in Börsch-Supan (2015), European welfare reforms in the 1990s combined "parametric" and "fundamental" changes, wherein parametric changes refer to small adjustments, such as reviews of the benefits indexation formula or increases in the retirement age, and fundamental changes refer to a change in the underlying philosophy of the welfare system, such as the introduction of private sector financing in retirement schemes. These changes came alongside the seminal shift from the Keynesian economic paradigm (demand-driven) to the neoclassical paradigm (supply-driven), brought about by the economic shocks of the mid-1970s and early 1980s. This new economic paradigm promoted a departure from the view of the state as major or sole provider of social protection and insurance toward a view that saw the state more as a promoter of the smooth functioning of markets. Along with the shocks came crucial changes in the global economy, including increased capital mobility, intensified competition between economies, and deindustrialization (Pallier 2010a).

As regards the welfare state more specifically, several socioeconomic transformations that had been unfolding since the 1970s favored this shift in economic thinking and policies. First, the economic stagnation and ensuing high unemployment brought about by the economic shocks of the mid-1970s and early 1980s unveiled the cracks of a welfare system designed at a time of robust economic growth and put a once and for all end to the assumption of full employment and lifetime work. Exacerbated by an aging population, a slow-growth environment entailed an increasingly higher number of benefit recipients (both unemployed and elderly), not always matched with an increasing number of contributors, despite higher female labor force participation. As a consequence, the productive capacity of many economies was insufficient to support the welfare system, due, among other thing, to a thinning tax base. Thus, for those countries that did not reduce welfare generosity, this entailed sizable increases in debt ratios in the early 1990s (in Greece, Finland, France, Italy, and Spain, for example). With such a toll on public finances and little fiscal space for countercyclical policies, the neoliberal perception that states were failing in managing welfare (as well as at controlling the economy at large) and that current systems were based on wrong incentives prevailed, paving the way to the entry of new and private economic agents in the welfare market.

Second, as discussed in Atkinson (2008), an effect of globalization was indeed increased international competition together with skill-biased technological change. This resulted in a reduced demand for low-skill workers in Europe and higher structural unemployment. In such a context, ordinary fiscal policies aimed at spurring aggregate demand through the cycle proved to be inadequate in addressing the needs of a low-qualified and long-term unemployed population. This triggered the design of several activation and training schemes and boosted the view in favor of a more targeted benefit system.

Third, rising female labor force participation entailed new household and gender role models, which included double-earner and single-parent families. Such change further complicated the systems for social contribution and benefit schemes and at the same time raised more needs for childcare and care services for the elderly.

Finally, a last factor that spurred the overhaul of European welfare systems around the 1990s was the creation of the European Monetary Union and the adoption of the Maastricht convergence criteria. The need for convergence in public finance as set by the Maastricht criteria entailed a heavy pressure for deficit and debt reductions. Such pressure resulted in a downsizing of the welfare states of many European economies, with substantial cuts and streamlining of social spending items. Albeit advocated for as beneficial for convergence of economic conditions within the EU, such a move toward smaller budgets was also in line with the new neo-classical economic paradigm that framed social policies and labor market reforms at the EU level in the years to come.

With welfare states designed for the social fabric prevailing in the 1960s, these trends created a dichotomy between insiders and outsiders, where insiders benefited from traditional labor relations (permanent contract) and the full spectrum of benefits, while outsiders were either excluded from the labor market (unemployed) or hired on a temporary basis, with precarious and unprotected contracts. Women, youth, and low-skilled workers tended to fill the rows of the outsider category. As the time span for unemployment lengthened, re-inserting the long-term unemployed became a serious challenge. Employability of these unemployed proved to be hard, given a loss of skills and/or a bias on the part of employers toward the long-term unemployed.

To address the social risks emerging from this new socioeconomic fabric, several EU countries embarked on profound reforms of their welfare systems during the 1990s. As argued in Pallier (2010b) and Hall (1986), some of these changes reflected a tendency to adapt to the new dominant macroeconomic paradigm anchored to the supply side, rather than demand. Within a shift in focus toward the firm rather than the individual or the household, emphasis and priority were given, for instance, to employability rather than to the support of the unemployed. Further, the role of the state changed from active economic agent (stimulating demand directly) to facilitator of business and production; a role that elicited a retrenchment of the public sector, and allowed new (private) players in the provision of welfare services. Although different across countries, changes to the welfare states were applied in an attempt to: (1) address the surge in the unemployed and boost competitiveness; and (2) reflect new household models and reduce the duality between insiders and outsiders.

To address the surge in the unemployed population, social systems started to complement unemployment benefit schemes (or passive labor market policies) with activation policies. This coincided with a new consensus toward an employment first approach. Within the broad realm of active policies, some countries, like France and Denmark, opted for investment in human capital and training of the labor force, while other countries chose labor market reentry policy, or employment support schemes, like in Sweden or Belgium, where the benefit recipients were encouraged to take up jobs usually priced out of the regular labor market (Hemerijck and Marx 2010; Bjorsted, Bova, and Dahl 2016).

In an attempt to boost competitiveness, activation policies were associated with labor market reforms that implied major changes in wage-setting and labor market flexibility. Many countries adopted wage moderation (or wage restraint) policies to lower unit labor costs. Similarly, regulations in terms of hiring and firing were relaxed to allow for more flexibility in the labor market. Overall, these reforms clearly coincided with periods of weakening of trade union powers across the board. After suspending wage indexation in the 1980s, the Netherlands made wage agreements more flexible in the early 1990s, cut security contributions, and introduced opening clauses that allowed firms to negotiate with workers a pay lower than minimum sets in collective contracts

(Hemerijck and Marx 2010; Barkbu et al. 2012). In the same year, Spain allowed for the issuance of fixed-term contracts, which already in the mid-2000s were used for 30 percent of salaried workers. Later on, Germany, through the 2000–2005 Hartz reforms, enhanced activation policies, cut unemployment insurance, introduced temporary contracts, and eased dismissal (Dustmann et al. 2014)

To reflect new family models, EU welfare states abandoned the traditional male breadwinner and female caregiver models and embraced new models of households, including dual earner and single parent (Hemerijck 2012). Given the new role of women at work, social services expanded to support female participation, for instance, in the form of spending on family services, childcare, and care for elderly. During the 1980s, the coverage of protection and insurance expanded in those EU countries that featured large gaps in social protection systems and high poverty and social exclusion indicators. Such expansion of coverage also reflected a departure from a male breadwinner model. For example, the Spanish welfare system expanded coverage for pensions and health care to all genders, not just to male workers, as had been historically the case in Spain. As a result, the protection gaps were successfully closed (Guillen 2010). Similarly, the Italian welfare system saw a large expansion over the 1980s and 1990s, due to an extension of coverage and more family allowance (Jessoula and Alti 2010).

To address the duality between insiders and outsiders, many countries designed schemes of labor and social protection policies targeted exclusively to the long-term unemployed, females, or youth. In France the government adopted several minimum income schemes to protect the poor. It lowered the level of social contribution for contracts that included some disadvantaged groups, such as the long-term unemployed, youth unemployed, or small companies; further, in 1993 all wages below 1.3 times the minimum wage were exempted of social contributions (Pallier 2010b). Similarly, in the 2000s, the Belgian government reduced social security contributions for low-paid employees (Hemerijck and Marx 2010). Portugal sought to address social protection gaps by introducing a guaranteed minimum income and measures against poverty and social exclusion (Ferrera 2010). Similarly, the Spanish government granted exemptions of social contributions and taxes for the young and the elderly and for the long-term unemployed (Guillen 2010).

Contrary to the recent austerity period, these transformations were not mostly determined by cost containment, and in some cases (like Spain and Portugal) the coverage and level of benefits were expanded. Overall, however, we can see a trend toward a better calibration of the benefit system, especially toward the outsiders and poor, more emphasis toward employability, and new (private) players in the social system. While arguably most changes affected the design of the welfare state, some countries started to embark in a cost-containment process during that time. EU economic policy played a major role in driving countries in this direction.

3. THE EU SOCIAL MODEL

As noted by Leibfried and Pierson (2000), while EU countries proceeded in adapting their welfare system to the new EU social fabric of the 1980s and 1990s, issues of work and welfare became much more intertwined with the European process of integration. More specifically, under the stability and growth pact requirements of small deficits and debts, many countries embarked in retrenchment processes and proceeded with cuts in social spending, including through the adoption of means-tested benefits, and adjusted pension systems to make them more sustainable over time and somehow more linked to population aging. Further, the EU influence also entailed a "recalibration" of welfare programs toward more active and service-oriented provisions (Petmesidou and Guillen 2015). In France, for instance, retrenchment consisted of stricter eligibility criteria, which in turn entailed lower coverage in terms of beneficiaries and in terms of benefits (Pallier 2010b). In the Netherlands, retrenchment had already occurred in the 1980s and entailed reduction in the levels and duration of insurance benefits (Hemerijck and Marx 2010). In the early 1990s, unemployment protection underwent drastic cuts in Spain, with coverage falling from 80 percent in 1992 to 51 percent in 1995 (Guillen 2010).

Looking more generally at the EU policy level, the social pillar had a fluctuating importance over time. During the second half of the 1980s, the European Commission under Delors brought into play the European social model to signal renewed commitment on the part of the EU to a social market economy, full employment, and social progress. As summarized in Busch et al. (2013), in the context of the social democratic and trade union debates, this encompasses: (1) pursuing macroeconomic policy aimed at full employment; (2) implementing both a wage policy in which real wage increases reflect productivity growth and EU minimum wages to reduce the low-wage sector; (3) adopting underlying social security systems that realize a high level of protection in pension, health care, and family policy as well as in unemployment benefits; and (4) providing for participation rights, promoting social dialogue, strengthening the public sector, and incorporating a social progress clause in EU treaties.

Further to this, a consistent, albeit timid, European employment strategy first appeared in the employment title of the Amsterdam Treaty establishing the European Community of 1997 (European Commission 2001). The treaty stipulated a high level of employment as one of the objectives of the EU (Article 2) and gave power to the council to design a coordinated strategy for employment, but also for social issues. The guidelines set were a promotion of investment in vocational training and more flexibility in the labor market, including in wage policy, reducing non-wage labor costs, and improving measures to sustain long-term unemployed, the youth, elderly, and women.

The importance of job creation and flexibility was then restated with the Lisbon Strategy of 2000 (and subsequently revised in 2005), launched as a response to job losses and deindustrialization brought about by globalization. The main underlying rationale was to create more cooperation regarding reforms aimed at generating growth and more and better jobs by investing in people's skills, the greening of the economy, and innovation. Regarding employment, the main strategy entailed investing in people in order to upgrade their skills in the EU's rapidly changing economy. In the same vein, the 2009 Lisbon Treaty officially endorsed the EU's normative commitment to a (highly competitive) "social market economy, geared toward employment and social progress." This was followed by the 2010 decision on the Europe 2020 Strategy. This defined five core objectives: increasing employment, reducing greenhouse gas emissions, reducing early school-leaver rates and improving education, reducing people at risk of poverty and social exclusion, and increasing research and development.

A crucial pillar of the European social dimension agenda was to help member states in their pension and health-care reforms. Related to this is the EU Charter of Fundamental Rights (2000), which introduces principles of social protection at the EU level, among others the right to maternity leave and the entitlement to social security benefits and social protection in cases of illness, accidents, or loss of employment. Overall, the Maastricht Treaty of 1992, which established the monetary union and the euro currency, has restricted the scope for fiscal policy in a way that may conflict with maintaining sound and sustainable social security systems. In line with this, the commitment to social market economy and social progress of the Lisbon Treaty had several setbacks, including wage-dumping policies that contributed significantly to the large current account imbalances of member states (Busch et al. 2013). The failure of the Growth and Stability Pact in assuring compatibility with social and economic standards emerged clearly during the crisis.

4. THE AUSTERITY PERIOD

The social dimension of the EU has been weakened tremendously during the crisis. Social policies fell to the bottom of the priority list of the EU strategies, a neglect that further contributed to the grim growth perfor-mances. The austerity policy proved to be a confirmation of the trend that EU social policies followed during the 1990s. As expressed in Busch et al. (2013), austerity policy primarily entailed an attack on wages, social services, and public ownership. The principles of centralized collective agreements and general applicability were undermined; decentralized, labor markets were liberalized; and public services, including pensions and health care, were downsized tremendously.

Between 2009 and 2014 the EU countries and the euro area went through fiscal consolidation of an average cumulative adjustment of 3 percent of GDP (in structural terms). In most cases, the adjustment entailed primarily cuts to expenditures, yet the crisis-affected countries (the three program countries of Greece, Ireland, and Portugal, plus Italy and Spain) also recorded substantial tax hikes. In Greece, Ireland, and Portugal the adjustment between 2009 and 2014 led to an improvement of the structural balance of about 16.6, 5, and 6.6 percent of GDP, respec-tively, and for Italy and Spain the adjustment amounted to more than 3 percent. Of this adjustment, expenditure cuts (still in structural terms) were 11.8 percent of GDP in Greece, 4.2 in Ireland, and 4.3 in Portugal. Expenditure cuts in Spain and Italy amounted to 1.4 and 2.5 percent of GDP (as shown in figure 8.1).

Expenditure cuts affected various budget items (see table 8.3). They ranged from cuts or freezing of public sector wages, reduction in the number of staff in the public sector, cuts in the costs of pensions and health care, reduction of unemployment benefits and other benefits, and finally, reduction in public investment, which bore the brunt of adjust-ment in many cases. Overall, the euro area saw a decline in the expansion of some benefit items, like benefits for old age and survivors, health-care

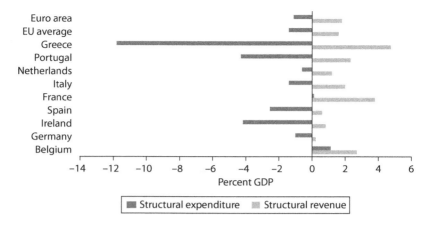

Figure 8.1 Fiscal consolidation: revenue increases versus expenditure cuts (2009–2014).

Source: Eurostat.

benefits, and housing (as shown in figure 8.2a). Considering the crisis-affected euro countries and France (figure 8.2b), disability benefits and family benefits were largely cut in all countries, with the exception of Portugal and France.

Measures adopted within the expenditure cuts vary substantially across member states (Avram et al. 2012). In broad terms, besides cuts in welfare, these reforms entailed reduction in public employment pay (either

Table 8.3 Expenditure Measures 2009–2012

	Public wage freeze/reduction	Control of the size of civil services	Pension savings	Health-care savings	Reduction in unemployment benefits	Reduction in other social benefits	Reduction in public investment	Other
France	x	x	x	x				x
Germany	x	x	x		x	x		
Greece	x	x	x	x	NA	x	x	x
Ireland	x	x	x	x	x	x	x	
Italy	x	x	x	x	NA	x	x	x
Portugal	x	x	x	x	NA	x	x	x
Spain	x	x	x	x	x	x	x	x
United Kingdom	x	x	x	x	x	x	x	x

Source: OECD database 2012; Kickert et al. 2013.

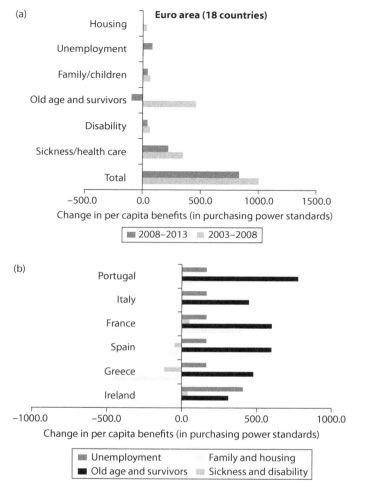

Figure 8.2   Cuts in EU welfare benefits between 2013–2008.

Source: Eurostat.

through freezes or cuts) and personnel, cuts in the costs of public administration, and savings in education spending and public investment.
Pay cuts for public sector workers (net of taxes and contributions) were
substantial in Greece, Latvia, and Portugal, and to a smaller extent in
Romania and Spain (Avram et al. 2012). Regarding cuts in public administration, some countries implemented cuts across the board. One example is Portugal, which cut budget funds for travel expenses by 25 percent,

budget funds for expert reports, projects and consultancy work, and acquisition of external services by 40 percent, and payment of overtime, extra pay for unusual working hours (often called *unsocial hours*), communication expenses, legal advice, and technical assistance by 20 percent (Hespanha and Portugal 2015).

Welfare reforms entailed cuts in the costs of pensions and health care and a reduction in unemployment benefits and other benefits. To reduce pension costs, many countries raised retirement ages, sometimes by accelerating previously scheduled increases (France, Greece, Ireland, Italy, Spain, and the United Kingdom), or by tightening eligibility for early retirement (Greece, Italy, and Spain); and some countries increased the taxation for high pensions and reduced or stopped the indexation of pensions (Greece, Italy, and Spain) (Callan et al. 2011; Fiscal Monitor 2012). In some cases, the application of means testing for the provision of basic pensions was tightened together with the link between contributions and pension benefits (Petmesidou and Guillen 2015). Pension spending was in many cases set to be automatically adjusted to demographic and economic trends. The effort to cut pension spending was often complemented by increases in revenues through higher contribution rates and shifts toward a multi-pillar system for pension benefits. When supplementary pension funds were underdeveloped, in Greece and Portugal, for example, reliance on a reduced public pension benefit system pushed work-related pensions to social assistance levels (Petmesidou and Guillen 2015). Increases in worker social insurance contributions were quite sizable in Estonia and Latvia and, in terms of the share, in the United Kingdom (Avram et al. 2012). In the case of Portugal, for example, the increases in the social security contribution rate paid by workers in the private sector was 7 percent and was partly compensated by a 5.75 percent decrease of contributions paid by employers (Hespanha and Portugal 2015).

In an attempt to reduce health spending, some reforms aimed at containing pharmaceutical spending (France, Germany, Greece, Ireland, Italy, Spain, and the United Kingdom) and others at increasing cost sharing (Greece, Italy, Portugal, and Spain) or reducing hospital operational costs (Portugal) (Fiscal Monitor 2012; Hespanha and Portugal 2015). In the case of Greece, public health-care spending was halved from 2009 to 2013, mostly by efficiency gains in hospital care, procurement methods, and pharmaceutical policies, in parallel with increasing fees and copayments, and drastic rollbacks of public provision (Petmesidou and Guillen 2015).

Regarding social protection benefits, some countries embarked on reforms that saw major cuts in social security budgets, especially in Greece, Portugal, Spain, and the United Kingdom. In 2011, Spain froze the indicator for social benefits, used for the calculation of unemployment benefits and childcare allowances. Similar changes to the base for calculating benefits were applied in Portugal. In 2012, the United Kingdom shifted the indexing of most benefits and tax credits from the Rossi indexes to the consumer price index (CPI), which resulted in a lower mean for the indexation. Greece halved all its tax credits in 2011 and drastically reduced the volume and duration of unemployment benefits (Callan et al. 2011). In Portugal, the duration of unemployment benefits was cut, and social unemployment benefits were capped (Hespanha and Portugal 2015). Child tax allowance was seriously curtailed in Greece; in 2011, Spain eliminated its universal birth grant and almost halved its child benefits; the United Kingdom froze child benefits rates in 2011 (Callan et al. 2011). In the United Kingdom, housing benefits were also cut.

The austerity packages coincided with a series of structural reforms that aimed primarily at liberalizing the labor market. This step was consistent with a general restriction of social rights implemented by governments to respond to an increasingly competitive global economy (Hespanha and Portugal 2015). Labor market liberalization was consistent with a view that regarded competitiveness as a major source for the European crisis. From this, the resulting main aim was to achieve comparative advantages through more flexibility (especially regarding wage policy) and less protection in the labor market and lower labor costs. In Portugal, the regime for individual dismissals was liberalized (Hespanha and Portugal 2015). Similarly, wages were repressed both in the public and private sector. In Greece, the minimum wage was cut by 22 percent for workers above 25 and 32 percent for workers below 25 in 2012 (Callan et al. 2011).

The crisis also brought a significant downsizing of the power of trade union and collective bargaining systems, especially in the crisis-affected countries. Regarding collective agreements, reforms included the legal extension of opening clauses for enterprise-level and deviations from branch-collective agreements (Italy, Portugal, and Spain); abolition of the favorability principle (Greece and Spain); and the possibility for deviating from company agreements with non–trade union workers' representations (Greece and Portugal) (Busch et al. 2013).

AUSTERITY CONSEQUENCES

The consequences for growth and living conditions of the austerity measures are well known. Studies show that the austerity measures were a major factor behind the double-dip recession that European countries experienced in 2011. Under the two bailout programs, Greek GDP shrank by a quarter between 2009 and 2013. Similarly, job losses were remarkably high. From 2009 to 2014, Spain lost about 3.2 million jobs (from a total of 17.2 million). In Greece, losses amounted to about 30 percent of the working population (1 million) for the same period. Employment in Italy declined by about 1.2 million and by half a million in Portugal. With a sluggish recovery, the unemployment spans were protracted, and the share of long-term unemployed over the total went from 34 percent of the total unemployed in 2008 to above 50 percent in 2014. Similarly, intergenerational differences expanded, and youth unemployment went from 15 percent of the corresponding labor force in 2008 to 22 percent in 2014 (OECD database).

Beside growth and jobs, the austerity policies inflicted a heavy toll on the European social model, with a severe impact on inequality, poverty, and ultimately, aggregate demand. As argued by Oxfam (2013), European austerity programs have dismantled the mechanisms that reduce inequality and enable equitable growth. As laid out in Hespanha and Portugal (2015), the measures entailed change both on the supply side and on the demand side. On the supply side the crisis entailed a transfer of responsibilities: changing the ways in which social services are delivered, moving from direct state delivery to indirect delivery via public/private partnership and outsourcing, and an increase in delegation to municipalities. On the demand side, this entailed a reduction in disposable incomes for households due to rising unemployment, higher taxation, cuts in wages and pensions, and increased expenditure on health care, education, housing, social security, and social assistance. Overall, many countries experienced a contraction and deterioration of public services at a time of growing demand for these services.

Income inequality widened as a consequence of the austerity measures (as shown in figure 8.3). While market income inequality deteriorated marginally, probably further due to cuts that altered predistribution (education, health care), most of the increase in inequality is due to changes in the Gini coefficient for disposable income, reflecting the role played by the tax and transfer mix. In Greece, inequality (based on the Gini

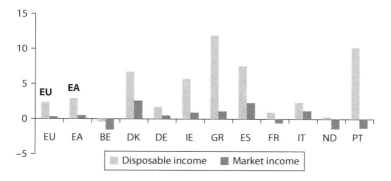

Figure 8.3   Gini coefficients in selected EU countries.

Source: Eurostat/SILC.

disposable income index) increased by 13 percent from 2009 to 2013. Median incomes fell across the board, and poverty rates increased. At present, almost one in ten working households in Europe lives in poverty, often referred to as "in-work" or "working poverty." Childhood poverty is worse, and indicators of social exclusion and material deprivation have also deteriorated in most countries. Access to health care and education and the quality of these services have declined. In Greece, over 2 million people are uninsured; infant mortality and incidences of mental disorders have increased.

As a consequence, countries are very much behind the attainment of the Europe 2020 Strategy (see figure 8.4). Despite some progress in climate policy and education, research and development spending remains very low and far from the target, and social indicators are still very disappointing. The employment rate fell from 70.3 percent in 2008 to 68.4 percent in 2013. The goal is to have 75 percent of the population aged 20–64 in employment. And the figures from the Eurostat report for persons threatened with poverty and social exclusion are nothing short of catastrophic. While this affected 116.6 million in 2008, the number for 2013 had increased to 121.4 million, far from the target of 96.6 million in 2020. A major focus of getting people out of unemployment by creating 20 million jobs by 2010 was not reached. As a reaction to these figures, the European Council expressed in 2012 a timid need for a road map of social Europe, but without much follow-up.

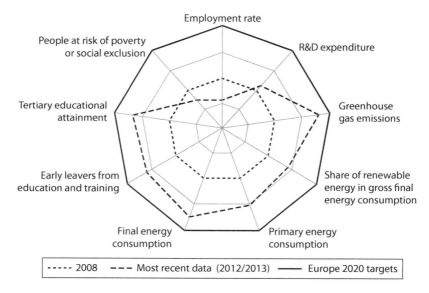

Figure 8.4   Europe 2020 strategy targets and progress.

Note: Since 2008 substantial progress has been made in the area of climate change and energy (through the reduction in greenhouse gas emissions and the increase in the use of renewable energy sources) and in the area of education (through the increase in the rate of tertiary educational attainment and the reduction in the number of early leavers from education and training). Progress has been more limited for R&D expenditure, while the distance to the employment and poverty targets has increased.

Source: Eurostat Press Release 38/2015 of 02.03.2015.

Across the EU countries, it is interesting to note that those with more comprehensive welfare like Germany and Sweden proved to be more resilient. As expressed in Hemerijck (2012), these countries benefited from near-universal social security benefits that acted as robust automatic stabilizers; also, the high quality of social services ensured that workers on short-term unemployment benefits could maintain the human capital. Some studies also point out that it was not the flexibility in the labor market that allowed more resilience to the crisis, but rather the presence of active policies (Bjorsted, Bova, and Dahl 2016). Regarding countries of southern Europe, Petmesidou and Guillen (2015) argue that while significant differences with respect to the roadmap and pacing of reform characterized the four countries in the two decades prior to the crisis, total social spending per capita in purchasing power standards remained significantly below the EU-15 average.

5. CONCLUSION AND THE WAY FORWARD

With an unemployment rate higher than 9 percent in the EU/euro area, a growth rate of around 1.5 percent, and inflation almost at zero, there is great need to stimulate aggregate demand. Against this backdrop, governments' room for maneuver to protect and sustain those in need has shrunken substantially with the retrenchment of the welfare systems brought on by the crisis and by earlier reforms. As the volume of welfare is no longer adequate, old social risks remain unaddressed. At the same time, new socioeconomic forces are unfolding and new risks are emerging, raising the need for a change in the design of the welfare system. Within the old social risks, the dualism between insiders and outsiders in the labor market was exacerbated during the crisis. This refers to both participation by women and youth employment. At the same time, there has been a surge in the precariat and short-term working conditions. Finally, all the challenges posed by an aging population remain. On a larger scale, international competition is challenging the redistributive scope of the welfare state, providing less room to maneuver. Within new social risks, skill depletion is rising, tension between work and family responsibilities is emerging, and new forms of unprotected labor (including digital) are expanding.

At the EU level, social dumping between countries with different welfare regimes is making the need for an EU-wide approach to welfare more compelling. In addition, a new political context characterized by the resurgence of national populism and old-style welfare chauvinism has emerged. Further, increased tax competition is reducing the provision of public goods. Within this state of affairs, aggregate demand remains low and policies for the recovery have been disappointing so far. More liquidity in the market has not helped, nor would the recently launched European investment plan. The effectiveness of both strategies—quantitative easing and investment policies—is limited by the prevailing sense of uncertainty in the EU countries. With weak economic prospects, investors and families are saving.

To address these problems, new strategies are needed. As argued by many, stepping up efforts in social investment spending should be a priority (Hemerijck 2012). This means higher and more targeted spending on ALMPs (active labor market policies), childcare, education, research, and the rehabilitation of the disabled.[2] Further, Europe is in deep need of stimulating aggregate demand. Priority should remain on fighting unemployment and poverty. The system of European economic and fiscal governance should be revised, and within this system, national tax and benefit systems have to be reviewed for improved efficiency, intergenerational equity, and fair sharing of financial burdens between the wealthy and the poor.

With no effective mechanism in place that could stop divergent economic developments across countries, a stronger political and social union, while delivering the much needed social assistance at the EU level, would also work in the direction of preserving the euro and its construct, as it will help reduce economic divergences that have frequently been the source of large economic imbalances within the EU. Such a step forward would probably require an EU treasurer or a sort of fiscal office that could raise taxes and have an enlarged budget. As put forward in this chapter, the Economic and Monetary Union setting generated major pressures on national labor markets and welfare states toward deregulation and liberalization of these markets, while weakening collective bargaining. We are of the view that a deepening and mutualization of the European social systems could repair major failures in the EU construct and resolve macroeconomic imbalances. As the appetite for such change is limited in the current context, at least at the national level, a new approach on a political level would be warranted, which would imply advancement toward a political union with a "decision-making body" and a social union as the "spending structure" to be achieved through a fiscal and monetary union with sound fiscal governance.

NOTES

1. At times these changes occurred in the 1980s and at times in the 2000s. Yet as the bulk took place in the 1990s, we will refer here to changes *around* the 1990s.

2. As defined by Hemerijck (2012), non–social investment spending includes old-age spending; survivors' and disability pensions, excluding the rehabilitation expenses; and unemployment spending, excluding expenses on ALMP.

REFERENCES

Atkinson, A. B. 2008. "The Economics of the Welfare State in Today's World." *International Tax and Public Finance* 15:5–17.

Avram, S., F. Figari, C. Leventi, H. Levy, J. Navicke, M. Matsaganis, M. Militaru, A. Paulus, O. Rastrigina, and H. Sutherland. 2012. "The Distributional Effects of Fiscal Consolidation in Nine EU Countries." European Commission, Research Note 01/2012. European Commission, Brussels.

Barkbu, B., J. Rahman, R. Valdés, and an IMF staff team. 2012. "Fostering Growth in Europe Now." IMF Staff Discussion Note, 12/07. International Monetary Fund, Washington, D.C.

Bjorsted, E., E. Bova, and S. Dahl. 2016. "Lessons Learnt from the Nordics: How to Fight Long-Term Unemployment?" *Intereconomics—Review of European Economic Policy* 51(3):172–78.

Börsch-Supan, A. 2015. "Challenges for European Welfare States." *International Tax and Public Finance* 22(4):534–48.

Busch, K., C. Hermann, K. Hinrichs, and T. Schulten. 2013. *Euro Crisis, Austerity Policy and the European Social Model.* Berlin: Friedrich Ebert Stiftung, International Policy Analysis.

Callan, T., C. Leventi, H. Levy, M. Matsaganis, A. Paulus, and H. Sutherland. 2011. *The Distributional Effects of Austerity Measures: A Comparison of Six EU Countries.* European Commission, Employment Social Affairs and Inclusion, Research Note 2/2011. European Commission, Brussels.

Cerami, A. 2010. "The Politics of Social Security Reforms in the Czech Republic, Hungary, Poland and Slovakia." In *A Long Goodbye to Bismarck? The Politics of Welfare Reform in Continental Europe*, ed. B. Palier, 233–54. Amsterdam: Amsterdam University Press.

Dustmann, C., B. Fitzenberger, U. Schönberg, and A. Spitz-Oener. 2014. "From Sick Man of Europe to Economic Superstar: Germany's Resurgent Economy." *Journal of Economic Perspectives* 28(1):167–88.

Esping-Andersen, G. 1990. *Three Worlds of Welfare Capitalism.* Cambridge, U.K.: Polity Press.

——. 1996. *Welfare States in Transition. National Adaptions in Global Economies.* London: Sage.

Esping-Andersen, G., Gallie, D., Hemerijck, A., and Myles, J. 2002. Why We Need a New Welfare State. Oxford: Oxford University Press.

European Commission. 2001. *Employment.* European Commission. Available at: http://eur-lex.europa.eu/legal-content/EN/ALL/?uri=URISERV:a13000.

Eurostat. 2015. *Europe 2020: Strategy.* Brussels: European Commission. Available at: http://ec.europa.eu/eurostat/web/europe-2020-indicators/europe-2020-strategy.

Fenger, H. J. M. 2007. "Welfare Regimes in Central and Eastern Europe: Incorporating Post-Communist Countries in a Welfare Regime Typology." *Contemporary Issues and Ideas in Social Sciences* 3(2):1–30.

Ferrera, M. 1996. "The "Southern Model" of Welfare in Social Europe." *Journal of European Social Policy* 6(1):17–37.

Ferrera, M. 2010. "Mapping the Components of Social EU: A Critical Analysis of the Current Institutional Patchwork." In *Europe, 2020*, ed. E. Marlier, D. Natali, and R. Van Dam, 45–67.

Fiscal Monitor. 2012. *Taking Stock: A Progress Report on Fiscal Adjustment, International Monetary Fund.* Washington, D.C.: International Monetary Fund.

Guillen, A. 2010. "Defrosting the Spanish Welfare State: The Weight of Conservative Components." In *A Long Goodbye to Bismarck? The Politics of Welfare Reform in Continental Europe*, ed. B. Palier, 183–206. Amsterdam: Amsterdam University Press.

Hall, P. A. 1986. *Governing the Economy: The Politics of State Intervention in Britain and France.* New York: Oxford University Press.

Hemerijck, A. 2012. "When Changing Welfare States and the Eurocrisis Meet." *Sociologica* 1:1–49.

Hemerijck, A., and I. Marx. 2010. "Continental Welfare at a Crossroads: The Choice Between Activation and Minimum Income Protection in Belgium and the Netherlands." In *A Long Goodbye to Bismarck? The Politics of Welfare Reform in Continental Europe*, ed. B. Palier, 129–56. Amsterdam: Amsterdam University Press.

Hespanha, P., and S. Portugal. 2015. "Welfare Cuts and Insecurity Under the Rule of Austerity: The Impact of the Crisis on Portuguese Social Services." *Oñati Socio-legal Series* 5(4):1110–32.

Jessoula, M., and A. Alti. 2010. "Italy: An Uncompleted Departure from Bismarck." In *A Long Goodbye to Bismarck? The Politics of Welfare Reform in Continental Europe*, ed. B. Palier, 157–82. Amsterdam: Amsterdam University Press.

Kickert, W., T. Randma-Liiv, and S. Riin. 2013. "Fiscal Consolidation in Europe: A Comparative Analysis." COCOPS Trend Report.

Leibfried, S., and P. Pierson. 2000. "Social Policy: Left to Courts and Markets?" In *Policy-making in the European Union*, 4th ed., eds. H. Wallace and W. Wallace, 267–92. Oxford: Oxford University Press.

Oxfam. 2013. "A Cautionary Tale: The True Cost of Austerity and Inequality in Europe." Oxfam Briefing Paper 174. Oxfam, Oxford.

Pallier, B. 2010a. "Ordering Change: Understanding the 'Bismarckian' Welfare Reform Trajectory." In *A Long Goodbye to Bismarck? The Politics of Welfare Reform in Continental Europe*, ed. B. Palier, 19–44. Amsterdam: Amsterdam University Press.

——. 2010b. "The Dualizations of the French Welfare System." In *A Long Goodbye to Bismarck? The Politics of Welfare Reform in Continental Europe*, ed. B. Palier, 73–99. Amsterdam: Amsterdam University Press.

Petmesidou, M., and A. Guillen. 2015. "Economic Crisis and Austerity in Southern Europe: Threat or Opportunity for a sustainable Welfare State?" Brussels: European Social Observatory 18, Research Paper.

Seeleib-Kaiser, M. 2013 "Welfare Systems in Europe and the United States: Conservative Germany Converging Toward the Liberal US Model?" *International Journal of Social Quality* 3(2):60–77.

——. 2015. *Quo vadis Social Europe? Options for Greece.* Presentation prepared for FEPS conference, *Greece Forward*, Athens, 14 October 2015.

CHAPTER 9

Visible Costs and Hidden Gains

Kalle Moene

Popular sentiments are not only based on what we wish to be true, but also on what we can directly observe. The economic costs of welfare spending are visible. The social and economic gains of welfare spending are less so. We cannot observe the gains directly. The gains can be identified by comparing the outcomes from the present state of affairs with the outcomes from circumstances that the welfare arrangements aim to remove, but that easily reemerge once we stop the spending.

Typically, participants in political debates highlight the cost side of welfare provisions and almost deny the existence of the benefit side. This *welfare denial* can be echoed with moral conviction all over the world— and not only by right-wing populists. Libertarians can be equally biased. If so, they are not in line with Adam Smith, who was an ardent enemy of welfare denial and instead emphasized the real gains of social policies: "What improves the circumstances of the greater part can never be regarded as an inconveniency to the whole. No society can surely be flourishing and happy, of which the far greater part of the members are poor and miserable" (Smith, 1776, 88).

As we proceed, I will try to make clear how welfare denial may block social programs that raise productivity, equalize power, and provide a head start on a good development path in poor countries.

THE POLITICAL ECONOMY OF VISIBILITY

In general, the welfare state can cover basic needs and necessary human investments that the market fails to cover. Skeptics of welfare arrangements for the poor may, of course, recognize that there are some social and economic gains of this kind, but without numbers it is too easy for them to claim that the welfare state is too expensive—that it is nice if we could afford it.

Even when the value of social insurance and productivity enhancement stemming from welfare arrangements is much higher than the cost, the political economy of visible costs and hidden gains might prevent good reforms from being implemented. Powerful elites may also have strong self-serving biases in the sense that they only see the gains that benefit themselves and compare these gains with the costs of welfare spending.

The bias can be grave. The gains from welfare state arrangements that go to the worst-off groups in society can be comprehensive. The benefits to them may change their social situation completely, by introducing a valuable element of economic security. The benefits may also increase their power in the workplace and raise their productivity and pay. The benefits may eliminate inefficiently low levels of wages and of work efforts.

What is eliminated, however, is no longer directly visible. In contrast, the cost side of welfare programs becomes more visible when the gains are not directly observed. This perception asymmetry of costs and benefits of welfare spending is important for the countries that plan to undertake welfare reforms. The financial costs of reform to cover health insurance, pensions, insurance of income loss, and so on are easy to calculate. The gains, however, seem more uncertain and vague, and they are actually much harder to quantify in a manner that is transparent to all.

To calculate the gains of welfare arrangements for developing countries requires an assessment of what would potentially happen with and without welfare arrangements. We therefore need more discussion of the relevant mechanisms. Focusing on workers and farmers, we need to imagine what poverty traps they can fall into, what kind of shocks and deprivation they can be exposed to, and how the employers and landowners can take advantage of their vulnerability. The improvements that a welfare state can contribute to stem in part from preventing such potential pitfalls, wherein a temporary worsening might have lasting consequences. The welfare state may also enhance the productivity of weak groups directly by raising their capabilities via education and health programs.

Accordingly, a welfare policy for the poor in developing countries can provide vulnerable groups with resources and services that they otherwise would not have. Northern European countries did not wait until they were rich before introducing such welfare benefits—they became rich after an early introduction of welfare systems.

Many European countries expanded their welfare systems after the crisis in the 1930s, at a time when they actually were poorer than many developing countries are today. In the 1930s Sweden and Norway had about half of the real GDP per capita that South Africa and Brazil have today. In Scandinavia, the early introduction of welfare programs expanded quickly into universal health-care systems and a generous social insurance against loss of income and unemployment.

Why did "asymmetric" visibility not block the Scandinavian welfare expansion? The uneven weight given to costs and benefits was present in the political debates, and may have slowed down the expansion, but not by much in the pioneering years of welfare spending after the mid-1930s and in particular just after the Second World War. One reason was the dominance of parliaments by social democratic parties with a strong commitment to welfare policies. Social organization in comprehensive unions also helped in giving weight to the gains of welfare to their members.

As a result, the reallocations of resources that the welfare programs provided became popular far beyond a core group of low-income earners. The balanced view of welfare programs was reinforced by high economic growth in Sweden and Norway. Even when we exclude Norwegian oil revenues, the economic growth of Scandinavia (from 1930 to 2016) was higher than economic growth in the United States (Barth, Moene, and Willumsen 2014).

CAPABILITY ENHANCEMENT: THE ROLE OF BALANCED POWER

Welfare arrangements can enable workers to take more control over their lives and thus become less vulnerable to abuse of power on the part of others. The possible individual productivity effect captures how the welfare state can make workers physically stronger, more able, and more powerful. These effects are the result of reducing the fear and suffering that people are exposed to and increasing their human capabilities.

One reason why support from outside can raise worker productivity and reduce vulnerability is that labor power in a sense is produced by inputs. When some of these inputs become cheaper and more readily available, workers become more valuable, more secure, and more productive. There are many anecdotal indications of the principle of how successful people have needed welfare support in early years. For instance, while J. K. Rowling was writing her first Harry Potter novel, she was getting single-parent benefits from the welfare state.

In the *Guardian* (30 September 2011) Peter Walker lists several similar stories of how successful entrepreneurs actually benefited from the welfare state while they were striving to establish themselves, including how financier Lord Ashford went on the dole in his twenties while waiting for a new opportunity to exploit. Walker concludes that "far from being a hindrance to entrepreneurship and economic growth, in many cases the welfare state actively promotes them." His conclusion is in line with how Hans Werner Sinn (1996) models the theoretical welfare state, which highlights how social insurance can realize hidden productivity gains and potential capabilities in the population (Moene and Wallerstein 2001).

THE TWO LINKS BETWEEN INCOME AND PRODUCTIVITY

In all societies, and in particular in societies in poor countries, there is a strong link from individual productivity of the direct producer to his or her individual income. Let us call it the I-link. The total productivity of the individual consists of the physical productivity of the means of production in the actual activity together with the producer's ability to work hard and leverage opportunities. Together, the two determine the individual's income and thus the I-link.

One often neglects, however, the reverse link from income to productivity where welfare policies may play an essential role. Let us call it the P-link. Formally, the P-link is often studied as the association between nutrition and productivity (Dasgupta and Ray 1987), but the changes needed to include several extensions are small. Clearly, the income of the producer determines not only his or her nutritional level but also the credit that he or she can obtain to acquire necessary inputs and the vulnerability he or she is exposed to without proper social insurance (Moene 1992). In any case, this reverse link from income to productivity exhibits how labor power, in a sense, is produced by personal income.

Let us first consider the pure links, one from productivity to income (the I-link) and the other from income to productivity (the P-link). We are interested in sustainable situations in which the productivity generates an income just high enough to sustain the productivity.

A low-productivity trap may emerge where low incomes generate low productivity. The resulting low productivity obviously produces low incomes, and the low incomes can maintain the low productivity. For instance, with a low income, the producer may be lean and hungry, with insufficient nutrition, and thus weak physical strength. He or she may therefore be constrained in the exercise of work and may therefore only be able to work with low effort and low intensity.

Similarly, with a low income, the producer may be unable to acquire important complementary inputs—everything from fertilizer and irrigation to electricity and health services—which may hamper the physical productivity for every level of work effort. This further constrains the ability to use actual opportunities effectively. The result may again be low productivity, and thus a low income that continues to constrain the access to complementary inputs maintains the low productivity and the corresponding low income in a self-enforcing equilibrium.

Equally important is the vulnerability to shocks that can lead individual households into the trap of low income and a low productivity. As a result they may become hopelessly indebted. Temporary shocks can thus have lasting consequences. The I-link from productivity to income may get a shift down due to a drought or a local famine, implying that the worker is unable to maintain the old productivity level and his or her ability to produce as income falls. To recover after such shocks can take years of suffering, trying to recoup by gradual saving and investments. The average income and productivity are, of course, highly affected by such disruptions.

It can make a difference to have a welfare state arrangement to prevent bad outcomes and to get out of the bad situation once there. The welfare state can, in short, change the self-enforcing low-productivity, low-income situation. It can affect the P-link, raising the capability of a worker for each level of income he or she earns.

Poverty and poor health erode the ability to work hard, but the welfare state can provide a remedy. It can offer social insurance and health services—and by doing so it may increase workers' strengths and help in preventing the poverty traps of bad health and severe destitution. With support from outside when it is needed the most, the direct producers may thus be able to avoid some of the worst pitfalls of poverty. In the longer run, the welfare state also provides more education, which again affects the productivity in each activity and each enterprise in which the producer participates.

As indicated, a welfare state can also affect the I-link from productivity to income. It can induce more risk-taking, which can be decisive in obtaining gains from specialization and investment in skills and equipment. In addition, the welfare state can empower producers, who then can dare to stand up against big landowners, strongmen, and employers, because the public provision makes them less vulnerable to abuses of power (Barth and Moene 2015).

HELP THE MILLIONS THAT GO HUNGRY EVEN IN GOOD YEARS

In India we find several policies that raise productivity and reduce vulnerability.[1] For example, India has the world's largest (but least known) school meals program—a program that lifts up the P-curve as it alters the link from income to productivity by providing one meal to all students every day. Thus, the child gets improved nourishment and the rest of household also gets more to eat, having fewer mouths to feed. The results are impressive. School enrollment in several areas increased by more than 20 percent, and nutrition has clearly improved. India also has a rural employment program—a program that lifts the I-curve—the link from productivity to income yields higher incomes for each productivity level. It guarantees 100 days of employment to every adult person in rural areas. In Kerala, 90 percent of the participants in the program are women who not only obtain better living conditions, but who also obtain more power in their villages as their incomes go up.

The former secretary of state for international development for the United Kingdom, Hilary Benn, clearly saw some of the benefits from programs like these—not only in India but more generally in Africa, Asia, and Latin America. In a presentation in 2006 (transcribed in the *Guardian* February 16, 2006), he emphasized how the welfare state "can stop a farmer selling precious assets—her livestock, farm tools—when she suffers a crisis, such as a drought or someone in her family becoming ill. It can help her and those many millions who go hungry even in the good years, when there is no drought. Social security can encourage her to take risks with higher yielding crops. It can encourage poor families to keep their children in school—as shown by very successful schemes in Brazil, Mexico, and South Africa. All of them contribute to growth, but also to a fairer and more equitable society."

A SOCIAL MULTIPLIER AT THE HOUSEHOLD LEVEL

Let us now return to our two-way links between income and productivity. As we have seen, welfare programs enhance capabilities compared with what they otherwise would have been. This means the P-curve is lifted upward as the link from income to productivity shifts up. Each income level of the worker now corresponds to a higher ability and productivity. The positive link from productivity to income, the I-link, can also be shifted up. What does it imply?

Consider first the case where the I-link remains unchanged, but where the P-link from income to productivity shifts up. The higher productivity for each income level generates a higher income that in the next round generates an even higher productivity and an even higher income—a self-enforcing process. Thus, there is a social multiplier at the household level that magnifies the initial improvement into positive adjustments in work efforts, incomes, and productivity.

Similarly, if the P-link remains unchanged and the I-link from productivity to income shifts up, a cumulative process of changes is set forth, adding up to a social multiplier at the household level. Now, no matter which of the two links get the initial boost, we clearly have magnified effects when one of the links changes and the other remains unchanged; we clearly have even stronger effects when both curves are lifted up simultaneously.

In other words, a welfare state arrangement can be a highly beneficial investment that not only improves the well-being of vulnerable groups but also expands the set of feasible opportunities and enhances the ability of all to take advantage of them. The public welfare provisions can spread the costs of necessary insurance. It can provide social protection against shocks, misuse of power, and the probability of becoming trapped in deprivation. It can help people avoid the slippery slope of poverty, as the welfare arrangement can stop temporary bad events from leading to chronic poverty.

The same two basic links between income and productivity may also give rise to two locally stable self-enforcing situations. They may sustain an outcome where a high productivity produces a high income that can maintain the high productivity. Whether or not there are two equilibria like this for each individual depends on the form of the two-way links between income and productivity. In any case, the welfare state can affect the situation in a way that magnifies productivity increases.

The effects become most dramatic when there are two locally stable equilibria and the introduction of welfare state provisions shifts the equilibrium from the poverty trap with low income and low productivity to the elevated level with high income and high productivity. But even when there is a unique equilibrium, welfare spending can have a significantly magnified effect. As we have shown, it first raises the income of vulnerable groups. Next, the higher income that each member of the group receives generates additional income growth. Greater access to resources raises productivity further, which again leads to higher income, and so on. Naturally, the process converges to a new and higher level of productivity and income than before.

EMPOWERMENT: THE CASE OF INEFFICIENTLY LOW WAGES

The interplay between the welfare state and the P-link can make bad jobs unprofitable and good jobs more profitable, encouraging structural change that enhances well-being and fairness and boosts the overall efficiency of the economy.

This mechanism depends on how high wages may give positive encouragement, and low wages may give negative encouragement. Such mechanisms were emphasized by Adam Smith (1776, 91) in his *Wealth of Nations*: "The liberal reward of labour, . . . encourages the propagation, so it increases the industry of the common people [. . .] Where wages are high, [. . .] we shall always find the workmen more active, diligent, and expedious, than where they are low."

The modern usage of efficiency wages emphasizes one side of this—namely the high effort when wages are high—and how the employer accordingly has reasons to raise wages to induce higher effort (as shown by Shapiro and Stiglitz 1984; Bowles and Gintis 1993). The perception we shall focus on here is the other side—namely, low effort when wages are low. But can any employer benefit from setting a low wage and obtaining a low effort when he or she knows that a higher wage would yield a higher effort?

The answer is yes, he or she can benefit from higher profits. A low-wage strategy is profitable as long as the decline in wage costs when wages are reduced is greater than the decline in the total revenue when efforts go down with lower wages. Thus, the employer needs to be powerful and must to some extent be able to force the workers into compliance with his or her terms. In low-productivity jobs, manned by vulnerable and low-skilled workers with few outside options, this may often be the case. Such bad jobs are prevalent in the informal sector in most developing countries. If the employer reduces the wage, the worker cannot easily retaliate by being less cooperative and impose costs on the employer. Or, which can amount to the same thing, the worker is so vulnerable that he or she does not dare to speak up against unfair treatment in fear of the consequences of not having a job.

When these conditions are present, it pays for the employer to lower the wage as much as possible, only constrained by the requirement that the worker is still willing to participate. The resulting wages can be classified as inefficiency wages. The name fits, as such low wages cause inefficiency; production goes down, and the workers become more miserable, but profits go up. Employers get a larger share of a smaller pie. Thus inefficiency wages are costly not only to the workers but also to society at large.

Good jobs with high productivity, in contrast, are often manned by more skilled workers, and it is important for the employer to motivate these workers to work hard and to take the right initiatives. If they are treated badly, high-skilled workers in high-productivity jobs have more retaliatory power in the workplace. As a consequence, it is most profitable for employers to offer them efficiency wages, while their brothers in low-productivity jobs get inefficiency wages.

Reciprocity can account for the behaviors in both good and bad jobs (Rabin 1993). Good jobs produce positive reciprocity: employers raise wages above the norm, and workers respond by a work effort above the norm. Bad jobs produce negative reciprocity: employers reduce wages below the norm, and workers respond by a work effort below the norm. The reason why wage reductions are profitable in these bad jobs is that the retaliatory power is low relative to the productivity of the jobs.

If all this is true and relevant, empowerment via welfare state programs would change the production relations. Workers would simply get more power and a stronger voice. Vulnerable workers would become less vulnerable as net receivers of welfare benefits and support. The consequences of being fired become less severe when they are socially insured. The health of their children is less dependent on their personal income when they have access to public health services. Workers become better trained when the education system improves.

Welfare state programs that empower workers and increase their short-term outside options and their long-term life chances would also raise the lowest wages that the workers would accept. As the lowest wage goes up, the inefficiency wage strategy becomes less profitable. Welfare state polices can also empower workers more directly. Workers may become more willing to stand up against unfair treatment and employers' abuse. As a consequence, workers get a stronger voice and more retaliatory power.

The profitability of bad jobs is high only when workers are weak and other wages are low. Empowering workers via welfare programs can put an end to this employer dominance. It may at least transform some of the bad jobs into good jobs. When the profitability of applying inefficiency wages declines, the low-wage strategy obviously become less attractive. In other words, the threshold level of productivity that separates good jobs from bad jobs goes down. Thus we get fewer bad jobs and more good jobs. In this way, welfare spending leads to structural change with higher productivity, higher average effort, and higher average wages. The changes are most dramatic at the bottom of the wage and skill distribution.

If this is right, formal welfare programs lead to a decrease in informal economic activities where workers work without any employment contract, and an increase in jobs with more well-ordered employment conditions. This comes on top of the empowerment effect and the productivity effects. So if welfare spending empowers weak groups in their life chances, and this empowerment provides society-wide gains, a pressing question must be: How can one implement such a system in poor countries?

IMPLEMENTATION: CONTINUOUS, POLITICALLY SUSTAINABLE, REDISTRIBUTION

How can one avoid visible costs and hidden gains situations? One may think that a possible remedy is to target welfare programs in favor of the worst-off groups. Such targeting may make the gains of welfare benefits more visible, as everybody can see to whom they go. This general visibility effect, however, can be countered by distributional concerns.

TARGETING ERODES POLITICAL SUPPORT

The comprehensive cradle-to-grave welfare state in European countries (Scandinavian countries in particular) is based on rather universalistic programs. The programs have benefits that go to all citizens—rich and poor—rather than only to the poor. Politically, the welfare state has benefited from this universalistic feature, even though it is rather expensive. Universal spending gathers wider support in the population than more targeted programs.

A targeted program that has benefits that go only to the needy would garner less support, unless one can rely on stable and strong altruism in the population. The insurance aspect of universal welfare spending extends the political support far up in the middle class, even among citizens who might pay more into the welfare system in the form of taxes than they expect to get out in the form of insurance benefits.

All these aspects are also important for implementing social policies in developing countries. One may ask which welfare state policy would lead to the highest empowerment of the poor and to the maximal reduction in poverty when the funding of the program is decided by majority vote in society? If the welfare budget was given, the answer is obviously the most targeted programs. But the welfare budget is endogenous, and it is not difficult to show that universal programs also lead to the highest benefits for the worst-off groups.

In fact, it can be demonstrated that with targeted programs, it is not clear that there would be any benefits to the worst-off groups in the absence of strong altruism in the population (Moene and Wallerstein 2003b). There would be so little self-interested support for such welfare programs from the middle class that the programs could easily vanish altogether.

Another pressing question for the implementation of welfare spending is how the overall support for the program is affected by changes in the income distribution and in the trust that people have in the public provider of welfare services.

INEQUALITY ERODES THE GENEROSITY OF WELFARE PROGRAMS

It should be clear by now that the welfare state is not a mechanism of pure redistribution from the rich to the poor. If it were, a huge inequality should generate high support for more welfare spending, as the majority in any country earns less than the average income.

The welfare state has never worked as simply as that, which is evident from the observation that even in the developed world it is those countries with the smallest pretax income inequality that have the largest and most generous welfare states (Barth and Moene 2015). Extending the picture to include developing countries, it is even clearer that countries with the most profound inequality and income divisions have almost no welfare arrangements at all (Lindert 2004).

As mentioned earlier, the welfare state is a provider of goods and services that the private sector often cannot supply equally efficiently, including social insurance, health care, and education. These welfare provisions are normal goods in the sense that the political demand for the provisions go up with higher income. The classification of welfare provisions as normal goods can be controversial for reasons that are not so easy to understand. A normal good is simply one that you like to have more of the higher your income is.

These public welfare provisions are paid for by taxes. The collective political demand for the provisions is a sum of individual demands. Consider a single mother. Her demand for welfare provisions depends on how high the total taxable incomes in the country are and on how much she earns. Her needs are important—how vulnerable she is to shocks and her sympathy for others who may be worse off. Finally, her demand for public welfare provisions would also depend on the trust that she has in the state apparatus and in local public providers.

Keeping all other things constant and just raising her income would raise her demand for welfare provision. Why? Simply because having a higher income, she can afford more of many things that she likes, and also those that the welfare state provides, such as health services, education, pensions, and social insurance for herself and others. With a lower income, her immediate needs would most likely be so pressing that she would be unable to pay much higher taxes to have more welfare provisions.

Now, with a lower income inequality for a given mean level, we raise the income to the majority of citizens. When the majority of the citizens get higher incomes, a majority of voters demand higher provisions by the welfare state.

Earlier we discussed a case in which structural change reduced inequality between good and bad jobs and the average income was raised as well. In that case, the political demand for welfare spending would go up, both because the tax base (the average wage) would increase and because the individual wage for most workers within the majority would go up as well—without necessarily altering individuals needs and the risks to which they are exposed. So welfare spending becomes higher when inequality (before taxes and transfers) is low, reinforcing the initial wage compression via political adjustments and structural change.

Welfare spending is therefore one of the clearest examples of how equality creates support for more equality—what can be called political reinforcement. I have tried to test this proposition in several joint research projects. All our work confirms the proposition that wage compression increases welfare spending (see Moene and Wallerstein 2001, 2003a; Barth and Moene 2015; Barth, Finseraas, and Moene 2015).

In fact, in northern European countries, this mechanism seems to be so strong that a generous welfare state is not dependent on a social democratic party being in power. Hidden gains of welfare can be a threat to this situation, in particular when the economy is exposed to demographic changes and external shocks. So far, however, it is still the case that to win elections in Scandinavia, political parties across the spectrum have to shift their policies in a social democratic direction as wage compression shifts the political center of gravity. And as incomes become more compressed, both right-wing and left-wing parties shift their policies toward higher levels of generosity (Barth, Finseraas, and Moene 2015). Rising inequality, however, may erode the support for welfare spending.

EQUALITY CAN MULTIPLY

To have a realistic view of a welfare state for the poor, we have to incorporate how welfare spending is both fueled by and fuels income equality by empowering weak groups in the labor market and via structural change in the economy. The generosity of social policies narrows wage differentials by altering the power between groups and the dispersion of productivity in the economy. Both reactions lead to more wage equality. In the next round, higher wage equality raises the political support for a more generous social policy by raising the income of the majority of the electorate.

This complementarity between social spending and earnings is an important example of the mutual dependence between politics and markets. It demonstrates how economic and social equality multiplies due to the complementarity between wage determination and welfare spending. Based on an elaborate model of these processes, Barth and Moene (2015) estimate an equality multiplier of more than 50 percent, using data for eighteen countries over thirty-five years. Any exogenous change in either welfare spending or wage setting is thus magnified in the long run by 50 percent by endogenous forces caused by social complementarity. A comparison of countries shows that the multiplier is highest in countries that start with a low level of welfare spending, like most developing countries to day.

The equality multiplier helps explain why almost equally rich countries differ so much in the economic and social equality that they offer their citizens, and why the divide in living standard between rich and poor countries may be widening. The equality multiplier can generate persistence of social policies. In the development context, this may be good news, as countries that embark upon social equality as a development strategy may be able to continue with the policy. The equality multiplier creates the conditions for further social improvements, even with shifting governments.

Thus, it may be seriously wrong to think that a country must first become more economically advanced and wait until it has become afflu-ent before it can distribute the fruits of its development to all citizens.

DEVELOPMENT FIRST, REDISTRIBUTION LATER

Indeed, some observers find it reasonable to think that it is important to become rich first, and then redistribute the fruits of labor via welfare spending. It might be tempting to reason like this. Yet it must be wrong for at least two different reasons.

First of all, this thinking is based on the idea that we can postpone necessary policies of health provision, education, and social insurance until a country is affluent. This gives priority to private consumption for the better off to an extent that is clearly absurd, and it might even undermine the possibility of earning high private incomes as well. If I am right that welfare spending has clear social gains for society in the form of empowerment and higher productivity, it must be important to start spending on welfare early. Postponement just means that potential gains are wasted, that people are deprived of the benefits they could have had.

Second, this thinking is based on the false assertion that becoming rich with a certain income distribution does not affect political ability to redistribute in the future. But economic development creates economic and political interests that tend to sustain the emerging distribution via the political processes. This is another aspect of political reinforcement where high inequality generates low support for redistributive welfare spending. So, postponing the policy can imply eliminating it altogether.

If political support for welfare spending declines as economic and social gaps increase, and if postponement further increases this inequality (some get rich first), then it follows that the emerging upper class may use their political power to preserve their privileges and thus block reforms of generous welfare benefits to the worst-off majority.

When Deng Xiaoping was China's de facto leader from 1978 until he died in 1997, he promoted economic liberalization under slogans such as "It doesn't matter if a cat is black or white, so long as it catches mice" and "Let some people get rich first." Both slogans seem innocuous, but they are not.

Economic growth (catching mice) is just a means to an end of higher well-being for everybody. Thus it matters to whom the benefits of growth are allocated. Welfare state arrangements can help in allocating more of the gains to the worst-off groups. As I have argued, it can pay to do so, not only for the worst-off groups but for the great majority of citizens.

Letting some get rich first is an argument for vested interests in policies that always let the same groups go first—all of the time—backed by the political support of redistribution and welfare state policies. Of course, among those who benefited the most at the earliest stage in China were officials of the Communist Party who quietly got rich, fast.

Generally, in all countries, letting some get rich first, before introducing welfare state arrangements, creates strong opponents of any egalitarian reforms of redistribution and empowerment. Letting some get rich first is the same as stimulating the rise of strong interests who are unable, and perhaps unwilling, to see the gains of redistribution and welfare policies, and who instead focus the most attention on the visible costs of the welfare state.

CONCLUSION

I have tried to make a case for the relevance of three interrelated effects of a welfare state for the poor in developing countries. The productivity effect emphasizes how the welfare state raises the labor productivity of poor workers. They become stronger and more able when they are better nourished and protected, when they have better health and more education. Higher productivity means higher incomes.

The empowerment effect emphasizes how the welfare state empowers weak groups. It enables them to take more control over their lives, to be more resistant against shocks and deprivation and better protected against the abuse of power by landowners and employers.

The head-start effect emphasizes how an early introduction of welfare spending is economically and politically advantageous. It can reap the benefits of empowerment and of higher productivity for a longer period. In addition, it can prevent those who have improved their income status from monopolizing political power and expressing an unwillingness to help others for the collective good of the great majority.

The three effects constitute a rather positive picture of the potential of the welfare state for the poor in poor countries. This is in contrast to views that emphasize how welfare spending can be difficult to implement in unstable developing countries where people do not trust the state apparatus, where there perhaps are dishonest and incompetent local providers who never forget themselves in allocating the benefits meant for others.

This criticism is easy to understand, but it can be raised against any policy that does not directly benefit the elite. Bad governance can be highly problematic for all policies to be implemented—not only welfare state policies. The basic question is whether welfare policies can improve politics and reduce favoritism and corruption—making the potential gains of welfare more politically visible.

The answer may depend on the design of welfare policies. Targeted programs with high levels of means testing, control, and monitoring would easily increase bureaucratic misuse of power. A more universal—and more expensive—welfare state may have a better chance of succeeding.

If it succeeds, empowering workers via welfare programs may increase production, reduce poverty, and reduce profits obtained through exploitation of low-wage workers. To achieve this, the benefits paid out by the welfare state need not be on Swedish levels in any absolute sense. The benefit levels have to be set in accordance with the local living conditions in a country.

Perhaps one should search for policies that make welfare spending as a share of GDP more or less the same across countries, both rich and poor. This share may well be at the Swedish level. In any case, no country needs to be rich before introducing welfare state programs—but a country may become rich by introducing such programs.

NOTE

1. A fine overview of all the social programs in India can be found in the compilation of articles and overviews by Dreze and Khera (2015), which provides a critical discussion of the results.

REFERENCES

Barth, E., H. Finseraas, and K. O. Moene. 2015. "Political Reinforcement: How Rising Inequality Curbs Manifested Welfare Generosity." *American Journal of Political Science* 59(3):565–77.

Barth, E., and K. O. Moene. 2015. "The Equality Multiplier. How Wage Compression and Welfare Spending Interact." *Journal of European Economic Association.* 14: 1011–37.

Barth, E., K. O. Moene, and F. Willumsen. 2014. "The Scandinavian Model—An Interpretation." *Journal of Public Economics* 117:60–72.

Bowles, S., and H. Gintis. 1993. "The Revenge of Homo economicus: Contested Exchange and the Revival of Political Economy." *Journal of Economic Perspectives* 7(1):83–102.

Dasgupta, P., and D. Ray. 1987. "Inequality as a Determinant of Malnutrition and Unemployment: Policy." *Economic Journal* 97(385):177–88.

Dreze, J., and R. Khera. 2015. "Readings in Social Policy and Public Action" [unpublished compilation]. Available at: http://hss.iitd.ac.in/faculty/reetika-khera.

Lindert, P. H. 2004. *Growing Public.* Vol. 1, *The Story: Social Spending and Economic Growth Since the Eighteenth Century.* Cambridge: Cambridge University Press.

Moene, K. O. 1992. "Poverty and Landownership." *American Economic Review* 82 (1): 52–64.

Moene, K. O., and M. Wallerstein. 2001. "Inequality, Social Insurance, and Redistribution." *American Political Science Review* 95(4):859–74.

Moene, K. O., and M. Wallerstein. 2003a. "Earnings Inequality and Welfare Spending." *World Politics* 55(4):485–516.

——. 2003b. "Targeting and Political Support for Welfare Spending." In *Conflict and Governance*, ed. Amihai Glazer and Kai A. Konrad, 33–54. Berlin: Springer.

Rabin, M. 1993. "Incorporating Fairness Into Game Theory and Economics." *American Economic Review* 93:1281–302.

Shapiro, C., and J. E. Stiglitz. 1984. "Equilibrium Unemployment as a Worker Discipline Device." *American Economic Review* 74(3):433–44.

Sinn, H. W. 1996. "Social Insurance, Incentives and Risk Taking." *International Tax and Public Finance* 3(3):259–80.

Smith, Adam. 1776. *An Inquiry Into the Nature and Causes of the Wealth of Nations.* Chicago: University of Chicago Press.

CHAPTER 10

Social Protection Systems in Latin America

TOWARD UNIVERSALISM AND REDISTRIBUTION

José Antonio Ocampo and Natalie Gómez-Arteaga

Latin America saw significant improvements in its social indicators over the 2003–2013 decade, including reductions in income inequality in most countries in the region—in sharp contrast to a global trend toward rising inequality both in developed and developing countries. These improvements were matched by a fair economic performance, particularly in 2003–2008, though with a slowdown in 2008–2013. Improvements in income distribution combined with a fair economic growth resulted in a massive reduction of poverty, the fastest since the 1970s. Aside from favorable external conditions (high commodity prices and ample access to external financing), improvements during this "golden social decade" can be attributed to the construction of stronger and innovative welfare states. New forms of social protection have been emerging in the region, including the universal basic pensions of Bolivia, Brazil, and Chile; the universal health system of Colombia; and the growing attraction of cash transfer programs and universal transfers, like child benefits in Argentina. The region has also experienced an expansion of contributory social security, in Ecuador and Uruguay among others, and reversals of pension privatizations in Argentina and Bolivia. These advances have also been matched by progress in other dimensions, such as significant increases of wages and rapid increase in access to education, despite remaining quality gaps.

With the recent improvements and innovations on social protection systems (SPS), the region is going back to the roots of the conceptions on which the welfare state was built in industrial countries, which underscores the universalism and solidarity of a social policy based on the principle of social citizenship. After an important debate and policies that emphasized targeting of state subsidies for the poor and the design of competitive schemes for social service provision with participation of both public and private agents, Latin American countries are moving back toward more universal and comprehensive SPS. This chapter reviews the targeting versus universalism debate and assesses recent improvements of eighteen Latin American countries in three dimensions of social protection aimed at measuring universality, solidarity, and public spending. Between 2002 and 2012, seventeen out of the eighteen Latin American countries improved their score in their Social Protection Index (SPI), meaning they increased coverage of both health and pensions, reduced coverage gaps between wage and non-wage earners, and increased social spending and/or had higher efficiency of social assistance. However, important inequalities remain, both by type of employment and income. Nonsalaried workers are always less likely to be affiliated to health and pensions, and pension coverage is still highly deficient, both in terms of low affiliation among the working population and low coverage of pensions during old age.

The incidence of social spending on poverty and inequality has been significant, especially that of the more universal benefits. The redistributive effect is higher for indirect transfers than for direct transfers, which shows that Latin American universal direct transfers are still limited, while targeted transfers, although highly progressive, have low benefits and coverage. In any case, Latin America achieves lower fiscal redistribution than developed countries due to a less progressive mix of taxes and transfers and limited benefits.

At a time when economic growth has already slowed down and is expected to remain weak in the immediate future, particularly in South America, continuing with the expansion of a stronger welfare state with universal benefits would be an essential strategy. This is supported by the evidence that there is no trade-off between redistribution and growth. In fact, Latin American countries with a higher score on the SPI, or even higher social spending, have had higher growth rates. This implies, however, that higher and more progressive taxes are needed.

This chapter is divided into six sections, aside from this introduction. The first one reviews the debate between universalism and targeting of social policies in Latin America and the return to the roots that inspired social policy in the past. The second shows the improvements of SPS during the last decade using a multidimensional index to measure their comprehensiveness and universality. The third analyzes the present state of SPS and gives an account of the persistent segmentations in the access to health care and pensions. The fourth assesses the incidence on poverty and inequality. The fifth shows the linkages between the expansion of social protection and economic development. Finally, the sixth concludes with some general recommendations.

1. UNIVERSALISM VERSUS TARGETING OF SOCIAL POLICY

The modern conceptions of social policy have their roots in the liberal views on the need to provide basic education and health services as inherent to the progress of modern societies. Since the late nineteenth century, the creation of modern social security systems under the leadership of Bismarck and, particularly, the increasing demands coming from the labor and socialist movements, led to the development of more encompassing views of social policy. The development of the welfare state in the major industrial economies since the 1930s was the result of this process, as well as of the competition with communism in the postwar years. A major corollary of this development was the unprecedented growth in the size of the state.

In Latin America, these views were manifested, but their impacts remained more limited. The reforms introduced in the 1910s in Uruguay by President José Battle are perhaps the earliest manifestations of this trend. However, the development of the most encompassing views of the welfare state remained limited to a few countries—the three Southern Cone countries (Argentina, Chile, and Uruguay) and Costa Rica[1]—and, even then, they never paralleled the welfare states of industrial countries, particularly in terms of the development of an encompassing tax and transfer system to reduce income inequality. For most Latin American countries, even the coverage of educational and health policies was low up to the mid-twentieth century, and social security came late and very restricted in scope, due to its association with formal employment and its corporatist tones. The result was a segmented and incomplete welfare state that irradiated its benefits to some middle sectors of society but tended to marginalize the poor, particularly in rural areas.

The market reforms of the 1980s and 1990s placed social policy in a subordinate status.[2] The new views of social policy that were disseminated throughout Latin America by the World Bank since the 1980s can be best summarized in three instruments for social policy reform: targeting, a more competitive system with private sector participation, and decentralization. The first tried to make social policy consistent with limited fiscal resources as it tried at the same time to benefit the poor. The other two instruments focused on the need to rationalize the state apparatus. To these we must add the multiplication of specific projects aimed at managing the social costs of structural reforms, the most important of which were perhaps the social emergency funds.

The application of the new principles was uneven throughout the region. Specifically, targeting had its best manifestation in the development of conditional transfer programs, which were developed first as an emergency mechanism ("Progresa" in Mexico) or as an instrument to guarantee broader coverage of basic educational services ("Bolsa Escola" in Brazil) but evolved through time into systems with broader coverage, which eventually aimed at the full coverage of the targeted population and were renamed as "Oportunidades" and "Bolsa Familia" and copied by other countries. The spread of this transfer is the spearhead of what Ferreira and Robalino (2011) have called the "social assistance revolution."

The result of these reforms is that the current systems of social policy combine three different models, sometimes in the same country. The first is the strict universal system with public sector organization and different degrees of decentralization that continues to characterize the educational systems; this also includes variable levels of private provision, particularly in the university system. The second is the segmented and corporatist system inherited from the past that continues to prevail in several countries in social security in its broader sense (health, pensions, and professional risks). The third is the strict targeting schemes, the best developments of which are the conditional cash transfer programs. Filgueira et al. (2006, 37) have characterized the resulting systems of social policies as "persistent corporativism mixed with liberal reforms." These systems lack a pillar of clearly designed entitlements, and perhaps most importantly, they lack the coherence and appeal of the old conceptions of the welfare state and thus the capacity to serve as central instruments of social cohesion.

The return of universalism as a paradigm in social policy is closely tied to the concepts of social rights and social citizenship. Internationally, this vision was reflected in the rise of the welfare state and the development of the economic, social, and cultural rights summarized in the Articles 22 to 27 of the Universal Declaration of Human Rights and later in the UN Covenant on Economic, Social and Cultural Rights. This new set of rights expresses the modern notions of equality, solidarity, and non-discrimination, which go back to T. H. Marshall's concept of social citizenship (see Marshall 1992, which reproduces his original 1950 essay).

Furthermore, as stated in the preamble to the in the UN Charter, they should be conceived as the manifestation of the determination of UN member states to "promote social progress and better standards of life in larger freedom"—a concept that, as we know, goes back to Franklin D. Roosevelt's "Freedom from Want" and that has most recently been conveyed by Amartya Sen's "development as freedom" (Sen 1999). In Latin America, this view has also been developed by UN Development Program in the concept of democracy as the extension of the three dimensions of citizenship (civil, political, and social) (UNDP 2004; see also Ocampo 2007).

The more precise formulation of this conception for Latin America is the chapter on the principles of social policy formulated by the UN Economic Commission for Latin America and the Caribbean (ECLAC) in its report *Equity, Development and Citizenship* (ECLAC 2000). The four principles are: universalism, solidarity, efficiency, and integrality. The first of them expresses the view that the entitlements associated with social policy are more than services or commodities: they are *rights* and should therefore be guaranteed to all citizens. The second indicates something that is obvious, particularly in highly unequal societies: that the guarantee of access by the poor to those entitlements should be based on the principle of solidarity, which furthermore expresses the basic objective of building more inclusive societies. The third indicates the resources available to society for its social welfare programs should be optimally used, whereas the last expresses the fact the there are many dimensions to poverty and inequality that should be tackled simultaneously.

Regarding social protection, in 2008 the International Labor Conference (ILC) adopted the landmark "ILO Declaration on Social Justice for a Fair Globalization." The declaration institutionalized the concept of "decent work," which has been developed by the International Labor Organization (ILO) since 1999 to promote a fair globalization. This concept puts forward an integrated approach that recognizes employment, social dialogue, rights at work, and social protection as strategic objectives, with the last including "the extension of social security to all" (ILO 2008, 9–10). As a follow-up to this declaration, at the 101st ILC in 2012, 184 members unanimously adopted Recommendation No. 202, which provides guidance to members for establishing and maintaining social protection floors as a core element of their national social security systems, guaranteeing universal access to essential health care and a basic income over the life cycle for all (ILO 2012).

As it will be seen in the next section, Latin American countries have made significant progress in moving toward more universal and comprehensive SPS during the last decade based on the concepts of social citizenship and decent work.

2. A MULTIDIMENSIONAL INDEX TO MEASURE SPS IN LATIN AMERICA

The SPI designed for this study[3] measures the achievement of eighteen Latin American countries in three dimensions of SPS: universality, solidarity, and social spending (see figure 10.1).[4] This index allows us to differentiate three groups of countries in terms of comprehensiveness and universality of their SPS: (1) Uruguay, Chile, Costa Rica, Argentina, and Brazil, with the highest scores, can be identified as having comprehensive systems; (2) Venezuela, Colombia, Peru, Mexico, Ecuador, the Dominican Republic, and Panama have intermediate systems; and finally (3) El Salvador, Paraguay, Bolivia, Nicaragua, Guatemala, and Honduras have relatively limited SPS (see figure 10.2).[5]

Between 2002 and 2012, fifteen out of the eighteen countries with available data improved their score in the SPI, meaning they had significant improvements in at least one of the dimensions of SP, moving toward a more universal and comprehensive system. In contrast, three did not experience any change in the indicator. Countries with intermediate SPS improved the most. Colombia experienced the strongest improvement in

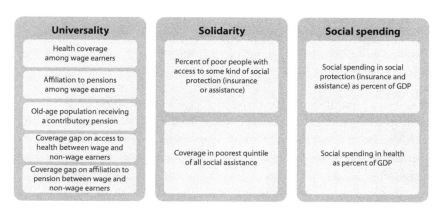

Figure 10.1   A social protection index for LAC.

Source: Ocampo and Gómez-Arteaga (2016).

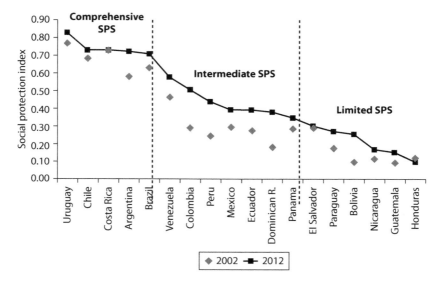

Figure 10.2   Social Protection Index score, circa 2002 and circa 2012.

Note: SPI as the arithmetic mean of the normalized achievements of each country in the nine indicators used to rank countries.

Source: Author's use of data from ECLAC (2013, 2014); Santos et al. (2015); and World Bank data on social protection (ASPIRE). Circa 2012 varies from 2010 to 2013.

the SPI score, followed by Peru, the Dominican Republic, and (a country with a limited SPS) Bolivia. In the case of Colombia, the improvement followed efforts to achieve universal health coverage using a subsidized insurance scheme to reach the poor and independent workers.[6] Colombia significantly increased health coverage for both salaried and nonsalaried workers, reducing the affiliation gap between both types of workers. While 53 percent of salaried workers had access to health care in 2002, coverage was 91 percent by 2012. Coverage also increased among nonsalaried workers, reducing the coverage gap between the two types of employment from 75 percentage points in 2002 to 5 in 2012. Peru, the country with the second-biggest improvement in the index, also had significant improvements in access to health care and pensions. Both indicators almost doubled between 2002 and 2012. Also, the coverage of the poorest quintile in social assistance increased from less than 10 percent to 70 percent. In turn, Bolivia significantly improved access to pensions among its old-age population, passing from coverage of 13 percent to 21 percent. Although this coverage is still low compared with other countries, Bolivia achieves almost universal coverage among the elderly (65 and older) with its noncontributory pensions (see section 3). Of the countries with comprehensive systems, Argentina is the one that improved the most. This was mainly driven by the expansion of pensions, establishing a mandatory minimum basic pension for all, independent of whether the beneficiary had reached the minimum contribution.[7]

The recent improvements in the SPI reflected efforts toward more universal SPS, with specific policies to include the poor and informal populations who have been traditionally excluded. However, as we will see, there is still high segmentation in the access and benefits of SPS by type of employment and income level.

3. A LOWER BUT PERSISTENT SEGMENTATION OF SPS IN THE REGION

There have been significant improvements in access to health care and pensions[8] across the region, with recent innovations in flexible contributory mechanisms, basic pensions like in Argentina, noncontributory pensions like in Bolivia and Chile, and universal health coverage with important solidarity mechanisms as in Colombia, among others.

Between 2002 and 2012, access to pensions and health increased throughout the region for both salaried and nonsalaried workers and at all income levels. Due to efforts to achieve universal health care and to solve the problem of limited coverage linked to formal employment, improvements have been higher on health coverage among non-wage earners and for the lower quintiles of income distribution (see figure 10.3).

The percentage of nonsalaried workers who had access to health care almost doubled during the past decade, while pensions increased by only 3 percentage points. Interestingly, independent of type of employment or income quintile, a person is always more likely to have access to health insurance than to be affiliated with a pension scheme, which reflects the higher redistributive impact of health care than transfers, as will be shown in section 4.

The recent innovations introduced to eliminate the segmentation or "truncation" in the access to protection by type of employment are a clear sign of the paradigm shift toward universalism that overtook the region in recent years. By the end of the twentieth century, when it became clear that the problem of limited coverage (only covering formal employment through contributory schemes) was not going to resolve itself as countries developed,[9] a wave of innovative mechanisms to provide some form

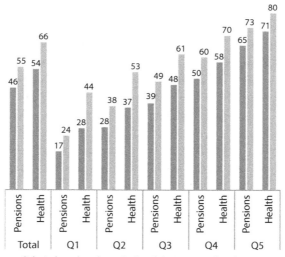

Salaried workers by quintile of the income distribution

2002 ■ 2012

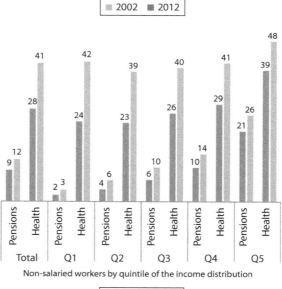

Non-salaried workers by quintile of the income distribution

2002 ■ 2012

Figure 10.3 **Affiliation to health and pension by type of employment in Latin America, circa 2002 and circa 2012.**

Source: ECLAC (2013).

of basic protection for all, especially for self-employed workers, spread throughout the region. Besides the example of the previously mentioned subsidized insurance scheme in Colombia, Uruguay implemented a monotax scheme in 2001 to improve coverage of self-employed workers by unifying different social security contributions and taxes into a single payment through a simplified process, allowing people covered by the monotax to have the same social security benefits as salaried workers based on a solidarity principle (ILO 2014b). Argentina had a similar experience with subsidization of social security contributions for self-employed workers and micro-enterprises, and in Brazil, SIMPLES (a simplified taxation scheme designed for micro- and small businesses) has significantly contributed to reducing the social security labor costs of micro-enterprises.

However, as can also be seen in figure 10.3, despite the improvements since 2002, there are still important segmentations in the access to social protection by type of employment and by income, especially for pensions. While 55 percent and 66 percent of salaried workers are affiliated to health services and a pension fund, respectively, only 12 percent and 41 percent of nonsalaried workers are. In 2012, access to pensions by nonsalaried workers in the lower quintile was less than 5 percent compared with 24 percent of salaried workers in the same quintile. Even in the highest quintiles, nonsalaried workers have lower access to both pensions and health.

Poor households are also less likely to be covered by both types of protection. This is true in all countries, even in countries with comprehensive systems, although the coverage gaps here are less marked. Interestingly, the coverage gap by type of employment in health is higher among the second-poorest 20 percent compared with the poorest 20 percent. This reflects the success of the conditional cash transfer programs, which were targeted to give the poorest population access to basic services. Thus, the coverage gap for the middle distribution is higher.

Protection for the elderly has also increased during the last years. However, according to data available on household surveys, the increases have been higher among the wealthier segments of the population. While 59 percent of the elderly on the top income quintile had access to a pension in 2012, only 21 percent of the elderly in the bottom 20 percent had. Inequality in the access to a pension during old age is not only associated with coverage but also with the amount of benefits. As seen in figure 10.4, benefits are significantly higher for the top 20 percent of the population—even in relation to the second quintile.

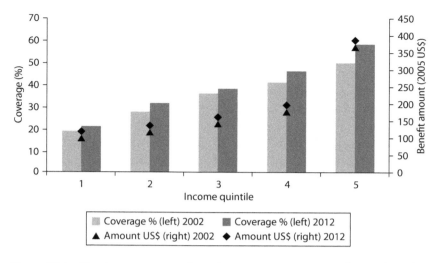

Figure 10.4   Pension coverage and pension amount among population 65 and older by income quintile in Latin America, circa 2002 and circa 2012.

Source: ECLAC (2013, 2015).

Given the low coverage of contributory pensions among the elderly, new schemes of noncontributory pensions are emerging in the region under the leadership of Brazil, Chile, and Bolivia. Coverage by this type of pension in Bolivia reaches 95 percent of the population. In other countries, like Mexico and Panama, noncontributory pensions exist, but as targeted subsidies conditioned on poverty status, and they reach less than 30 percent of the population, a proportion that has nonetheless increased since 2002 (ECLAC 2015)

Efforts to expand social protection have come with an increase in social spending. Social spending as a percentage of GDP increased by almost 5 percentage points between 1990 and 2013; 70 percent of the increase was achieved between 2002 and 2013. The increase was driven mainly by health and social security (insurance and assistance) (ECLAC 2014). However, although Latin America ranks second in the emerging and developing world in terms of social spending as a percentage of GDP, it allocates fewer resources relative to developed countries, both for direct transfers (which include social insurance and assistance, noncontributory pensions, and other benefits like child benefits) and for health and education (see figure 10.5).

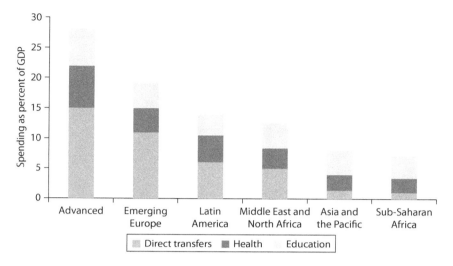

Figure 10.5   Social spending as percentage of GDP.

Source: Bastagli, Coady, and Gupta (2012), based on IMF data.

When looking at the access to health care and pensions by the three categories of SPS (see figure 10.6), two conclusions emerge. First, on average, countries with comprehensive systems have higher coverage and do not have important segmentation by income quintile or type of employment in health, although gaps remain in the access to pensions. Second, the differences in coverage between the three categories of SPS are wider when looking at coverage of nonsalaried workers. Countries with limited SPS still have the majority of the nonsalaried working population excluded from social protection. In these countries, social security is only available for a small proportion of workers with formal employment, in contrast to countries with intermediate and comprehensive systems, which have been advancing in this regard. For example, while 80 percent and 46 percent of nonsalaried workers in countries with comprehensive and intermediate systems, respectively, have access to health coverage, only 10 percent in countries with limited systems do. This gap is much higher than the gap for salaried workers across all types of SPS.

In any case, there is still much to be done. Although targeted programs have been successful in reducing poverty, their effect in reducing income inequality is smaller than in the area of universal benefits (see section 4). The next step is to go beyond narrow targeting mechanisms toward more

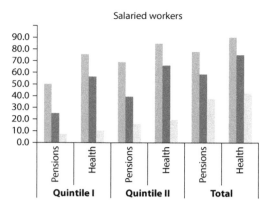

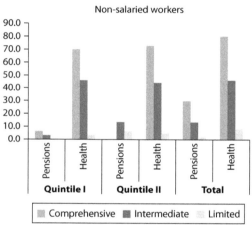

Figure 10.6   Affiliation to health and pensions (total and bottom two quintiles; average by SP category [in %], circa 2012).

Note: Countries with comprehensive systems include Argentina, Chile, Costa Rica, and Uruguay; those with intermediate systems include Colombia, Ecuador, Mexico, Panama, Peru, and the Dominican Republic; and those with limited systems include Bolivia, El Salvador, Guatemala, Honduras, Nicaragua, and Paraguay.

Source: Author's use of data from ECLAC (2013).

universal SPS, including an expansion of social insurance as countries develop. A universal SPS that protects people from all types of risk is necessary, not only to continue with massive poverty reduction, but also to increase the resilience of the population above the poverty line, including even the middle class (Ferreira et al. 2013), and construct social citizenship. Without universal protection mechanisms, previous gains could be reversed. This implies, of course, that more resources are needed for social spending.

4. THE REDISTRIBUTIVE EFFECTIVENESS OF PUBLIC SPENDING

The redistributive effect of public spending varies with the characteristics of the SPS. Higher social spending, universal coverage, and progressive transfers are associated with a higher redistributive impact.

Using the national studies of the Commitment to Equity Project (CEQ) of Tulane University and the Inter-American Dialogue,[10] it can be estimated that, on average, countries with comprehensive SPS for which information is available reduce inequality by 0.021 points of the Gini coefficient through direct transfers and by 0.085 through in-kind transfers. Intermediate systems do so by 0.01 and by 0.037 points, respectively, while countries with limited systems have almost no incidence on inequality through direct transfers (0.006) and a very small redistributive effect (0.03) through in-kind transfers (see figure 10.7).

Interestingly, regardless of the type of SPS, the redistributive effect of in-kind transfers is higher than the effect of direct transfers, which reflects the higher budget allocated to this type of transfers and, in most cases, the higher coverage. The budget allocated to health and education as a percentage of GDP is, in all countries, more than twice that allocated to direct transfers, and in several countries, much more. The budget for in-kind transfers varies from almost two times the budget of direct transfers in Paraguay (3.5 percent versus 6.7 percent) to 14 times in Peru (0.4 percent to 5.9 percent). Countries with comprehensive SPS tend to have also a higher incidence on poverty reduction through direct transfers. For example, according to CEQ data, direct transfers reduce the head-count ratio by 7.5 percentage points in Argentina, by 3.1 percentage point in Ecuador, and by less than 1 percentage point in Paraguay.

Most of the differences in the effectiveness of SPS can be explained by differences in the coverage rates, the share of social spending, and the progressivity of transfers. As figure 10.8 shows, there is a clear relation between size of budget for social transfers and their redistributive impact for the countries for which CEQ has published data. The higher the share of resources allocated to social transfers, the higher the incidence on income distribution. In fact, the four countries with a comprehensive SPS also have the highest redistributive impact.[11]

The progressivity of transfers, which measures the percentage of benefits that go to the poorest households, also account for the differences between the redistributive impacts of direct or in-kind transfers. Figure 10.9 shows the concentration (quasi-Gini) coefficients[12] for the different types of social spending. While all direct and in-kind transfers

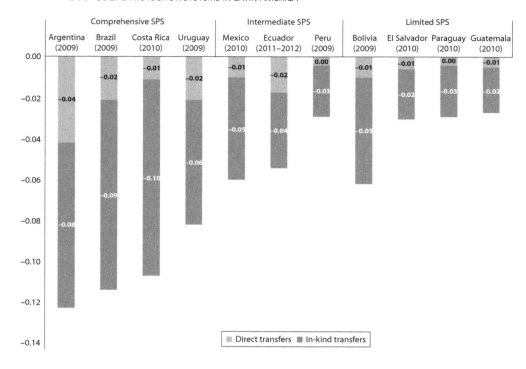

Figure 10.7   Redistributive effect of social spending (direct and in-kind transfers) showing absolute change in Gini.

Note: The difference in the Gini coefficient of the net market income (which is market income less the personal income tax and employee contributions to social security) and disposable income (which is net market income plus direct public transfers) is the redistributive effect of direct transfers. The difference between net market income and final income (which includes pensions) is the effect of all direct transfers and in-kind transfers. Final income is defined as disposable income plus in-kind transfers minus copayments and user fees. For a detailed explanation of the methodology see the handbook of the estimation methodologies (Lustig and Higgins 2013).

Source: Commitment to Equity Project (CEQ) based on the working paper for each country. Contributory pensions considered as market income.

in countries with comprehensive systems are progressive, only direct cash transfers in countries with limited systems are. In countries with limited systems, the progressivity of direct transfers is due to the conditional cash transfers (CCT) program, which on average account for more than 70 percent of direct transfers (Higgins et al. 2013). In turn, in-kind transfers are regressive in these countries, given their lower coverage, as shown, for example, by the SPI in health.

In turn, direct transfers are more progressive than in-kind transfers in all countries, except for Brazil. This is highly driven by the CCT program

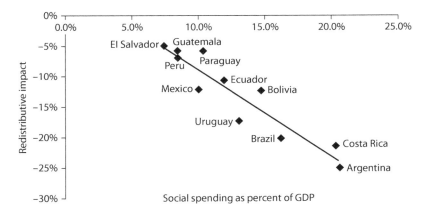

Figure 10.8   Relation between social spending (direct and in-kind transfers) and its redistributive impact.

Note: The redistributive impact equals the reduction in the Gini coefficient from net market income to final income expressed as a percentage of the Gini for net market income, to account for differences in the initial inequality. Final income is defined as disposable income plus in-kind transfers minus copayments and user fees.

Source: Estimated from the country studies of the Commitment to Equity Project (CEQ).

of each country, which is targeted to low-income families to meet a poverty reduction goal, and also by noncontributory pensions in the countries where they exist. However, despite being highly progressive, the overall redistributive impact of direct transfers is lower than the effect of in-kind transfers, as was shown in figure 10.9. This is due to the lower spending and coverage of these types of transfers.

In-kind transfers (education and health) achieve the highest redistributive impact when they are universal, like primary education and, in most countries, health care (except mainly countries with limited systems, where it is still linked to formal employment). In all cases, basic education is highly progressive and is also the most universal in-kind transfer and has a high share of social spending. This combination results in a very high redistributive impact. Health is also highly progressive in countries with comprehensive systems, as it is linked to universal coverage.

The high redistributive impact of social policy in countries with comprehensive systems is achieved through a combination of high social spending, universal coverage, and progressive benefits (e.g., Argentina). Conversely, countries with limited systems spend a lower budget in both direct and in-kind transfers, and although direct transfers are highly

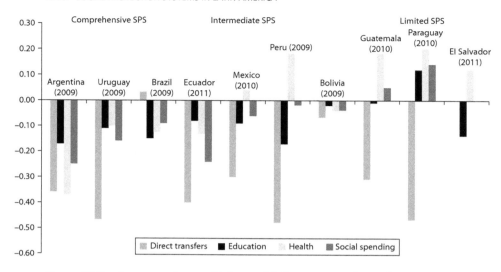

Figure 10.9 **Concentration coefficients of different types of spending.**

Note: The concentration coefficient (CC) measures how progressive or regressive each transfer is. A CC below −0.4 means that a transfer is absolutely progressive (relatively more concentrated on the lower quintiles). A CC between −0.1 and −0.4 means the transfer is moderately progressive. A CC between −0.1 and 0.1 indicates the transfer is neutral (evenly distributed between income deciles). Finally, a transfer with a CC above 0.1 is regressive. Direct transfers include noncontributory pensions, CCT, and other direct transfers.

Source: Commitment to Equity Project, based on the working paper for each country.

progressive, as they target the poorest households, in-kind transfers are regressive (especially health, as they have limited coverage), and thus the total effect is a low redistributive impact. In any case, the redistributive effect of fiscal policy in Latin American countries is much smaller than in Organisation for Economic Co-operation and Development countries (OECD 2011).

5. THE MYTHS REGARDING THE LINKS BETWEEN ECONOMIC GROWTH AND REDISTRIBUTION

Although national SPS around the world have achieved important reductions in poverty and inequality (ILO 2014a), there are still some myths regarding the relationship between social protection and economic performance.[13] These are:

1. At each stage of development, societies can only afford a certain level of social expenditure (the affordability myth).

2. There is a trade-off between social expenditure (redistribution) and economic growth (Okun's famous trade-off—which, as we will show, is also a myth).
3. Economic growth will automatically reduce poverty (trickle-down myth).

Based on the recent experience of Latin America, it is possible to refute these myths. First, there is high heterogeneity in the SPS in the region even when per capita GDP differences are taken into account. Second, there is no clear evidence that countries that expanded their SPS experienced lower growth. And third, there is stronger correlation between the improvements in the SPI and poverty reduction than between growth and poverty reduction.

Although there is a positive association between higher GDP per capita and a higher SPI score,[14] there is high variation in the SPI by level of GDP per capita (see figure 10.10). The best comparisons are Costa Rica versus Panama and Uruguay versus Mexico. Costa Rica, with a little more than the region's average GDP per capita, has the second-highest SPI score. Since 1941, Costa Rica has promoted universal coverage of both health and pensions as mandatory pillars of the welfare state. With lower GDP per capita, Costa Rica has always excelled at social inclusion indicators. On the other hand, Panama has a higher GDP per capita but

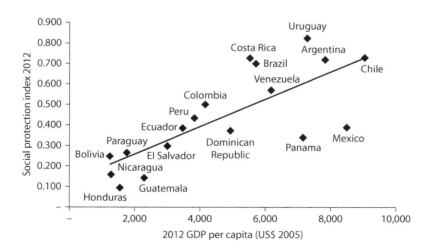

Figure 10.10   GDP per capita and Social Protection Index (circa 2012).

Source: GDP data from ECLAC.

relatively low social spending and ranks low in the SPI. The same is true when we compare Uruguay and Mexico. Mexico, despite having the second-highest GDP per capita in the region, has an intermediate SPS, even more limited that many countries with lower GDP per capita.

Thus, it is not true that at each level of GDP, countries can only afford to spend a certain amount in social protection. In fact, given the time it takes to build well-functioning social protection systems, waiting for the introduction of comprehensive SPS until high levels of GDP have been achieved is not an efficient option (Cichon and Scholz 2009).

In turn, figure 10.11 shows the change in the SPI between 2002 and 2012 and the average annual growth rate of GDP per capita. As can be seen, there is no negative association between improvement in SPS and economic growth. Rather, the correlation between these two variables is close to nil (–0.007). And, in fact, the three countries that increased their SPI the most—Peru, the Dominican Republic, and Colombia—grew at faster rates than the average for Latin America over the period analyzed. There is, therefore, no evidence of a trade-off between expanding SPS and growth.

This is in line with recent studies that find no evidence of a trade-off between redistribution and growth (Ostry, Berg, and Tsangarides 2014)

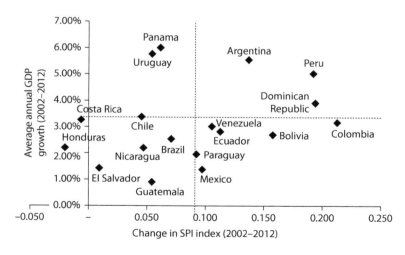

Figure 10.11 Average annual growth rate of GDP per capita and change in the Social Protection Index (2002–2012).

Source: GDP data from ECLAC stats. Lines refer to averages for each indicator.

and has, of course, major implications for public policy. According to this International Monetary Fund study: "Redistribution appears generally benign in terms of its impact on growth; only in extreme cases is there some evidence that it may have direct negative effects on growth" (Ostry et al. 2014, 2). This means that the combined direct and indirect effects of redistribution—including the growth effects of the resulting lower inequality—are, on average, pro-growth.

Finally, the last myth argues that economic growth will automatically reduce poverty. Poverty in Latin America decreased significantly during the 2003–2013 decade. While 43 percent of the population in the region lived in poverty at the beginning of the 2000s, the poverty rate in 2013 was only 28 percent, according to ECLAC data. The rapid poverty reduction of the region during this decade relied on a combination of both high economic growth and redistribution. Economic growth was significantly pro-poor, in the sense that incomes of the lowest deciles of the distribution grew relatively more than the incomes at the top; also, faster growth translated into higher formal employment. In turn, higher social spending had important redistributive effects, thus reducing poverty and also the inequality among the poor[15] (Lustig et al. 2013a).

As can be seen in figure 10.12, both higher SPI (high social spending) and higher GDP per capita reduce poverty. However, and interestingly, the correlation in Latin America seems to be higher between changes in the SPI and poverty reduction (figure 10.12a) than between annual growth rate of GDP per capita and poverty reduction (figure 10.12b).[16]

This indicates that poverty reduction is more strongly associated with an increase in the SPI than with GDP growth rates. Based on a regression analysis (see table 10.1), although both economic growth and the SPI are positively correlated with the poverty level, when looking at the standardized beta coefficient, which represents the change in the poverty rate for every one standard deviation change in the explanatory variable, it can be seen that the effect of one standard deviation change in the SPI is stronger than that for GDP capita on poverty reduction (models 3 and 4). This should not be interpreted as a choice between transfer-based poverty reduction and growth-based poverty reduction, but rather as evidence of their strong complementarities. Without well-designed redistributive mechanisms, such as comprehensive SPS, economic growth may not have important effects on poverty, and these effects may not be automatic.[17]

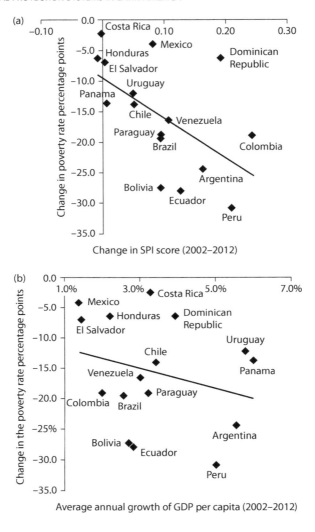

Figure 10.12 Poverty change and average annual growth rate of GDP (a) and change in the Social Protection Index (b) (2002–2012).

Source: GDP and poverty data from ECLAC.

Given the expected lower economic growth of the region in the next year, continuing with the expansion of SPS and universal coverage may be the best possible strategy for poverty reduction and for continuing the positive social trends of the 2003–2013 decade.

Table 10.1 Regression Analysis on the Determinants of Poverty Reduction

Variables	1	2	3	4	5	6
GDP per capita	-2.332^a		-2.353^b	-2.179^a	-2.562^a	-1.568^a
	(-0.372)		(-0.375)	(-0.347)	(-0.408)	(-0.250)
Social Protection Index		-1.384^b	-1.392^b	-1.181^b		
		(-0.464)	(-0.466)	(-0.396)		
Adjusted SPI						-0.423^c
						(-0.454)
Social spending					-0.077	-0.019
					(-0.244)	(-0.059)
Dependency ratio				0.157	0.337	0.228
				(0.071)	(0.151)	(0.103)
Gini				1.057^c	1.254^c	1.093^c
				(0.574)	(0.681)	(0.594)
Constant	-0.081^b	-0.105^c	-0.037	0.016	0.109	0.032
	(.)	(.)	(.)	(.)	(.)	(.)
Observations	18	18	18	18	18	18
R^2	0.138	0.215	0.356	0.658	0.561	0.719

Note: The adjusted SPI is the SPI excluding the social spending dimension. Robust normalized beta coefficients are given in parentheses.

[a] $p < 0.1$.

[b] $p < 0.05$.

[c] $p < 0.01$.

8. CONCLUSIONS

Given the continuing high levels of labor market informality in most Latin American countries and low mandatory contributions, low coverage of contributory social protection, and low redistributive impact of fiscal policy, the challenges of social policy in an era of slower economic growth will be large. New solutions with regard to both transfers and taxes are needed. Moving toward universal benefits and an expansion of noncontributory social protection mechanisms are needed, in parallel with labor formalization efforts and flexible mechanisms to increase social insurance contributions and benefits. The rising middle class has come with new demands for social protection and more of the same will not be enough: more resources (increasing contributions but also taxes) and universal coverage (with a mix of contributory and noncontributory schemes) are essential. Social assistance programs with targeted benefits, a large focus of attention in recent decades, are simply not enough.

Universal coverage of social services should thus be the essential objective of social policy and is the best guarantee that the redistributive impact of social spending is progressive. Universal benefits will be more effective in reducing income inequality and creating more equal societies. Causality goes both ways in this case: more equal societies demand more universal systems of social policy, but the latter contribute, in turn, to equality. A further advantage of universal social policies is their political appeal, and particularly their appeal to the middle classes, which is in turn essential to get the political backing for the public sector resources necessary to make universal policies effective.

The major challenge is, however, on the fiscal regime, and the crucial issue in this regard is the low tax income of Latin America, particularly of personal income taxes, as well as its mix with low transfers, as pointed out extensively by ECLAC, the World Bank, and the IMF (see, for example, IMF 2014, 2015). In fact, according to a recent study, there is "fiscal impoverishment" in Latin America due to the fact that benefits from transfers can be lower than the incidence of taxes, and thus fiscal policy may hurt the poor (Higgins and Lustig 2015). The capacity to raise taxes—and, particularly, more redistributive taxes—to achieve more universal systems of social spending is thus the domain where the battle of equity should be fought in years to come.

NOTES

This chapter borrows from a longer paper prepared by the authors for the International Labor Organization (Ocampo and Gómez-Arteaga 2016).

1. We should add to this list Cuba after its 1958 revolution, but due its entirely different economic, social, and political system, we leave Cuba out of this paper.

2. This is reflected, for example, in the lack of any special mention of social policy in the ten principles of the "Washington consensus," as summarized by Williamson (1990), except as a priority of public sector spending.

3. The index goes from 0 to 1, where 1 represents the most comprehensive system with relatively higher universal coverage, less inequality in affiliation to health and pensions for different types of employment, high social inclusion, well-targeted social assistance, and high social spending.

4. The dimensions in the index try to reflect the principles of a robust welfare state. Although efficiency and integrality could not be approximated, public spending on

SPS is used as a proxy. Cross-country evidence suggests that the higher the budget of social spending, the higher the benefits incidence on poverty and inequality reduction. Furthermore, the size of the budget also reflects the social contract and type of institutions in a given country and the universality of the system. "The hypothesis here is that the size of the budget available for redistribution is not fixed and that the institutional structures of welfare states are likely to affect the definitions of identity and interest among citizens. Thus, an institutional welfare state model based on a universalistic strategy with higher budget intended to maintain normal or accustomed standards of living is likely to result in greater redistribution than a marginal one based on targeting" (Korpi and Palme 1998, 663).

5. This classification goes in line with different rankings on the topic, all concluding that countries in the Southern Cone have built up more comprehensive welfare states. Costa Rica in itself has always excelled as having a fairly universal welfare state despite its much lower GDP per capita (Cecchini and Martínez 2012).

6. See the case study on universal health coverage in Colombia for the World Bank (Montenegro, Acevedo, and Bernal 2013).

7. See Lustig and Pessino (2013). Moratoria Previsional (the pension moratorium), introduced in 2004–2005, allowed workers of retirement age to receive a pension regardless of whether they had completed the full thirty years of required social security contributions through formal employment.

8. Access to health and pensions is a measure of the working-age population (15 years and older) that is affiliated to some kind of health insurance (regardless of type of financing schemes) and affiliated to a pension scheme (public or private). Pensions are also measured by the percentage of elderly receiving this benefit.

9. As a consequence of economic growth, it was expected that the informal sector would gradually disappear as workers shifted from more traditional (mainly informal) to more modern (formal) sectors. See Kaplan and Levy (2014).

10. The Commitment to Equity Assessment (CEQ) uses standard incidence analysis to assess the questions of how much redistribution and poverty reduction is being accomplished in each country through social spending, subsidies, and taxes, and how progressive revenue collection and government spending are. The incidence analysis measures the changes in Gini coefficient and poverty indicator between different income concepts (that is, before taxes and transfers, after direct taxes, and after direct and in-kind transfers). See in the reference section all working papers of the CEQ Project. The data for each country comes from the working paper of each specific country.

11. The relationship also applies to coverage. Ocampo (2008) shows the higher the Human Development Index (excluding per capita income), the higher the redistributive the effect of transfers on income distribution—that is, the more universal the coverage of SPS, the more redistributive it is.

12. The quasi-Gini coefficient of social spending fluctuates between –1 (perfect targeting of spending to the poor) and 1, with zero representing a situation in which spending is equally distributed among all social groups.

13. See Cichon and Scholz (2009) for a revision of these myths in OECD countries

14. The same results for myth 1 and 2 hold when looking only at percentage of social spending.

15. See Cecchini 2014; Fiszbein et al. 2009.

16. Even running some simple regression, the R^2 of the SPI is higher and more significant than the regression with GDP per capita.

17. Cichon and Scholz (2009) arrive at the same conclusions on a similar analysis for other countries studied.

REFERENCES

Bastagli, Francesca, David Coady, and Sanjeev Gupta. 2012. "Income Inequality and Fiscal Policy." IMF Staff Discussion note SDN/12/08. International Monetary Fund, Washington, D.C.

Beneke, Margarita, Nora Lustig, and José Andrés Oliva. 2015. "El impacto de los impuestos y el gasto social en la desigualdad y la pobreza en El Salvador." CEQ Working Paper No. 26. New Orleans, La.: Center for Inter-American Policy and Research and Department of Economics, Tulane University and Inter-American Dialogue.

Cabrera, Maynor, Nora Lustig, and Hilcías e. Morál. 2015. "Fiscal Policy, Inequality, and the Ethnic Divide in Guatemala." In *World Development* 76, 263–79.

Cecchini, Simone. 2014. "Social Protection, Poverty and Inequality A Comparative Perspective." *Journal of Southeast Asian Economies* 31(1):18–39.

Cecchini, Simone, and Rodrigo Martínez. 2012. *Inclusive Social Protection in Latin America: A Comprehensive, Rights-Based Approach*. Libros de la CEPAL No. 111. Santiago: ECLAC.

Cichon, Michael, and Wolfgang Scholz. 2009. "Social Security Social Impact and Economic Performance: A Farewell to the Three Famous Myths." In *Building Decent Societies: Rethinking the Role of Social Security in State Building*, ed. Pete Townsend, 80–98. Basingstoke, U.K.: Palgrave Macmillan.

Economic Commission for Latin America and the Caribbean (ECLAC). 2000. *Equity, Development and Citizenship*. Santiago: ECLAC.

———. 2013. *Social Panorama of Latin America*. Santiago: ECLAC.

———. 2014. *Social Panorama of Latin America*. Santiago: ECLAC.

———. 2015. *Inclusive Social Development: The Next Generation of Policies for Overcoming Poverty and Reducing Inequality in Latin America and the Caribbean*. Santiago: ECLAC.

Ferreira, Francisco H., and David Robalino. 2011. "Social Assistance in Latin America: Achievements and Limitations." In *Handbook of Latin American Economics*, eds. José Antonio Ocampo and Jaime Ros, 836–62. Oxford: Oxford University Press.

Ferreira, Francisco H., Julian Messina, Jamele Rigolini, Luis-Felipe López-Calva, Maria Ana Lugo, and Renos Vakis. 2013. *Economic Mobility and the Rise of the Latin American Middle Class*. Washington, D.C.: World Bank.

Filgueira, Fernando, Carlos Gerardo Molina, Jorge Papadópulos, and Federico Tobar. 2006. "Universalismo básico: una alternativa posible y necesaria para mejorar las condiciones de vida." In *Universalismo básico: Una nueva política social para América Latina*, ed. Carlos Molina, 19–55. Washington, D.C.: Inter-American Development Bank.

Fiszbein, Ariel, Norbert Shady, Francisco H. G. Ferreira, Margaret Grosh, Niall Keleher, Pedro Olinto, and Emmanuel Skoufias. 2009. "Conditional Cash Transfers: Reducing Present and Future Poverty." Washington, D.C: World Bank. Retrieved from: https://openknowledge.worldbank.org/handle/10986/2597.

Higgins, Sean, and Nora Lustig. 2015. "Can a Poverty-Reducing and Progressive Tax and Transfer System Hurt the Poor?" CGD Working Paper 405. Center for Global Development, Washington, D.C. Retrieved from: www.cgdev.org/publication /can-poverty-reducing-and-progressive-tax-and-transfer-systemhurt-poor%03 -working-paper.

Higgins, Sean, Nora Lustig, Julio Ramirez, and Billy Swanson. 2013. "Social Spending, Taxes and Income Redistribution in Paraguay." CEQ Working Paper No. 11. New Orleans, La.: Center for Inter-American Policy and Research and Department of Economics, Tulane University and Inter-American Dialogue.

International Labor Organization (ILO). 2008. *ILO Declaration on Social Justice for a Fair Globalization*. Geneva: International Labor Office.

———. 2012. *Social Security for All: Building Social Protection Floors and Comprehensive Social Security Systems. The Strategy of the International Labour Organization*. Geneva: International Labor Office. Retrieved from: www.socialsecurityextension. org/gimi/gess/RessFileDownload.do?ressourceId=34188.

———. 2014a. *World Social Protection Report*. Geneva: International Labor Office.

———. 2014b. "Monotax: Promoting Formalization and Protection of Independent Workers." Policy Brief No. 02/2014. International Labor Office, Geneva.

International Monetary Fund (IMF). 2014. "Fiscal Policy and Income Inequality." Policy paper, January 22. International Monetary Fund, Washington, D.C.

———. 2015. *World Economic Outlook: Uneven Growth, Short- and Long-Term Factors*. Washington, D.C.: International Monetary Fund.

Kaplan, David, and Santiago Levy. 2014. "The evolution of social security systems in Latin America." In *Social Insurance, Informality, and Labour Markets: How to Protect Workers While Creating Good Jobs*, ed. Marcus Frolich, David Kaplan, Carmen Pagés, Jamele Rigolini, and David Robalino, 33–57. New York: Oxford University Press.

Korpi, Walter, and Joakim Palme. 1998. "The Paradox of Redistribution and Strategies of Equality: Welfare State Institutions, Inequality and Poverty in the Western Countries." *American Sociological Review* 63(5):661–87.

Llerena, Pinto, Freddy Paul, María Christina Llerena Pinto, Roberto Carlos Saá Daza, and María Andrea Llerena Pinto. 2015. "Social Spending, Taxes and Income Redistribution in Ecuador."New Orleans, La.: CEQ Working Paper No. 28. Center for Inter-American Policy and Research and Department of Economics, Tulane University and Inter-American Dialogue.

Lustig, Nora, and Sean Higgins. 2013. "Commitment to Equity Assessment (CEQ): Estimating the Incidence of Social Spending, Subsidies and Taxes. Handbook." CEQ Working Paper No. 1. New Orleans, La.: Center for Inter-American Policy and Research and Department of Economics, Tulane University and Inter-American Dialogue.

Lustig, Nora, and Carola Pessino. 2013. "Social Spending and Income Redistribution in Argentina in the 2000s: The Rising Role of Noncontributory Pensions." CEQ Working Paper No. 5 [revised August 2013]. New Orleans, La.: Center for Inter-American Policy and Research and Department of Economics, Tulane University and Inter-American Dialogue.

Lustig, Nora, George Gray Molina, Sean Higgins, Miguel Jaramillo, Wilson Jiménez, Veronica Paz, Claudiney Pereira, Carola Pessino, John Scott, and Ernesto Yañez. 2012. "The Impact of Taxes and Social Spending on Inequality and Poverty in Argentina, Bolivia, Brazil, Mexico and Peru: A Synthesis of Results" CEQ Working Paper No. 3. New Orleans, La.: Center for Inter-American Policy and Research and Department of Economics, Tulane University and Inter-American Dialogue.

Lustig Nora, Luis, F. Lopez-Calva, and Eduardo Ortiz-Juarez. 2013a. "Deconstructing the Decline in Inequality in Latin America." Policy Research Working Paper 6552. Washington, D.C.: World Bank.

Lustig, Nora, Carola Pessino, and John Scott. 2013b. "The Impact of Taxes and Social Spending on Inequality and Poverty in Argentina, Bolivia, Brazil, Mexico, Peru and Uruguay: An Overview" CEQ Working Paper No. 13. New Orleans, La.: Center for Inter-American Policy and Research and Department of Economics, Tulane University and Inter-American Dialogue.

Marshall, T. H. 1992. *Citizenship and Social Class*, ed. T. B. Bottomore. London: Pluto Press.

Montenegro Torres, Fernando Acevedo, and Oscar Bernal. 2013. "Colombia Case Study: The Subsidized Regime of Colombia's National Health Insurance System." Universal Health Coverage (UNICO) Studies Series No. 15. World Bank Group, Washington, D.C. Retrieved from: http://documents.worldbank.org /curated/en/2013/01/17207398/colombia-case-study-subsidized-regime-colombias -national-health-insurance-system.

Ocampo, José Antonio. 2007. "Market, Social Cohesion, and Democracy." In *Policy Matters: Economic and Social Policies to Sustain Equitable Development*, ed. José Antonio Ocampo, K. S. Jomo, and Sarbuland Khan, 1–31. Himayatnagar, India: Orient Longman; London: Zed Books; Penang: Third World Network.

——. 2008. "Las concepciones de la política social: universalismo versus focalización." *Revista Nueva Sociedad* No. 215.

Ocampo, José Antonio, and Natalie Gomez-Arteaga. 2016. "Social Protection Systems in Latin America: An Assessment." Working Paper No. 52. Geneva: ILO, Extension of Social Security.

Organisation for Economic Cooperation and Development. 2011. *Divided We Stand: Why Inequality Keeps Rising*. Paris: OECD.

Ostry, Jonathan D., Andrew Berg, and Charalambos G. Tsangarides. 2014. "Redistribution, Inequality, and Growth." IMF Staff Discussion Note, SDN/14/02. International Monetary Fund, Washington, D.C.

Santos, Maria Emma, Pablo Villatoro, Xavier Mancero, and Pascual Gerstenfeld. 2015. "A Multidimensional Poverty Index for Latin America." OPHI Working Paper 79. Oxford University, Oxford.

Sen, Amartya. 1999. *Development as Freedom*. New York: Knopf.

UN Development Program (UNDP). 2004. *La democracia en América Latina: hacia una democracia de ciudadanas y ciudadanos*. Buenos Aires: UNDP, Aguilar, Altea, Tauros, Alfaguara.

Williamson, John. 1990. "What Washington Means by Policy Reform." In *Latin American Adjustment. How Much Has Happened?*, ed. John Williamson. Washington, D.C.: Institute of International Economics.

CHAPTER 11

Social Protection in Latin America

SOME CHALLENGES FOR REDUCING INEQUALITY

Ana Sojo

Risks such as illness, restrictions that endanger adequately addressing the care needs of children and vulnerable or disabled people, unemployment and underemployment, and the loss or dramatic decline of income during old age are factors that determine the present and future well-being of all individuals. Although these circumstances are crucially influenced by the asymmetries that characterize the socioeconomic conditions enjoyed by different people, to different degrees they nevertheless escape their control: the timing of the occurrence of such risks and the availability of access to necessary protection are uncertain, while the time during which services will have to be provided, the costs involved, and the extent to which personal integrity and income will be strained, all remain indeterminate. Moreover, the demand for services, by its very nature, also tends to be uneven and unpredictable.

Social protection facilitates dealing with the "welfare economics of uncertainty" and diversifying the risks involved, while the market is severely limited in its ability to address them, due to the prevalence of uncertainty and profit-driven orientation (Arrow 1963, 2000). Both in individual and social terms, it is desirable to narrow the gap between income and desired levels of insurance. The nature of the good to be protected also determines the type of insurance. Contributory pension systems must reasonably reflect personal saving efforts, which narrows the redistributive dimension of the system, because savings are correlated to people's labor path; but from a rights-based approach, solidarity pensions must be guaranteed to those who have had very low incomes during their working life. In the case of health, due to the role it plays in improving people's quality of life and overall human liberty and range of opportunities (Sen 2004, 23, 29), solidarity and the economic allocation of resources must look after equity in this realm, which should enable redistribution between different income, age, and risk strata and contribute to easing household expenditures and strengthen their savings capacity.

In Latin America, efforts of diverse nature and magnitude will be required to expand social protection's coverage, to improve its quality, and to increase the solidarity of its financing in the different countries. The strategy of universalization of social protection cannot be focused exclusively on an increase in resources, but must rather act upon the institutional morphology of social protection itself: institutional change is a crucial part of the locus of innovation, because fragmentation and segmentation are built into the very structures of social protection systems. In this chapter I will address some of the main challenges in this area.

COVERAGE EXPANSION

Until 2012, the decrease in unemployment and the increase in levels of activity and formalization, as well as the flexibilization of eligibility criteria for contributory coverage, contributed in general terms to expand contributory mechanisms in numerous countries, which led to a broadening of social protection in the areas of health care and pensions. In a complementary fashion, to correct the exclusions generated by traditional contributory regimes, subsidized regimes linked to contributory ones were strengthened through the creation of solidarity pillars of social protection.

Affiliation coverage evidences a great heterogeneity throughout the region; affiliation in health-care and pension systems are used as a proxy for coverage. Inequality varies dramatically from country to country; clearly there are countries with high, low, and intermediate rates of affiliation in health-care and pension systems. It is disquieting to witness the virtual stagnation in countries that have very low coverage that does not manage to cover even half of salaried people. Further, in three countries ranked in diverse gradients of coverage, there is evidence of a regression in the pension affiliation.

As for coverage expansion, recent increases are more inconspicuous in countries with higher coverage, while an interesting dynamism can be observed in some countries with intermediate coverage, with some notable improvements in health care and pensions. In some cases, the increases have taken place in both dimensions; in others, the trends diverge from one another, which can point either to a difference in emphasis or perhaps to variations in the effectiveness—in terms of coverage—of the solidary or individualist character of social protection.[1] The coverage of unsalaried individuals, although noticeably lower, has also improved; in some countries that have high health coverage and in one with intermediate coverage, the affiliation in health care of unsalaried individuals increased at a higher rate compared with salaried individuals during the period analyzed (see tables 11.1 and 11.2).

With the exception of four countries, an analysis of trends at the regional scale reveals that in the case of salaried workers, the current differences by gender generally favor women: the increases in affiliation in the last few years have proportionally benefited them to a greater extent in many countries.

On the other hand, in the region large disparities of access can be identified among quintiles: between extreme quintiles, in the last year of measurement, the affiliation gap is 36 percentage points in health care and 49 in pensions; in health care, the gap decreased by 7 percentage points and in pensions it increased by 2 percentage points. The access gap according to levels of educational attainment is very large, though a decreasing trend can be observed, especially in the case of health care: the comparison of extreme categories—university-educated, salaried individual versus salaried individual with incomplete primary education—shows that the differences in pension affiliation, which remain almost unchanged, are 55 percentage points, while in health care they are 40 percentage points, which represents a decrease of 11 percentage points. As for the trends by age group, although an increase in affiliation was registered in both pension and health-care systems, the higher rates of affiliation are observable in the middle years of working life (CEPAL 2015).

Recent multivariate analyses of the determinants of pension system affiliation in Latin America have demonstrated that, to a very significant extent, the disparities of pension affiliation are correlated with the characteristics of job profiles, and not merely with characteristics of individuals.[2] Some common patterns emerge, although of diverse magnitude in different countries: in contrast with industry, employment in construction and, to a lesser extent, in commerce and agriculture, is associated with lower probabilities of affiliation; something similar occurs with half-time workers and with domestic service workers. As can be expected, the probability of affiliation increases in accordance with both the income and educational levels of the household. The characteristics

Table 11.1   Latin America (18 Countries): Affiliation to the Pension System and Health Care among Wage Earners Aged 15 or Older, by Sex (Expressed as Percentage)

Country	Year	Both sexes		Men		Women	
		Pensions	Health care	Pensions	Health care	Pensions	Health care
Argentina (urban areas)	2004	54.7	65.1	59.3	66.4	49.0	63.5
	2012	68.5	77.8	70.9	77.3	65.4	78.4
Bolivia (Estado Plurinacional de)	2002	26.3	29.8	25.6	27.5	27.6	34.1
	2011	39.6	45.4	38.2	42.1	41.8	51.0
Brazil[a]	2001	65.0		65.6		64.2	
	2013	77.4		77.6		77.2	
Chile	2000	76.9	92.1	79.0	91.2	73.4	93.5
	2013	83.5	96.0	85.3	95.3	81.1	97.0
Colombia	1999	40.8	53.2	36.4	48.5	47.7	60.4
	2013	60.1	92.8	60.5	91.6	59.4	94.4
Costa Rica[b]	2002		83.7		81.6		87.2
	2013	76.9	87.8	79.5	85.9	72.8	90.7
Ecuador (urban areas)	2002	42.0	45.0	40.7	43.6	44.2	47.5
	2013	65.6	66.0	61.9	62.3	71.5	72.1
El Salvador	1999	48.6	50.0	45.0	45.6	54.6	57.5
	2013	48.5	51.0	46.3	47.7	52.2	56.6
Guatemala	2002	35.1	37.8	33.5	36.2	38.6	41.4
	2006	38.5	44.5	36.4	42.5	42.8	48.9
Honduras	2006	38.0	36.0	30.8	30.2	51.8	47.1
	2010	38.8	37.2	32.4	31.8	51.2	47.7
Mexico	2002	41.0	53.8	39.5	52.0	44.0	57.0
	2012	39.8	77.0	40.0	75.0	39.3	80.3
Nicaragua	2001	33.2	28.8	28.6	24.9	42.4	36.5
	2005	34.0	36.3	28.0	30.2	45.6	48.3
Panama[b]	2000		73.2		71.6		75.6
	2013		79.0		76.5		82.7
Paraguay	2000	28.1	33.2	27.2	30.9	29.6	36.9
	2013	38.8	45.6	38.8	43.4	38.9	48.7
Peru	2001	27.1	39.3	27.1	38.9	26.9	40.0
	2013	52.8	67.9	56.0	66.7	48.0	69.7
Dominican Republic	2005	42.5	51.1	42.5	52.6	42.4	49.0
	2013	63.0	77.7	67.2	76.6	58.0	79.1
Uruguay (urban areas)	2002	76.3	98.2	79.6	97.8	72.5	98.6
	2013	86.4	99.1	88.3	98.8	84.3	99.4
Venezuela (República Bolivariana de)	2002	61.0		57.4		66.5	
	2013	55.9		52.9		59.9	
Latin America[c]	2002	46.3	54.4	45.2	52.5	48.5	57.9
	2013	55.7	67.6	55.1	65.2	57.3	71.6

Source: Economic Commission for Latin America and the Caribbean (ECLAC), based on special tabulations of household surveys of the respective countries.

[a] The surveys used do not make it possible to distinguish membership of health-care systems independently.
[b] The surveys used do not make it possible to distinguish membership of pension systems independently.
[c] Simple average that excludes countries that do not have data for the two points in time taken as the reference.

Table 11.2 Latin America (14 Countries): Affiliation to Pension and Health Systems among Non-Wage Earners Aged 15 Years and Older, by Sex (Expressed as Percentage)

				Sex			
		Both sexes		Men		Women	
Country	Year	Pensions	Health care	Pensions	Health care	Pensions	Health care
Argentina (urban areas)	2004		44.0		42.5		45.6
	2012		53.0		50.0		56.3
Bolivia (Plurinational State of)	C	1.4	7.8	2.1	6.7	0.7	8.9
	2011	2.9	19.3	4.4	16.7	1.5	21.9
Brazil[a]	2001	20.6		22.4		18.3	
	2013	30.2		29.9		30.5	
Chile	2000	28.0	78.3	25.6	71.8	31.0	86.3
	2013	26.0	91.4	25.9	87.3	26.2	95.8
Colombia	1999	7.0	14.3	7.0	14.1	7.0	14.6
	2013	11.9	88.4	12.2	86.2	11.6	91.2
Costa Rica[b]	2002		65.3		60.7		72.1
	2013	40.6	77.7	54.3	75.2	24.6	80.5
Ecuador (urban areas)	2002	11.0	13.4	12.8	15.5	8.9	11.0
	2013	21.8	23.0	22.0	23.3	21.6	22.7
El Salvador	1999	3.1	10.6	4.5	7.7	1.9	13.3
	2013	3.4	11.7	4.8	8.7	2.1	14.4
Honduras	2006	0.8	0.9	0.9	1.0	0.6	0.8
	2010	0.8	1.0	0.6	0.9	1.1	1.1
Nicaragua	2001	1.9	2.7	1.9	2.3	1.8	3.3
	2005	0.5	2.7	0.5	2.2	0.4	3.3
Panama[b]	2002		21.8		17.5		30.5
	2013		24.7		19.6		31.8
Paraguay	2000	0.3	9.7	0.4	7.5	0.3	12.2
	2013	1.3	15.5	1.7	12.1	0.9	19.1
Peru	2001	2.9	14.2	4.6	13.4	1.4	14.9
	2013	14.4	57.2	21.0	52.2	8.5	61.6
Uruguay (urban areas)	2002	35.6	95.2	34.1	93.1	37.3	97.5
	2013	47.9	96.1	43.0	93.8	52.5	98.3
Latin America[c]	2002	10.2	29.1	10.6	27.2	9.9	31.6
	2013	14.7	43.2	15.1	40.6	14.3	46.0

Source: Economic Commission for Latin America and the Caribbean (ECLAC), based on special tabulations of data from household surveys conducted by the respective countries.

[a] Health-care system affiliation could not be determined from the surveys used.
[b] Pension system affiliation could not be determined from the surveys used.
[c] Simple average for 14 countries. Excludes countries on which no data are available for the two points in time taken as a reference.

of predominantly female occupational categories, given the conditions of labor segmentation, lead to lower levels of female affiliation; the greater rates of informality among women that can be verified in some countries can be ascribed to determine characteristics of the workers (such as levels of educational attainment and age group) and to the particular job in question; when these aspects are controlled for, there is usually an increase in the probability that women will contribute. Nevertheless, the values are negative in the case of female-headed households, reflecting their greater vulnerability and need to accept low-quality employment opportunities (CEPAL 2014; Amarante and Sojo 2015; Sojo 2015).

Coverage expansion entails efforts to eliminate certain barriers of access to contributory systems that involve the implementation of changes in the architecture of those systems, but also requires continued improvements in the process of employment formalization. Among other mechanisms, the flexibilization of eligibility criteria for contributory coverage has had redistributive effects. The most salient of the implemented policies include: simplified tax schemes that combine contributions and tax components; procedures that facilitate the registration of workers and their employers and their oversight; a diverse reduction of employers' contributions for small enterprises; simplified regimes for special categories of workers (such as domestic workers) and tax deductions to incentivize their contributory payments; tax deductions to companies that undergo formalization processes; measures for people without income that are devoted to unpaid domestic work, i.e., the recognition of care work; reductions in prior periods of nonentitlement to access to health services; broadening of family coverage plans at the contributor's charge; and investment laws that encourage formalization (OIT 2014; Amarante and Arim 2015).

IMPROVING SOME NONCONTRIBUTORY SERVICES

Subsidized regimes linked to contributory systems have also been strengthened, as can be observed in the case of the health-care systems in Colombia and Costa Rica, and in the case of the solidarity pillars of social protection systems, as in the case of Chile's pension system.

Several countries have noncontributory pension systems, which are compared in table 11.3 for six countries of the region.[3] As can be seen, Chile is the country that provides the highest solidary pensions, followed by Costa Rica, while Bolivia has the lowest noncontributory pensions, with the

Table 11.3   Latin America (6 Countries): People above 65 Years of Age Who Receive Noncontributory Pensions According to Sex and Average Monthly Pension Amount

		Total		Sex Men		Women	
Country	Year	Coverage (%)	Amount (US$)	Coverage (%)	Amount (US$)	Coverage (%)	Amount (US$)
Bolivia (Plurinational State of)[a]	2002	69.5	9.3	72.3	9.6	67.1	9.1
	2011	95.5	15.6	94.6	15.4	96.3	15.8
Chile	2000	14.0	67.0	11.6	67.1	15.9	67.0
	2013	30.4	107.6	22.3	105.0	36.3	108.8
Costa Rica	2013	17.7	83.1	15.1	83.5	19.8	82.9
Ecuador (urban areas)	2002	14.8	41.8	13.1	37.2	16.4	45.3
	2013	30.3	35.1	26.7	35.1	33.5	35.1
Mexico	2012	33.6	36.0	33.0	35.3	34.0	36.5
Panama	2013	26.3	69.4	22.9	69.4	29.3	69.4

Source: Economic Commission for Latin America and the Caribbean (ECLAC), based on special tabulations from household surveys conducted by the countries

[a] The data for 2002 for the Plurinational State of Bolivia refer to the Bonosol Bono Solidario, which provided an annual pension of 1,800 bolivianos, converted here into monthly values to enable comparison with the 2011 figures. The amounts for 2011 refer to the Renta Dignidad, which provides a monthly benefit of 200 bolivianos.

highest coverage, which contrasts with the low coverage of its contributory pensions. In general, a slightly higher proportion of women receive this type of pension; the most significant difference can be observed in Chile's case, due to the solidary pillar's recognition of unremunerated household and childcare work. In real terms, the value of solidary pensions in Bolivia and Chile have increased, while in Ecuador they have decreased.

The low levels of these pensions stand out to varying degrees. The improvement of the provision of services afforded by these systems requires channeling greater fiscal resources to them.

OVERCOME PROFIT INCENTIVES AS THE ARTICULATOR OF PUBLIC-PRIVATE COMBINATIONS

Social protection systems can be constructed on the basis of diverse public-private sector mixes. Strictly speaking, the equality of social protection is not guaranteed by the legal ownership status of the entities in charge, but is rather determined by the characteristics of welfare states, by the principles and objectives that articulate the public-private mixes within the systems, and by the rules of the game that govern and regulate their functions. In conjunction with the characteristics and the development of the markets with which they interact, this determines a broad and heterogeneous spectrum of situations (Sojo 1999). Due to the inherent complexities of social protection systems, the application of the principles of universality, solidarity, and efficiency to their design, financing, provision, and regulation is not exempt from critical dilemmas, whose solutions are not uniform, particularly in the context of the participation of private actors.

Compulsory or obligatory insurance has had the rationale of achieving a sufficiently broad pool of risks with redistributive purposes, which differs from profit-driven market-based private insurance that adjusts to individual risk in terms of the prices and the coverage of the insurance policy. It follows that dualist public-private combinations, that with certain adjustments were propagated from Chile to the rest of Latin America, have a paradoxical characteristic: they use obligatory contributions and public cross-subsidies, but in conformity with the profit-motive principle, to which insurance is subordinated, and the principles of social security are thereby abandoned or dramatically curtailed. The profit-motive argument emphasizes, in systemic terms, the proportionality, rationality, and magnitude of the gains accrued by the actors involved in relation to the resources available for effective social protection. Driven by the maximization of private economic gain as the supreme principle and objective, at the expense of the system's insurance functions, these dualist public-private combinations, despite the compulsory character of the obligatory contributions that distinguish them from a typical voluntary market insurance scheme, break with the principles of social security. Clearly stated, the economic gains of the business entities involved in the administration, insurance, and provision of social services must be contrasted with the gains in well-being of the system's members and the effective diversification of risks (Sojo 2014).

In these terms, Chile's health-care system is sui generis at the international level. Due to its dual logic, the obligatory contribution, that is the worker's sole responsibility, facilitates affiliation either to the public health-care system through the National Health Fund (Fondo Nacional de Salud, or FONASA), whose distributive rationality favors solidarity, or to the private health insurance companies (Instituciones de Salud Previsional, or ISAPRES) that function according to the logic of private insurance, despite the compulsory character of the contributions that nourish them. The FONASA grants access to the public provision of services through the so-called institutional modality, or to the private provision of services through the modality of free choice, which is subject to a diverse variety of copayments and complements the contributions with additional funds drawn from the public budget. The ISAPRES, in contrast to the inherent logic of compulsory insurance, provide insurance through individual plans that are renewed on a yearly basis and that adjust their prices and coverage to the age, health risks, and sex of the insured/ policyholder, which reflects the plan's actuarial risk assessment. The public sector plays a global reassurance role in the system, because it insures the lower-income and higher-risk populations who might otherwise be barred from having insurance. Throughout the years, the ISAPRES's risk assessments have been curtailed through palliative measures, encouraged primarily by the litigation of the right to health care.

Another prominent aspect of the Chilean case is the dualist design of the country's pension system, which is structured primarily on the basis of profit incentives, whose very logic has culminated in a situation in which the obligatory contributions to the system of individual capitalization has translated into pensions with low replacement rates, accompanied by substantial returns for the for-profit pension fund managers (Administradoras de fondos de pensiones, or AFP), for the insurance companies in charge of providing annuities, and for related businesses, such as the banks and private companies that pay very low interest rates to the pension funds (Rivera 2014). Rather than accomplish the essential objective of maximizing retirement income security through the provision of the best possible replacement rates achievable through the optimal use of the pension fund's investments, the dualist rationality of the system ultimately generates sumptuous returns for the pension fund managers.

The potential reform of these systems is challenged by the presence of strong veto possibilities on the part of a spectrum of powerful actors because their development has gone hand in hand with the economic and political strengthening of the actors in charge of managing the system's constitutive institutions (in Chile the ISAPRES and AFPs; in Colombia the entidades promotoras de salud or health-promoting entities [EPS] and instituciones prestadoras de salud or health-provisioning institutions [IPS]) as well as actors "external" to the system who nevertheless benefit immensely from the status quo (such as the pharmaceutical companies in Colombia, or the companies and banks in Chile that pay low interest rates to the pension funds). The power of such actors and their ability to establish alliances have so far curtailed substantial changes. However, some potentially transformative reforms have recently been proposed—reforms that would have been unthinkable a short time ago due to the hegemonic ideas that justified the current institutional structure—which reflect the general citizenry's highly critical evaluation of the existing institutions. Given the complexity of the political situation, the outcome of this process of contestation remains enigmatic; on the near horizon we can glimpse certain strategies for change that, confronted by strong negating forces, could try to subvert existing systems through new rules superimposed upon current ones that, despite operating on the margins, could ultimately result in substantial changes through processes of "layering" (Streeck and Thelen 2005; Mahoney and Thelen 2009). Such is the case in the proposal of a state-run AFP in Chile. In Colombia, an intense litigation of the right to health care highlighted the new regulation of prices and the licensing of medications and the introduction of a negative list of health services excluded.

LIMITED CHOICE IN SOCIAL PROTECTION AND GRATUITOUS AND FEIGNED COMPETITION ASSOCIATED WITH INCREASED COSTS

Broadening the spectrum of options available to consumers and their ability to choose on the basis of market competition has been a cornerstone of the communicative discourse that has laid the foundations for the privatization of social protection, or the eminent participation of private for-profit entities in its administration and provision. However, Latin America's experience evidences severe restriction on competition with very high associated costs, the abundance of moral risk behaviors on the part of several actors, and the fact that, empirically, the majority of people do not truly exercise their freedom to choose, or rather practice it for erroneous motives, due to, for example, the influence of advertising campaigns.

For example, in the case of the ISAPRES, the plans allow the adjustment of premiums and copayments to expected individual costs and profitability expediencies; if the contribution is insufficient, additional amounts are paid in, the so-called voluntary contribution, and that gap is greater between lower-income and elderly insured individuals. The plan's price increase dispersion is regulated through a band. There are more than 12,000 commercialized plans, and a stock of more than 53,000 that are differentiated by the financial coverage offered for different types of services, as well as by the use limits and copayments: the freedom to choose is curtailed by such abundance and, in fact, the policies are concentrated in a reduced number of plans (Chile, Comisión Asesora Presidencial para el Estudio y Propuesta de un Nuevo Marco Jurídico para el Sistema Privado de Salud 2014, 21–22). This bears witness to the fallacy of the principle of perfectly informed consumers, as well as to the obstacles embodied by the proliferation of plans of a superfluous or feigned diversity, which are in fact not conducive to well-informed decision-making processes on the part of consumers, and that infinitely raise the temporal transaction costs of those who desire to make well-informed decisions.

In the case of pensions in Chile, most people do not understand the relationship between the replacement rates they will receive with the fees they pay in exchange for the management of their individual accounts and, therefore, do not make their decisions on this basis. In many cases the correspondent information is neither transparent nor comprehensible for consumers, nor are they aware of the profits generated by the AFPs and the businesses that have access to the latter's resources. In opposition to the interest of the consumer, increases in management costs have been observed due to the presence of a misleading and false competitive environment, which demonstrates the urgent role public efforts must play in assisting the system's members to comprehend the relevance prices such as those associated with management fees will have on the pensions they will ultimately receive (Chile, Comisión Asesora Presidencial sobre el Sistema de Pensiones 2015a, 2015b, 2015c). Due to the pervasiveness of information asymmetries and the lack of incentives conducive to effective competition, one would be hard-pressed to claim that it is the pension fund managers' reputation in the achievement of better replacement rates or the level of the management fees they charge that shape consumers' behavior, but rather that such behavior is in fact shaped by questionable advertising campaigns.

In Colombia, in addition to the information asymmetries inherent in the health-care system, consumers' freedom of choice is further compromised by the sheer amount of insurance entities and health service providers, which are territorially concentrated and have weak regulatory and supervisory structures. In 2013, the system comprised a wide network of actors: approximately 66 (EPS) private and public insurers that receive a fixed amount by member, denominated "unit of payment by capitation," and that hire health services both in the private and public networks. There were 30,000 service providers (IPS) and more than 30,000 independent professionals. The sheer number of entities, besides hindering the presumed freedom of choice associated with competitive markets, complicates the state's accreditation, monitoring, inspection, vigilance, and control functions that must jointly protect the citizen, which also evidence lax standards. A great asymmetry has been identified, for example, between the territorial entities' and the Secretariats of Health's regulatory and governance capabilities, especially in remote and isolated areas, in relation to those of the EPS and the IPS. This also obstructs the establishment of networks. Clearly there have been some interventions that have sought to strengthen the insurance and service provision systems and to purge them on the basis of quality, capability, and financial responsibility criteria (República de Colombia, Ministerio de Salud 2013, 75).

In these terms, and in relation to the presumed advantages a competitive system allegedly offers consumers, the results are disappointing. On this basis, it is reasonable to discuss the arguments that have been advanced in the international debate in favor of curtailing excessive instances of choice in social protection systems. Information asymmetries and the characteristics of human behavior explain the considerable observed divergence between actual performance and the optimal outcomes predicted by certain economic theories: in practice, observed behavior is characterized by indecisiveness, inertia, and immobility (Barr 2013). On the other hand, it is a myth that competition per se will reduce costs; for example, the management fees may increase due to the decentralization of the management of the individual pension accounts, which implies that the profitability rates of a decentralized private system can be lower than that of a public system (Orszag and Stiglitz 2001, 24, 35–37).

FACING THE STRUCTURAL CAUSES OF THE ABUNDANT JUDICIAL ENSHRINEMENT OF THE RIGHT TO HEALTH CARE

In Latin America, the judiciary has been swept into a protagonist role in the defense of the right to health care, a situation that expresses the underlying tensions and conflicts stemming from individual demands concerning subjects of law related to the spectrum of health services fixed by the state, or rather, of effective access to them. An active jurisprudence has emerged that interprets and protects social rights, and that has in various instances forced the executive to redefine its policies, reinforcing further dynamics of the judicial enshrinement of rights. Some disquieting chiaroscuro effects have also emerged in this area, especially considering how insurers, service providers, and pharmaceutical companies have benefited, sporadically or recurrently, from certain rulings.

The reiterated judicial rulings stemming from the same pattern or type of service demonstrate the failure to solve the problem of equal access through more structural means (Maestad, Rakner, and Motta Ferraz 2011, 297). The reiteration of litigation increasingly enfeebles factual arguments and weakens the ability to scrutinize the structural reasons underlying the complaints. When litigations become massive or recurrent and prone to inertia, they become almost a precondition of access to determined services and lead to a postponement of both regulatory authorities' identification of the causes underlying the problem and their attempt to develop structural solutions to rectify them (Gloppen 2011; Uprimny and Durán 2014).

Different countries' experiences demonstrate a highly varied spectrum of experiences with respect to the changing situation of vulnerable groups: in Argentina, Brazil, Colombia, and Costa Rica, some cases have involved systemic changes that have benefited such groups, while in other countries, the inequalities that characterize the provision of services have been exacerbated (Maestad, Rakner, and Motta Ferraz 2011, 299, 301; Uprimny and Durán 2014). Individual demands seem to favor those who have more resources and can more easily access courts and lawyers, while resolutions of a structural character related to the system's inequalities have had more positive effects from the point of view of equality (Gloppen 2011; Uprimny and Durán 2014).

It has been proposed that the nature and volume of judicial processes are related to the organization of health-care systems: the more universal and public and, in principle, available to the entire population, the lower the amount of litigation; the more fragmented and more reliant on competition and predominantly private mechanisms in financing and/or in-service provision, the greater the amount of litigation (Gloppen 2011, 19). On the other hand, it has been critically pointed out that judges do not necessarily consider the virtually universal effects of their rulings or the associated costs (Yamin 2011, 368).

Judicial activism has also been pertinently explained by limited abilities to design just and solid benefit packages and to establish priorities in health care (Cubillos et al. 2012): because of this, the courts would consider that the administrative inefficiencies and prioritization processes of the health-care system curtail the protection of people's access to health services and therefore violate this right, thereby transforming the courts into the guarantors of such rights and the supervisors of the institutions responsible for satisfying them (Iunes, Cubillos, and Escobar 2012). Prioritization allows certain variations: exclusions may be explicit, or rather implicit, in the case of those services that are not included in the lists of service provision and are rather given in a dynamic framework in which, in the course of scientific research and in market contexts, a series of innovative services emerge that could potentially be included.

Hence it is important that the exclusion of the provision of certain services enjoys a high level of legitimacy and that exclusions should not be "closed" measures, but rather the result of participative deliberative processes. Against an unwarranted rigidity in terms of consumer's rights, it has been proposed that such exclusions do not imply an absolute prohibition of access to the provision of particular services, but rather that its access deserves a special judicial deference, because the exclusion would be the product of a transparent and participative procedure that, in principle, would be respected by the judges. To overcome the dichotomy of broadening health coverage due to litigation and the difficulty of imposing barriers that are insurmountable to it, some "intermediate options" have been proposed that seek to improve health-care protection. These options seek to maintain some degree of flexibility, using barriers and exclusions only in clearly justified cases.

It is also imperative to consider the different options for the financing of service provision that may emerge due to the litigation. It is reasoned that the "lists of services" must have an endurable legal basis: in the Colombian case, its inclusion has been recommended for both ordinary and statutory health laws.

Colombia is undergoing a transition from a detailed and rigid stipulation of benefits toward a system of implicit rationing and the use of a negative list of nonfinanced services (Gaviria 2015).

TRANSFORMING CARE INTO A NEW PILLAR OF SOCIAL PROTECTION

In relation to the public or private provision of care, it is important to remember that the state, the market, and the family jointly structure the production and distribution of people's well-being, while the community plays a complementary role. But care has been an eminently private responsibility, while the delay of its translation into concrete policies is also notable, because with a few exceptions, the risks associated with care remain concentrated in families, and within families, in women.

An implicit gender contract underlies both the division of social labor between families and societies and the division of labor at the family scale in relation to both income generation and care-related tasks (Saraceno 2008, 2). It is worth emphasizing that intergenerational reciprocities crystallize social inequalities and add new ones that, to a significant extent, are idiosyncratic and depend on the individual's biography within the social context, to the extent that the availability of resources is interconnected with and depends on the quality, density, and intensity of private relationships. The disentanglement of the provision and quality of care from their dependence on people's unequal social positions would allow the rupture of certain vicious circles. In Europe, systems with broader coverage rates have been associated with more redistributive outcomes (Kohli and Albertini 2008; Saraceno 2008; Sarasa and Billingsley 2008). Facing these types of inequality is a crucial challenge in Latin America.

Public policies in care provision involve new equilibria in the interrelationships among the state, markets, and families and can point to highly diverse objectives that in the course of time might generate positive reciprocal feedback mechanisms. Some prominent objectives include: taking a leap forward in the development of infant's skills and capabilities through early interventions that are critical for cognitive development and that may play a role in diminishing social inequalities; striving for the well-being of vulnerable and dependent elderly persons through a spectrum of interventions that would provide care and would promote their activity and autonomy, thereby safeguarding them from social isolation; strengthening the vital options of those family members responsible for the provision of care; narrowing opportunity gaps between men and women; contributing to broadening women's employment possibilities so as to generate positive externalities for employment creation and productive capacity; diminishing households' poverty or their vulnerability to fall into poverty by increasing low-income women's ability to seek higher quality employment; contributing to accomplishing a rejuvenation of the population that reflects the free exercise of people's right to motherhood and fatherhood, by leveling the obstacles that prevent the reconciliation between family and work life; and favoring the financial sustainability of social protection (Sojo 2011).

The institutional development of the social protection and educational systems related to the provision of care in the region's different countries is very diverse, as are the constellations of actors that can influence public policies. The configuration and institutional structure of care provision must consider these aspects. Due to the transversal character of care, this institutional structure can initially operate fundamentally through interfaces associated with the systems of social protection and education to progressively accomplish a more singular profile through new services that may be related to it or by redefining old services that, in accordance with their objectives, may become weightier in determining sectoral policies and may engender institutional changes concomitant to strengthening the resilience of such policies and protecting them from the volatility of political life. It can be stated with great certainty that the entrenchment of such sectoral policies is an imperative task.

NOTES

This chapter synthesizes approaches developed in Sojo (2017).

1. For example, in Colombia the contrast between health care and pension coverage is very pronounced. The health-care system reform included a subsidized regime, while the pension reform was directed toward a system of individual capitalization; moreover, noncontributory pensions have only been developed very recently.

2. Probit models have estimated the determinants of affiliation for workers between 15 and 64 years of age. The dependent variable refers to affiliation and the independent variables include personal characteristics of the workers (such as age, sex, educational attainment, and marital status) and the household (size and headship) and those pertaining to the workplace (occupational category, branch of activity, part-time work, type of labor insertion, and labor income quintile). Other variables such as race and location (urban or rural) in the countries with available data were also considered, as were interactions between the variables of educational attainment level and sex and between those of household headship and sex. The estimates were corrected for selection biases, including in the selection equation the sex, education, age, quantity of minors in the household (from 0 to 4 years and from 5 to 12 years of age), and the interaction between the quantity of minors under age 4 in the household and the presence of members between 15 and 64 years of age who are outside the labor force.

3. Brazil's polls have information about noncontributory pensions in special modules, whose breakdown does not allow meaningful comparisons with other countries' household polls.

REFERENCES

Amarante, Verónica, and Rodrigo Arim, eds. 2015. *Desigualdad e Informalidad*. Un análisis de cinco experiencias latinoamericanas, Libros de la CEPAL 133. Santiago: CEPAL.

Amarante, Verónica, and Ana Sojo. 2015. "Protección social y afiliación a los sistemas de pensiones en América Latina." In *Desigualdad e Informalidad*, ed. Verónica Amarante and Rodrigo Arim. Un análisis de cinco experiencias latinoamericanas, Libros de la CEPAL 133. Santiago: CEPAL.

Arrow, Kenneth. 1963. "Uncertainty and the Welfare Economics of Medical Care."*American Economic Review* 53(5):941–73.

———. 2000. "Insurance, Risk and Resource Allocation." In *Foundations of Insurance Economics. Readings in Economics and Finance*, compiled by G. Dionne and S. E. Harrington. Boston: Kluwer Academic.

Barr, Nicholas. 2013. *The Pension System in Sweden. Report to the Expert Group on Public Economics*. Stockholm: Ministry of Finance.

Chile, Comisión Asesora Presidencial para el Estudio y Propuesta de un Nuevo Marco Jurídico para el Sistema Privado de Salud. 2014. *Estudio y Propuesta de un Nuevo Marco Jurídico para el Sistema Privado de Salud*, October 8. Santiago.

Chile, Comisión Asesora Presidencial sobre el Sistema de Pensiones. 2015a. *Resumen Ejecutivo*, September. Santiago.

———. 2015b. *Antecedentes de la industria previsional*, September. Santiago.

———. 2015c. *La opinión y percepción del sistema de pensiones en Chile*, September. Santiago.

CEPAL. 2013. *Social Panorama of Latin America 2012*, Santiago: CEPAL.

———. 2014. *Social Panorama of Latin America 2013*. Santiago: CEPAL.

———. 2015. *Desarrollo social inclusivo. Una nueva generación de políticas para superar la pobreza y reducir la desigualdad en América Latina y el Caribe*. Santiago: CEPAL

Colombia, República de, Ministerio de Salud. 2013. *Exposición de motivos del Proyecto de ley por el cual se redefine el Sistema general de seguridad social en salud y se dictan otras disposiciones*. Retrieved from: https://www.minsalud.gov.co/Documents/Ley%20Reforma%20a%20la%20Salud/Exposicion-Motivos-%20Proyecto-leyre definicion-sistema-General-SeguridadSocial-Salud%20pdf.pdf.

Cubillos, Leonardo, Maria-Luisa Escobar, Sebastian Pavlovic, and Roberto Iunes. 2012. "Universal Health Coverage and Litigation in Latin America." *Journal of Health Organization and Management* 26(3):390–406.

Gaviria, Alejandro. 2015. "Fortalecer la capacidad de discernimiento de los gobiernos: una necesidad para enfrentar la presión tecnológica en salud." Webinar presentation organized by Criteria (Priorización y planes de beneficios en salud), Social Protection and Health Division, Interamerican Development Bank, December.

Gloppen, Siri. 2011. "Litigating Health Rights: Framing the Analysis." In *Litigating Health Rights: Can Courts Bring More Justice to Health?*, ed. Siri Gloppen and Alicia Yamin, 17–42. Cambridge: Harvard University Press.

Iunes, Roberto, Leonardo Cubillos, and Maria-Luisa Escobar. 2012. "Universal Health Coverage and Litigation in Latin America." En breve No. 178. Washington, D.C.: World Bank.

Kohli, Martin, and Marco Albertini. 2008. "The Family as a Source of Support for Adult Children's Own Family Projects: European Varieties." In *Families, Aging and Social Policy. Intergenerational Solidarity in European Welfare States*, ed. Chiara Saraceno. Northampton, Mass.: Elgar.

Maestad, Ottar, Lise Rakner, and Octavio Motta Ferraz. 2011. "Assessing the Impact of Health Rights Litigation: A Comparative Analysis of Argentina, Brazil, Colombia, Costa Rica, India and South Africa." *In Litigating Health Rights: Can Courts Bring More Justice to Health?*, ed. Siri Gloppen and Alicia Yamin, 273–303. Cambridge: Harvard University Press.

Mahoney, James, and Kathleen Thelen. 2009. "A Theory of Gradual Institutional Change." In *Explaining Institutional Change, Ambiguity, Agency, and Power*, ed. James Mahoney and Kathleen Thelen, 1–37. New York: Cambridge University Press.

OIT. 2014. "Experiencias recientes de formalización en países de América Latina y el Caribe." Notas sobre Formalización, Lima, Programa de Promoción de la Formalización en América Latina (FORLAC).

Orszag, Peter, and Joseph Stiglitz. 2001. "Rethinking Pension Reform. Ten Myths about Social Security Systems." In *New Ideas About Old Age Security*, ed. Robert Holzmann and Joseph Stiglitz, 17–56. Washington, D.C.: World Bank.

Rivera Urrutia, Eugenio. 2014. "La situación del sistema previsional privado al inicio del nuevo gobierno: el debate que viene." *Barómetro de política y equidad* No. 8. Santiago de Chile: Fundación Equitas y Fundación Friedrich Ebert.

Saraceno, Chiara. 2008. "Introduction: Intergenerational Relations in Families—A Micro-Macro Perspective." In *Families, Aging and Social Policy. Intergenerational Solidarity in European Welfare States*, ed. Chiara Saraceno. Northampton, Mass.: Elgar.

Sarasa, Sebastian, and Sunnee Billingsley. 2008. "Personal and Household Caregiving from Adult Children to Parents and Social Stratification." In *Families, Aging and Social Policy. Intergenerational Solidarity in European Welfare States*, ed. Chiara Saraceno. Northampton, Mass.: Elgar.

Sen, Amartya. 2004. "Why Health Equity?" In *Public Health, Ethics, and Equity*, ed. Sudhir Anand, Fabienne Peter, and Amartya Sen, 21–34. New York: Oxford University Press.

Sojo, Ana. 1999. "Principios generales y pautas de buenas prácticas en política social. Una propuesta de la CEPAL para la discusión." Unpublished background paper for CEPAL (2000), Equidad, desarrollo y ciudadanía, IV versión, 1.10. 1999, mimeo.

——. 2011. "De la evanescencia a la mira. El cuidado como eje de políticas y de actores en América Latina." Serie Seminarios y Conferencias Nº 67. Santiago: CEPAL.

——. 2014. "The Chilean System of Contributory Pensions as Locus of Rivalry and of a New Social Compact." Series Social Policy 211. Santiago: ECLAC.

——. 2015. "Including Informal Economy Workers in Contributory Social Protection: Current Challenges in Latin America." *International Social Security Review* 68(4):69–92.

——. 2017. *Protección social en América Latina. La desigualdad en el banquillo.* Libros de la CEPAL 143, Santiago: CEPAL.

Streeck, Wolfgang, and Kathleen Thelen. 2005. *Beyond Continuity. Institutional Change in Advanced Political Economies.* New York: Oxford University Press

Uprimny, Rodrigo, and Juanita Durán. 2014. "Equidad y protección judicial del derecho a la salud en Colombia." Serie Políticas Sociales No. 197. Santiago: CEPAL.

Yamin, Alicia. 2011. "Power, Suffering and Courts: Reflection on Promoting Health Rights Through Judicialization." In *Litigating Health Rights: Can Courts Bring More Justice to Health?*, ed. Siri Gloppen and Alicia Yamin, 333–72. Cambridge: Harvard University Press.

CHAPTER 12

Do Competitive Markets of Individual Savings Accounts and Health Insurance Work as Part of the Welfare State?

Andras Uthoff

Chile is known for its liberal economic policy, which was introduced under the military regime (1973–1989) and was a characteristic that spread into social security and was not sufficiently revised after the recovery of democracy in 1990. Recovering political rights has taken time, and the consideration of social and social security rights have taken a backseat.

Compulsory individual savings accounts and individual health insurance markets were introduced in 1981 to replace social insurance in providing for health and retirement benefits. Huge economic interests have been developed around these industries, capturing the interest but also the ideology of many professionals and academicians. It is my opinion that they have produced misleading papers, which enhanced the financial and macroeconomic effects around the development of this industry and avoided the real purpose of these tools. Namely, poverty relief, consumption smoothing, insurance in the case of pensions, and insurance and prevention in the case of health.

The issue is simple. Private market solutions in social security have demanded in Chile the implementation of individual contracts, which themselves enhance the equivalence principle, where every single contract needs to be actuarially fair. This implies that the affiliate is transformed into a consumer of financial services, who maximizes his/her individual welfare function by selecting options within his/her individual contract. This principle conflicts with the solidarity principle. The latter is needed to provide (in unequal societies such as Chile) universal access under a social insurance contract. In the meantime, academic and public policy debates have been centered on the new industries created and their efficiency conditions and macroeconomic effects through long-term savings, labor supply, and insurance, diverting attention from a real discussion on social security outcomes that deal with coverage and sufficiency of benefits.

Chile must show the world that transforming citizens with rights into consumers of different financial services industries with freedom to choose among providers does not represent a true social security reform. Since early 2016, massive protests in the streets, research done on alternative reforms, and the conclusions of two presidential advisory commissions (Comisión Asesora Presidencial para el Estudio y Propuesta de un Nuevo Régimen Jurídico para el Sistema Privado de Salud, Comisión CID [2014] and Comisión Asesora Presidencial sobre el Sistema de Pensiones, Comisión Bravo [2014–2015]) are building an increasing recognition that social security in Chile is in a severe historical crisis that will not be overcome unless the real causes behind it are tackled. Structural changes are needed.

This chapter addresses this issue. It does not review the large list of papers that have been produced, most of them funded by the same industry and written by members of their boards. I leave it to the interested reader to search these out and read them, along with World Bank papers and reports from the 1990s that tried to introduce similar reforms in emerging economies. Instead, based on my personal view and experiences as member of three presidential commissions called to review these systems (Comisión Marcel in 2006, Comisión CID in 2014, and Comisión Bravo in 2015, named after their president's last name), I would like to discuss the inconsistencies between the equivalence principle concept in individual insurance and saving contracts offered in competitive markets and the solidarity principle needed for universal coverage.

The chapter is organized in three parts. Section 1 summarizes how these industries were introduced in Chile and recent findings on the relevant outcomes for which these markets replaced social insurance schemes. Section 2 conceptualizes the main trade-offs between unregulated incentives in these markets and the principles of social security. Section 3 presents my conclusions.

1. REPLACING SOCIAL INSURANCE BY MARKETS: FALSE PROMISES, POOR RESULTS

PENSION SYSTEM

THE FIRST AND WORST-EVER REFORM

Decree Law 3500 of 4 November 1980 created in Chile an old age, survivor, and disability pension system derived from individual capitalization and established the norms for its development. In short, it replaced multiple and heterogeneous funds operating under pay-as-you-go (PAYG) schemes with a single competitive market of compulsory savings accounts. To do this, all funds, except those for the armed forces, were merged into a single account, after homogenizing and quantifying the affiliates' acquired rights. The latter were split into current retirees and current workers who had contributed to the old system and needed to convert to the new.

This structural change implied that future contributions would be directed into individual savings accounts and would not be available to finance benefits for those retired under the old system. Thus, two liabilities were created: one with current and future beneficiaries willing to remain in the old system, and one with current contributors willing (or obliged) to move into the new system. The first was labeled *operational costs* and is represented by the net flow between benefits paid and contributions received by the stock of actual beneficiaries and those to come remaining in the PAYG system. The second was labeled *recognition bond* and is a debt instrument introduced into those who moved into the new system individual accounts and representing the present value of past contributions made into the replaced PAYG system.

These flows represent present and future liabilities due to the change from a PAYG into a fully funded system (individual savings account). The present value of such flows is labeled as the *implicit debt* of the replaced PAYG and has been estimated to equal 136 percent of Chile's GDP (Bravo and Uthoff 1999).

In the reformed system, affiliates would put savings into the system during the entire work life cycle and, at retirement, opt for either a programmed retirement benefit funded out of their accumulated capital or an annuity bought from an insurance company with the same capital. If eligible (after having contributed twenty years) they could apply for a minimum guaranteed benefit. Otherwise they would apply to old-age assistance benefits. The industry was strongly regulated in both its market structure and the risk exposure of the portfolios the firms could manage.

Results were poor. In 2006, after twenty-five years of the system being in operation, authorities could show that only 45 percent of affiliates had self-financed a pension benefit, an additional 5 percent would receive the minimum guaranteed benefit (after having contributed for twenty years), and the remaining 50 percent would end up with no guarantee, except for the right to apply for assistance transfers that were limited by fiscal budget restrictions and delivered by quotas.

THE SECOND, "FINE-TUNING" REFORM

Based on such poor results, Law 20255 of 17 March 2008 created a solidarity pension system for old age, survival, and disability, complementary
to the existing pension system of DL 3500 (1980).

The interesting issue about this law is the process by which it was created. All presidential candidates for the 2006–2010 period were in agreement about the poor performance of the existing pension system, and all
campaign platforms included a review of the system. Once elected candi-
date Michelle Bachelet was in power, she named a commission (Comisión
Marcel) to provide guidelines to improve the system.

The commission argued that after a large and costly transition, the
system was providing poor results, and additional fiscal resources could
be justified to guarantee solidarity benefits for the poor. This was the
main improvement of Law 20255, the creation of a noncontributory and
complementary solidarity pillar.

The new complementary system offers basic solidarity pension benefits
to those having no contributory histories and solidarity-topped benefits
for those with contributory histories but not enough accumulated savings. Both these benefits are targeted to beneficiaries who are among
families in the poorest three quintiles.

The new law also included market bidding for the flow of new affiliates with the aim of reducing excess profits in the account manager industry. It also introduced a set of gender- and age-specific transfers and/or
subsidies to reduce gender inequalities and improve young workers' entry
into the system.

CONTINUING POOR RESULTS

The new solidarity pension system is believed to provide appropriate benefits for those who have complete contributory histories and poverty alleviation for the aged through the solidarity pillar. Nevertheless, 70 percent of all
citizens believe that benefits financed by the system are substandard.[1] In fact,
44 percent of all beneficiaries receive benefits below the Chilean poverty line,
and 79 percent receive benefits below the minimum wage. Consumption
smoothing, as measured by replacement rates, also reports poor results. Fifty
percent of all beneficiaries receive benefits that represent less than 38 percent
of their last ten years' average wage. This is worse among women (less than
59 percent for men and less than 24.5 percent for women).

These results are said to be biased because beneficiaries include those who participated in the old system (previous to 1981), and their benefits are not from the purely individual capitalization regime. Instead, if these are computed for older age cohorts who spent their working lives within the capitalization system, replacement rates for beneficiaries in 2025 and 2035 would average only 39 percent, and for 50 percent of beneficiaries it would not be higher than 37 percent.

Six characteristics that cannot be solved via individual savings accounts explain these results:

1. *Weak densities of contributions.* Despite improved coverage (69.3 percent contributors over the total occupied; and 84.5 percent of those aged 65 and over receiving some benefit [CASEN 2013]), contribution densities[2] are less than 50 percent for all affiliates. This result is related to labor histories characterized by informality, unemployment, abandoning the labor force along the life cycle, and elusion and evasion. These problems are most extreme for women.

2. *Population aging.* Increasing life expectancies at age of retirement contrasted with fixed savings capacities imply lower annuities offered by insurance companies and greater vulnerability for the aged.

3. *Lack of competition in the saving managers' industry.* The bidding process has not resulted in better efficiency, and commissions remain high. Only the newcomers are benefiting from the bidding process, and the large stock of old affiliates pay high commissions. There is no mobility incentivized by lower commissions.

4. *Historical financial returns.* Historic returns from pension funds have been higher than those predicted when the system was created (4 percent). Nevertheless, these returns are lower than those reported as the gross returns of the funds and have a falling trend.

5. *Choice in pension benefit.* At retirement, an affiliate faces new risks that affect optimal smooth consumption when choosing among benefit alternatives. Programmed retirement benefits reduce benefits whenever life expectancy is higher than expected. Annuities bought by insurance companies are sensitive to financial outcomes at retirement.

6. *Gender biases.* Individual savings accounts are biased against women. Sex-specific life tables and early age of retirement without compensation imply higher life expectancies at retirement for women. For similar accumulated savings amounts at retirement, this implies lower self-funded benefits for women. Saving capacity along the working life is also

lower for women due to both discrimination when economically active and when performing the cultural roles that limit labor force participation.

Two hidden lessons arise from these events. The 1981 (DL 3500) reform implied large public finance resources, which were made available under special political conditions and a reshuffling of the budget to fit the transition costs. In fact, such accommodation was done via a combination of tax reform, social expenditure cuts, and debt emission. It is estimated that the large burden of these measures was supported by the current generation by means of fiscal cuts, although there is yet a balance to be funded until 2050.

The new solidarity pillar instead is funded out of general taxes, which in turn are raised through income taxes (43 percent) and value-added taxes (45 percent).

After more than six years of application, a poll of citizens shows very poor satisfaction ratings.

• Seventy-two percent believe that only a major change in the system would improve pension benefits.
• Sixty-six percent believe that pension fund managers or administradoras de fondos de pensiones (AFPs) are solely responsible for the low benefits.
• As reported in the Diálogos Ciudadanos and Audiencias Públicas, the system is permanently criticized for its origin under the military regime; for not accomplishing promises for higher rates of replacement; for the lack of information and education needed to make choices; and for the large and non-related to performance profits of AFPs.
• It was also mentioned that the system does not meet the basic principles of social security (solidarity, sufficiency, and universality) included in ILO's 102 Agreement on Social Security.

HEALTH SYSTEM

THE WORST INTERNATIONALLY KNOWN REFORM

As of 1981 a market of competitive health prevention institutions (ISAPRES) offering individual health insurance was instituted to replace the multiple corporate and public health funds. The latter were unified and kept as an option of last resort for those who could not afford to pay the market premiums.

These firms sold insurance to each individual based upon his or her individual risk as defined by actuarial tables with an eye to efficiency and profit. Lack of proper regulation within this industry ended in a large cream skimming of the population, on the basis of risk selection. Income distribution took its toll. As of today, merely 18 percent of the beneficiaries are insured by the private industry, 76 percent are insured by the public fund, and another 6 percent are insured either by the armed forces system or other alternative insurance.

The main result was the immediate development of a dual system that segmented the population by health risks and income factors. Those determined to be high risk and/or those with lower incomes were insured through the public fund, and those determined to be low risk and/or those with higher incomes were insured through individual private health insurance.

As shown in table 12.1, the private system excludes more than 76 percent of the population from private health coverage, forcing those people into the public fund. Cream skimming takes place by way of health status requirements that identify preexisting factors for noneligibility. Efficiency is sought by tailor-made health plans that increase premiums for the worst risks up to a level that obliges them to leave the system. Today, the industry offers more than 10,000 different plans, and there are more than 50,000 in stock. The industry has only seven insurers; the largest three have captured over 60 percent of the market, and their half-year profits, although small in the form of revenue, represent a larger share of capital and reserve and double each firm's own capital. Half-year profits of these insurers amount to the cost of building a medium-sized hospital in Chile.

Original price regulation made affiliation compulsory and eligible for coverage by paying 7 percent of taxable income, intended to avoid adverse selection (i.e., forcing good risks to demand insurance). Nevertheless, private insurance pricing excluded a large share of consumers: first by income factor and then by risk factor. Unilateral premium setting and discrimination by income and risk factors ended in a dual model. A large share of consumers and the destitute are covered by the public health fund (known as FONASA), while a small share of the richest and/or lowest-risk consumers are covered by the private insurers (ISAPRES).

The Chilean case is a clear example of the competitive private health insurance market being driven exclusively by efficiency, with risk ratings, risk segmentation, and risk selection making insurance less affordable for the majority of the population.

Table 12.1 Market Characteristics of Health Insurance in Chile

	Distribution of beneficiaries (%)			Half-year industry profits as % of:			Market concentration (out of 7) (%)			Number of plans offered				
	FONASA	ISAPRES	Other	Capital	Capital + reserves	Income	Larger	Two largest	Three largest	Existing	In stock	In market	Individual	Group
2010	74.4%	16.5%	9.1%	100.9	40.9	3.6	22.2	44.3	64.3	49,448	37,538	11,910	30,329	19,119
2011	76.4%	16.9%	6.7%	137.6	53.6	3.6	21.8	43.0	62.9	50,246	37,698	12,548	30,649	10,597
2012	76.7%	17.6%	5.8%	138.9	56.6	4.8	22.4	43.7	63.9	51,747	39,540	12,207	30,823	20,889
2013	76.3%	18.2%	5.5%	63.6	19.1	2.1	22.4	43.3	64.8	52,706	38,555	14,151	30,941	21,765
2014	75.7%	18.6%	5.7%	99.8	17.6	2.9	21.3	42.5	63.4	55,830	44,226	11,604	32,277	23,553
2015				63.5	10.6	1.6	21.3	41.7	62.0	60,057	45,007	15,050	32,816	27,242

Source: Author's estimates with official data from Superintendencia de Salud and FONASA, Chile.

After the return to democracy, several attempts have been made to overcome this dualistic system.

LAW AUGE-GES

The first attempt was a law that defines a set of explicit health guarantees (Garantías Explícitas en Salud AUGE-GES, universal access to explicit guarantees). Any insured beneficiary from either FONASA or ISAPRES who is suffering an illness that is included in the AUGE-GES list must get a medical certificate. If certified to be suffering one of the illnesses listed, he or she can demand his or her right to receive treatment within the existing providers' network of his or her insurance segment (either FONASA or ISAPRES). The rights and guarantees secure the proper treatment with guaranteed financial coverage and opportunity as set by law.

The AUGE-GES law created a mechanism that prioritizes prevention, treatment, and rehabilitation for specific illnesses. These illnesses are defined as those having major health impacts on Chilean citizens. GES is a set of benefits guaranteed by law for those insured in both FONASA and ISAPRES. It implies four guarantees:

1. *Access*: All who are eligible are guaranteed treatment protocols for each illness listed.
2. *Opportunity:* All treatments must be provided according to established timing.
3. *Financial coverage*: Affiliates are financially covered in an inverse proportion to the level of taxable income. The destitute and those with lower incomes have 0 percent copayments (these are called FONASA A and B groups). Those in the next income stratum have 10 percent copayments (FONASA C group). Those in the upper-income stratum in FONASA (FONASA D group) and all those insured by ISAPRES have 20 percent copayments.
4. *Quality:* Providers of treatments and services must be registered and certified by the Health Superintendent.

All insured beneficiaries from either any group in FONASA or ISAPRES who suffer one of the eighty AUGE-GES pathologies are eligible. They must certify their age, health status, and other conditions identified for each health problem. They must be covered by providers in the original insurer's network and for treatments that are duly certified for the prescribed pathologies.

RICARTE SOTO LAW

Named after activist Ricarte Soto (who passed away after a long and costly illness), this law establishes financial coverage for high-cost treatments and diagnoses. It provides financial coverage for high-cost medicine, medical instruments, and medically prescribed diets that are effectively proven (scientifically, economically, and socially). The list of treatments and diagnoses may be increased after certified by a medical commission.

The Ricarte Soto law complements the AUGE-GES law to the extent that it covers non-frequent illness excluded from the AUGE-GES list. In their certification, health burden or high prevalence that are important in the AUGE-GES law are not considered. To the contrary, it is based on studies that justify risk-sharing treatments. The number of beneficiaries is expected to grow exponentially from two to twenty thousand people, demanding significant resources. The coverage is said to be universal and includes those insured under the armed forces and ISAPRES schemes.

As for AUGE-GES, beneficiaries must be certified by their primary physician and treatments must be provided by a network certified by the Ministry of Health on the basis of technical qualification and feasibility. High-cost medicine, medical instruments, and special diets must be also certified, with all medical, economic, social, and security factors taken into account. New components to this social security scheme will be evaluated and certified by a panel of experts overseen by commissioners, including patients. The listing will be updated every three years, with exceptional cases examined separately. This panel and the medical commission will follow transparency rules, and public response will be demanded by health authorities.

The scheme is universal and funded out of general taxes.

LEGAL CLAIMS

Since the reform in 2005 that enhanced social security rights, the Chilean dual system has been faced with important legal claim processes, mainly against the private insurers. Cases have increased year by year as people became aware of their rights. The claims are against unilateral individual products indexation and also argue that discrimination by age and sex has occurred.

The cases arise during the yearly indexing efforts that insurers do on their clients' product premiums. The number of judicial demands have increased by thousands each year. The cases are based on the property right on all components of the health plans (products), and not accepting reductions due to arbitrary costing. In the public sector, legal cases are rare and mainly address access to medicine.

2. INDIVIDUAL CONTRACTS AND SOCIAL SECURITY: CONFLICTS BETWEEN BASIC PRINCIPLES

When the welfare state is replaced with private health insurance operating in a poorly regulated, competitive market, as is the case in Chile, the health insurance system faces obvious problems. But solutions have been constrained by constitutional threats and economic interest surrounding the private health insurance and private savings account management industries.

Individual health insurers and savings account managers in a competitive market seek efficiency through actuarially fair individual contracts. There is a trend in the health insurance market to rate the premiums on risk; and in the savings account management market to transfer all risks involved in savings along the life cycle to the consumer. This is called the equivalence principle, implying that both insurers and managers actuarially balance each individual contract. The main problem with individual contracts in competitive health insurance and savings account management is the incompatibility between the equivalence and solidarity principles.

The principle of solidarity implies that high-risk individuals receive a cross-subsidy from low-risk individuals in order to improve their access to an affordable insurance and/or pension benefit.

THE CASE IN COMPETITIVE INDIVIDUAL HEALTH INSURANCE MARKETS (ISAPRES)

Figure 12.1 plots the age-specific relative health expenditures over the life cycle for males and females against the market structure of beneficiaries in either FONASA or ISAPRES by age. For those ages at which expected expenditures increase, the share of insured persons in the private sector decreases, and with aging and higher expected health expenditures, the share of insured in the private sector fades out.

THE CASE IN COMPETITIVE INDIVIDUAL SAVINGS ACCOUNTS MANAGEMENT MARKETS (AFP)

Table 12.2 reports on the effect on replacement rates of diverse factors that affect consumers along the life cycle. Self-financed replacement

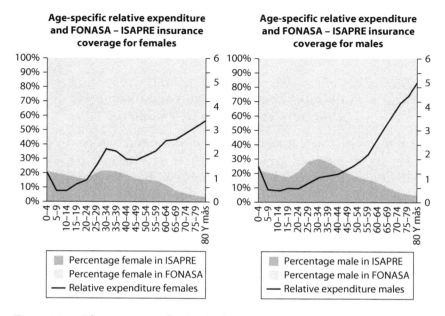

Figure 12.1   The outcomes of individual savings contracts managed by unregulated competitive firms.

Source: Chile, Superintendencia de Salud and FONASA, age-sex-risk costs tables and age-sex affiliation in insurance schemes.

rates vary by sex, favoring males due to cultural discrimination factors in the labor market. But then replacement rates increase in direct proportion to the density of contributions, thus affecting those more exposed to factors that affect labor force participation—unemployment and underemployment—affecting full employment for all. Replacement rates for a beneficiary also have implicit the financial risks and demographic risks associated with the fact that individual contracts are actuarially fair. The solidarity pillar improves replacement rates, especially for those with lower contributions, who by definition are those facing higher labor market risks along the life cycle and end up in poverty when aged.

By not including an internal solidarity component, the Chilean pension system cannot compensate for lifetime inequality and poverty in old-age benefits. It is for the extreme poor that the solidarity pillar has an after-retirement scheme for alleviating poverty through transfers funded with general taxes.

Table 12.2 Median Replacement Rates in Chile by Sex and Number of Months Having Contributed (2007, 2014)

Number of months contributing	Interval	Self-financed benefits			With subsidies		
		Female	Males	Total	Female	Male	Total
Low (≤25%)	(1–35)	4%	5%	4%	21%	128%	64%
N		20,877	11,588	32,465			
Medium low (26–50%)	(36–46)	10%	23%	13%	14%	69%	33%
N		43,499	29,493	72,942			
Medium high (51–74%)	(147–285)	23%	45%	33%	27%	57%	42%
N		51,797	54,435	106,232			
High (>75%)	(286–386)	36%	55%	46%	37%	59%	48%
N		53,819	71,963	125,782			
No information	(0)	7%	41%	9%	170%	53%	159%
		369	29	398			
Total		24%	48%	34%	31%	60 %	45%
N		170,311	167,508	337,819			

Source: Informe Comisión Bravo (cuadro 13).

The commission's (Comisión Asesora Presidencial sobre el Sistema de Pensiones, Comisión Bravo, 2014–2015) recently released report is very clear:

1. Compared with other OECD members, the Chilean system shows lower replacement rates for all intervals of contribution and for both sexes. The differences are less severe for the lower intervals where the solidarity pillar operates.
2. Concerning sufficiency, the report states that 79 percent of benefits are below the minimum wage, and 44 percent are below the poverty line. When the same exercise is performed exclusively for those eligible for the solidarity pillar, it shows that only 14 percent receive benefits below the poverty line, but 93 percent receive benefits below the minimum wage.
3. Things are worse for women:
   a. Fifty-nine percent of them receive benefits below the poverty line, whereas only 26 percent of men are similarly affected.
   b. When only beneficiaries of the solidarity pillar are examined, it is seen that 22 percent of women receive benefits below the poverty line compared with 9 percent of men.

   c. Eighty-five percent of women receive benefits below the minimum wage compared with 72 percent of men.

   d. When only beneficiaries of the solidarity pillar are examined, it is seen that 95 percent of women and 92 percent of men get benefits below the minimum wage.

5. The 2008 reformed system mildly alleviates poverty in old age:

   a. 60 percent of those in the solidarity pillar belong to poor families (below the poverty line), and 28 percent of them belong to families with no income.

   b. From all 1,281,628 beneficiaries:

      i. Forty-five and a half percent (583,202) correspond to a flat rate (solidarity basic pension benefit [PBS]) and 54.5 percent (698,426) to a complement (supplementary pension benefit [APS]). They are provided to women in a larger proportion (66.5 percent PBS and 57.6 percent APS for women).

      ii. Fifty-two percent of the PBS beneficiaries fall within the poorest 20 percent of households, and 87 percent are among the poorest 60 percent. Within the APS cases, 32 percent fall within the first quintile and 82 percent fall within the poorest 60 percent.

      iii. Ninety-six percent of the pillar beneficiaries belong to the poorest 60 percent of families.

      iv. The pillar reduced poverty and destitution in old age by 2.1 percentage points of poverty incidence and 0.5 percentage points of destitution incidence.

3. CONCLUSIONS

In Chile, a country where private insurance and private savings managements markets have been used to replace social insurance, the poor results in terms of universal access raise the following question: How can we guarantee access to affordable coverage for high-risk people in the individual insurance market and provide sufficient benefits for the poor and vulnerable in the individual savings account management markets?

The answer in both cases is the same. If political and constitutional constraints prevent a return to a public social insurance, then public policies must be created that reconcile the principles of equivalence and solidarity in both markets.

1. In the individual health insurance market this implies:
   a. A threefold strategy based on (i) premium regulation to access a single and open health plan, with open affiliation (no health condition restrains); (ii) a pooling to compensate across insurers by risk exposure; and (iii) a combination of both.
   b. The commission (Comisión Asesora Presidencial para el Estudio y Propuesta de un Nuevo Régimen Jurídico para el Sistema Privado de Salud, Comsion CID 2014), in order to break the wall that segments the system, recommended creating a universal plan; eliminating health condition certificates to enter the system; creating an inter-insurers compensation fund with all the compulsory contributions; allowing a flat additional premium for non–health risk related differential factors to be paid voluntarily; allowing extra financial coverage; and expanding the use of pooled funding for pathologies that are universal (see figure 12.2).

2. In the individual savings pension system, this implies:
   a. A three-step plan, as suggested by the ILO, to provide (i) an universal flat benefit for all; (ii) a tripartite contributive benefit funded under defined contributions, with cross-subsidies topped to a level that guarantees a progressive scaling to the large replacement rate for the minimum wage; and (iii) a self-funded benefit out of individual savings managed by AFPs selected by the consumer.
   b. The commission recommended (i) expanding the basic solidarity benefit with an affluence test (that is, to reach the poorest 80 percent of all beneficiaries, or alternatively, to exclude the richest 20 percent); (ii) separating affiliates according to income levels; (iii) applying a social insurance scheme for the low-income affiliates and for the lower part of the higher income taxable income; (iv) using a progressive distributive formula to cross-subsidize in favor of the more vulnerable, provided they make contributive efforts; (v) regulating the financial management of the social insurance reserve fund; (vi) providing each beneficiary with three benefits if eligible (the universal benefit; the social security tripartite-funded benefit; and the individual savings benefit). (See table 12.3.)

Chile has wrongly been praised for the "wonders" of its liberal economic policy. I leave experts in other fields to judge those. However, spreading market solutions toward social security has proven to be

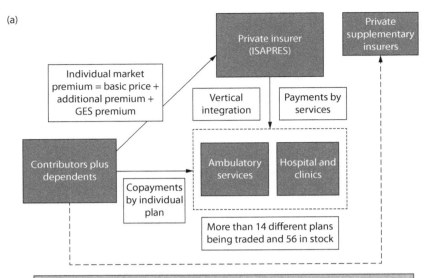

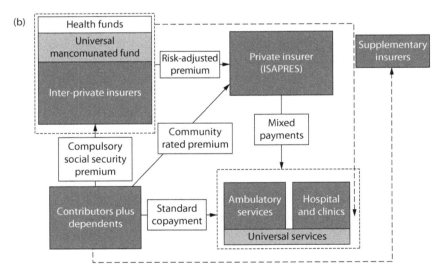

Figure 12.2 Private health insurance reform scheme: (a) existing situation and (b) proposed situation.

Source: Author's schemes based on Informe Comision CID.

Table 12.3 Schematic Reform Proposal for the Individual Savings Account Managers' System in Chile[a]

Existing system				Reformed system (proposal B)				
							Contributive	
Beneficiaries	Targeting criteria	Noncontributive	Contributive	Beneficiaries	Sorting criteria (CH $1,000)	Noncontributive	Social insurance	Individually funded
Ordered by contributive effort	60% Poorest	PBS		Ordered by taxable income	Never contributed	PBS		
	60% Poorest	APS	ICB		Taxable income < 400	PBS	SSB	
	Non-60% poorest		ICB		Taxable income > 400	PBS excluding 20% richest	SSB	ICB
Finance		General taxes	Contribution from taxable income	Finance		General taxes	Tripartite contributions	Individual contribution
Administration		Social security institution	Account managers and insurance companies + regulations	Administration		Social insurance institution	Social insurance institution + pension reserve fund administration	Social insurance institution + account managers and insurance companies

Source: Based on commission report, proposal B (2015).

[a] APS, supplementary pension benefit; ICB, self-funded capitalization benefit; PBS, solidarity basic pension benefit; SSB, social security benefit.

extremely wrong. The reason is simple: a badly regulated or constitutionally restrained competitive market of individual health insurance and individual savings account managements hampers the degree of solidarity needed to provide affordable coverage for those bearing the larger risks and burdens of inequality.

In the future, Chile's public policy innovations will experience radical changes from its current social insurance schemes (providing the political conditions are apt for such change).

NOTES

1. As was reported to the Survey on Opinions and Perceptions on the Chilean pension System. Presidential Advisory Commission on the Pension System (Comisión Bravo 2015).

2. Density of contributions is defined as the ratio between the number of months he/she contributed to the system and the total number of months in active ages.

REFERENCES

Bravo, Jorge, and Andras Uthoff. 1999. "Transitional Fiscal Costs and Demographic Factors in Shifting from Unfunded to Funded Pension in Latin America." 1999, Serie Financiamiento del Desarrollo 88 (LC/L.1264-P), CEPAL, Santiago.

Comisión CID: Comisión Asesora Presidencial para el Estudio y Propuesta de un Nuevo Régimen Jurídico para el Sistema Privado de Salud. 2014. Retrieved from: http://www.gob.cl/comision-isapres/.

Consejo Asesor Presidencial Para La Reforma Previsional (Comisión Marcel). 2006. El derecho a una vida digna en la vejez: Hacia un contrato social con previsión en Chile. Retrieved from: http://www.sbif.cl/sbifweb/servlet/DBiblioteca?indice =6.5&TXT_CORRELATIVO=L3252&CTR_CORRELATIVO =XXXXXXXXXXXXXXX.

Presidential Advisory Commission on the Pension System (Comisión Bravo). 2015. "Final Report" Retrieved from: www.comision-pensiones.cl/Documentos /InformeFinal.

Presidential Advisory Commission on the Pension System (Comisión Bravo). 2015a. "Executive Summary." Retrieved from: www.comision-pensiones.cl/Documentos /ResumenIngles.

Presidential Advisory Commission on the Pension System (Comisión Bravo). 2015b. "Encuesta de Opinión y Percepción del Sistema de Pensiones en Chile." Retrieved from: http://www.comision-pensiones.cl/Documentos/encuestadeopiniony percepciondelsistema.

CHAPTER 13

Innovations in Protecting the Old

MOSTLY SOCIAL INSURANCE AND SOME ASSETS

Teresa Ghilarducci

The risk of being poor or near-poor in old age is growing for the first time in two generations because the American pension system has failed. The American system evolved into a patchwork of loosely connected private-public programs many people try to rationalize using various metaphors of stability—a three-layered stool, a multipillar system, and a layered pyramid. But, for most workers the system is not stable. The stool metaphor is misleading because the importance of each source of retirement income, unlike the legs of a stool, is not of equal size. The pyramid metaphor is much better to describe the relative sizes of the sources of income to middle-class elderly—Social Security is the most important, so it sits on the bottom; employment-based retirement plans sit in the middle; and personal assets are the least important—that layer sits at the very top. But the system is a crumbling; it is an unstable pyramid creating serious sources of inequality in retirement security. The main cause of the erosion of American retirement security is the transformation of employer-based pensions based on social insurance principles to a system based on "do-it-yourself" financial accounts.

This chapter describes how the American retirement system collapsed, in part because of ideological commitments to individual asset building. The emphasis on individual wealth to insure the known risks of retirement and superannuation embedded fatal flaws in old-age income support programs. Some of the consequences were new sources of inequality, such as access to retirement and government retirement subsidies.

Eroding pension security for low- and middle-income workers "commodifies" their labor in old age (compels them to work for pay), as the normal retirement age to qualify for Social Security benefits started to increase with the reforms of 1983 from 65 to 67 for people born between 1954 and 1960 and 401(k) income became less ample, more insecure, and more unequally distributed. Additionally, the wages of older boomers will be suppressed—as boomer wages have always been suppressed throughout their labor market experience, mainly because of the sheer size of the cohort—as 7 million boomers who would have retired under the former more secure and generous pension plans may now remain in or re-enter the labor market (Ghilarducci, Papadopoulus, and Radpour 2017).

The chapter closes with a way forward to a system that is better designed, the "guaranteed retirement account" (GRA), which combines social insurance elements and asset accumulation to shore up the crumbing second layer of retirement income (Ghilarducci and James 2017). The GRA will help mitigate the problem of inequality of retirement time, assets, tax breaks, and the coming problem of old-age poverty. The GRA stabilizes the economy over business cycles relative to 401(k)s and IRAs, which act as automatic destabilizers, inducing households to save and work more in downturns, behavior that would perversely make the recession worse.

1. THE RISE OF ASSETS REPLACING SOCIAL INSURANCE

The changing second tier of the American retirement income security system fails to deliver the three elements of any good pension system. An effective and efficient pension system smooths lifetime consumption in three basic steps: the system helps workers accumulate assets, invest the assets efficiently, and convert them to annuities—pensions for life. The U.S. financial-based system is flawed on all dimensions: coverage is incomplete; the investments underperform; and the payments are lumps and not lifelong annuities. Voluntary coverage and permitted preretirement leakages mean people do not accumulate enough. Liquid accounts mean long-term savings are not matched to long-term investments and appropriately diversified portfolios, and in old age retirees are expected to manage their lumps sums so the income lasts their lifetime. (Uthoff, in chapter 12 of this volume, discusses the same problems in the Chilean pension system.)

Most workplace retirement plans are 401(k)-type plans and most assets in individual retirement accounts (IRAs) (administered not by employers but by financial institutions) come from 401(k)s. The three-decade-long decision of employers and policy makers to switch from actuarially funded defined benefit plans to commercial, voluntary, and individual directed accounts has shifted financial, investment, and longevity risk to individuals who are the people least able to insure against them. Thus, the "asset ownership society" is a process that shifts risk to individuals and households with no added return or benefit to them. (In Chile, the financial industry benefited greatly [Uthoff, this volume].)

Despite the fatal flaws in the design, the financialization of retirement income security was part of a movement for an asset-based social welfare state which took off in the 1980s as both the Left, liberal scholars (Sherradan 2003), and the ideological Right promoted an asset-based welfare state.

The rhetoric of the "ownership society" had become the motivational frame behind the reform of Social Security through private savings account. Here, former president George W. Bush and former vice president Richard Cheney describe the importance of assets:

> Ownership, access to wealth and independence, should not be the privilege of the few. They are the hope of every American, and we must make them the foundation of Social Security. (George W. Bush, as quoted in Stevenson 2001)

> One of the great goals of our administration is to help more Americans find the opportunity to own a home, a small business, a health care plan, or a retirement plan. In all of these areas, ownership is a path to greater opportunity, more freedom, and more control over your own life. (Richard Cheney, as quoted in Rosenbaum 2005).

The Left also supported asset-based social welfare programs. Ed Wolff, a leftist economist at New York University and his coauthor are quoted in a publication from a Russell Sage (Wolff and Shapiro 2005) project supporting asset-based social welfare policy: "Assets for the Poor is the first full-scale investigation into the importance of family wealth and the need for policies to encourage asset-building among the poor."

Progressive philanthropic institutions, such as the Ford Foundation, promoted individual savings accounts as an important element of social welfare policy:

> [Individual accounts] help community residents develop their own, long-term wealth-generating capacity. They promote education, homeownership and small, local business development—critical elements of vibrant,

sustainable neighborhoods. By teaching participants key financial skills, they empower people to make informed choices and secure their own financial wellbeing. (Ford Foundation 2016)

Pierson's (2001) dichotomy of social welfare reform divides welfare state reform into three camps: retrenchment for cost-containment sake, recalibration to bring some benefits back into line, and commodification to take away sources of non "labor-selling" income. The changes to the U.S. system of retirement income was mostly aimed at commodification. Financializing pensions—supported by the asset movement—resulted in an unraveling of widespread support for the proposition that all workers— not just the well-off—are entitled to paid time off at retirement age. The one important source of resistance to commodification of the labor time of the elderly was the labor movement, AARP, and Democratic Party's success in stopping President Bush's push to privatize Social Security in 2005 (Avsar 2008).

2. THE FAILURE OF THE CURRENT SYSTEM

Individual directed, commercial liquid accounts underperform for everyone, but low- and middle-income workers are especially hard hit because they pay disproportionately higher fees (Ayers and Curtis 2015). The tax breaks also underperform for low- and middle-income workers, as the highest-paid receive a disproportionate share of the benefits. Because of the inequality of underperformance and lopsided tax breaks, retirement account access and retirement wealth are becoming more unequal.

The first aspect of the system's failure is lack of coverage, resulting in too little accumulation. Only 53 percent of American workers between the ages of twenty-five and sixty-four have a retirement plan at work, despite the generous indirect subsidies from federal and state governments, which totaled over $140 billion in 2015. Those who do have 401(k)-type retirement plans or IRAs have only accumulated a median value of $104,000 in those accounts. In retirement, this yields only $2,500 per year for life (Ghilarducci et al. 2015). Including all households with and without a plan, the median account balance is $12,000. Most people in the bottom 90 percent of the income distribution have no plan.

But lack of access and participation, taken together, represent only one cause of inadequate accumulations. Because pensions are not mandatory and can be withdrawn before retirement, life events can disrupt the best intentions. The inequality this structure causes is covered in section 4 on inequality.

3. THE RISE OF BOTH PRIVATIZED SOCIAL INSURANCE THROUGH TAX BREAKS AND BEHAVIORAL ECONOMICS

The financialization of American pension plans was abetted by the rise of asset ownership ideology, which lubricated a series of congressional acts: permissive regulations by the Labor Department and Treasury on 401(k) plans and IRAs (Weller 2016); entrepreneurial activity by 401(k) brokers (Anderson 2013); and employers who discovered their employees did not either understand the value of their defined benefit (DB) plans or had no means or motivation to fight against their erosion (Madland 2007).

It was not always thus. Workplace benefits that paid workers for time off (paid time off includes vacation, sickness, and family leave, but the largest form of paid time off is for "superannuation") were parts of compensation that were luxury-type goods, meaning they are income elastic, and demand for paid time off increased with income. The labor movement always included shorter working times, including retirement, paid holidays, funeral leave, vacations, and weekends, in their lists of demands. The song, "Too Old to Work: Too Young to Die" (Glazer 1950), written during the 1950 United Automobile Workers' strike against Chrysler, summed up the anger over unequal access to retirement: "Your boss gets a pension when he gets too old. You helped him retire. You're out in the cold."

The demand for retirement time backed by insurance plans is also evinced by the democratic acceptance and expansion of Social Security from 1935 to 1985. When workers were represented by unions and could express their views collectively about their financial futures, they voted to divert some compensation into defined benefit plans, which are mandatory and pay out annuities at retirement. DB plans are not used as loan collateral and DB assets cannot be withdrawn before retirement. A DB sponsoring employer bears three risks workers bear alone in 401(k) plans: (1) investment risk—investing in inadequate portfolios; (2) financial risk—retiring when the market is on a down cycle; and (3) longevity risk—outliving your pension.

Starting in about 1980, as the labor movement waned, employers embraced 401(k) plans and retrenched their defined benefit plans, resulting in an overall decrease in employer retirement plan contributions.

Risks were transferred to workers, and wealth was transferred to employers. The onus of failure was also transferred to the individual. When the individual worker has control, it is seamless to blame the worker when the system fails. Instead of the design coming under scrutiny, individuals were criticized. Behavioral economics explained that the 401(k) system failed because workers make heuristic mistakes.

With the rise of behavioral economics and asset-based social welfare ideology, policy took a wide swing (Amir et al. 2005) into psychology and behavioral finance in the early 2000s, and the "better design" or "choice architecture" became the preferred and professed stronger ways to design social programs (Orenstein 2013; The *Economist* 2015). The argument was that tweaking human decisions is a cheaper way to solve expensive social problems than through politically difficult, and perhaps costly, mandates. Clever design of options could solve social problems for free. Free, just like fusion. Fusion releases great clean energy with no pollution: all the benefits of energy and none of the costs. In like manner, polices designed to nudge humans to make the socially optimal choices through "choice architecture" offers up social policy "fusion" solutions. Here are three problems solved cheaply with choice architecture:

1. Problem: Dirty toilets. Cass Sunstein (Obama's chief regulation advisor) explains that the power of "choice architecture" overcomes collective action problems, it makes individuals—in this case men—make slight private "improvements" that will save millions of dollars in janitorial money. Sunstein explains, "In a busy airport restroom used by throngs of travelers each day, the unpleasant effects of bad aim can add up rather quickly. Enter an ingenious economist who worked for Schiphol International Airport in Amsterdam. His idea was to etch an image of a black house fly onto the bowls of the airport's urinals, just to the left of the drain. The result: Spillage declined 80 percent. It turns out that, if you give men a target, they can't help but aim at it" (Thaler and Sunstein 2008).

2. Problem: Expensive and unnecessary surgeries. Wellness programs aim to make people healthier with lower costs and encourage second opinions about expensive courses of action. For decades, companies paid for wellness programs and second opinions. But, workers did not join up or seek second opinions. By changing the reward into a penalty, participation in wellness programs surged and so did the use of second medical opinions. "Employers that used penalties or surcharges for not

participating boosted their median employee participation rates to 73 percent" (Zabawa 2015).

3. Problem: Half of the workforce not being covered by pensions. Behavioral economics encourage the same voluntary structure, but by making people opt out of their 401(k) rather than opt in, studies show people's tendency toward inertia raises the participation rate. Therefore, the Obama administration pushed for auto-IRAs, whereby everyone would be auto-enrolled in an IRA, and individuals could opt out, rather than individuals having to take the affirmative step to actively opt in (Madrian 2014). But many people eventually opt out of retirement plans. Imagine the failure and the expense if Social Security relied on "inertia" to keep people in Social Security during recessions and times of household turmoil. If voluntary, Social Security participation would have to be tax incented with all the complications and inequity tax preferences create.

The design of asset-based, voluntary, individual-directed pension systems was the source of its failure to perform, but behavioral economics focused on blaming individual behavior rather than innovating for better design. The design of asset-based, voluntary, individual-directed pension system also caused inequality to grow in two ways.

4. THE RISE OF INEQUALITY BECAUSE OF THE FINANCIALIZATION OF PENSIONS

The rising inequality in retirement time is occurring because: savings shocks are unequally distributed; tax breaks are unequally distributed; and the social legitimacy of being retired is unequally distributed.

UNEQUAL DISTRIBUTION OF EXPOSURE TO LIFE COURSE SHOCKS

The first pathway to inequality is shocks. The design of the system and the facts of life make the saving process much more onerous for those at the bottom 90 percent of the income distribution. Lower-income people suffer more shocks that interfere with their saving than wealthy people. The second pathway from design to inequality is the tax preference that subsidizes higher-income workers relative to lower-income workers.

First, shocks. One study followed a special group of workers who were aged 51–65 and who did not lose their jobs in the years after the

Table 13.1   The Unequal Distribution of Lifetime Shocks that Affect Accumulation

	Account balances: 2012	Number of times income fell 10% over work career	Weeks unemployed: 2009–2011	Percent who lost retirement wealth in recession
Bottom 40% of income distribution	$65,006	7.37	2.86	44%
Middle 50% of income distribution	$132,510	5.86	2.44	39%
Top 10% of income distribution average	$218,556	6.06	1.40	39%

Source: Ghilarducci, Saad-Lessler, and Fisher (2016)

recession of 2009–2012 (Ghilarducci, Saad-Lessler, and Fisher 2016). This study found inequality, not only in the life events that cause retirement account leakages, but also in the intensity of the responses to those life events. Low earners were more likely to have reduced their asset balances during the 2007–2009 recession. Forty-four percent of the bottom 50 percent of the income distribution reduced their 401(k) account balances during the recession, compared with 39 percent in the higher income groups. Lower-income people had more income shocks in their lifetime, 7.37 compared with less than 6 in the middle- and top-income groups. The top 10 percent had many fewer lifetime weeks unemployed than the bottom 90 percent: 1.4 total weeks unemployed compared to 2.86 weeks (see table 13.1).

Ghilarducci, Webb, and Radpour 2016 found in just two years (2009–2011), one-fifth of low-income 401(k) participants were likely to experience job loss, divorce, health problems, or a job change. In contrast, middle-income workers experienced a 17 percent risk, and high earners had an 11 percent risk. Shocks trigger 401(k) and IRA withdrawals, and low- and moderate-income households are more likely to withdraw, conditional on experiencing a shock. Furthermore, since workers in low-income households were more likely than those in middle- and upper-income households to respond to an economic shock by withdrawing money from their retirement savings, the ordinary conduct of economic life in the American economy results in an unequal distribution of retirement wealth and access to retirement.

UNEQUAL ACCESS TO GOVERNMENT RETIREMENT SUBSIDIES

The second pathway to retirement wealth inequality is the structure of tax expenditures for retirement savings. Tax expenditures are revenue losses to federal or state treasuries from tax exclusions and deferrals.[1] Aimed at promoting a social goal, tax expenditures are designed to induce the voluntary provision of a positive externality. In 2014, federal retirement plan tax expenditures totaled $94.6 billion. Spending on defined-contribution plans, such as 401(k) plans, made up the largest share of this total. The costs of these tax subsidies are projected to increase to $222.1 billion in 2018, for a total of $805.1 billion over five years (U.S. Treasury 2015).

People with the highest balances garner the most in tax expenditures: 70 percent of the tax benefit goes to the top 20 percent of taxpayers. The top 10 percent hold a vast majority of all the retirement and they have the highest tax rate so the retirement account tax expenditures are highly skewed to the highest-income savers.[2] And the lopsided tax expenditures are ineffective in achieving the social goal of retirement security. In 1980, the tax expenditure per worker was $406 in 2016 dollars, and the retirement plan coverage rate was 46 percent. By 2015, the coverage rate had fallen slightly to 45 percent of all workers having a workplace retirement plan, but the tax expenditure per worker more than doubled to $997 (see table 13.2).

Table 13.2 More Than Doubling Tax Expenditures Did Not Improve Coverage

		2016 dollars			
Year	Coverage rate (1)	Tax expenditures (2)	Workforce (3)	Tax expenditures per person covered	Tax expenditures per worker covered and not covered
1980	0.46	$43,550,000,000	107,352,000	$882	$406
1990	0.47	$111,670,000,000	126,142,000	$1,884	$885
2000	0.52	$129,220,000,000	143,248,000	$1,735	$902
Present	0.45	$157,400,000,000	157,833,000	$2,216	$997

Sources: (1) Morrissey, M. 2016 Retirement Inequality Chartbook. Economic Policy Institute, Washington, D.C. Accessed August 9, 2017, www.epi.org/publication/retirement-inequality-chartbook; (2) Joint Economic Committee. 2017. "Estimates of Federal Tax Expenditures for Fiscal Years 2016–2020." Accessed August 9, 2017 www.jct.gov/publications.html?func=select&id=5; Bureau of Labor Statistics. 2017. "Employment, Summary Table B. Establishment Data, Seasonally Adjusted Accessed August 9, 2017, https://www.bls.gov/web/empsit/ceseesummary.htm.

Replacing ineffective tax deductions with refundable tax credits would provide 88 million workers with $607 to save for retirement. An additional $197 would go to 70 million people who live in states with an income tax, for a total of $804.

UNEQUAL ACCESS TO RETIREMENT LEGITIMACY

The third pathway to retirement wealth inequality is the unequal distribution of legitimacy, the social approval of retirement before ill health is increasingly only available for the wealthy (Estes 2001). The legitimacy of retirement, a form of paid time off, is under challenge for working-class people (Moulaert and Biggs 2012).

More people age 55 and older are working than ever before in America, because most of the population growth since the mid-1980s has been among older Americans and the labor force participation rate among men and women aged 55-plus is higher than ever before, mainly due to women's increasing participation. Between 1985 and 2013, the labor force participation rate for women age 55 and older increased from 22 percent to just over 35 percent. Men's participation rate rose from 41 percent to nearly 47 percent. Experts identify the two reasons more older people are working. First, people want to be needed, want to be productive, want to develop new skills, and want to meet new challenges. Some jobs meet these desires. Second, people work because they need money.

The good news about older workers is that they are more educated, and work effort increases with education. Burtless (2013) estimates that the increase in older Americans education levels accounts for almost half of the increase in older worker labor force participation. In 1985, less than 20 percent of workers between the ages of 60 and 64 had college degrees. In 2013, 35 years later, over 36 percent did. Enfranchising older women into mainstream economic life is part of the trend. Labor income gives women some independence and more equal footing with men, and that is good news for men and women.

But many older people are working because their reservation wage (the minimum wage required to lure someone into the workforce) fell. The availability of income from non-wage sources is a key factor determining a person's reservation wage. If "non-labor" income (e.g. pension income) falls a person's reservation wage falls and work effort increases. And non-labor income to the elderly is falling. Social Security benefits are decreasing, replacing less retirement income as the "full benefit age" increases to

67 and Medicare premiums increase. Furthermore, most older workers have no traditional pension and only little over half have a 401(k) or IRA. As mentioned earlier, almost half of older workers have nothing except Social Security, and the half with an account have a median amount of $111,000 (2013), which would yield a $400 per month annuity. A part-time, minimum-wage job will pay almost twice that.

The disturbing part of the new work reality for older workers is that nonexistent too-small 401(k) account balances reduce older workers' bargaining power, limiting their power to quit a job or find a job they want. With less bargaining power older people accept lower wage jobs with poorer working conditions because having a low wage, low quality job is not as bad as not having one when pension income is inadequate.

In addition, the quality improvements in old people's jobs has stopped. The share of older workers who say they have "very" physically demanding jobs is increasing, and the share of jobs reported as "easy" is falling. Job requirements for stooping, bending, and using keen eyesight and intense concentration is increasing for older people.

Some groups of workers are likely to enter retirement with poor health because continuing to work in their poor quality will degrade their health. Lauren Schmitz (2015) found that older workers who have less control over their jobs suffer worse health outcomes so that continuing to work will shorten their life spans. A straightforward characteristic of a good job—one with less stress—is one that allows workers to control the pace and content of their time and work. For many people, the only way to get the control they want and avoid the stress of not having control is to retire with a decent pension.

Consider this: Americans already work more years and more weeks per year than most people in many other advanced industrialized countries. The Organisation for Economic Co-operation and Development reports the United States ranks in the bottom third in achieving a balance between work and life (OECD 2015): Americans work more hours per year, at 1,790 hours per year. The OECD average is almost a week less, and the United States ranks eighth out of thirty-three nations in the percentage of adults working long hours: 11.8 percent versus the average of less than 8 percent. For example, less than 1 percent of Dutch workers work more than 50 hours a week. The United States leads rich countries in low-wage jobs—paying two-thirds of the median wage; over 22 percent of jobs in the United States pay less than $23,000 per year. Older people face this labor market reality as many find work in the service and retail sectors.

Further evidence that American workers have lost bargaining power is that Americans say they want to work more than older people in other nations, even though older Americans have poorer health (Heiland and Yin 2015). Older American people have more severe health problems but are less likely to say they are severely restricted from working (see table 13.3)

The correlation between self-reported work ability and having diabetes is negative: people with diabetes are more likely to report they can't work than people without. But the correlation is less negative for Americans than the correlation in other nations. For all countries reported in table 13.3, the correlation between diabetes and workability is negative 38 percent. But excluding the United States from the calculation, the negative correlation is stronger, −52 percent. Compared to older people in other nations, older Americans are more likely to say they can work even when they require assistance with many tasks of daily living (ADLs). For all countries reported, the correlation is −7 percent. But without the United States, the negative correlation between ADLs and readiness to work is stronger, −17 percent.

Table 13.3 Older Americans Are Sicker but Less Likely to Report Limitations on Work and Work More

	Labor force participation of 65- to 69-year-olds: 2000 (OECD)	Labor force participation of 65- to 69-year-olds: 2014 (OECD)	Education attained	Diabetes incidence	ADL limitations	Self-reported limitations of work none	Self-reported limitations of work: extreme severe and severe
United States	24.5	31.6	12.7	0.18	0.22	0.45	0.14
Sweden	14.5	21.8	10.4	0.07	0.09	0.56	0.15
Netherlands	6.0	15.7	11.5	0.07	0.09	0.54	0.06
Germany	5.1	14	13.1	0.11	0.09	0.42	0.08
Europe (Average)	8.6	12.4	9.6	0.09	0.13	0.48	0.09
Italy	6.4	8.4	7.2	0.09	0.17	0.47	0.1
France	2.1	5.9	8	0.09	0.16	0.51	0.08
Belgium	2.9	4.7	10.2	0.08	0.17	0.38	0.09
Spain	3.9	4.6	7.1	0.12	0.13	0.45	0.13

Sources: Heiland and Yin (2015) and OECD 2015 stats.

Many may not consider American elderly and impaired workers willing to work a problem to be solved. The National Research Council (2012) views getting older workers to work as one of the key drivers to long-term growth (more on this in section 6). Older workers choosing to work because work provides hours, wages, and opportunities for skill enhancement in comparison to an adequate retirement is likely to have the effect on productivity that the added worker effect has. Attracting workers—what Henry Aaron (2013) at the Brookings Institution calls "bribing" older workers—will have a better effect on productivity than "mugging," or forcing people without pensions to work.

The next section assumes that public policy makers prefer employers to boost older labor force participation by tackling age discrimination (Neumark, Burn, and Button 2016) and encouraging employers to make work more inviting. The policy solution in section 5 of this chapter constructs an approach that aims to boost the reservation wage of older people by securing their pensions.

5. SOLUTIONS: INNOVATIONS WILL HAVE TO BE HYBRIDS

I recommend a new pension system that is a hybrid design of asset-based accounts with insurance-like features. Innovations are a combination of previous good ideas: the comprehensive policy recommendation is to prop up Social Security and implement GRAs. In sum, the problems to solve are not just inadequate retirement assets for many, but an unequal distribution of retirement readiness and access to retirement that results in downward mobility of middle-class workers and poverty and chronic deprivation among the old. Other problems to be solved are the ineffective use of tax expenditures and the unintended consequences of lowering the reservation wage of older Americans. The causes of these problems are badly designed retirement plans and policies, not badly designed humans.

An optimal pension system (Barr and Diamond 2009) embeds key design features of social insurance. A pension system should also help stabilize and grow the economy, as detailed in a small section of the chapter before the conclusion.

ACCUMULATION

The GRA aims to strengthen retirement security by increasing accumulation. Low- and moderate-income families are especially helped by mandatory contributions into private asset-based accounts. GRAs apply to all 1,099 workers and full-time and part-time workers. In 2016, Senator Elizabeth Warren called for all employee benefits and protections to be delinked from employers—the GRA plan does that—although savings and contributions occur only when people work for pay. The contributions to GRAs are 3 percent of wages, with half paid by employer and half paid by employee. To ease the burden on low-wage earners, all workers would receive a tax credit equal to their annual contribution up to $600 per year so that the after-tax cost to workers earning $40,000 or less would be zero. For high-income workers, the obligation to contribute is capped—the 1.5 percent mandate for employees and employers would apply only to the first $250,000 of income. Workers would be encouraged to contribute additional funds to their GRAs.

Employers would be required to offer a defined benefit pension or contribute to a GRA. The proposal assumes most employers would choose the GRAs because the costs would be lower. Pension mandates, like most labor regulation, would protect many employers by taking this particular form of worker compensation—retirement income security—out of competition, thus more pensions will be provided and employers who provide workplace retirement plans will no longer be at a disadvantage.

Retirement wealth accumulation will grow when current tax breaks for 401(k) plans and IRAs are repurposed into a refundable retirement tax credit. The costs of the new tax credit would be offset by the savings from eliminating existing tax deductions for 401(k) plans and IRAs. Existing 401(k)-type savings accounts would be rolled over into the new GRAs.

INVESTMENT

The GRAs will be invested better than existing 401(k) and IRA plans because long-term savings will be matched to diversified portfolios containing long-term investments. Now, all 401(k) and IRA assets are entirely liquid so that people pay for liquidity they don't need. Each year individuals could choose (or change) their federally licensed and regulated money managers from a national exchange of managers administered by the federal government. The GRA's key feature is investment pooling, which reduces administrative fees and allows investments in less-liquid, higher-yielding, higher-return asset classes, including real estate, managed futures, and commodities.

The proposal assumes the GRAs would earn a 6 to 7 percent nominal rate of return. In order to reduce workers' risk, the government could guarantee the preservation of principal or even a minimal return of, say, 2 percent. The government could assess the accounts for the small cost of the insurance.

DEACCUMULATION

To solve the problem of individuals bearing too much longevity risk at retirement, each worker's account would be automatically annuitized to provide lifetime income. The Social Security Administration would administer the annuity payments, adding them on to Social Security benefit disbursements. Workers could choose to annuitize their GRA at any age from 62 to 70, with or without collecting Social Security benefits. Each worker's annuity would take age and marital status into account. Before annuitization, GRA balances would be inheritable. But once the account had been annuitized, it would not be inheritable. Affluent retirees with annual incomes of $250,000 or more from sources other than the GRA would not be eligible to receive any annuity income from their accounts, though they could deduct the value of the annuity not received from their taxable income.

Workers, employers, and repurposed tax deductions from federal (and presumably state) governments pay for the GRAs. Also, annual distributions withheld from affluent retirees would be used to fund annuities topping up accounts of low-wage or part-time workers if need be, offsetting administrative costs of the GRAs and the guarantee.

6. ASSET-BASED PROGRAMS MAKE RECESSIONS A GREATER RISK

A guaranteed pension system serves as an automatic stabilizer over the business cycle. Unlike 401(k) plans and IRAs that destabilize the economy, defined benefit plans and social insurance plans do not. In the Great Recession of 2008–2009, the gap between real gross domestic product (GDP) and potential output fell precipitously in 2009—by $504 billion. Additionally, because of the decline in household and business spending between December 2007 and December 2009, employment fell by 5.7 percent—a loss of 8.3 million jobs—and the unemployment rate peaked at 10 percent.

To counter the recession, the U.S. federal government spent $700 billion for stimulus programs. But the largest source of recession mitigation—built-in automatic stabilizers—quietly did their thing by injecting billions of dollars into the spending stream of the economy. Traditional automatic stabilizers such as unemployment insurance, means-tested programs, and the progressive tax system (which has the largest stimulative effect, because the average marginal tax rate shrinks as more people fall into the lower brackets)—all helped mitigate the effects of the downturn.

Nontraditional automatic stabilizers, such as Social Security's Old-Age and Survivors Insurance (OASI), Social Security Disability Insurance (SSDI), Medicare, and defined benefit (DB) and 401(k) plans, also had an effect. People use these programs in recessions as income and lifestyle support, and the taxes used to finance those programs reduce spending in expansions. Five government automatic stabilizers—progressive income taxes, unemployment insurance (UI), Social Security, Social Security Disability, and Medicare—reduced the number of jobs lost in 2009 by a low of 81,456 and a high 967,506; the range depends on which marginal propensity to consume data is used.

Over half of households own IRAs, 401(k)s, and 401(k)-type accounts, and the values of those accounts fell by an average of 14 percent in 2008. Middle-class and lower-income households, whose current and future retirement income wealth derives primarily from OASI, SSDI, defined benefit pension plans, and Medicare lost almost nothing in the 2008– 2009 period.

While 401(k) plans work in the opposite, destabilizing direction, OASI, SSDI, UI, Medicare, and federal taxes temper the output gap's effect on unemployment by injecting more net household spending in recessions and dampening spending in expansions. Those programs are automatic stabilizers. In contrast, 401(k) plans and other financial market–based retirement accounts have a destabilizing effect; financial market declines reduce wealth and income in financial accounts so that in recessions people who own these accounts tend to cut their spending even more than they would otherwise. Also, people with these accounts, everything else equal, would seek more hours of work in a recession because of lost income and wealth. Spending less and looking for work is exactly the opposite of what anyone would want people to do in a recession. Such behavior—spending less and job seeking—just makes the recession worse and unemployment rate higher.

The bottom line is that the existence of 401(k) plans and other financial market–based retirement wealth—whose values fluctuate with the business cycle—made the last recession deeper and caused slightly more unemployment than would have happened otherwise if 401(k) plans did not exist (Ghilarducci and Saad-Lessler 2015). Annuity-based retirement accounts backed by government programs also helped the economy, while financial market–based retirement programs, such as 401(k)-type programs, hurt the economy.

7. CONCLUSION

Extending large tax breaks and encouraging more voluntary participation in individual-directed, commercial, liquid 401(k) and IRA accounts may boost participation, but the investment and distribution aspects of the system mean it is doomed to be ineffective, very expensive, and a source of more inequality. The inequality is made worse because the system relies on tax deductions to encourage participation. Tax deductions are largest for those with the most money, and they are extended to those people with the smallest risk of not having enough retirement assets. Although pension systems with automatic enrollment, automatic investing in safe instruments, and auto-annuitization depend on most people not opting out, they do not work, because they are still voluntary systems.

The Obama administration spent eight years trying to implement the auto-IRA in keeping with a libertarian, paternalistic philosophy (White House 2015). The Trump administration eliminated the program in a series of actions to protect the retail money-management industry from competition and regulation from the government, including slowing down the fiduciary rule and chilling actions in the states to create state-regulated alternatives to commercial IRAs. But like many large problems, the solution to most our social problems will take real money. We can get real money from progressive taxation—or in the case of comprehensive pension reform—by reducing the regressivity of our current tax system.

A well-designed system has important macroeconomic features. It restores and maintains sources of net wealth for households. A well-designed pension system allows the household sector to be the savers, while the business and government sector are deficit spenders.

The 401(k) structure is not suited for pensions, and the government subsidies are perversely incented. The problem is not bad human decisions or financial illiteracy. Life events happen to people that disrupt the best-laid plans. The consequences of too many voluntary, commercial financial accounts to back pensions are the following:

- An unequal distribution of work at older ages (work for old people *can be* bad; choice about retirement is good).
- Employers could use elders as substitutes for younger workers because the time of older people is being recommodified with uncertain retirement income.
- Lump sum payouts themselves, rather than annuities, can induce more anxiety and depression among the old, while annuities make old people more comfortable.
- Last, asset ownership induces shame, blame-the-victim narratives, and lack of political will.

A pension system does three simple things to smooth life-course consumption. One, it accumulates sufficient assets over the life course; two, it invests those assets well; and three, it distributes the assets in a lifelong stream of income (Orszag and Stiglitz 2001). The GRA plan outlined by Ghilarducci and James (2016) satisfies all three functions. Sufficient accumulation is achieved through mandatory participation and banning all leakages before retirement; investments are low fee, pooled, and invested to match the long-term liabilities; and payouts are in the form of an annuity.

NOTES

1. Tax expenditures are entitlement spending: the size is determined by the number of taxpayers who participate in the preferred activity and claim the benefit on their taxes. As part of the tax code, tax breaks are immune from "sunset provisions" that automatically terminate unless extended through a process of legislative oversight and action. Experts criticize entitlements, as they allow the growth of government spending without appropriate scrutiny and evaluation and, in part because of the lack of scrutiny, retirement savings tax expenditures have been widely criticized as ineffective and regressive (U.S. Government Accountability Office 2005).

2. For example, a worker earning $2,000 a month has a marginal tax rate of 10 percent, pays a $200 tax bill, and has $1,800 remaining in after-tax income. But if this worker contributes $200 to a 401(k), his or her taxable income is $1,800, and he or she owes only $180 in taxes. There will be less after-tax income—$1,620 versus $1,800—but the worker now has $200 in a retirement account and has saved $20 on his or her tax bill. Tax is not paid on the investment gains in the account during accrual. When he or she withdraws the savings—presumably when retired and paying a lower tax rate—he or she will pay less in taxes.

REFERENCES

Aaron, Henry. 2013. "Nudged, Pushed, or Mugged. Policies to Encourage Older Workers to Retire Later." In *Closing the Deficit: How Much Can Later Retirement Help?*, 72–120. Washington, D.C.: Brookings Institution Press.

Amir, On, Dan Ariely, Alan Cooke, David Dunning, Nicholas Epley, Uri Gneezy, Botond Koszegi, Donald Lichtenstein, Nina Mazar, Sendhil Mullainathan, Drazen Prelec, Eldar Shafir, and Jose Silva. 2005. "Psychology, Behavioral Economics, and Public Policy." *Marketing Letters* 16(3):443–54.

Anderson, Tim. 2013. "Your 401(k): When Was It Invented and Why." Retrieved from: www.learnvest.com/knowledge-center/your-401k-when-it-was-invented-and-why.

Avsar, Rojhat B. 2008. "A Critique of Neoliberal Autonomy." Retrieved from: http://content.csbs.utah.edu/~mli/Graduate%20Placement/Avsar_The%20rhetoric%20of%20ownership%20society.pdf.

Ayres, Ian, and Quinn Curtis. 2014. "Beyond Diversification: The Pervasive Problem of Excessive Fees and 'Dominated Funds' in 401(k) Plans." *Yale Law Journal* 124:1476–552.

Barr, Nicholas, and Peter Diamond. 2009. "Reforming Pensions: Principles, Analytical Errors and Policy Directions." *International Social Security Review* 62(2):5–29.

Burtless, G. 2013. "Future of Labor Force Participation Among the Aged." In *Closing the Deficit: How Much Can Later Retirement Help?*, ed. G. Burtless and H. Aaron, 36–45. Washington, D.C.: Brookings Institution Press.

Center for Budget and Policy Analysis. "Policy Basics: Federal Tax Expenditures." Retrieved from: www.cbpp.org/research/federal-tax/policy-basics-federal-tax-expenditures.

Economist, The. 2015 "Behavioural Economics: The Limits of Nudging." July 24. Accessed 22 May 2016. www.economist.com/blogs/freeexchange/2015/07/behavioural-economics.

Estes, Carroll L. 2001. "Inequality of Aging: The Creation of Dependency." In *Social Policy and Aging: A Critical Perspective*, chap 7. New York: Sage.

Ford Foundation. 2016. "Overview: Individual Wealth Building." Retrieved from: http://community-wealth.org/strategies/panel/individuals/index.html.

Ghilarducci, T., B. Fisher, S. Radpour, and A. Webb. 2016. "Policy Options for Cutting Retirement Plan Leakages." Schwartz Center for Economic Policy Analysis and Department of Economics, The New School for Social Research, Policy Note Series. Funded by the National Endowment of Financial Education (NEFE). accessed October 25, 2017. http://www.economicpolicyresearch.org/images/docs/research/retirement_security/Policy_Options_for_Cutting_Retirement_Plan_Leakages.pdf

Ghilarducci, Teresa, Michael Papadopoulos, and Siavash Radpour. 2017. "Relative Wages in Aging America: The Baby Boomer Effect." Schwartz Center for Economic Policy Analysis and Department of Economics, The New School for Social Research, Working Paper Series 2017-5. Retrieved August 10, 2017 from: http://www.economicpolicyresearch.org/images/docs/research/retirement_security/Relative_Wages_Aging_.pdfFradpour.

Ghilarducci, T., S. Radpour, B. Fisher, and J. Saad-Lessler. 2015. "Inadequate Retirement Account Balances for Workers Nearing Retirement." Schwartz Center for Economic Policy Analysis and Department of Economics, New School for Social Research, Policy Note Series. New School for Social Research, New York.

Ghilarducci, Teresa, and Joelle Saad-Lessler. 2015. "How 401(K) Plans Make Recessions Worse." In *Inequality, Uncertainty, and Opportunity: The Varied and Growing Role of Finance in Labor Relations*, 9–30. Champaign, Ill.: Labor and Employment Relations Association.

Ghilarducci, T., J. Saad-Lessler, and B. Fisher. 2016. "Winners and Losers in the Recovery: Older Workers' Defined Contribution Retirement Accounts after the Great Recession." Schwartz Center for Economic Policy Analysis, New School for Social Research, Report Series. New School for Social Research, New York.

Ghilarducci, Teresa, and Hamilton "Tony" James. 2017. *Rescuing Retirement*. New York: Columbia University Press.

Glazer, Joe. 1950. *Eight New Songs for Labor*. CIO Washington, D.C.: Department of Education and Research.

Heiland F., and N. Yin. 2015. "Anchoring Vignettes in the Health and Retirement Study: How Do Medical Professionals and Disability Recipients Characterize the Severity of Work Limitations?" *PLoS One* 10(5):e0126218.

Madland, David. 2007. "The Politics of Pension Cuts." In *Employee Pensions: Policies, Problems, and Possibilities*, ed. Teresa Ghilarducci and Christian E. Weller, chap. 10. Ithaca, N.Y.: Cornell University Press.

Madrian, Brigitte C. 2014. "Applying Insights from Behavioral Economics to Policy Design." *Annual Review of Economics* 6(1):663–88.

Moulaert, T., and S. Biggs. 2012. "International and European Policy on Work and Retirement: Reinventing Critical Perspectives on Active Ageing and Mature Subjectivity." *Human Relations* 66(1):23–43.

National Research Council. 2012. *Aging and the Macroeconomy. Long-Term Implications of an Older Population*. Washington, D.C.: National Academies Press.

Neumark, David, Ian Burn, and Patrick Button. 2016. "Experimental Age Discrimination Evidence and the Heckman Critique." *American Economic Review* 106(5):303–8.

Orenstein, M. A. 2013. "Pension Privatization: Evolution of a Paradigm." *Governance* 26:259–81.

Organisation for Economic Co-operation and Development. 2015. *How's Life? 2015 Measuring Well-Being*. Retrieved 22 May 2016. www.oecdbetterlifeindex.org/topics/work-life-balance.

Orszag, Peter, and Joseph Stiglitz. 2001. "Rethinking Pension Reform: Ten Myths About Social Security Systems." In *New Ideas About Old Age Security: Towards Sustainable Pension Systems in the 21st Century*, ed. Robert Holzmann and Joseph Stiglitz. Washington, D.C.: World Bank.

Pierson, P. 2001. "Coping with Permanent Austerity: Welfare State Restructuring in Affluent Democracies." In *The New Politics of the Welfare State*, ed. P. Pierson. Oxford: Oxford University Press.

Rosenbaum, David. 2005. "Bush to Return to 'Ownership Society' Theme in Push for Social Security Changes." *New York Times*, January 16.

Schmitz, L. 2015. "Do Working Conditions at Older Ages Shape the Health Gradient?" New School for Social Research. Paper for the 17th Annual Joint Meeting of the Retirement Research Consortium, August 6–7, 2015, Washington, D.C.

Sherradan, Michael. 2003. *Shelterforce Online* issue 128 (March/April). Retrieved from: www.nhi.org/online/issues/128/socialinvest.html.

Stevenson, Richard. 2001. "Social Security Panel Faces Challenges." *New York Times*, May 3. Retrieved from: http://www.nytimes.com/2001/05/03/us/social-security -panel-faces-challenges.html.

Thaler, Richard H., and Cass R. Sunstein. 2008. *Nudge: Improving Decisions About Health, Wealth, and Happiness*. New Haven, Conn.: Yale University Press.

U.S. Government Accountability Office. 2005. *Government Performance and Accountability: Tax Expenditures Represent a Substantial Federal Commitment and Need to Be Reexamined*. Retrieved from: www.gao.gov/assets/250/247901.pdf.

U.S. Treasury. 2015. Tax Policy for Pensions and Tax Expenditures. "Green Book" lists all the federal tax expenditures) Retrieved from: www.treasury.gov/resource-center/ tax-policy/Documents/General-Explanations-FY2015.pdf.

Weller, Christian. 2016. *Retirement on the Rocks*. New York: Palgrave.

White House. 2015. "Executive Order—Using Behavioral Science Insights to Better Serve the American People." Office of the Press Secretary. September 15.

Wolff, Edward, and Shapiro. 2005. *Assets for the Poor: Benefits of Spreading Asset Ownership*. New York: Russell Sage Foundation.

Zabawa, Barbara J. 2015. "Legally Incentivizing Health Assessment and Biometric Screen Participation." Paper presented at the National Wellness Conference, June 27, 2016, St. Paul, Minn.

CHAPTER 14

Universal Basic Income and the Welfare State

Richard McGahey

Welfare states are struggling with slow economic and job growth, fiscal pressures from rising benefit costs, demographic changes, and fears of structural economic transformation and job losses caused by information technology and computerization. This combination of factors has led some analysts to explore new ways to deliver welfare state benefits or reconfigure them to reduce fiscal pressures.

But others speculate that existing welfare state policies may have run their course, and cannot be easily repaired to cope with these multiple challenges, especially in the face of slower and less labor-intensive economic growth. In the face of these problems, some advocates are calling for introducing a universal basic income (UBI) as a floor to provide a basic level of subsistence, as a complement to existing welfare state policies, or in some cases as a replacement for the welfare state.

Much of the current interest in UBI stems from a belief that technology is rapidly eliminating jobs faster than new ones can be created, and future job growth will be much lower. But the evidence on technological displacement seems too uncertain to justify major disruptions in the welfare state. Rather, the UBI debate might better focus on the over thirty-year strengthening of business's economic power relations over labor. Rather than a historically unique event, advanced technology may just be the latest factor to harm both labor's ability to bargain and also overall macroeconomic performance by contributing to weaker overall demand and growing inequality.

In fact, using the single term "universal basic income" masks several important differences not only in specific proposals, but also in their underlying logics and rationales. This chapter describes the range of ideas included under the concept, highlights the economics associated with different versions of the idea, discusses the social welfare policy issues associated with a UBI (with special reference to the United States), and ends by outlining an agenda for future economic research into how UBIs would function in relation to existing welfare state policies.

UBI AND THE WELFARE STATE

At its simplest, a UBI can be defined as "an income paid by a political community on an individual basis, without means test or work requirement" (Van Parjis 2000, 2). While simple, each clause in this definition immediately raises a number of considerations.

- "Income" means, to most proponents, cash, and not some set of in-kind benefits (housing, medical care, vouchers for food or education, etc.). Most versions also assume a periodic ongoing payment (e.g., monthly), not a onetime lump sum, although some examples cite annual payments.
- "Political community" raises the question of who are recipients: Only citizens?[1] What about immigrants with some type of legal status? Only adults? If minors are included, should payment go to household heads, and at what age does that stop? Are those under criminal justice supervision included? What about mentally disabled people?
- "Political community" also usually means a nation-state, although there are examples of payments made to people in subnational governments or independent Native American tribal governments.[2]
- "On an individual basis" means that each person gets some fixed amount, although again, the question of payments to minors or disabled people arises.
- "Without means test or work requirement" signals that the payment is meant to be universal, or at least not conditioned on any level of income or work history or status. This has raised concerns among some advocates who want to make basic incomes progressive, as "universal" means payments made to higher-income and wealthy people, but that can be addressed by taxing basic incomes. Advocates argue that adjusting the payment prior to distribution based on poverty or income status would be a means test.

Providing a basic income to all citizens (at a minimum), including children, raises obvious tensions with existing welfare state policies. Some existing welfare state policies share features of a UBI—payment in cash, no means test, broadly awarded. But other welfare state policies differ—providing in-kind benefits (housing, health care, food, medical care), means tested, or requiring behavior (often work related) to qualify with potentially intrusive periodic status reviews that can result in a reduction or withdrawal of the benefit.

For example, in November 2016, the U.S. Social Security system paid out cash every month to over 45 million older people in the United States without a means test, around 14 percent of the population.[3] Payments are calculated based on a work record accumulated over decades, although the program has a progressive payment structure, with a larger replacement rate for lower-income workers. Benefits are treated like ordinary income and subject to income tax.

In contrast, the American Supplemental Nutrition Assistance Program (SNAP, or "food stamps") is highly categorical and means tested, with time limits and work requirements for participation, and the benefits vary further depending on a person's state of residence. Assistance is given in the form of vouchers to buy foods identified on a predetermined list but not nonfood items, alcohol, cigarettes, or restaurant or fast-food meals. In fiscal year 2015, 45.7 million people benefited from this assistance, close to the number receiving Social Security.[4]

So Social Security, even with its work history and age restrictions, has some UBI-like features—namely, monthly cash payments to all participants. But in contrast SNAP funds are dedicated to a specific set of purchases and come with a complex array of qualification tests and ongoing, and often intrusive, reassessment and monitoring. These two brief examples underscore that specific existing welfare state policies, in the United States and in every country, grew up under different historical and economic circumstances, and often without one underlying logic. This has led some to characterize the totality of welfare state policies as a "hodgepodge of issue specific instruments and benefits" (Nullmeier and Kaufmann 2010, 99).[5]

Others, following Esping-Andersen, argue for a tripartite classification of welfare states, while recognizing that all real welfare states share some of these features:

- Liberal (the United States, Australia, Canada), with policies that feature "means-tested assistance, modest universal transfers, or modest social-insurance plans," with benefits going to "mainly a clientele of low-income, usually working class state dependents."

- Conservative or corporatist, centered on social insurance, often "earned" by previous work experience and notional contributions, and also influenced by the religious institutions that emphasize family support and charity.
- Social democratic, with the state playing the central role in providing a wide range of benefits, including care for children, the sick, and the elderly (Esping-Andersen 1990).

A UBI would play out differently in each of these regimes, and in relation to the diverse set of existing policies in each.

But much of the new interest in a UBI stems less from how it would replace or supplement existing welfare state policies.[6] Instead, many UBI advocates see it as necessary because of dramatic changes in the economy, and specifically the labor market, that are reducing or eliminating jobs faster than the economy can replace them, due to technological change.

ARE JOBS DISAPPEARING? ROBOTS, TECHNOLOGY, AND UBI

Although people have advocated some type of universal basic livelihood or support for centuries, usually tied to concerns about poverty, recent advocacy is closely linked to fears about extensive job losses due to technology, especially artificial intelligence (AI) and robotization of work. Of course, most people get their income to purchase the necessities and luxuries of life, save for retirement, and take care of their children and other dependents through paid employment. But some scientists and technology observers believe the AI revolution is starting to threaten that long-standing model of the economy and society, fueling their support for a UBI.

Moishe Vardy (2015), a computer scientist at Rice University, argues that "by 2045 machines will be able to do much of the work that humans do," and he wonders, "What will humans do?" Venture capitalist Vinod Kholsa (2014) says flatly that "it seems likely that humans will lose this 'race against the machine' in many, if not most work domains," on a scale not seen since the transition from agriculture to manufacturing, and that unlike in previous transitions, there could be few new jobs created that machines cannot do.[7]

The concern is not limited to technologists or venture capitalists. Andy Stern, former head of the Service Employees International Union (SEIU), foresees an almost "jobless future," with "tens of millions" fewer jobs, divided among a few well-paying ones and a lot of bad ones, with labor market competition for the bad ones overwhelming any ability to unionize or guarantee benefits for even the employed workers (Stern 2016).

Three major studies undergird these concerns. Frey and Osborne's (2013, 44) work gained significant attention when they concluded that "47 percent of total U.S. employment" is at risk of being "automated relatively soon, perhaps over the next decade or two." The authors used estimates of more rapid growth in machine learning and applied those to a detailed index of specific job tasks for 702 occupations in the U.S. economy.

Jobs across the spectrum were found to be vulnerable, but they argue that the displacement risks are "principally confined to low-skill and low-wage occupations," in contrast to previous epochs of technological displacement, which occurred in higher-wage, higher-skill work (Frey and Osborne 2013, 45). They also link the job risks to probability of offshoring, meaning that although the United States may lose the jobs, some of them could well survive, but in a cheaper non-U.S. location (Frey and Osborne 2013, 36).

Brynjolfsson and McAfee (2014, 36) published *The Second Machine Age*, in which they argued that "computers and other digital advances are doing for mental power" what steam and internal combustion power did in substituting for physical human work, leading the economy into "the second machine age" (the first being the Industrial Revolution). This new age is an "inflection point" that will bring "bounty instead of scarcity, freedom instead of constraint," but also will "leave behind some people, perhaps even a lot of people, as it races ahead."

But their forecast is less dire than Frey and Osborne's in terms of total job losses. Rather, they argue that the new technology will displace many workers with "ordinary" skills, and the key to predicting changes in total employment will be aggregate economic demand, not technological substitution. Jobs instead will shift to a more bimodal distribution, with poorly paid service jobs increasing along with a smaller number of higher-skilled (and higher-paying) jobs that increasingly depend on education in digital technology.

The relevance of these forecasts for UBI comes from the authors' explanation of how wages as a share of GDP have fallen since the year 2000, in what they label as the "great decoupling" of living standards and economic growth. They attribute this decoupling to a "hollowing out" of the middle class, which they see as driven by technology that sharply reduces middle-income jobs that depended on a set of skills machines can now replace. They see technological displacement continuing and likely growing, implying that further income declines and perhaps outright net job losses will continue, with the "middle class . . . hollowing out in country after country" (Bernstein and Raman 2015, 70). But the authors are not certain about the pace of economic displacement. Commenting on basic income proposals, Brynjolfsson said that "the idea of a basic income is a good one in a world where robots do most of the work, but we probably won't be there for thirty to fifty years" (quoted in Freedman 2016, 50).

An even more dystopian view was put forward in Martin Ford's *Rise of the Robots: Technology and the Threat of a Jobless Future*, which won the 2015 Financial Times/McKinsey Business Book of the Year award. Ford argues that "robots, machine learning algorithms, and other forms of automation are gradually going to consume much of the base of the jobs skills pyramid," and that as AI progresses, "even the safe area at the top of the pyramid is likely to contract over time" (Ford 2015, 251).

In particular, Ford sees "machine learning" (a form of AI where the software can respond to new situations, mimicking human learning) as potentially empowering computers to take on an ever-increasing range of tasks and jobs, and also using that capacity to take on new jobs created by the technology, rather than having those jobs go to humans. He sees the new technologies as pushing the economy toward "permanent technological unemployment," implying that some form of UBI is necessary, although "you'd have to phase it in at a relative low level" so it acts as a "free market alternative to a safety net" but not so high or costly as to deter work effort or overwhelm government budgets (quoted in Dashevsky 2015).

Corporations and governments are increasingly worried about the impact of changing employment on the economy and society. The 2016 World Economic Forum (WEF) in Davos, Switzerland, an annual gathering of world's top corporate, economic, and political leaders, was devoted to "the future of jobs." The Davos organizers argued that the world has entered a "fourth industrial revolution," where technological change "will lay the foundation for a revolution more comprehensive and all-encompassing than anything we have ever seen." Somewhat paradoxically, their report also says that "overall, there is a modestly positive outlook for employment across most industries" (WEF 2016, v).[8] Perhaps because the report's analysis envisions modest macroeconomic total employment growth, the report focuses on human resource policies, especially training and education, as a response.

So the Davos report accepts the prediction of sweeping technological change, but not the forecast of major disruptive employment loss. Furthermore, the WEF is not alone in downplaying fears of massive job loss, or at least fears that no net new jobs will be created to replace those displaced by technology. Several economists argue that while some jobs and sectors are being disrupted by technology, we are not seeing significant net displacement, and as in the past, new technologies can lead to increased prosperity and employment. A report from the McKinsey Institute concluded that "automation will cause significant labor displacement" in many sectors but that it also could "contribute meaningfully" to economic growth, especially as the labor force ages (Manyika et al. 2017, 14–15).

Many economists claim support for this view from the long history of technology, accepting that technology does eliminate jobs (often of lower productivity and greater drudgery), but displacement allows movement of capital and labor to higher-value activities. As David Autor (2015, 5) puts it:

> Automation does indeed substitute for labor—as it is typically intended to do. However, automation also complements labor, raises output in ways that lead to higher demand for labor, and interacts with adjustments in labor supply.

In this view, robots and AI can raise total economic output and also improve job quality and the overall quality of life.

Automation also can increase productivity and hence get more output for the same amount of labor. Increasing productivity can lead to more jobs with economic expansion, but also less labor inputs, which can be positive, principally through lowering the amount of work needed by society and increasing total economic goods and services with the same amount of labor. Hal Varian captures this view well when he says that he expects more robots to reduce the average workweek so "there will be the same number of jobs (adjusted for demographics, of course)." Varian argues "this is what has been going on for the last 300 years and I see no reason that it will stop in this decade" (quoted in Smith and Anderson 2014, 12).

For these economists, the rise of robotics and AI are just another episode in the long history of technology replacing human labor in some specific occupations and industries. While they expect displacement will occur in specific occupations and industries, they view dire forecasts of massive net job losses as being wrongly static, and specifically disagree with the argument that middle-skill jobs are the most threatened. Autor argues that "a significant stratum of middle-skills jobs . . . will persist in coming decades" and cites other empirical analyses that find such jobs growing, not declining (quoted in Smith and Anderson 2014, 27).[9] These economists (like the Davos report) see improved education and employment and training policies as ways to address displacement, since they do not envision massive net job losses over time.

As a result, these analyses provide relatively weak justification for UBI policies, instead calling for adjustment policies principally in the form of increased education and training for both displaced workers and for younger labor market entrants. These economists believe the displacement effects of new technology can be dealt with by workers developing new skills in working with AI, or being more effective in group activities that rely on human initiative, or working in human service occupations.

But other economists, while not blaming AI and robotics per se for job losses, find the belief in skill-based adaptation inadequate and support calls for a UBI. In this view, capital's share of national income has been growing at the expense of the labor share since the 1980s, well before the most recent technological wave. But the reasons are largely rooted in institutional change and political and economic power, not in neutral technological substitution of capital for labor. So a UBI is justified to help redistribute the total economic output produced in part by new technology, which is not being adequately shared with labor

These economists share the skepticism of AI and robotics driving a profound transformation in the labor market, especially when compared with older technological changes. Ha-Joon Chang writes that "the impact of the internet, which many think has totally changed the world, has not been as fundamental" as the impact of the washing machine, which has freed up "mountains of time" (almost entirely for women). Mechanization of household production like washing and cooking, along with other key technologies (especially control over reproduction through contraception and abortion) allowed women to enter the labor force in huge numbers (Chang 2010, 34–35). While potentially good for women's standard of living, this large number of new workers shifted the balance of negotiating power toward capital and business.

A second major labor force impact that shifted power was the entry into the global market during the 1990s of China, India, and the former Soviet Union. Freeman estimated that those changes increased the global labor force by over 1.5 billion workers, what he has called the "great doubling" (Freeman 2007). Since the amount of capital did not double, the terms of trade between labor and capital shifted abruptly in favor of capital. The ability of businesses to reach these new workers and build supply chains linking them to advanced economies was made possible in part by technological change and new developments in logistics, but in this view the logistics and production technologies were facilitators, not fundamental causes (Milberg and Winkler 2013).

Finally, this line of analysis notes that labor's share of real national income has been falling for decades, well before the spread of computer-based technologies into many economic sectors. In the United States, labor's share of non-farm business income peaked in 1960, with a long, downward trend since then. Although labor share would rise on a cyclical pattern, each successive peak was lower than 1960, and troughs also have become deeper over the same period. Inequality also has grown over this period, with the Gini ratio for all U.S. households rising steadily from its lowest point in 1968 (Federal Reserve Bank of St. Louis 2017). Wage and income trends in other advanced economies are similar (International Labor Organization 2013).

The fall of labor's income share occurred at the same time that labor protection and other social insurance were weakened. Union membership declined, it became harder to organize unions, and unemployment insurance covered fewer workers.[10] Cash welfare was reduced and work requirements were increased, part-time and temporary employment rose, pension coverage (especially for defined benefit plans) declined, existing labor regulations were modified or eliminated or just not enforced,[11] and it became easier for employers to classify workers as contractors or assign some other nonemployee status that deprived them of job stability and benefits. This dramatic increase in labor market "flexibility" occurred during the increased internationalization of the economy, well before the latest wave of technological innovation.

Guy Standing calls 1975 to 2008 the "globalization" era that has given rise to a workforce more and more unmoored both from stable employment (either with a secure employer or in a profession) and from adequate social benefits—what Standing calls the "precariat," the term reflecting the precarious position of a growing share of the workforce (Standing 2011, 43). For Standing and others, the story of labor market change is not new technology but changes in the relative power of business and workers, with a parallel reduction in social benefits for those not working.

These economists concede that increased technology is affecting the labor market now, but see the key problem as labor's inability to capture an adequate share of income or rents from the new technology. Companies, especially labor brokers like Uber but also more typical employers like Walmart, are using these technologies to intensify the trends disadvantaging workers. But in this view, technology is enabling and intensifying ongoing inequities of relative economic and political power, rather than being an entirely new force in the labor market.

THE VARIETIES OF UBI

Advocates blaming technology for declining jobs, and using those declines to argue for a UBI, are not supported by many economic analysts. But there is a broad consensus that the rewards from paid employment have weakened over the past decades. Economists who explain those declines as driven by the weakening of labor's economic and social power often support some form of UBI to help correct these market trends (Standing 2011, 295).[12]

But there are several trends in the UBI debate that pull advocates in different directions. Three positions are especially relevant in thinking about how UBIs might intersect with existing welfare state policies and affect the economy.

First, UBIs could be a *supplement* to existing welfare state policies, with the cash from a UBI awarded alongside most of the existing range of housing, medical, food support, and other welfare state programs. A second group of advocates are libertarians who would accept UBIs as a *replacement* for most or all welfare state spending. And a third group prefers *targeted* basic income policies directed at the poor, because UBIs contain an implicit threat to successful existing antipoverty welfare state policies. This last group fears an alliance wherein the libertarian, anti–welfare state position is legitimated or blended with UBI advocacy, turning UBIs into an erosion of support and protections for the poor.

For many advocates, UBI is a policy to address the effects of technological displacement, income inequality, and slow economic growth. A variety of UBI-type experiments are taking place or being considered in Finland, Kenya, and other jurisdictions. But in a major political test in June 2016, Switzerland voted on (and decisively defeated, with opposition reaching 78 percent) a national ballot initiative for a universal UBI grant. Advocacy articles, policy proposals, and academic analyses are published almost daily.[13]

The Basic Income Earth Network (BIEN) argues for "some sort of economic right based upon citizenship" through a "universal and unconditional, if modest, continuous stream of income." Although BIEN has taken no formal position on how basic income would relate to other welfare state programs, the tenor of most writing they distribute strongly sees a UBI as a supplement to existing programs. A June 2016 posting at BIEN catches this tone by arguing that basic income proposals from libertarians that sharply reduce or eliminate social protections and welfare spending and programs would be a project "that most anti-poverty activists oppose" (Murphy 2016). Details of UBI proposals often are left to specific national advocacy groups, but most envision maintaining a good part, if not virtually all, of current welfare state programs, especially in health care.

Two major economic objections often put forward against UBIs are high costs and work disincentives. The fiscal objection argues that any UBI with a meaningful income level will be very expensive, resulting in a concern about the source of such tax revenue to pay for a UBI and the impact on public debt and increased taxation. Second, providing income not linked to work is seen to reduce work effort, leading to fewer work hours and higher wage levels for those working, and possibly lower output as a result.

Advocates are divided on the work disincentive question. Most economists rely on labor economics to argue that any source of non-labor income, like a UBI, will reduce hours of work and overall labor force participation. Empirical results from U.S. welfare reform and other income transfer programs support that theory, while finding a range of negative empirical magnitudes (Ben-Shalom et al. 2012). There are wide-ranging estimates of how much work effort would fall, but a general consensus is that a UBI would have that effect. The negative effects are amplified if an income supplement is added to existing welfare programs.

Advocates for UBIs respond in two ways. Some claim that little or no reduction in work effort would take place, relying on data from a 1970s Canadian program in the province of Manitoba that provided a guaranteed annual family income and more recent results from cash transfer programs in developing countries. But in an evaluation of the Manitoba case that looked explicitly at work effort, the analysts found "modest reductions in hours worked as predicted" (Hum and Simpson 1993, S289).[14] Similarly, developing country projects were onetime cash transfer programs, not ongoing income programs, and transitory short-term income supplements are not expected to induce permanent changes in labor market behavior.

But other advocates explicitly embrace a UBI-induced reduction in work hours and labor supply, especially those who argue that we may see large-scale technological displacement. Erik Olin Wright (2002, 8) argues that a "UBI would contribute to a greater symmetry of power between labor and capital," even without increased formal organization, and would be especially beneficial for low-wage sectors. Tighter labor markets might also make employers more willing to bargain with unions or other new forms of worker organizations to raise wages, reduce hours, and improve working conditions to attract and retain workers who could otherwise fall back on a UBI.

Other economists support UBIs for their effect on increasing innovation, which in turn boosts productivity. Tighter labor markets mean that employers will want to substitute capital for labor to control labor costs. Since most UBI proposals would be partly paid for by taxing back income from wealthier people, UBIs also would reduce inequality. The reduction in inequality redistributes income to lower-income households, which increases aggregate demand, because lower-income people have higher marginal propensities to consume. This boost in aggregate demand could also help spur innovation and productivity.[15]

This first type of UBI proposal envisions largely keeping existing welfare state programs, with a UBI providing a modest spending allowance. But there is a second trend in UBI advocacy that instead wants to dramatically reduce or altogether eliminate welfare state programs, turning them into cash grants as a way of funding UBIs.

The intellectual root of these proposals rests with Milton Friedman, in the form of a "negative income tax" that would replace all existing welfare state programs. Friedman saw this idea as a "second best" that would have the added virtue of reducing the size and scope of the modern state. In 1967, when challenged by conservatives opposing the idea, Friedman (1967, 239) responded:

> We now have a governmentally guaranteed annual income in substance though not in name . . . that is what our grab-bag of relief and welfare measures is. . . . If we lived in a hypothetical world in which there were no governmental welfare programs at all and in which all assistance to the destitute was by private charity, the case for introducing a negative income tax would be far weaker than the case for substituting it for present programs . . . that is not our world and there is not the remotest chance that it will be in the foreseeable future.

When Richard Nixon was president, he implemented a negative income tax (NIT) experiment as part of his drive to create the Family Assistance Plan (FAP), replacing existing welfare programs with a single guaranteed payment that would be means tested, phasing out as incomes rose. Unlike some current UBI proposals, maintaining work incentives was a key political goal, so a central design feature was keeping payments low enough to encourage people to work.

The NIT also was the first major random assignment experiment in social policy. The empirical results consistently found reduced work effort. Although these negative impacts were not high enough to affect aggregate labor supply in the entire economy (because welfare recipients were a small share of the overall labor force), the reduced work effort was relatively high for the subset of poor family households receiving NIT. This reduced work effort for NIT recipients helped kill conservative political support, while liberal advocates wanted to make the program more generous and include more poor individuals without children. Even with these countervailing political forces, the Nixon proposal passed the U.S. House of Representatives but failed to pass the Senate (Steensland 2006).

An additional unexpected empirical outcome that greatly contributed to the death of NIT and other income programs was the finding from the Seattle-Denver Income Maintenance Experiment that family dissolution and divorce rose sharply for program participants. Although a major objective of FAP was encouraging intact families in order to improve the lives of poor children, the experiments resulted in reduced work effort and family breakup, killing any political chance of passage (Munnell 1986).[16]

Senator Daniel Patrick Moynihan, an early major advocate of the NIT, recanted his support in 1978, saying, "But were we wrong about a guaranteed income! Seemingly it is calamitous. It increases family dissolution by some 70 percent, decreases work, etc." Moynihan was reflecting what American opinion polls showed. Although there was support for providing subsistence to the poor, most people wanted those who could to "work for it" (Moynihan 1978).[17]

Current libertarian support for a UBI explicitly follows Friedman's model—the UBI is meant to replace most, or all, welfare state spending. Replacing not only cash welfare but also SNAP, Medicare, and other major programs allows small-government advocates to minimize the cost and any associated taxation, because their version of a UBI would be mostly financed by transferring existing budget expenditures.

Others recognize that some additional revenue might be needed, but oppose getting it through progressive income taxes, preferring either regressive consumption taxes or land taxes (Zwolinski 2016). Libertarians also attract Left advocates by criticizing existing welfare state programs as intruding on people's freedom through behavioral and work requirements and means testing for current welfare state benefits (Stern and Kravitz 2016, 186–187). Reducing government programs also would feed a second libertarian goal, to reduce governmental oversight powers and overall government employment.

The potential alliance between some progressive UBI advocates and conservatives worries defenders of the existing welfare state, leading them to question or even oppose UBIs. These defenders advocate strengthening existing targeted welfare state programs, seeing those programs as helping the poor precisely because they are targeted. Instead of seeing any UBI as further helping the poor, these analysts fear it will weaken the effectiveness of targeted programs by draining income and political support from them.

Additionally, any affordable UBI cannot award significant incomes per person without massive tax increases that do not seem politically feasible. The feared net result is that providing even a modest UBI will therefore make poor people worse off. These critics argue that reforming existing welfare state policies can achieve many of a UBI's benefits, while not exposing effective welfare state programs to political risk (Gaffney 2015).

Robert Greenstein has articulated this pro–welfare state criticism of UBI proposals in the United States. An individual UBI of $10,000 per year—17 percent below the official poverty line—for the American population of over 300 million people would cost over $3 trillion annually. Greenstein sets that amount against current U.S. federal budget expenditures: "This single-year figure equals more than three-fourths of the entire yearly federal budget. . . . It's also equal to close to 100 percent of *all* (italics in the original) tax revenue the federal government collects" (Greenstein 2016, 1). Even a $5,000 UBI would only be 41 percent of the poverty line for individuals and would still cost as much as the entire federal budget absent Social Security, Medicare, defense, and interest payments. John Kay states this perspective succinctly, arguing that "either the basic income is impossibly low, or the expenditure on it is impossibly high" (Kay 2016).

Since Greenstein doesn't believe that tax increases of the magnitude required for a UBI could be passed, he argues that the libertarian goal of "cashing out" many welfare state programs would become a major funding source and could attract support from progressives as well. And such a shift in funding from targeted programs for the poor to a universal income would mean "you are redistributing income *upward*."[18] A significant amount of UBI payments would be taxed back from higher-income households, lessening the overall budget impact, but potentially undercutting political support for UBIs.

Greenstein instead argues that effectively helping the poor means continuing to expand specific programs, many of which are means tested. He notes that the U.S. safety net now "lifts *42 percent* [italics in the original]" of people who otherwise would be poor above the poverty line. Instead of a UBI he advocates a strategy to "substantially strengthen the income floors . . . in ways that are far likelier than UBI to succeed politically and much less fraught with danger to the very people we most want to help" (Greenstein 2016, 3).

ECONOMISTS' QUESTIONS FOR A UBI

So there is serious disagreement about whether a meaningfully sized UBI would strengthen welfare states or end up reducing their scope and impact, thus hurting poor and disadvantaged people. Indeed, one explicit objective of libertarian UBI supporters is sharp reductions in the welfare state, not only in total fiscal expenditure but also in government employment and regulatory powers.

But the economics of a UBI are less studied, and there are several important economic questions about any UBI proposal that need further investigation.

1. What effects would reduced labor supply have on the economy? If UBIs would allow people to take fewer low-paying jobs or reduce their work hours on a substantial basis, there could be major economic impacts. Some advocates would welcome such responses, arguing that it would induce further technological substitution, especially in low-wage and low-skilled work. Others worry that it would reduce human capital acquisition, especially for low-income workers, with negative effects both on their individual career paths and also on long-term productivity.

2. Would UBIs be inflationary? Adding basic income would add to demand pressures in the economy, as basic income for many lower- and modest-income households would be entirely spent, boosting consumption and aggregate demand. Again, in our current economic circumstances, this

is seen by many as a benefit, given weak macroeconomic demand and wealth concentration.

3. Would UBIs add to long-term debt and fiscal burdens? Unless UBIs would be paid for entirely by tax increases, there would have to be some increased debt financing, adding to high levels of debt to GDP and creating future uncertainty about how such debts would be paid off. Some advocates hope that UBI could be part of shifting the economy onto a higher growth path, with the sustained increased output helping to pay for UBI costs.

4. Would UBIs encourage productivity? Some advocates argue that as people have to work less, they will invent more productive goods and services through rising entrepreneurship and engage in more public activity. Most economists emphasize another channel for aggregate productivity gains, through the increased demand along with decreased labor supply that together would encourage businesses to employ more capital and innovative processes.

5. What about a guaranteed job option? Some advocates argue that a universal public jobs guarantee is a superior way to address the labor market problems of the poor and technologically displaced. With basic employment rights and a reasonable wage, public jobs could help address such critical needs as human services for a growing elderly and "green" jobs to help mitigate climate change, while maintaining the skills base of the labor force. At least in the United States, it also would have the benefit of tying income provision for the poor to actual jobs, as political scientists remain skeptical that American voters will endorse a UBI without a work requirement (Tcherneva 2003).

CONCLUSION

Consideration of a substantial UBI presents challenges to all three types of welfare states. For the *liberal* state, it undercuts paid work as the core behavior for most able-bodied people, which is at the heart of both political ideology and welfare state design. For *conservative/corporatist* states, it diminishes people's social bonds and obligations and undercuts social insurance linked to work and private charity. And for *social democratic* states, it can be seen as weakening ties to the state and to political communities, turning active political participants into mere income recipients.

Much of the current interest in UBI stems from a belief that robots and technology will rapidly eliminate jobs faster than new ones will be created. But the evidence thus far is too uncertain to justify a major disruption of the welfare state. Rather, the UBI debate might be better linked to the analysis of changing economic and power relations between business and labor and the growth of the "precariat." Advanced technology in this view is just the latest in a string of developments that have weakened not only labor's ability to bargain, but also overall macroeconomic performance by contributing to weaker overall demand and inequality.

Focusing on the continuing decline of job quality, labor standards, and dependable income returns us to the core arguments about the design and efficacy of the welfare state. Technology, especially if it reduces dangerous, monotonous, or ineffective work, can be a liberating force. But debate over the distribution of profits and rents from technical change or any other form of work reorganization, and the welfare state's role in buffering or confronting those changes, should not be reduced to a debate over robotization and Internet platforms.

NOTES

1. See Van Parjis and Vanderborght (2015); Boso and Vancea (2012).

2. The state of Alaska provides an annual payment to state residents from the Alaska Permanent Fund, which is financed by oil exploration and production leases on state-owned lands. Some Native American tribes in the United States also provide annual payments to individual members, often from casino gaming revenues. See Native Assets Research Center (2011).

3. In addition, over 14 million nonelderly disabled people receive a monthly means-tested benefit from Social Security, which also requires an administrative certification of disability for recipients. http://retiredamericans.org/social-security-medicare-current-facts-figures-2016.

4. Many people receive both Social Security and SNAP, but the eligibility rules for SNAP are extremely complex and vary from state to state. It is possible that a high enough level of Social Security income could prevent receipt of SNAP.

5. In 1956, F. A. Hayek dismissed welfare state regimes as a "hodgepodge of ill-assembled and often inconsistent ideals," although his critique was more philosophical than programmatic. See "Foreword to the 1956 American Paperback Edition" in Hayek (2007).

6. There is the distinct case of conservative or libertarian support for UBI, which envisions it as replacing much or all of existing welfare state spending and programs, discussed later.

7. He also believes that machines may largely replace investors and hedge fund traders.

8. The three previous "revolutions" are identified as "(1) 1784 to 1870, steam, water power mechanical production equipment; (2) 1870 to 1969, division of labour, electricity, mass production; (3) 1969 to present, electronics, IT, automated production; (4) ? cyber-physical systems" (WEF 2016).

9. See also Holzer (2015). Holzer does see declines in "traditional" middle jobs in construction, production, and clerical jobs, but also growth in health care, mechanical maintenance, and repair and some services.

10. U.S. workers went from nearly half being eligible for unemployment benefits to under 30 percent (Wenger 2012).

11. To take just one example of lax enforcement, researchers have estimated that failure to pay U.S. workers their legally entitled wages—"wage theft"—was over $50 billion in 2012, three-and-a half times the amount lost to the crimes of robbery, burglary, larceny, and auto theft (Meixell and Eisenbrey 2014).

12. See also Standing (2015).

13. The best source for tracking UBI advocacy information is the Basic Income Earth Network (BIEN), which lists events, opinion polls, and research; has sponsored fifteen global and many regional conferences; and publishes a peer-reviewed journal now in its eleventh year. See their website: www.basicincome.org.

14. UBI advocates often cite Evelyn Forget, who has said that in the Canadian project, "few people stopped working and hardly anyone with a full time job reduced the hours they worked at all," although she also notes that her own research, "did not look at work effort" (she analyzed health outcomes) and that there were reduced work hours in the Canadian program. Hum and Simpson were unable to disentangle reduced work hours from general economic effects reducing hours, in part because the Manitoba research was not a true experimental design. See Jourdan (2013).

15. OECD 2015; Millemaci and Ofria 2012.

16. There is a vast literature on the NIT experiments; Widerquist (2002) identified "at least 345 scholarly articles" on them.

17. On opinion polls, see Munnell (1986, 13).

18. For example, Stern and Kravitz (2016, 212) explicitly endorses such a funding mechanism. On shifting income upward, see Greenstein (2016, 2) (italics in the original).

REFERENCES

Autor, David. 2015. "Why Are There Still So Many Jobs? The History and Future of Workplace Automation." *Journal of Economic Perspectives* 29(3):3–30.

Ben-Shalom, Yonatan, Robert A. Moffitt, and John Karl Scholz. 2012. "An Assessment of the Effectiveness of Anti-poverty Programs in the United States." In *The Oxford Handbook of the Economics of Poverty*, ed. Phillip N. Jefferson, 709–749. Oxford: Oxford University Press.

Bernstein, Amy, and Anand Raman. 2015. "The Great Decoupling: An Interview with Erik Brynjolfsson and Andrew McAfee." *Harvard Business Review* 93(6):66–74.

Boso, Àlex, and Vancea, Mihaela. 2012. "Basic Income for Immigrants? The Pull Effect of Social Benefits on Migration." *Basic Income Studies* 7(1):1–24.

Brynjolfsson, Erik, and Andrew McAfee. 2014. *The Second Machine Age: Work, Progress, and Prosperity in a Time of Brilliant Technologies.* New York: Norton.

Chang, Ha-Joon. 2010. *23 Things They Don't Tell You About Capitalism.* New York: Bloomsbury.

Dashevsky, Evan. 2015. "How Long Until a Robot Takes Your Job? An Interview with *Rise of the Robots* Author, Martin Ford." *PC Mag*, December 30. www.pcmag.com /article2/0,2817,2496733,00.asp.

Esping-Andersen, Gosta. 1990. *The Three Worlds of Welfare Capitalism.* Cambridge: Polity Press.

Federal Reserve Bank of St. Louis. 2017. FRED Economic Data. "Nonfarm Business Sector: Labor Share, 1947–2016"; "Income Gini Ratio for Households by Race of Householder, All Races." https://research.stlouisfed.org/fred2/series/PRS85006173 and series GINIALLRH. Accessed on August 10, 2017.

Freedman, David H. 2016. "Basic Income: A Sellout of the American Dream." *MIT Technology Review* 119(4):48–53. www.technologyreview.com/s/601499 /basic-income-a-sellout-of-the-american-dream.

Freeman, Richard. 2007. "The Great Doubling: The Challenge of the New Global Labor Market." In *Ending Poverty in America: How to Restore the American Dream*, ed. John Edwards, Marion Crain, and Arne L. Kalleberg, chap. 4. New York: New Press.

Friedman, Milton. 1967. "The Case for the Negative Income Tax." *National Review*, March 7, pp. 239–41.

Ford, Martin. 2015. *Rise of the Robots: Technology and the Threat of a Jobless Future.* New York: Basic.

Frey, Carl Benedikt, and Michael A. Osborne. 2013. "The Future of Employment: How Susceptible Are Jobs to Computerization?" September 17. University of Oxford, Martin School.

Gaffney, Declan. 2015. "Even in Finland, Universal Basic Income Is Still Too Good to Be True." *The Guardian*, December 10. www.theguardian.com/commentisfree/2015 /dec/10/finland-universal-basic-income-ubi-social-security.

Greenstein, Bob. 2016. "Universal Basic Income." Paper prepared for Open Society Foundations, Universal Basic Income Convening, March.

Hayek, F. A. 2007. "Foreword to the 1956 American Paperback Edition" in *The Road to Serfdom*. In *The Collected Works of F. A. Hayek*, ed. Bruce Campbell. Chicago: University of Chicago Press, 2:39–52.

Holzer, Harry J. 2015. " Job Market Polarization and U.S. Worker Skills: A Tale of Two Middles." Brookings Institution Economic Studies Working Papers, April. Washington, D.C.: Brookings Institution.

Hum, Derek, and Wayne Simpson. 1993. "Economic Response to a Guaranteed Annual Income: Experience from Canada and the United States." *Journal of Labor Economics* 11(1; part 2):S263–S296.

International Labor Organization. 2013. *Global Wage Report 2012/2013: Wages and Equitable Growth.* Geneva: ILO.

Jourdan, Stanislas. 2013. "A Way to Get Healthy: Basic Income Experiments in Canada." Basic Income. August 7, 2013, http://basicincome.org.uk/2013/08/health-forget -mincome-poverty.

Kay, John. 2016. "With a Basic Income, the Numbers Just Do Not Add Up." *Financial Times*, May 31.

Kholsa, Vinod. 2014. "The Next Technology Revolution Will Drive Abundance and Income Disparity." *Forbes*, Tech/Valley Voices, November 6. www.forbes.com /sites/valleyvoices/2014/11/06.

Manyika, James, Michael Chui, Mehdi Miremadi, Jacques Bughin, Katy George, Paul Willmott, and Martin Dewhurst. 2017. *A Future That Works: Automation, Employment, and Productivity*. New York: McKinsey Global Institute.

Meixell, Brady, and Ross Eisenbrey. 2014. "An Epidemic of Wage Theft Is Costing Workers Hundreds of Millions of Dollars a Year." Economic Policy Institute. September 11. www.epi.org/publication/epidemic-wage-theft-costing-workers-hundreds.

Milberg, William, and Deborah Winkler. 2013. *Outsourcing Economics: Global Value Chains in Capitalist Development*. Cambridge: University of Cambridge Press.

Millemaci, Emanuele, and Ferdinando Ofria. 2012. "Kaldor-Verdoon's Law and Increasing Returns to Scale: A Comparison Across Developed Countries." FEEM Working Paper No. 92, January. http://dx.doi.org/10.2139/ssrn.2192520.

Moynihan, Daniel Patrick. 1978. "Letter to William H. Buckley." *National Review*, September 29.

Munnell, Alicia H. 1986. "Lessons from the Income Maintenance Experiments: An Overview." In *Lessons from the Income Maintenance Experiments*, ed. Alicia A. Munnell, 1–21. Brookings Institution, Conference Series no. 30, September. Washington, D.C.: Brookings Institution.

Murphy, Jason Burke. 2016. "Basic Income as Proposal, as Project, and as Idea." Basic Income Earth Network. June 10. www.basicincome.org/news/2016/06 /basic-income-as-proposal-as-project-and-as-idea.

Native Assets Research Center. 2011. *Developing Innovations in Tribal per Capita Distribution Payment Programs*. Longmont. Colo.: First Nations Development Institute.

Nullmeier, Frank, and Franz-Xaver Kaufmann. 2010. "Post-war Welfare State Development." In *The Oxford Handbook of the Welfare State*, ed. Francis G. Castles, Stephan Leibfried, Jane Lewis, Herbert Obinger, and Christopher Pierson, 81–101. Oxford: Oxford University Press.

Organization for Economic Cooperation and Development. 2015. *In It Together: Why Less Inequality Benefits All*. Paris: OECD. http://dx.doi.org/10.1787/9789264235120-en.

Smith, Aaron, and Janna Anderson. 2014. "AI, Robotics, and the Future of Jobs." Pew Research Center. August 6. www.pewinternet.org/2014/08/06/future-of-jobs.

Standing, Guy. 2011. *The Precariat: The New Dangerous Class*. London: Bloomsbury.

——. 2015. "The Growing Precariat: Why We Need a Universal Basic Income." Singularity Hub, March 30. http://singularityhub.com/2015/03/30/the-growing-precariat -why-a-basic-income-is-needed.

Steensland, Brian. 2006. "Cultural Categories and the American Welfare State: The Case of Guaranteed Income Policy." *American Journal of Sociology* 111(5):1273–1326.

Stern, Andy. 2016. "Moving Towards a Universal Basic Income." *The World Bank Jobs and Development Blog*, April 12. http://blogs.worldbank.org/jobs/moving-towards -universal-basic-income.

Stern, Andy, and Lee Kravitz. 2016. *Raising the Floor: How a Universal Basic Income Can Renew Our Economy and Rebuild the American Dream*. New York: Public Affairs.

Tcherneva, Pavlina R. 2003. "Job or Income Guarantee?" Center for Full Employment and Price Stability, University of Missouri at Kansas City, Working Paper No. 29, August. www.cfeps.org/pubs/wp-pdf/WP29-Tcherneva.pdf.

Van Parjis, Phillipe. 2000. "Basic Income: A Simple and Powerful Idea for the 21st Century." Background paper, Basic Income European Network, VIIIth International Congress, Berlin, October.

Van Parjis, Phillipe, and Yannick Vanderborght. 2015. "Basic Income in a Globalized Economy." In *Inclusive Growth, Development, and Welfare Policy: A Critical Assessment*, ed. Reza Hasmath, 229–247. New York: Routledge.

Vardy, Moishe. 2015. "The Future of Work: But What Will Humans Do?" *Pacific Standard*, September 11. https://psmag.com/the-future-of-work-but-what-will-humans-do-5b9ca56d6c61#.tfd3d73s4.

Wenger, Jeffrey B. 2012. "Why State Unemployment Insurance Is Broken—Can We Fix It?" Scholars Strategy Network. April, www.scholarsstrategynetwork.org/brief/why-state-unemployment-insurance-broken-%E2%80%93-can-we-fix-it.

Widerquist, Karl. 2002. "A Failure to Communicate: The Labour Market Findings of the Negative Income Tax Experiments and Their Effects on Policy and Public Opinion." Basic Income Earth Network (BIEN). September. www.ilo.org/public/english/protection/ses/download/docs/wider.pdf.

World Economic Forum (WEF). 2016. "The Future of Jobs: Employment, Skills, and Workforce Strategy for the Fourth Industrial Revolution." January. http://reports.weforum.org/future-of-jobs-2016.

Wright, Erik Olin. 2002. "Basic Income, Stakeholder Grants, and Class Analysis." Paper for the Real Utopias Conference on Rethinking Redistribution. University of Wisconsin, May. www.ssc.wisc.edu/~wright/EOW%20RR%20essay.pdf.

Zwolinski, Matt. 2016. "Libertarianism and the UBI." Paper prepared for Open Society Foundations, Universal Basic Income Convening, March.

CHAPTER 15

Employment Guarantee in the Age of Precarity

THE CASE OF INDIA'S NATIONAL RURAL EMPLOYMENT GUARANTEE ACT

Amit Basole and Arjun Jayadev

India's employer of last resort program, the National Rural Employment Guarantee Act (NREGA, later Mahatma Gandhi NREGA or MGNREGA), guarantees 100 days of wage employment in a year to every rural household whose adult members volunteer to do unskilled manual work. Work is undertaken on public or private land to produce durable assets that will contribute to environmental conservation, irrigation, and infrastructure. In terms of its coverage of people, MGNREGA is perhaps one of the largest social safety programs in the world. It covers up to 15 percent of the Indian population, and recent estimates suggest that in 2012 it benefited 50 million households (Carswell and Neve 2014). Apart from its size, however, it is unusual in another way: it is one of the few jobs programs adopted in a nonindustrialized country context.

Employment guarantees have a long history in economics and policy making, beginning in the seventeenth century with William Petty's support of public works as a solution to the social and economic depredations of unemployment (Petty 1899). Arguments in favor of the idea of the government as the employer of last resort (ELR), however, became more pronounced only after the Industrial Revolution and the understanding of the business cycle as being demand-led. If periods of insufficient private demand led to higher unemployment and poverty, the state could step in to limit deflationary spirals by guaranteeing employment. In doing so, they could maintain growth and alleviate poverty.[1]

Employment guarantees in the context of developing economies have had less of a history. While relief through employment under public works programs has been part of poverty alleviation in many pre-industrial contexts, including in developing economies, the idea of a programmatic ELR has not been advocated to the same extent.[2] Unemployment in developing countries has been argued to not be Keynesian, but rather classical, arising out insufficient capital and slow structural transformation. State efforts therefore need to be directed to the problem of structural transformation, allowing for an economy to move from a primarily agrarian one to a modern, industrialized one. Indeed, in such a view, attempting to support rural labor markets through employment guarantees may serve to retard the necessary (if painful) transition to an industrialized working force necessary for development.[3] With capital accumulation and free mobility of labor, economies would go through the Lewisian transition and surplus labor from the "traditional" sector would be absorbed into the "modern sector" at higher levels of output.

While several countries have indeed gone through such a transformation, the optimistic vision of the transition to a largely industrialized economy, less subject to decreasing returns in which labor is absorbed naturally and made more secure, is more questionable now than in decades. The return to an emphasis on the provision of jobs,[4] as opposed to simply income transfers, has been driven at least in part by three conjoint factors.

First, as Rodrik (2015) points out, peak industrialization is actually occurring at lower levels of per capita output across the world, except in East Asia. In Latin America, sub-Saharan Africa, and India, peak manufacturing employment has been reached at lower incomes than in Western Europe. This has meant that the pace of labor absorption into the modern sector has been slower, since manufacturing has been historically a much larger absorber of surplus labor. Again, with some exceptions in Asia, developing countries have experienced falling manufacturing shares of output in both employment and real value added. Moreover, the decline has been more pronounced for employment than output. This has meant the rise of service sector–led growth. The problem is especially severe in India. As Amirapu and Subramanian (2015) show, India's largest state, Uttar Pradesh, reached its peak share of manufacturing in output at 10 percent of GDP in 1996 at a per capita state domestic product of about $1,200. By way of comparison, Indonesia attained a manufacturing peak share of 29 percent at a per capita GDP of $5,800. Furthermore, virtually no Indian state has a continuously increasing manufacturing share of employment, and labor movement has been primarily from agriculture straight into (informal) services.

Second, across the industrial sectors of the world, there has been increasing informalization that increases precarity of job tenure and vulnerability. Shrinking manufacturing, growing informality, low productivity, and sharp increases in urban migration have created jobs crises in many countries. The labor displaced from the agrarian sector now crowds into petty services rather than, as might be hoped, into high-productivity, high-labor-absorbing industrial sectors. This has economic and political consequences; as Standing (2011) has noted, a global "precariat" is also a volatile political force. In India, rapid urbanization and the attendant difficulties that it brings in its wake have become pressing policy concerns.

Finally, across countries that have large agricultural sectors, the forms of globalization that have been adopted have led to increased volatility and, in some cases, extreme distress (for an overview on India's agrarian distress see Vakulabharanam and Motiram 2011). Therefore, in countries like India, there are serious and continuing push factors and demographic changes that make labor absorption crucial.

It is in this context that the MGNREGA serves as a vital social insurance mechanism. It serves to buffer the economy against the particular challenges its development pattern has generated: an agricultural sector with low productivity and that is shedding labor, and an informal sector that is absorbing most of this labor, all in the context of a demographic challenge raised by a large youth population.

One might imagine, of course, other social insurance programs (in particular, income transfers) that serve to ameliorate the strains associated with the nature of Indian growth. Indeed, several recent criticisms of the MGNREGA offer income transfers or income grants as a superior alternative. From the viewpoint of theory and some empirical literature, these forms of social insurance have the clear advantage in that they are self-targeting and allow for more choice in labor supply. While there is no reason to oppose cash transfers, there are at least two reasons to be in favor of a job guarantee program. First, while the pressing problem with unemployment is often the attendant poverty, a major concern is *the fact of unemployment itself.* To the extent that work confers self-worth, status, and purpose, being unemployed has far more corrosive effects than simply a fall in income. A job guarantee scheme allows for not only the maintenance of these nonmonetary benefits but also the building of a sense of community, capacity building, and skill development within the paid work environment. Second, to the extent that there is genuine slack in the economy and a desperate need for public infrastructure, job guarantees are an effective way to provide these assets, which may not be forthcoming under a simple income transfer program.

Given these larger concerns, in this chapter we do not aim for a full appraisal of the MGNREGA in terms of all the competing pressures of social insurance. We instead highlight some key features, successes, and challenges and make a case for its expansion in the current context. We begin by elaborating on its adoption as a result of "jobless growth" in India before moving on to a short appraisal and concerns. We conclude by arguing for its expansion along some key dimensions.

1. JOBLESS GROWTH IN INDIA

The significance and impact of MGNREGA needs to be understood in the context of India's ongoing structural transition from a largely agrarian economy to an industrial and service economy. The Indian growth story has been widely celebrated in the academic and popular literature since the early 2000s. The standard narrative on offer paints a picture of a sluggish "Hindu" rate of growth in the planning period (1950–1980) giving way to an acceleration in growth in the 1980s as a result of pro-business policies of the Rajiv Gandhi government (1984–1989) and a further picking up of the pace in the late 1990s after the pro-market reforms of 1991 (Kotwal, Ramaswami, and Wadhwa 2011). Figure 15.1 shows that, as far as GDP growth is concerned, this narrative is correct. A continuation of the trend from the 1960s and 1970s (straight line) differs drastically from

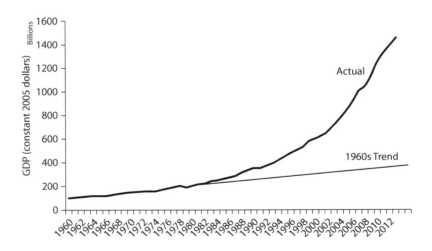

Figure 15.1   India's growth path.

Source: World Development Indicators, World Bank.

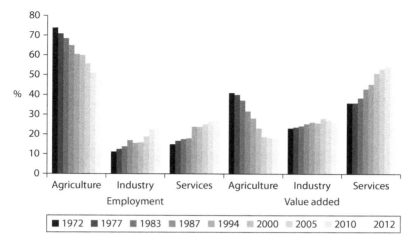

Figure 15.2   Sectoral shares in output and employment.

Source: World Development Indicators, World Bank.

the actually observed trend, indicating the vast increase in rates of growth during the post-1980s period.

However, seen through the lens of structural transformation (à la Arthur Lewis) and stable employment, and in particular of formal sector jobs, the Indian experience leaves much to be desired. We can understand the pattern of structural change by seeing that sectoral employment shares have been changing far more slowly than output shares. Between 1972 and 2012, share of value added coming from the primary sector (composed of agriculture and allied activities) fell from 41 percent to 17.5 percent. Over the same period, the share of employment in the primary sector declined from 74 percent to 47 percent (figure 15.2). This has resulted in a large proportion of the labor force being trapped in low-productivity agricultural work.

Over the past two decades, there has been virtually no growth of formal sector employment. Figure 15.3 contrasts GDP growth with formal employment growth. As the growth rate of GDP increased from an average annual rate of 4.7 percent during the 1970s to 5, 6, and then 9 percent in the 2000s, the employment growth rate plummeted from an already low 2.4 percent to an abysmal 0.22 percent per year. Papola and Sahu (2012) report that employment elasticity (ratio of employment growth to growth in value added), which was 0.52 in the 1970s, declined

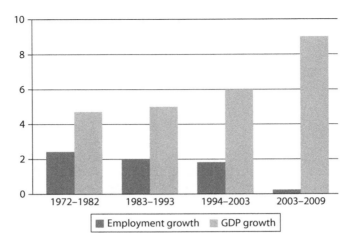

Figure 15.3 Jobless growth: Output and employment elasticities.

Source: Papola and Sahu (2012).

steadily (0.41 in the 1980s, 0.29 during 1993–2004), until it reached almost zero during 2005–2010. Recent growth was thus almost entirely jobless, at least in terms of formal jobs.

On the other hand, for the first time in India's post-Independence history, between 1999 and 2004 there was a decline in the absolute number of people employed in agriculture (Mehrotra et al. 2014). Bhaduri (2008) notes that, for example, during 1994–2000, aggregate employment elasticity was low because agriculture, with an output weight of about 60 percent, had an elasticity of only 0.02. The corresponding elasticities for industry and services were 0.38 and 0.35. Unfortunately, while the move out of agriculture per se may be desirable within a Lewisian framework, in India this has been the result of push factors rather than pull factors. Agricultural land holdings, which were already small, have declined further in size due to demographic pressures and land fragmentation. Between 1961 and 2003, average area of ownership holding declined from 2.01 to 0.81 hectares. Over the same period, the proportion of households owning less than 1 hectare of land increased from 75.22 percent to 90.4 percent; the proportion of total area owned by such households increased over this four-decade period from 20 percent to 43 percent (Basole and Basu 2011). Exhaustion of the Green Revolution's gains and collapse of public investment in agriculture after the 1980s resulted in a steady decline in viability of agriculture, acute agrarian distress, and a collapse of rural incomes by the early 2000s.

Piecing together these trends, we get the picture of an economy in which people are being pushed out of agriculture but there are no formal jobs available to absorb them. Hence this labor force, as well as the new entrants, have been absorbed into the ranks of the informal precariat. Between 1991 and 2011, the total labor force in India increased from 338.67 million to 476.66 million (World Development Indicators). Over the same period, as per the Economic Survey of India (2012–13), total (that is, private and public) employment in the organized sector increased from 26.73 million to 28.99 million. Thus, over this two-decade period of rapid economic growth, more than 98 percent of the increase in the labor force was absorbed in informal employment. Informal employment as a whole (including informally employed workers in formal sector enterprises) accounts for 92 percent of the workforce (Sengupta 2009). A large part of this is accounted for by the construction industry. Mehrotra et al. (2014) show that 37 million workers left agriculture between 2005 and 2012 and another 15 million were added to the labor force in the same period. In this same period, the labor force in construction increased by a whopping 25 million. In other words, nearly half of the newly available workers were absorbed in this sector alone.

Thus, at the time it was launched in 2006, MGNREGA intervened in a rural economy that was badly in need of stable wage employment. In this context, the surety and dignity of a government employment program went a long way in accounting for its popularity.

2. MGNREGA: DESIGN, ACHIEVEMENTS, AND CRITICISMS

We now provide a brief introduction to the way the program is designed and how it operates. A detailed review of its functioning and a thorough assessment is outside the scope of this chapter. We refer the reader to other more detailed treatments on these issues (Dreze and Khera 2009; Viswanathan et al. 2014; Sharma 2015).

MGNREGA is part of a set of rights-based legislation promulgated by the United Progressive Alliance governments (2004–2009 and 2009–2014). Other examples include the Right to Education (2009), Right to Information (2005), Forest Rights Act (2009), and Food Security Act (2013). The MGNREGA takes earlier rural employment schemes, expands them, and translates them into a "right to livelihood" framework. It is:

> An Act to provide for the enhancement of livelihood security of the households in rural areas of the country by providing at least one hundred days of guaranteed wage employment in every financial year to every household whose adult members volunteer to do unskilled manual work. (Ministry of Law and Justice 2005)

Although coming on the heels of several other employment guarantee programs (such as the Maharashtra Employment Guarantee Act, the Sampoorna Gramin Rozgar Yojana, and the National Food for Work Program), MGNREGA is different in seeing employment as a right and therefore legally binding the government of India to provide employment to those who demand it, within fifteen days of the demand being officially made. The primary objective is enhancing livelihood security in rural areas by providing 100 days of guaranteed wage employment in a year to every household. In addition, rural asset creation (public and private) is an important aspect of the program, with activities such as school building, water conservation and water harvesting, drought proofing, flood control, micro-irrigation works, sanitation, rural roads, and development of land owned by households belonging to the Scheduled Castes (SCs) and Scheduled Tribes (STs) or below poverty line (BPL) families or other disadvantaged groups.[5] The program has been recognized as "unique in global context of social protection policies" (Carswell and Neve 2014, 567). In addition to taking a rights-based approach to employment provisioning, it includes several other innovative features, such as equal pay for men and women, onsite childcare facilities, an attempt at grassroots democracy, and participatory governance. It has generated tremendous interest in academic, policy, and activist circles. Several studies have come out, especially in the past five years, examining almost all aspects of its design and functioning: employment generated, infrastructure created, the impact on wage rates and household incomes, impact on local social relations, and problems with implementation, corruption, and so on.[6]

MGNREGA is currently active in 262,232 villages in 661 districts of India. Since its inception, cumulatively it has provided employment to 273.9 million workers and currently (in 2015–2016) 72 million are active workers. Twenty-five percent of rural households have accessed MGNREGA.[7]

One important distinguishing feature of MGNREGA from earlier employment guarantee programs is that it legally binds local administrative bodies (Gram Panchayats) to provide work on demand to any worker within fifteen days of receipt of a work application. If the local bodies fail to provide work, the state government must pay an unemployment allowance to the worker. The statutory minimum wage is the same for both men and women, and under law at least one-third of the workers should be women. There is also a provision for childcare facilities when more than five children under six years of age are present at the worksite. The program is locally managed, self-targeted, demand driven, universal, and year-round. Work is provided within fifteen kilometers of residence and there is a commuting provision if the worksite is more than five kilometers from a worker's residence (Ministry of Law and Justice 2005).

The act was passed into law in 2005, and the program was first implemented in rural areas of 200 of the most "backward" districts in 2006.[8] This was followed by 130 more districts in 2007 and all districts by 2008.

Figures 15.4 and 15.5 use official MGNREGA data[9] to map state-level performance in terms of two key indicators: number of days that participating households were provided work (maximum 100) and wages received per person per day. Both figures make apparent that there is significant state-level variation, which is in part due to differences in implementation that we will briefly discuss later. It is also interesting to see that states that have otherwise been noted to be good performers with respect to program implementation (for example, Tamil Nadu and Rajasthan) do worse in terms of labor expenditure per person-day compared to less well-performing states such as Orissa.[10]

The most direct and expected effect of MGNREGA at the national level has been a reduction in poverty and enhancement of rural incomes (especially during the agricultural lean season). Studies have also found general equilibrium effects on agricultural and rural wages at large and a strengthening of the bargaining position of the most vulnerable sections of rural India by reducing their reliance on local employers. Finally, there are productivity and welfare gains due to investment in durable assets under the program.

Four recent studies have examined the impact of MGNREGA on rural wages. Azam (2012), Zimmermann (2012), and Imbert and Papp (2015)

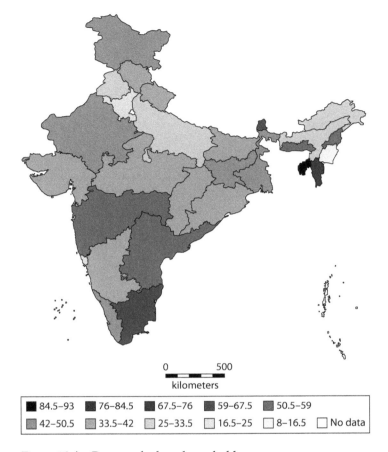

Figure 15.4   Days worked per household.

use household-level National Sample Survey (NSS) data, while Berg et al. (2012) use a district-level monthly data set called Agricultural Wages in India (AWI). All four studies use the phased rollout as an identification strategy but reach slightly different conclusions. Berg et al. (2012) find no immediate jump in agricultural wages after introduction of MGNREGA, but instead report a positive and significant increase in the rate of growth of agricultural wages to the tune of 5.3 percent in MGNREGA districts. They interpret this as an effect of a gradual increase in the demand for labor in the district. This is close to the estimate of Imbert and Papp (2015), which is 4.7 percent per annum increase in earnings (in NSS data). Azam (2011) found that real wages of female casual workers increased 8 percent more in

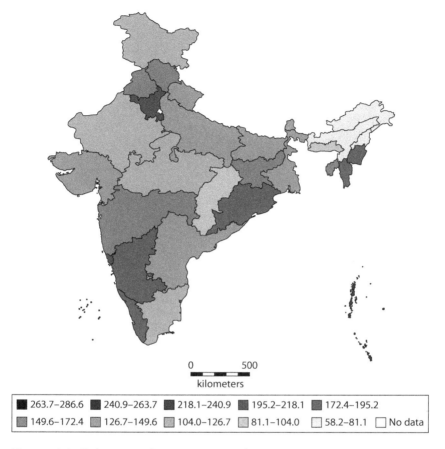

Figure 15.5   Labor expenditure per person-day.

MGNREGA districts compared to non-MGNREGA districts. However, he did not find a significant impact on male wages. Zimmermann (2012) finds similar results. Part of the difference in findings is likely due to differences in data and methodology. But it is also possible that wage effects are heterogeneous due to variation in program implementation, and hence national trends are difficult to identify with certainty.

Klonner and Oldiges (2014) approach program effects from the perspective of consumption smoothing rather than income enhancement. Relying on NSS data and also taking advantage of the phased rollout of the program, they use a regression discontinuity design and find no significant effect on the level of consumption or on consumption-based poverty figures for all rural households; however, they do find strong effects for SC and ST households. They estimate that MGNREGA participation increased consumption of SC/ST households by 30 percent and halved poverty in the spring season. One caveat here, as the authors themselves note, is that they use the "thin" rounds of the NSS, which are not representative at the district level, in order to perform district-level estimation. Thus, lack of statistical power may lie behind the negative overall result. That workers see the program as important to smoothing income and consumption is clear from ethnographic work. For example, an agricultural worker in Tamil Nadu noted,

> I do 10 days of agricultural work and 10 days of this work . . . If I use up my 100 days in one go, I will only have work for 4 months and be without income after that! (Carswell and De Neve 2014, 572)

Indeed, going beyond secondary data-driven studies, primary surveys usually find a positive attitude toward the program, at least among the agricultural workers at whom it is targeted. Dreze and Khera (2009), reporting on a 2008 survey, found that 50 percent of respondents felt the program "brought significant change in their lives," and 69 percent said it had helped them avoid hunger. It also helped in avoiding migration (59 percent), sending children to school (38 percent), coping with illness (50 percent), repaying debt (32 percent), and avoiding demeaning or hazardous work (35 percent).

From both secondary data studies and primary surveys as well as journalistic accounts, it is clear that MGNREGA is reaching socially disadvantaged groups such as women, SCs, and STs, albeit with significant interstate variation. Khera and Nayak (2009) reported that in states such as Kerala, Tamil Nadu, and Rajasthan, 70–80 percent of workers were women. At the other end, women workers were less than the stipulated one-third in states like Assam (31), Bihar (27), West Bengal (17), Uttar Pradesh (15), Himachal Pradesh (30), and Jharkhand (27). Figure 15.6 shows more recent data (2015–2016) for women's participation. Kerala, Tamil Nadu, and Rajasthan continue to lead with 70–90 percent women's participation. Somewhat expectedly, given social norms, the poorly performing states are Uttar Pradesh, Bihar, Jharkhand, and Orissa. Surprisingly, the northeastern states, usually known for higher status for women compared to the heartland, are also at the bottom of the list. A possible reason is that women are already significantly employed in wage work in these areas and need not rely on MGNREGA for such work.

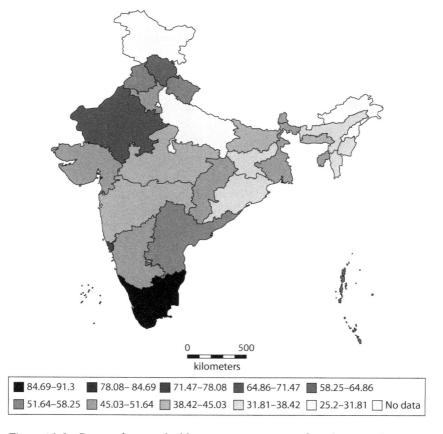

■ 84.69–91.3	■ 78.08– 84.69	■ 71.47–78.08	■ 64.86–71.47	■ 58.25–64.86
■ 51.64–58.25	■ 45.03–51.64	■ 38.42–45.03	■ 31.81–38.42	□ 25.2–31.81 □ No data

Figure 15.6 Person-days worked by women as percent of total person-days worked.

The study by Khera and Nayak (2009) is an early study that looks at reasons for high women's participation in the program. Important factors include nonavailability of any other wage work in the village, the prestige attached to government work, regular hours, and wages substantially higher (sometimes double or more) than the going rate for women's work. Dignity associated with doing government work and having an option to escape potentially exploitative work from private landlords or contractors is also a very significant benefit for women. Based on the same survey data, Dreze and Khera (2009) report that 79 percent of women workers report collecting their own wages, and 68 percent report keeping them. In a primary district-level study of Rajasthan, Bihar, Himachal Pradesh, and Jharkhand, Pankaj and Tankha (2010) showed that the contribution of MGNREGA wages in the total annual income of woman workers' households ranged from 13 percent to 27 percent. In interviews, women report being able to manage their needs and their families' needs better and relief from migrating in search of work and from strenuous and poorly paid work. But as the data presented in figure 15.6 show, several challenges still remain in program implementation, especially with regard to ensuring women's participation in those states where gender norms do not permit women to work outside the home.

Figures 15.7 and 15.8 show the performance of different states in enabling the participation of two other socially disadvantaged groups: scheduled castes (former untouchables) and scheduled tribes (tribals).

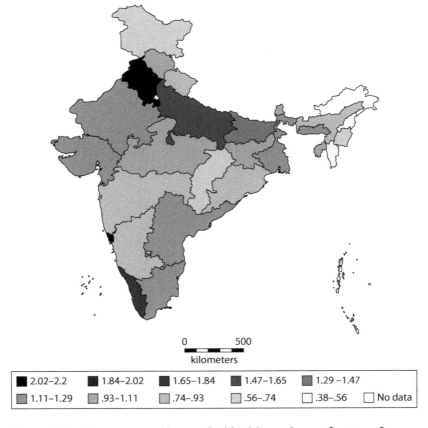

2.02–2.2	1.84–2.02	1.65–1.84	1.47–1.65	1.29–1.47
1.11–1.29	.93–1.11	.74–.93	.56–.74	.38–.56	No data

Figure 15.7   Percent person-days worked by SC members as fraction of percent state SC population.

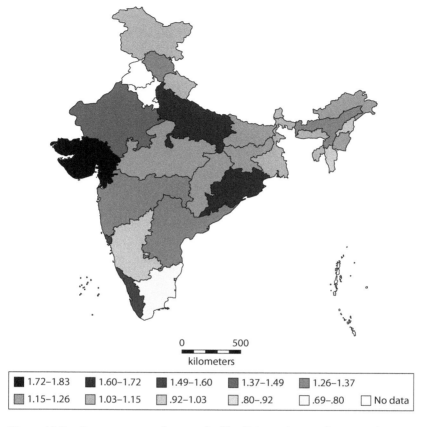

| ■ 1.72–1.83 | ■ 1.60–1.72 | ■ 1.49–1.60 | ■ 1.37–1.49 | ■ 1.26–1.37 |
| ■ 1.15–1.26 | ■ 1.03–1.15 | ■ .92–1.03 | □ .80–.92 | □ .69–.80 | □ No data |

Figure 15.8 Percent person-days worked by ST members as fraction of percent state ST population.

We show percent person-days worked by SCs and STs as a fraction of percent state population accounted for by these groups. In this measure, a value of 1 indicates that SCs and STs are proportionately represented in MGNREGA. Values greater than 1 indicate overrepresentation, and values less than 1 indicate underrepresentation. Knowing the prevalence of poverty among these two groups and their social exclusion, overrepresentation can be taken as an indication of a well-run program. For SCs the major states that meet this criterion are Gujarat, Rajasthan, Punjab, Haryana, Uttar Pradesh, Bihar, Bengal, Karnataka, Tamil Nadu, and Kerala. For STs most states fall into this category, with the exception of Karnataka and Tamil Nadu.

We now briefly discuss the assets being created under the program. As noted earlier, the primary focus on MGNREGA and its public reputation relates to providing wage employment. However, since the beginning, the act has envisioned that work undertaken in the program will create durable rural assets, especially for natural resource management and improvement of rural productivity. After a spate of studies analyzing the program's effects on rural wages and empowerment of marginalized groups, recent attention has focused on assessing the quality of work undertaken as well. Since MGNREGA is thought of primarily as a poverty alleviation and social protection program, this aspect is relatively understudied. Ranaware et al. (2015, 53) noted that "there is a widespread belief that the works created under the MGNREGA are of dubious usefulness." The Ranaware et al. (2015) study is a nonrandom study of over 4,000 works undertaken under MGNREGA in the state of Maharashtra. It finds that small and marginal farmers (median landholding 1.6 hectares) were most likely to benefit from the program. Interestingly, this was true for private assets developed as a part of the program as well. Seventy-five percent of works on private lands were on lands that belonged to small (53 percent) and marginal (22 percent) farmers. The authors conclude that "fears of elite capture of MGNREGA works, or large farmers and absentee landlords benefiting disproportionately . . . appeared to be misplaced" (56). One important cautionary note, however, is that SCs, STs, and "Other Backward Classes" or OBCs (lower castes who are higher in status than SCs) were underrepresented among the beneficiaries.

An often overlooked and interesting aspect of the MGNREGA works program is that assets can be constructed not only on public lands but also on private lands that belong to a program participant. In the latter case, the landowner works alongside other workers who offer themselves for MGNREGA employment. Wages and material costs are provided by the government, and the asset becomes the private property of the land owner. A common asset thus constructed is a well for irrigation and household uses. Bhaskar, Gupta, and Yadav (2016) undertook a randomized evaluation of wells constructed under the program in the state of Jharkhand. They found an excellent correspondence between official statistics and on-the-ground reality as far as completed wells are concerned. Statistics do not agree, however, on in-progress wells, with many officially "in progress" wells actually being abandoned for lack of funds. Importantly, they found that almost 95 percent of completed wells are being used for irrigation purposes. This has led to "a near tripling of agricultural income of those in the command area." They estimate the real rate of return on these assets to be around 6 percent. While many more such studies are needed, it seems clear that asset creation, even if it is a secondary goal of the program, has not been the complete failure that it is often portrayed to be in the popular media.

CRITICISMS

Notwithstanding the positive effects described earlier, like most large-scale public programs in India, MGNREGA has had its share of concerns raised around issues such as corruption and elite capture. One of the most frequent criticisms, not surprisingly, is that India cannot afford such an ambitious program. With increasing emphasis on fiscal consolidation, this has become almost common wisdom. But is MGNREGA in fact unaffordable? The expenditure is countercyclical as expected, and the peak cost of the program is around 0.3 to 0.5 percent of GDP. We can contrast this with the size of what have been termed "non-merit subsidies" to various industries such as fertilizer and petroleum production that are regressive in nature (they benefit the relatively well-off more than others) and that account for 9 percent of GDP. Thus, while the most recent fiscal commitment to MGNREGA is Rs. 38,500 crore,[11] the fertilizer subsidy is nearly twice that at Rs. 70,000 crore, and the fuel subsidy is Rs. 27,000 crore. Indirect subsidies such as tax concessions can also be taken into account here. Estimated revenues forgone due to corporate tax concessions usually come to another Rs. 70,000 crore annually. P. Sainath has estimated the total corporate giveaways in the 2013–14 budget to be Rs. 532,000 crore (5 percent of GDP).[12] This includes the already mentioned tax revenue forgone plus forgone revenues from excise and customs duties and is twice the size of the food, fuel, and fertilizer subsidies combined for that year (Rs. 240,000 crore). Thus it would seem that there is room for a significant increase in the MGNREGA budget using monies saved from ending such giveaways. Further, the revival in rural incomes would reduce the need for other subsidies. Note also that India has historically spent a much lower proportion of national income on social expenditure (4–5 percent as compared with other South Asian countries such as Nepal). Finally, to the extent that productive assets are actually created (as studies show is the case), the macroeconomic expense is further reduced.

Another concern that was frequently cited at the outset of the program was that it was responsible for the high levels of inflation in the period 2011–2013. Rising rural wages, as a consequence of MGNREGA, it was argued, had led to a classic wage-price spiral. But this argument does not stand up to evidence. First, as researchers have observed, while wage rates rose by 5 percent, inflation was in double digits. Further, food inflation was primarily in commodities such as milk, eggs, and protein and unlikely to have been due to grain wages. Work by the Reserve Bank of India (Nadhanael 2012; Sonna et al. 2014) shows that agricultural wage increases were at best a small contributor to rising inflation, and even to the extent that they were a factor, there were several other confounding factors at the same time that may have led to rising wages independent of the MGNREGA (for example, loan waivers and the implementation of the pay-commission government-servant wage increases.). Finally, even if it wages had increased food inflation, the government did have a way to reduce inflation, since India had been building up substantial food stocks throughout the period (that it chose not to is a different matter).

The third biggest category of criticisms is program implementation. Household surveys and social audits reveal many complaints involving nonissuance of dated receipts, nonpayment of unemployment allowance, payment of less than full wages, and especially, delayed payments. Estimating leakages by comparing officially reported person-days of employment provided with person-days of employment reported by rural households in NSS data, Imbert and Papp (2015) report that while the government disbursed funds for 1.84 billion person-days as per MGNREGA statistics, in NSS data respondents reported working 1.02 billion person-days (56 percent of the official figure) in public works (NREGA and non-NREGA). The randomized sample study of MGNREGA wells in the state of Jharkhand alluded to earlier found that 87 percent of well owners had to incur private costs due to delays in official payments, nonpayment, siphoning off of money meant for materials and wages, or bribes paid to get work sanctioned.

These concerns must of course be taken seriously and addressed. "Leaky buckets" are a feature of every scheme or policy. But if the scheme is fundamentally sound, attention can be focused on minimizing problems. Indeed, that has been the attitude of program supporters from the early days. One reason why the state of Rajasthan has been a star performer in the program is that local civil society groups and activists took it upon themselves to ensure that implementation was carried out as intended in the legislation. Official employment generation figures are also increasingly consistent with independent household survey data, suggesting leakages are going down.

One particularly thorny aspect of the program shows up only when rural society is analyzed from a class perspective. Rural classes have long been stylistically divided into three, viz. the landless and marginal farmers who primarily earn wage incomes, the large landholders who practice at least partially mechanized farming and produce comfortable surpluses, and the small to middle landholders who hire in labor and produce surpluses of a precarious nature. Roy (2015) has used such a class framework along with ethnographic work in four districts to analyze where MGNREGA succeeds and where it fails. He notes that small and middle landholders are often opposed to the program, because it results in higher labor costs that they cannot afford given the small size of their surpluses. Larger landholders are less concerned, and therefore even support the program, either because they can afford to pay higher wages or have less need for labor on mechanized farms. Fear of labor shortages (since MGNREGA is not restricted only to the agricultural lean season) and fear of rising wages often mobilize the small farmers against the program. However, rather than being a problem with the program, this is instead an indication that better designed agricultural policy is needed to boost farm output and incomes.

Finally, we alluded earlier to the criticism that MGNREGA's welfare aspect takes precedence over asset creation. In this view, much work undertaken is for the sake of providing employment only. Carswell and Neve (2014) in an ethnographic study on MGNREGA in Tamil Nadu note that

> Given that all tasks are unskilled and merely consist of pulling out weeds and clearing surfaces, no skills are created for the participants either, and no lasting investments are made to enhance the rural economy more broadly.

They quote a worksite supervisor as saying:

> We can't be too strict [in what we ask them to do] . . . they have to dig one foot deep according to the rules, but nobody is doing that. If we are strict, nobody will turn up for work. We really can't be too strict . . . it's for Rs 100 only!? (578)

Sharma (2015) shows that the problem of productive work taking a backseat to employment provisioning is structural. The program has been structured to guarantee employment within a strict fifteen-day time period, but sustainable and productive work may not always be found within this period. Under such circumstances, "the need to provide work will gain precedence over the search for sustainable productive work, if a choice has to be forced" (Sharma 2015, 28).

Relatedly, the program has been criticized for top-down implementation. Once again, the Tamil Nadu study noted:

> While schedules are presented at Panchayat meetings, workers were not actively engaged in coming up with ideas or designs for new projects. There appeared to be no input at all from the wider village population. (Carswell and Neve 2014, 576)

Similarly Sharma (2015, 31) noted,

> The functions are the heaviest at the bottom—GP level and the leanest at the top—ministry level. But the control of funds on which the entire guarantee rests is inverse to the distribution of functions, resting maximally with the centre and reducing with each lower level, with the GP having least control over access to funds.[13]

Despite these problems and criticisms, on the whole we feel that the program has succeeded in its intentions and the time is right to think about expanding it. In the next section, we offer some suggestions along these lines.

3. EXPANDING MGNREGA

Even after six decades of development, the Indian economy is still characterized by a large informal sector. Of a 475-million-strong labor force, 439 million (92 percent) are informally employed (Mehrotra et al. 2014). The lack of job creation in the private formal sector commensurate with the increasing labor force as well as the declining size of the public sector has meant that informality has persisted and is expected to remain dominant for the foreseeable future. Most of these jobs also fall under the category identified by the National Commission on Enterprises in the Unorganized Sector (NCEUS), the 77 percent of the Indian population that spent under Rs. 20 a day in 2005 (Sengupta 2009). Nearly half of the informal workers are self-employed workers to whom minimum wage laws do not apply, and the rest are employed in micro and small enterprises where conditions of work are precarious and minimum wages are difficult to enforce. Incomes in the informal economy are an order of magnitude lower than the formal economy. While this is partly due to differences in productivity, differences in market structure (entry-exit barriers in factor and product markets) are also important. Specifically, the existence of surplus labor in the informal sector keeps wages tied to subsistence. Even if productivity gains do occur, under conditions of surplus labor they do not accrue to workers, but instead manifest as higher profits further up in the value chain or as lower prices for consumers. Thus, from a welfare perspective, ending this surplus labor regime is imperative.

An employment guarantee program for the entire informal economy—rural and urban—can perform this task. It can provide an effective income floor and increase informal incomes. The accompanying demand effects are also likely to be significant. One important dimension that a few commentators have already raised is expansion beyond unskilled labor. Sharma (2015, 64) notes that confinement to unskilled labor is really a way of managing or coping with poverty, not ending it. Limiting the program to unskilled labor is, of course, a targeting mechanism, as Sharma also recognizes. However, she notes that the same feature of MGNREGA that makes it effective as a safety net fails to offer those at the bottom of the wage hierarchy a chance to upgrade skills and perpetuates the lack of opportunity and capability; not only that, it can destroy existing skills.

But is not the informal economy largely a site of low-skilled or unskilled work? In policy literature, this view is common. For example, the NCEUS took the position that the vast majority of the informal workforce is unskilled (Sengupta 2009, 3). This belief relies on two empirical facts: the low levels of formal education and training among informal sector workers and low wages as well as low productivity prevailing in this sector. Basole (2014) argues that neither of these two facts can be taken as proof of absence of skills. Informal business often perform poorly by measures such as value added because of hypercompetition among many informal entrepreneurs in product markets and subordinate position in value chains. Wages are low not only because productivity is low, but also because of surplus labor. While informal qualifications are difficult to capture in standard large-scale surveys, smaller primary surveys and ethnographic work repeatedly demonstrate that informal workers do not lack skills, what they lack is formal certification of their (informally acquired) skills. From agriculture and animal husbandry to food processing, weaving, and other small industry, everything demands skilled work and varied knowledge of the environment, the soil, materials, and markets. This knowledge has increasingly become visible in the development literature over the past two decades under labels such as "traditional knowledge," "indigenous knowledge," "poor peoples' knowledge," and "lokavidya" (Warren, Slikerveer and Brokensha 1995; Finger and Schuler 2004; Basole 2015). Diverting workers possessing such knowledge to manual labor leaves skills unused and can even destroy them. Sharma (2015, 64) makes this point:

> If Mahatma Gandhi NREGA continues in the way it is, as unskilled manual labour with large funds, and a quick fifteen day time-bound, work allocation, it tends to become a major employer in the market. Even without a guarantee incentivising the choice of unskilled labour, *exigencies of poverty often force skilled artisans to stone-crushing* [emphasis added].

Indeed, in some parts of the country, the collapse of the rural economy means that skilled workers often earn less than MGNREGA wages. During fieldwork in Varanasi district, Uttar Pradesh, in 2009–2010, skilled handloom weavers often complained to one of this chapter's authors (AB) that they would earn more "throwing dirt" under MGNREGA than they did weaving. Availability of work under MGNREGA thus means that skilled workers are drawn into manual labor such as digging ditches.

What if, instead, MGNREGA were to be extended to these occupations? This will create employment for all types of rural informal workers in the trades that they have already been trained for and potentially give them space to improve their skills. By offering to employ people in their own trades at a minimum wage, the government can create a wage floor in these occupations, with the important added benefit of formally recognizing these skills. This can have spillover effects on the private sector both in terms of wages and dignity of work. It is worth recalling that even for marginal and small farmers, up to 20 percent or more of income derives from non-farm sources (Basole and Basu 2011). Thus, boosting incomes in weaving and other secondary occupations is likely to have a wide impact on the rural economy.

Even more ambitiously, we can conceive a job guarantee program that provides a genuine income floor for the entire rural and urban informal sector. This would be a right to livelihood for all, based on the skills and knowledge they already possess and would like to improve. Assuming a program that supports every informal sector worker who wishes to participate, for a third of the year (as in the current form of the program), this would increase the size of the job guarantee program around three- or fourfold from its current level.[14]

But scale is not the only consideration. Such an expansion may also require some rethinking of the concept of an employment guarantee program, because workers will not only be involved in public works but will also be producing private goods. The program could match workers with (self-declared) skills to appropriate local employers and bear the wage costs, or perhaps provide these as a form of a long-term, low-interest loan. In this regard, note that MGNREGA already involves the use of publicly funded labor in producing private durables such as wells on privately owned land. In such a scenario, effectively, a private employer (the landholder) is employing local labor paid for by public funds. The proposal is to generalize such activity to a wider set of occupations. Another way to think about this is that instead of taxing (or borrowing from) the rich and the middle classes to subsidize consumption for the poor, the government will instead pay the poor to produce private goods. Such a scheme has been suggested at least by one team as far as we have been able to ascertain. The writers of the *2013 State of India's Livelihoods Report* refer to a statement by the Indian textile minister who suggests a tie-up with garment manufacturing companies. The idea, according to the authors, is that companies would provide workers jobs as well as skills training, while the wages would be paid by the MGNREGA scheme under the proposal. Similar options could be explored with respect to agriculture: large farmers could register with Panchayats for workforce requirements, and the wages could be paid through MGNREGA (Babu et al. 2013, 97)

The first objection to such a proposal is likely to be that the fiscal burden will be unsustainable. We do not think this is the case. As mentioned earlier, in 2013–2014 the cost of MGNREGA was around 0.3 percent of GDP. In contrast, as we also saw earlier, forgone tax revenues and other corporate concessions in that same fiscal year came to 5 percent of GDP, not to mention subsidies such as the one on fertilizer, which is double the MGNREGA budget. Thus fiscal room does not seem to be a constraint. Political will and ideological "won't" are much more likely to be the problems.

The second objection we foresee is that targeting the program becomes more complicated once skilled labor is introduced. Identifying informal skills is not straightforward. However, this can be done if all the government does is provide income support to privately employed workers, since marketability considerations are already at work in identifying skilled workers. Even if they do not need to pay wages, private employers are unlikely to keep unproductive workers in their firms. As a spillover effect, an MGNREGA for skilled workers will have the benefit of bringing to the fore a much-neglected issue: how to formally recognize informal skills. Such as program would force the government to take cognizance of skills that the market already recognizes.

A third concern is the incentives that such a program will create. If a subset of a private firm's workforce is on public payroll, does this create incentives for private employers to extract as much work as possible for these employees, firing the rest? For this, note that public funds will cover wage costs for only around a third of the year. This means that an employer who needs the firm to function the entire year will have to keep the regular workforce employed if he or she is to avoid repeated hiring and firing, losing firm-specific knowledge and employee loyalties in the process.

A fourth concern is what happens to the significant portion of informal workers who are self-employed? This is a trickier issue to resolve and may not be amenable to a solution at the very start of the program. Instead, one may expect, as the program establishes itself, for the prevalence of self-employment to decline as existing firms absorb workers who are self-employed only out of necessity as opposed to entrepreneurial spirit.

The foregoing is only an initial outline. Clearly, much further work is needed to draw out a feasible program and understand its possible general equilibrium effects. We hope that the points we have laid out can provide a path for further research.

4. CONCLUSION

India's peculiar structural transition has created a unique employment challenge. A very large labor force of over 450 million people is in search of stable, decent jobs and living wages. The current pattern of development has failed to deliver this in an effective manner, especially in the last two decades. Supporting and expanding the MGNREGA would be a step toward reversing this malign state of affairs and allowing the country's workers some security and dignity. Such an intervention also has the advantage over an unconditional income transfer in that it will create meaningful work, develop skills, and provide goods for the private economy.

NOTES

1. The fundamental argument and many proposals in this vein are described in Kaboub (2007).

2. In India in particular, they were central in medieval times as a measure to provide social security in case of famine and other catastrophes, in colonial times as an enshrined part of the constitution at Independence, and central to poverty alleviation proposals in post-Independence India (Dandekar and Rath 1971).

3. Indeed, at the outset of the program, the World Bank criticized the NREGA as constituting a "policy barrier" with respect to development (World Bank 2009).

4. Other programs similar to the NREGA are the expanded public works program in South Africa and the Jefes de Hogar program in Argentina.

5. SC and ST are administrative terms for former untouchable (Dalit) and tribal populations, respectively.

6. See, among others Adhikari and Bhatia (2010); Banerjee and Saha (2010); Berg et al. (2015); Bhaskar (2016); Bhatia and Dreze (2006); Carswell and Neve (2014); Dreze and Oldiges (2011); Dutta et al. (2014); Imbert and Papp (2015); Khera and Nayak (2009); Pankaj and Tankha (2010); Ranaware et al. (2015); Sudarshan et al. (2010); and Vanaik (2008).

7. See http://mnregaweb4.nic.in/netnrega/all_lvl_details_dashboard_new.aspx. Accessed May 2016.

8. According to a "backwardness index" developed by the Planning Commission of India. See Report of the Task Force, Identification of Districts for Wage and Self Employment Programmes: Planning Commission, May 2003.

9. MGNREGA Public Data Portal, accessed May 2016, http://mnregaweb4.nic.in /netnrega/dynamic2/dynamicreport_new4.aspx.

10. All rupee values are nominal. In PPP terms, 1$ = Rs. 20.

11. Fiscal year 2015–2016. One crore is equal to 10 million.

12. P. Sainath, "Corporate Karza Maafi at Rs. 36.5 Trillion," *Follow the Money*, July 13, 2014, http://psainath.org/corporate-karza-maafi-at-rs-36-5-trillion.

13. The reader is referred to Sharma (2015), in particular table 1 (p. 32), for a detailed account of the structure of responsibilities and the consequences of this structure.

14. If we assume that around half of the 450-million-strong informal workforce demands work under the job guarantee program and take into account the fact that in 2015–2016 72 million workers worked under MGNREGA, this is around three times the current coverage. The assumption of 50 percent workers demanding work seems reasonable given that around 30 percent of the rural workforce demanded work under MGNREGA in 2015–2016. Of course, wages paid would need to be higher in the urban areas, so actual program costs may increase further.

REFERENCES

Adhikari, A., and K. Bhatia. 2010. "NREGA Wage Payments: Can We Bank on the Banks?" *Economic and Political Weekly* 45(1):30–37.

Amirapu, A., and A. Subramanian. 2015. "Manufacturing or Services? An Indian Illustration of A Development Dilemma." Center for Global Development Working Paper No. 408.

Azam, M. 2012. "The Impact of Indian Job Guarantee Scheme on Labor Market Outcomes: Evidence from a Natural Experiment." IZA Discussion Paper, No. 6548. IZA, Bonn.

Babu, S., R. Bhaskaran, A. Kumar, T. Nair, S. Roul, O. Ruthven, A. Sircar, K. Vardhana, and G. Vasudevan. 2013. *State of India's Livelihoods Report*. New Delhi: Sage.

Banerjee, K., and P. Saha. 2010. "The NREGA, the Maoists and the Developmental Woes of the Indian State." *Economic and Political Weekly* 45(28):42–47.

Basole, A. 2014. "The Informal Sector from a Knowledge Perspective." *Yojana: A Development Monthly* 58(October):8–14.

———, ed. 2015. *Lokavidya Perspectives: A Philosophy of Political Imagination for the Knowledge Age*. New Delhi: Aakar Books.

Basole, A., and D. Basu. 2011. "Relations of Production and Modes of Surplus Extraction in India. Part I: Agriculture." *Economic and Political Weekly* 46(14):41–58.

Berg, E., S. Bhattacharyya, R. Durgam, M. Ramachandra. 2012. "Can Public Works Increase Equilibrium Wages? Evidence from India's National Rural Employment Guarantee." Working Paper WPS/2012-05. Centre for the Study of African Economies, Oxford University, Oxford.

Bhaduri, A. 2008. "Growth and Employment in the Era of Globalization: Some Lessons from the Indian Experience." ILO Asia-Pacific Working Paper Series. International Labour Organization, New Delhi.

Bhaskar, A., S. Gupta, and P. Yadav. 2016. "Well Worth the Effort: Value of MGNREGA Wells in Jharkhand." *Economic and Political Weekly* 51(19):40–48.

Bhatia, B., and J. Dreze. 2006. "Employment Guarantee in Jharkhand: Ground Realities." *Economic and Political Weekly* 41(29):3198–3202.

Carswell, G., and G. Neve. 2014. "MGNREGA in Tamil Nadu: A Story of Success and Transformation?" *Journal of Agrarian Change* 14(4):564–85.

Dandekar, V. M., and N. Rath. 1971. "Poverty in India. I: Dimensions and Trends." *Economic and Political Weekly* 6(1):25–48.

Dreze, J., and R. Khera. 2009. "The Battle for Employment Guarantee." *Frontline* 26(1):3–16.

Dreze, J., and C. Oldiges. 2011. "NREGA: The Official Picture." In *The Battle for Employment Guarantee*, ed. Reetika Khera, 21–39. Oxford: Oxford University Press.

Dutta, P., R. Murgai, M. Ravallion, and D. Van de Walle. 2014. *Right to Work? Assessing India's Employment Guarantee Scheme in Bihar*. Washington, D.C.: World Bank Publications.

Finger, J. M., and P. E. Schuler. 2004. *Poor People's Knowledge: Promoting Intellectual Property in Developing Countries*. Washington, D.C.: World Bank and Oxford: Oxford University Press.

Imbert, C., and J. Papp. 2015. "Labor Market Effects of Social Programs: Evidence from India's Employment Guarantee." *American Economic Journal: Applied Economics* 7(2):233–63.

Kaboub, F. 2007. "Employment Guarantee Programs: A Survey of Theories and Policy Experiences." Levy Economics Institute Working Paper No. 498. Levy Institute, New York.

Khera, R., and N. Nayak. 2009. "Women Workers and Perceptions of the National Rural Employment Guarantee Act." *Economic and Political Weekly* 44(43):49–57.

Klonner, S., and C. Oldiges. 2014. "Safety Net for India's Poor or Waste of Public Funds? Poverty and Welfare in the Wake of the World's Largest Job Guarantee Program." Discussion Paper Series/University of Heidelberg, Department of Economics, No. 564. Available at: www.ub.uni-heidelberg.de/archiv/16875.

Kotwal, A., B. Ramaswami, and W. Wadhwa. 2011. "Economic Liberalization and Indian Economic Growth: What's the Evidence?" *Journal of Economic Literature* 49(4):1152–99.

Mehrotra, S., J. Parida, S. Sinha, and A. Gandhi. 2014. "Explaining Employment Trends in the Indian Economy: 1993–94 to 2011–12." *Economic and Political Weekly* 49(32):49–57.

Ministry of Law and Justice. 2005. "The National Rural Employment Guarantee Act, 2005." *The Gazette of India* 48.

Nadhanael, G. 2012. "Recent Trends in Rural Wages: An Analysis of Inflationary Implications." *Reserve Bank of India Occasional Papers* 33(1):89–112.

Pankaj, A., and R. Tankha. 2010. "Empowerment Effects of the NREGS on Women Workers: A Study in Four States." *Economic and Political Weekly* 45(30):45–55.

Papola, T. S., and P. P. Sahu. 2012. "Growth and Structure of Employment in India: Long Term and Post Reform Performance and the Emerging Challenge." Study prepared as part of research programme on Structural Changes, Industry, and Employment in the Indian Economy. New Delhi: ICSSR.

Petty, W. 1899. *The Economic Writings of Sir William Petty*, vol. 1. Cambridge: Cambridge University Press.

Ranaware, K., U. Das, A. Kulkarni, and S. Narayanan. 2015. "MGNREGA Works and Their Impacts." *Economic & Political Weekly* 50(13):53–61.

Rodrik, D. 2015. "Premature Deindustrialization." *Journal of Economic Growth* 21(1):1–33.

Roy, I. 2015. "Class Politics and Social Protection: The Implementation of India's MGNREGA." ESID Working Paper No. 46.

Sengupta, A. 2009. *The Challenge of Employment in India: An Informal Economy Perspective*. New Delhi: National Commission for Enterprises in the Unorganized Sector.

Sharma, A. 2015. *Rights-Based Legal Guarantee as Development Policy: The Mahatma Gandhi National Rural Employment Guarantee Act*. Technical report, eSocialSciences. Retrieved from: http://www.ipc-undp.org/pressroom/files/ipc163.pdf

Sonna, T., H. Joshi, A. Sebastian, and U. Sharma. 2012. "Analytics of Food Inflation in India." https://ideas.repec.org/s/ess/wpaper.html.

Standing, G. 2011. *The Precariat: The New Dangerous Class*. Bloomsbury, U.K.: A&C Black.

Sudarshan, R. M., R. Bhattacharya, and G. Fernandez. 2010. "Women's Participation in the NREGA: Some Observations from Fieldwork in Himachal Pradesh, Kerala and Rajasthan." *IDS Bulletin* 41(4):77–83.

Vakulabharanam, V., and S. Motiram. 2011. "Political Economy of Agrarian Distress in India Since the 1990s." In *Understanding India's New Political Economy: A Great Transformation*, ed. Sanjay Ruparelia, Sanjay Reddy, John Harriss, and Stuart Corbridge, 101–26. New York: Routledge.

Vanaik, A. 2008. "Bank Payments: End of Corruption in NREGA?" *Economic and Political Weekly*, 43(17):33–39.

Viswanathan, P., R. N. Mishra, M. Bhattarai, and H. Iyengar. 2014. "Mahatma Gandhi Rural Employment Guarantee (MGNREGA) Programme in India: A Review of Studies." IGIDR Occasional Paper Series, Indira Gandhi Institute of Development Research.

Warren, D. M., J. Slikkerveer, and David. Brokensha, eds. 1995. *The Cultural Dimension of Development: Indigenous Knowledge Systems*. London: Intermediate Technology Publications.

World Bank. 2009. *World Development Report*.

Zimmermann, L. 2012. "Labor Market Impacts of a Large-Scale Public Works Program: Evidence from the Indian Employment Guarantee Scheme." IZA Discussion Paper No. 6858. IZA, Bonn.

José Antonio Ocampo is a codirector of the central bank of Colombia, chair of the UN Committee for Development Policy, and professor (on leave) from Columbia University. He was UN undersecretary-general for economic and social affairs; executive secretary of the UN Economic Commission for Latin America and the Caribbean; and minister of finance, minister of agriculture, and director of the National Planning Department of Colombia.

Joseph E. Stiglitz is professor at Columbia University, cochair of the High-Level Expert Group on the Measurement of Economic Performance and Social Progress at the Organisation for Economic Co-operation and Development, and chief economist of the Roosevelt Institute. A recipient of the Nobel Memorial Prize in Economic Sciences (2001) and the John Bates Clark Medal (1979), he is a former senior vice president and chief economist of the World Bank, and a former member and chairman of the U.S. Council of Economic Advisers.

Torben M. Andersen is professor at Aarhus University and associate research fellow at CEPR, CESifo, IZA, and PeRCent. He has published widely on the economics of the welfare state, labor economics, and public economics, and has been extensively involved in policy advice in the Denmark, the Nordic countries, and the EU Commission.

Amit Basole is associate professor of economics at the School of Liberal Studies, Azim Premji University, Bangalore, where he teaches development economics and political economy. He has previously taught at Bucknell University and the University of Massachusetts. His research focuses on poverty and inequality, informality, structural change, and the economics of knowledge.

Teresa Ghilarducci is director of the Schwartz Center for Economic Policy Analysis and the Retirement Equity Lab, and professor of economics at the New School for Social Research. She was previously professor of economics at the University of Notre Dame and was twice appointed by President Clinton to serve on the Pension Benefit Guaranty Corporation advisory board. Her most recent book is *Rescuing Retirement*, with Tony James (Columbia University Press, 2018).

Natalie Gómez-Arteaga is coordinator of the special group of territorial studies at the National Planning Department of Colombia. She contributed to this volume when she was research associate at the Initiative for Policy Dialogue at Columbia University and consultant to the International Labor Organization and the UN Development Program.

Jody Heymann is dean of the University of California–Los Angeles Fielding School of Public Health, Distinguished Professor of Public Policy at the Luskin School of Public Affairs, Health Policy and Management at the Fielding School of Public Health, and Medicine at the Geffen School of Medicine. Heymann is an elected member of the U.S. National Academy of Sciences. She held Canada Research Chair in Global Health and Social Policy and was Founding Director of the McGill University Institute for Health and Social Policy.

Arjun Jayadev is an associate professor of economics at Azim Premji University and director of the Research Center. His work is on distribution, finance, and innovation, with publications in several major economic journals. He is also a senior economist at the Institute for New Economic Thinking.

Ravi Kanbur is T. H. Lee Professor of World Affairs at Cornell University. He is the current president of the Human Development and Capability Association, a member of the Organisation for Economic Co-operation and Development High Level Expert Group on the Measurement of Economic and Social Progress, and chair of the board of UNU-WIDER. He was president of the Society for the Study of Economic Inequality and worked at the World Bank, including as chief economist for Africa.

Nora Lustig is Samuel Z. Stone Professor of Latin American Economics and director of the Commitment to Equity Institute at Tulane University. Her current research focuses on assessing the impact of taxation and social spending on inequality and poverty in low- and middle-income countries and on the determinants of income distribution in Latin America.

Richard McGahey is a senior fellow at the Schwartz Center for Economic Policy Analysis, New School for Social Research. He has served as executive director of the U.S. Congress's Joint Economic Committee, as Economic Policy Advisor to Senator Edward M. Kennedy, as assistant secretary for policy at the U.S. Department of Labor, and as a program officer and director of impact assessment at the Ford Foundation.

Kalle Moene is a professor of economics at the University of Oslo, where he also has been the leader of the Research Center on Equality Social Organization and Performance, funded as a center of excellence by the Norwegian Research Council. His research interests include income distribution and comparative economic institutions, both in rich and poor countries.

Isabel Ortiz is director of social protection at the International Labor Organization (ILO), where she is responsible for the ILO's flagship publication, the *World Social Protection Report*, and the ILO's policy work on social protection. Earlier in her career she was a senior official at UNICEF, UN DESA, and the Asian Development Bank.

Sandra Polaski is an expert on labor and social policy issues at national and global levels. She was the deputy director-general for policy of the International Labor Organization from 2012 to 2016, U.S. deputy undersecretary of labor in charge of international labor affairs from 2009 to 2012, and director of the Trade, Equity and Development Program at the Carnegie Endowment for International Peace.

Ana Sojo is an independent consultant and expert in social protection, poverty, social cohesion, and care policies. From 1989 until 2016, she was senior expert at the UN Economic Commission for Latin America and the Caribbean. From 1981 to 1988, she was a researcher, professor, and director of the master's program in sociology at the University of Costa Rica.

Aleta Sprague is a senior legal analyst at the WORLD Policy Analysis Center at the University of California–Los Angeles Fielding School of Public Health. Previously, she worked on anti-poverty policy with the Asset Building Program at the New America Foundation and served as a fellow at the Congressional Hunger Center.

Ernst Stetter is an economist and political scientist, and since 2008, secretary-general of the European think tank Foundation for European

Progressive Studies and visiting fellow at Greenwich University, London. He began his career as a lecturer in economics at the DGB Trade Union Centre for Vocational Training in Heidelberg and worked for the Friedrich Ebert Stiftung.

Andras Uthoff is an independent consultant and a member of the Social Security Consultative Council (Consejo Consultivo Previsional) of Chile. He was formerly head of the Social Policy Division at the UN Economic Commission for Latin America and the Caribbean and regional advisor of the International Labor Organization.

of, 99–101; healthy development in childhood and, 103–9; "inequality of opportunity," 148; laws and policies on, global progress in, 102–19; legal protections, 101; paid leave and, 99–100; pillars of, 101, *101*; policies supporting, 120; policy implementation and, 121; resilience and, 114–16; supporting, through laws and policies, 98–122; in workplace, 99–100, 113

equal pay, *172*, 174–75; constitutional protection of, 112; discrimination and, 111–12; wage gap, 111–12

equal rights, 101, 102, 117, 119

equity: efficiency and, 178; individual, 53

equivalence principle, 277, 291

Ethiopia, 135

EU. *See* European Union

Europe: employment strategy in, 199–200; labor market reforms in, 197–98; pension system in, 82; tax system in, 31; unemployment in, 196–97; welfare state in, xi, xiv, 214–15

Europe 2020 Strategy, *208*

European Monetary Union, 196

European Union (EU): aggregate demand in, 209–10; Charter of Fundamental Rights, 200; expenditure cuts in, 201–4, *202*, *203*; fiscal consolidation in, 201–3, *202*; Gini coefficient in select countries, 206–7, *207*; health-care reforms, 200, 204; labor market liberalization in, 205; pension reforms, 204; social dumping in, 209; social investment spending in, 209; social model, 199–201; socioeconomic fabric of, changes in, 195–99

EU welfare state, xviii, 191–210; austerity measures and, 192, 201–8; changes in, 191–92; child benefits in, 205; cradle-to-grave, 222; elements of, 192–94; family models and, 198; health-care reform, 204; pension

reform, 200, 204; reforms, 195, 201–4, *203*; regime types and, *193*, 193–94, *194*; social protection benefits and, 205; social security in, 204; socioeconomic transformations and, 195–96

excise tax, 135

Fair Labor Standards Act (FLSA), 41–42, 65*n*17; employer/employee definitions under, 49–50

Family and Medical Leave Act, 1993, 47

family structures, changes in, 175

final income, 137, 139

financial crises, 78, 82; inequality and, 185*n*9. *See also* Great Recession of 2008-2009

financial deregulation, capital and, 40

financial sector, 31, 34*n*25

Finland, basic income in, 66*n*32

fiscal consolidation: in EU, 201–3, *202*; validity of, 94*n*9

fiscal impoverishment, *133*, 134–35; in Latin America, 252

fiscal incidence analysis, 137–41; household surveys for, 140–41; welfare indicator used in, 140

fiscal systems: net payers and receivers in, 135, *136*; poverty and, 128–32, *129*, *132*

five presidents report, 184*n*1

FLSA. *See* Fair Labor Standards Act

FONASA, Chile, 265–66, 283; age-specific relative expenditure, *288*; AUGE-GES law and, 285

food: assistance, poverty reduction through, 74; caloric intake, 152; consumption, cash transfers and, 94*n*3. *See also* hunger and nutrition

food stamps. *See* Supplemental Nutrition Assistance Program

401(k) plans, 296; failure of, 300; during Great Recession, 309–10; regulations on, 299; structure of, 311–12; tax breaks for, 308, 312*n*2; withdrawals from, 302

composition patterns across, 157–59;
income, equivalized, 175; income
sharing within, 157–59; taxation of,
160–61
household surveys, 140–41, 150–51
housing: financing, 29–30; low-income,
30; middle-class life and, 29–30;
substandard, 5; 2008 crisis and,
29–30
human capital, 185n10; accumulation
of, 176; distribution of, 168, *168*;
economic growth and, 176–77;
inequality and, 165, 175–77;
persistence in, 186n12
Human Development Index, 253n11
hunger and nutrition: BMI and,
intrahousehold inequality measured
with, 151–52; caloric intake, 152;
school meals program in India, 218;
social protection on, 74

ILO. *See* International Labor
Organization
incentives: children and, 20; UBI and,
326; welfare state and, xi, 4
income: concepts, 137, *138*; consumable,
141n4, 142n5; fetishism, xvii,
16; final, 137, 139; GMI, 88–90;
household, equivalized, 175; labor's
share of, 323–24; per capita,
140; post-fiscal, 137; productivity
and, 216–20; programs, 47;
social spending and, 225. *See also*
disposable income; market income;
universal basic income
income-contingent loans, xv, xxii$n$8, 23;
college access and, 27–28
income distribution, xviii, 148–49,
184n3; education and, 174–75, 178;
factors determining, 166; inequality
and, 47; labor, 166; market, 167–69,
168
income protection, 46, 56, 115, *115*.
See also unemployment insurance
systems

independent contractor, 41–42, 61, 63n8,
64n10; employee compared with, 50
India: agriculture in, 342–43; economic
growth in, *340*, 340–41; inflation
in, 354; informal economy, 356–57;
jobless growth in, 340–43, *342*;
manufacturing employment,
338; NCEUS, 356–57; NREGA,
xvii, xx–xxi, 337–61; rights-based
legislation, 343–44; school meals
program, 218; sector shares in output
and employment, *341*; structural
transformation in, 341
indirect subsidies, poverty reduction
and, *129*
individual equity, 53
individual-level distributions, 151
individual responsibility and choice,
xv, xvii
individual retirement accounts (IRAs),
296–98; auto-enrolled, 301, 311;
during Great Recession, 309–10;
regulations on, 299; tax breaks for,
308; withdrawals from, 302
individual savings accounts: in Chile,
277–79, 281–82, 291; competitive
market of, 277–94; gender bias and,
281–82, 289–90; pension system,
291; reform, *293*
Indonesia, 141n4
industrialization: in developing
countries, 338; "fourth industrial
revolution," 90–91
inequality, xi, 15; analytics of, 148–50;
austerity measures and, 206–7;
"between-group" and "within-group"
components, 147; causes of growing,
165; decomposition of, 147–48, 170,
171, 185n4; distribution of, 149–50;
economic growth and, 14, 58, 165,
176, 178–79; economic performance
and, xv–xvi, 13; education, market
incomes, disposable incomes and,
169; EU welfare regimes and, *194*;
financial crises and, 185n9; generosity

CPSIA information can be obtained
at www.ICGtesting.com
Printed in the USA
LVHW08*0142040818
585922LV00001B/3/P